ABOUT THE AUTHORS

Born in Greensboro, NC, noted author and black studies scholar Jessie Carney Smith is a librarian and the William and Camille Cosby Professor at Fisk University in Nashville. Her work includes *Epic Lives* and *Black Firsts*, both published by Visible Ink Press. A book on African American men is forthcoming. Among Dr. Smith's numerous honors are the 1992 Women's National Book Association Award, the Candace Award for excellence in education and *Sage* Magazine's Anna J. Cooper Award for *Epic Lives*.

Jessie

Carney

Smith

Born in Washington, D.C., Camille O. Cosby is a philanthropist, entrepreneur, and chief executive of Cosby Enterprises, a foundation that supports black colleges and the education of black youth. In addition to a master's degree and a doctoral degree in education from the University of Massachusetts School of Education, Dr. Cosby has received honorary doctorates from Howard University and Spelman College. Beyond her philanthropic work, Dr. Cosby has also produced albums, videos, a play, and a documentary. A feature film based on *Having Our Say* is in the planning stages for 1997.

Camille O. Cosby

"Reading it was like having a steaming cup of tea with some of the most ... creative and bold women in our nation."

—*Detroit Free Press*

"Information to heal our ignorance, about lives luminous with courage."

—*Ms.* **Magazine**

EPIC LIVES

One Hundred

Black Women

Who Made

a Difference

A unique contribution to both black studies and women's studies, *Epic Lives* is an inspiring glimpse into the lives of 100 remarkable women, many of whose stories are related for the first time in this book. *Epic Lives* heralds the achievements of such women as Pan-African scholar Anna J. Cooper, astronaut Mae C. Jemison, opera soprano Leontyne Price, abolitionist Sojourner Truth, educator Mary Church Terrell, singer Marian Anderson, folk artist Clementine Hunter, activist Mary McLeod Bethune, dancer and anthropologist Katherine Dunham, "Queen of Soul" Aretha Franklin, founding president of the Children's Defense Fund Marian Wright Edelman, poets Maya Angelou and Gwendolyn Brooks, Olympic gold medalist Wilma Rudolph, talk show host, actress, and producer Oprah Winfrey, sculptor Barbara Chase-Riboud, politician and lawyer Barbara Jordan, aviator Bessie Coleman, Spelman College president Johnetta B. Cole, and Anglican bishop Barbara Harris, and gives them the recognition they have long deserved.

Foreword by Stephanie Stokes Oliver, editor, *Essence* magazine. By Jessie Carney Smith, 7 1/4" x 9 1/4", paperback, 661 pages, 100 photos, ISBN 0-8103-9426-X, $18.95.

ALSO AVAILABLE FROM VISIBLE INK PRESS

The Essential Black Literature Guide

"Essential is the key word for this treasure."—*Copley News Service*

Published in association with the Schomberg Center for Research in Black Culture, one of the world's foremost facilities dedicated to the preservation and interpretation of black cultural artifacts.

By Roger M. Valade III, 6" x 9" paperback, 446 pages, 138 illustrations and photos, ISBN 0-7876-0734-7, $17.95.

Lay Down Body Living History in African American Cemetaries

Anyone who has ever tried to trace their African-American heritage understands the frustration of not knowing where to start to or where to look. This unique glimpse into African American culture blends moving, personal accounts with painstaking research to describe and help locate 300 cemeteries.

By Roberta Hughes Wright and Wilbur B. Hughes III, 7 1/4" x 9 1/4", paperback, 330 pages, 75 photos, ISBN 0-7876-0651-0, $17.95.

Black Firsts

"A superb historical study of black achievement."—*Houston Chronicles*

By Jessie Carney Smith, 7 1/4" x 9 1/4", paperback, 556 pages, 200 illustrations, ISBN 0-8103-9490-1, $16.95.

African America: Portrait of a People

"Thoughtfully addresses the challenges and triumphs of Black Americans during the last 400 years."—*Christian Science Monitor*

By Kenneth Estell, 7 1/4" x 9 1/4", paperback, 811 pages, 200 photos, ISBN 0-8103-9453-7, $18.95.

Historic Black Landmarks A Traveler's Guide

"An important contribution to American society."—*Washington Post*

Foreword by Robert L. Harris, Jr., Africana Studies and Research Center, Cornell University. By George Cantor, 6" x 9", paperback, 408 pages, photos and maps, ISBN 0-8103-9408-1, $17.95.

Milestones in 20th-Century African American History

"An illustrated, detailed account of the struggles and triumphs of Blacks in the past nine decades."—*Syracuse, NY Herald-Journal*

By Alton Hornsby, Jr., 7 1/4" x 9 1/4", paperback, 542 pages, 100 photos, ISBN 0-8103-9180-5, $17.95.

Powerful Black Women

Jessie Carney Smith, editor

Foreword by Camille O. Cosby

VISIBLE

INK
PRESS

DETROIT   NEW YORK   TORONTO

Published by **Visible Ink Press**™
a division of Gale Research
835 Penobscot Building
Detroit, MI 48226-4094

Visible Ink Press is a trademark of Gale Research

Most Visible Ink Press™ books are available at special quantity discounts when purchased in bulk by corporations, organizations, or groups. Customized printings, special imprints, messages, and exerpts can be produced to meet your needs. For more information, contact the Special Markets Manager at the above address. Or call 1-800-877-4253.

Art Directors: cover design, Mary Krzewinski; interior pages Tracey Rowens

Cover photo of Gay Johnson McDougall by Dayna Smith

Prayer by Marian Wright Edelman, copyright © 1995 Beacon Press, reprinted by permission

Library of Congress Cataloging-in-Publication Data

Powerful Black Women / Jessie Carney Smith, editor; foreword by Camille Cosby.
    p.   cm.
  Includes bibliographical references and index.
  ISBN 0-7876-0882-3
  1. Afro-American women—Biography. I. Smith, Jessie Carney.
E185.96.P69 1996
920.72′08996073—dc20   96-11062
                                           CIP

CONTENTS

PHOTO CREDITS

CONTRIBUTORS

Tanty R. Avant
Dawn Cooper Barnes
Kathleen E. Bethel
Jacqueline Brice-Finch
Cynthia Stokes Brown
Phiefer L. Browne
Bettye Collier-Thomas
Sarah Crest
Richelle B. Curl
Althea T. Davis
Vanessa D. Dickerson
Margaret Duckworth
Joan C. Elliott
Sharynn Owens
 Etheridge
Elizabeth Hadley
 Freydberg
Erica L. Griffin
Debra Newman Ham

D. Antoinette Handy
Lynda Roscoe Hartigan
Carolyn Hodges
Felicia H. (Felder)
 Hoehne
Phyl Garland
Elwanda D. Ingram
Dona L. Irvin
Jacquelyn L. Jackson
Laura C. Jarmon
Barbara Williams
 Jenkins
Robert L. Johns
Adrienne Lash Jones
Casper LeRoy Jordan
Juanita Karpf
Karen Cotton McDaniel
Dolores Nicholson
Leslie A. Norback

Margaret Perry
William D. Piersen
Bobbie T. Pollard
Margaret Ann Reid
Florence Robinson
Marva L. Rudolph
Vivian O. Sammons
Brenda Robinson
 Shaw
Jessie Carney Smith
Lisa Studier
Patricia Turner
Marsha C. Vick
Nagueyalti Warren
Julie Winch
Kari Winter
Phyllis Wood
Barbara Lynne Ivey
 Yarn

Heartfelt •

thanks to these

chroniclers

of history

FOREWORD

Powerful Black Women. Women. African American Women. Victori-   **Defining power** •

ous, tenacious; responsible overseers of home and families; educators;

lovers and partners; beside *a lover,* beside *a partner (not behind);*

protectors of families and friends; annihilators of obstacles; splendid

shades of cream, caramel, honey and chocolate; respecters of life

because life blooms in our bodies; resplendent straight, curly and twisty

hair textures; political, business, and community leaders; activists,

peacemakers... oh, yes, our human spirits have prevailed.

Power. That word has been misused and abused in different forms of media as well as from some of the people who consider themselves to be powerful. The most common definition of power from the aforementioned entities is the ability and desire to control and oppress people. My preferred definition of power is the "ability to do, act, or produce" (Webster's New World Dictionary, 1988). Power is the ability to listen as well as to speak. Power is to live honestly. Power is to have reciprocal trust and love. Power is to share one's joy. Power is to not let racial and sexual obstacles get in one's way. Power is to be decisive and to make timely choices. Power is to be knowledgeable. Power is to give of oneself as to receive from others. Power is to pursue one's goals. Power is to laugh and to be connected. Power is to be open-minded to new ideas. Power is to accept people's ethnic differences as well as human similarities. Power is to be flexible. Power is to speak one's mind. Power is voting.

Two of the women who are featured in this book have had pronounced effects on my life. Some of the wisdoms that Dr. Bessie Delany and Ms. Sadie Delany have imparted to me and to the world are as follows: First, Dr. Delany and Ms. Delany have taught me the importance of knowing American history from the diverse viewpoints of the people rather than the one-sided perspectives of the aristocrats. Second, Dr. Delany and Ms. Delany have been the antitheses of the perceived stereotypical notions about elderly women. They are not cute, old women; indeed, they have lived lives full of profundities which are embodied in this book's profiles of them. Third, the Delany sisters have been models of positive reciprocity. They believe that healthy relationships are rooted in giving and receiving. Last, the sisters have a way of cutting to the core, to speak clearly and honestly; they have overcome racial and sexual obstacles to achieve their ambitions and have managed their lives without accommodating the opinions of any particular day.

Furthermore, during my visits, when Dr. Delany held my hand, she would stare straight through at my very soul. When Ms. Delany held my hand, her warmth permeated my body. Without question, the Delany sisters have been self-defining and inspiring women.

Women have so many choices to make... choices about men, choices about exercise, choices about money, choices about schools for our children, and choices about friendships, among others. Those choices protect our independence, energies, spirit, and wholeness.

Camille O. Cosby
January 1996

A friend once said, "One cannot congratulate rightful thinking." I agree, but I feel that Black women should congratulate themselves for mobilizing people with hope, love, and vision.

INTRODUCTION

"We have many estimable women of our variety, but not any famous **Recognition** •

ones," wrote the abolitionist and orator Frederick Douglass more than **for African-**

one hundred years ago. He was answering a request from Monroe **American**

Majors, who was gathering information for his pioneering book Notable **Women**

Negro Women, *published in 1893. Majors had asked Douglass, the most*

famous black man of his era, to suggest additions to the list of women to

be included in the book. In his reply, Douglass defined a famous person

as one who was "celebrated in fame or public" and "much talked of."

He cautioned: "It is not well to claim too much for ourselves before the

public." Douglass continued in his letter, now in the possession of

Majors's great-granddaughter, Eleanor Boswell-Raine of El Sobrante, California, that he had seen "no book of importance written by a Negro woman" and that he knew "of no one among us who can appreciably be called famous."

That Douglass could not recognize the fame of Sojourner Truth and Harriet Tubman, who doubtlessly were "much talked of" during his lifetime, causes concern. Both Douglass and Truth were abolitionists and proponents of women's rights and had even appeared at the same gatherings on occasion. In her work as underground railroad conductor, Harriet Tubman led over two hundred of Douglass's black brothers and sisters from bondage to freedom. Refusing to acknowledge that the lack of recognition of women reflected a prevailing male chauvinism, Douglass excused himself from expanding Majors's list and said that while many of the women listed were admirable, "it does not follow that they are famous." Thus one of the nation's most renowned black leaders, Frederick Douglass, demonstrated a limited view of the importance of black women and passed up an opportunity to contribute to an important area of research—black American women's biography.

Thirty-three years later, in 1926, Hallie Quinn Brown published her seminal work, *Homespun Heroines and Other Women of Distinction*. The biographical sketches written by various women for the book presented information on other notable black American women, some of whom may not have been widely known at the time. In one of these sketches, a biography of Elizabeth N. Smith, contributor Maritcha Lyons questioned Frederick Douglass's advice "not to claim too much for ourselves before the public." In fact, Lyons pointed out that "we know so little about ourselves," that we have neglected our history and failed to preserve facts and incidents especially of those who "lived lives of strenuous endurance." Prominent in this category have been black women. Since their stories remained untold, many black American women, enslaved and free, died "unhonored and unsung." In the pre-Civil War era, black women founded schools and trained other young women and men who would, in turn, train others and become educators of renown. We also find among black women of that era concert musicians, linguists, and elocutionists. These women began a tradition of strenuous effort that continues to the present day.

Lyons praised the work of black women throughout the country. She recognized African–American women of the South who "fought the stars in their course, to step out of the darkness of bondage into the light of personal liberty." She said those of the North and other sections of the country "lived clouded lives, made dim by the tales of the indescribable sufferings endured by their sisters by blood and lineage. Their tears have flowed in sympathy and their characters have been molded by large sacrifices cheerfully made upon demand to alleviate distress which at best could only be surmised."

The history of black women in America is the history of such strife and success. Lyons's conclusion in *Homespun Heroines* is a fitting tribute to the black women profiled in this book, *Powerful Black Women,* and other accomplished women not presented here. As she said, "they all have done their duty, much better than they knew. They have left a broad foundation upon which their successors are obligated to raise an enduring superstructure of character, one that will exhibit the progress of the much maligned 'black woman of America,' and so conserve the toils, vigils and prayers of the many whose lives have been lived in shade, who only in lives of others saw 'the shine of distant suns.'"

We extended the work of Monroe Majors and Hallie Q. Brown through the publication in 1992 of *Notable Black American Women,* in 1993 with *Epic Lives,* in 1996 with *Notable Black American Women,* Book II, and now with *Powerful Black Women.* Some of these women set their own foundation while others built upon the structures set by black women pioneers. Whatever they achieved, they make a powerful statement that we would do well to read, study, and benefit from. The women in this book had unbelievable determination and courage: In the 1800s, slave woman Alethia Browning Tanner purchased her own freedom as well as that of seventeen other family members and friends, and in 1833 Maria W. Stewart was perhaps the first black woman to speak publicly on women's rights. The range of women—by time period and area of contribution—is broad. Included are early black educators Charlotte Hawkins Brown and Nannie Helen Burroughs; public officials Jocelyn Elders and Hazel O'Leary; pioneer doctor Justina L. Ford; philanthropist Camille O. Cosby; journalist Hazel B. Garland; calligrapher and illustrator Louise E. Jefferson; early preacher Florence Spearing Randolph; contemporary conductor Kay George Roberts; ice skater Debi Thomas; and singers Marion Williams and Ma Rainey.

Powerful Black Women is the product of many writers who conducted research and wrote painstakingly so that the lives of the women chronicled here could be available to advance scholarship. In many instances the writers pieced together fragments of information, discovered a history that seemed to be lost, and produced a portrait that enlightens and informs. This volume would not have been possible without their important contributions.

This work is also the product of the work of several advisors and countless researchers in libraries and repositories throughout the land.

Expressions of •

Gratitude

The many who worked with the writers are unrecognized individually in this book, and they remain silent contributors to black women's scholarship. Three of the leading institutions that gave support deserve special recognition: Moorland-Spingarn Research Center, Howard University, Washington, D.C.; Schomburg Center for Research in Black Culture, New York Public Library; and Special Collections Department, Fisk University, Nashville, Tennessee. Associated Press/Wide World Photos and the Bettmann Archives also eased the search for illustrations. Despite a diligent search, we were unable to locate photographs for Sarah Forten Purvis and Maria W. Stewart. Due to the importance of their contributions and their life stories they remain part of the collective voice of *Powerful Black Women*.

I thank Robert L. Johns, my Fisk colleague, who created useful computer files, edited essays, wrote essays, conducted bibliographical and biographical research, and offered a sympathetic ear and comforting words as I faced the usual obstacles encountered in such a research project. President Henry Ponder of Fisk University made possible the completion of the project while I was involved in administrative duties. To these supporters and facilitators I am especially grateful.

The staff at Visible Ink Press/Gale Research provided advisory, editorial, and technical expertise. They are all to be recognized for their efforts, particularly Leslie A. Norback, developmental editor; Marie Ellavich, editor; Mary Krzewinski, cover design; Andy Malonis, research specialist; Tracey Rowens, interior page design; and Kim Smilay, permissions associate. I also thank Kevin and Laurie Hillstrom of Northern Lights Writers Group for accurate copyediting and indexing; and Casey Roberts for efficient and precise typesetting.

Jessie Carney Smith,
editor of
Powerful
Black Women

Finally, I acknowledge the gifts of patience, encouragement, and understanding from my family and friends, who allowed me time away from the activities we share so that I could complete this work and who share my enthusiasm for scholarship about African–American women.

God, protect us from and keep
    us from being
Hypocrites
Experts
Attention huggers
Blamers and complainers
Snake oil salespeople
Takers and just talkers
Lone rangers
Excuse makers
Fair-weather workers
Braggers
Magic bullet seekers and sellers
    and
Quitters.
God, send us and help us to be
Righteous warriors
Moral guerrillas
Scut workers
Nitty-gritty doers
Detail tenders
Long-distance runners
Energetic triers
Risk takers
Sharers
Team players
Organizers and mobilizers and
Servant leaders,
to save our children.

Marian Wright Edelman
from, *Guide My Feet: Prayers and Meditations on Loving
and Working for Children*, Beacon Press, 1995

DEBBIE ALLEN

*T*he multi-talented Deborah "Debbie" Allen has arrived as one of

the brightest stars in American show business. For years she honed her

varied skills in obscurity, waiting for an opportunity to display them. She

was patient, though, abiding by her philosophy that "luck is when

opportunity meets preparation" (Current Biography Yearbook, 3). First

catapulted to stardom on the strength of her dancing ability, Allen made

the most of her rising fortunes, establishing herself as a notable actress,

singer, director, and producer as well.

1950– •

Actress, •

dancer,

producer

Allen was born in Houston, Texas, on January 16, 1950, to Vivian (Ayers) Allen, a Pulitzer Prize nominee for poetry, and Andrew Allen, a dentist. She is the third of four children (one sister and two brothers) in an artistic family that also includes actress Phylicia Rashad, known for her role as Clare on *The Cosby Show,* and jazz musician Andrew "Tex" Allen.

At the age of three, Allen began her dance training. By age eight she had settled on a future in musical theater, inspired by a performance of *Revelations* by Alvin Ailey's ballet troupe. Her mother, whom she considers her mentor, was an active participant in her training. After her attempt to enroll Allen in the Houston Foundation for Ballet was denied due to what she perceived to be segregation practices of the time, Vivian Allen contracted a former dancer with the Ballet Russe to give her daughter private lessons. Later she took her three older children and moved to Mexico City, where Allen trained with the Ballet Nacional de Mexico. There Allen became fluent in Spanish and attended perform-ances of the Ballet Folklorico de Mexico. Back in Houston, at age fourteen, she was finally admitted to the Houston Foundation for Ballet on full scholarship. Allen was the only black in the company.

The Houston Foundation for Ballet was not the only institution to erect racially-motivated obstacles to Allen's training. As her senior year of high school approached, she sought but was denied admission to the North Carolina School of the Arts in Winston-Salem. Though the director cited inappropriate body type as the reason for refusal, Allen credited this rejection to a racial quota system. She had, after all, been asked to demonstrate appropriate technique to others auditioning at that time, hardly an indication that she was lacking in talent. This rejection proved difficult for the young dancer to accept. She stopped training for a year, devoting her time instead to studies of Greek classics, speech, and theater arts at Howard University in Washington, D.C.

At Howard, choreographer Mike Malone reintroduced Allen to dance. After recruiting her for his dance troupe, he gave her a part in the Burn Brae Dinner Theater's production of *The Music Man*. Allen began to perform with student groups at the university while also studying at the National Ballet School. She was then named head of the dance department at the Duke Ellington School of the Performing Arts. She received her bachelor of fine arts degree cum laude from Howard in 1971.

Although Allen loved teaching, she also yearned for the stage and decided to go to New York after her graduation. Her first Broadway performance there was in the chorus of the musical adaptation of Ossie Davis's play *Purlie Victorious*, titled *Purlie*. After just six weeks in that show, Allen left to become a principal dancer in George Faison's modern dance troupe, the Universal Dance Experience.

In 1973 Allen returned to the Broadway stage in *Raisin*, a musical rendering of the Lorraine Hansberry classic *A Raisin in the Sun*. She "added a kick and a turn to her dance assignment whenever possible" and was quickly elevated to the featured role of Beneatha (*Current*

Biography Yearbook, 4), where she attracted the attention of reviewers. *New York Post* theatre critic Richard Watts noted that "I liked the attractively humorous and zestful Debbie Allen as the ambitious [young woman]." *Women's Wear Daily*'s Martin Gottfried found her "enchanting . . . and [with] chance enough to show a special talent for dance and a delightful quality altogether" (*New York Theatre Critic's Reviews*, No. 26).

After a nearly two-year run in *Raisin*, Allen began working in television. Her first commercial gave her an opportunity to work with her sister. Her next effort, a role in a comedy-variety series titled *3 Girls 3* was a critical success, but it sagged in the ratings and was quickly canceled. Undeterred, she performed in television specials, working with Ben Vereen on his special *Stompin' at the Savoy* and with Jimmie Walker in the made-for-television movie *The Greatest Thing That Almost Happened*.

Back on stage in 1977, Allen starred with Leslie Uggams and Richard Roundtree in a revival of *Guys and Dolls*. In 1978 she was selected for the lead in a disco version of *Alice in Wonderland*. The production was a disappointing failure and closed after only a short run. Allen described the *Alice* flop as devastating.

Displaying Texas-sized enthusiasm and energy, Allen returned to television in 1979 as Alex Haley's wife in the top-rated miniseries *Roots: The Next Generation*. On stage, she joined the cast of *Ain't Misbehavin'*. That year also marked Allen's film debut in *The Fish That Saved Pittsburgh*. The hard-working actress and dancer worked in duel capacities on the film, acting and serving as the film's choreographer.

In 1980 Allen returned to Broadway in a revival of *West Side Story*. Her dazzling performance placed her in that charmed circle of stars who could name their own projects. Her peers agreed with the laudatory public and critical assessment of her performance. Allen was nominated for the Antoinette Perry ("Tony") Award and awarded the Drama Desk Award for her performance.

That year Allen also took a bit part in the hit movie *Fame,* playing the dance instructor Lydia Grant in the fictionalized look at New York City's High School for the Performing Arts. The movie became a television series and Allen reprised her role as the strong yet empathetic dance instructor while simultaneously serving as the show's choreographer. *Fame* achieved critical acclaim, winning five Emmy Awards (two to Allen for choreography) and a Golden Globe Award for best actress in a series. Anemic ratings, though, led NBC to cancel the show in 1983 after two years. The show gained a new level of popularity in America in

TV Show **Fame**

Allows Allen to

Branch Out

syndication, and emerged as a number one show in syndication in several international markets. For the show's fourth season (1985-1986), Allen added to her duties, serving as producer and director.

Allen maintained a presence in films during the early 1980s as well, taking on roles in *Ragtime* and *Women of San Quentin.* In 1985 she again made time for television production, choreographing, cowriting, and performing in the special *Dancin' in the Wings.*

Back on the big screen in 1986, Allen starred with Richard Pryor in his "semi-autobiography," *Jo Jo Dancer, Your Life is Calling.* Bob Fosse's choreography in the revival of *Sweet Charity* beckoned her back to the Broadway stage that same year. The show won Allen her second Tony nomination. She also filled out her busy year by directing episodes of *Family Ties* and *Bronx Zoo.*

Allen then turned her attention to the television series *A Different World.* The 1987-1988 season was a rocky one for the show, which was a *Cosby Show* spin-off. Blessed with a strong time slot on the heels of *The Cosby Show, A Different World* enjoyed top ratings, but it was battered by critical jeers. Executive producer Bill Cosby challenged Allen to take over behind the camera. Accepting the challenge, she was able to revive the show through creative directing and the introduction of meatier, more realistic plots.

Allen's natural talent and effervescence was most visible in her choreography for *Polly* and *Polly—Coming Home,* a black adaptation of the Polly Anna stories, which aired on ABC in 1989 and 1990. For the 1990 *Motown 30 Special,* a chronology of the thirty years of the black-founded record company, Allen created a dance retrospective that traced the roots of break dancing. The versatile performer also recorded her first album, *Special Look* (1989) around this time.

Despite her whirlwind career, Allen has not sacrificed her personal life. She has been married twice. Her first marriage, in 1975 to CBS Records executive Winfred Wilford, ended in divorce in 1983. In 1984 she married Norman Nixon, a former pro basketball star, with whom she has had two children, Vivian Nichole and Norman Nixon, Jr. Debbie Allen credits Nixon with supporting her in a way that allows her to aggressively pursue her career. "Being rooted in a really good family life situation allows me creative freedom.... I've found myself even more creative since I've had my children," she remarks of her family ("Debbie Allen," *Ebony,* 57).

**Profile by
Sarah Crest**

DEL MARIE NEELY ANDERSON

*I*n July 1991, Del Marie Neely Anderson was appointed president of **1937–** •

_____

San Jose City College in California. She became one of the small group of

_____

black women college presidents who call themselves "sister presidents," **College** •

_____

along with Johnetta Cole of Atlanta's Spelman College and Niara **president,**

_____

Sudarkasa of Lincoln University in Pennsylvania. Anderson worked a **educator, model**

_____

variety of jobs to finance her own education, and she was a college

professor and administrator at various schools in California for sixteen

years prior to her appointment as president. Her decision to pursue a

career in academia may seem somewhat unusual because she was once

a highly successful Ebony *Fashion Fair model who graced the cover of*

the December 7, 1961, issue of Jet *magazine.*

Anderson was born on November 6, 1937, in Vicksburg, Mississippi. Her parents, Frank and Emma Williams, worked as urban laborers, and her great-grandmother lived on a farm where the young girl spent her summers. Reminiscing about her childhood in *Ebony*, Anderson said that she "did everything from cutting down trees to slaughtering animals and curing meats and canning foods."

Anderson was an honor student in elementary school and high school in Vicksburg. She then attended Alcorn Agricultural and Mechanical College for two years, where she supported herself by working as a secretary and maintained her spot on the honor roll. As she came to realize that her education in Mississippi would not prepare her for the future she envisioned, Anderson decided to move to California. She attended school on a part-time basis and again financed her studies by working in various secretarial and other positions.

Anderson once considered a nursing career, but she eventually decided that it would be too taxing physically and emotionally. Although it took her ten years, she completed her undergraduate degree in 1965 and then earned a master's degree in social work in 1967, both at San Diego State University. Anderson humorously related in an interview that she still does her own personal correspondence and can still type faster than the average secretary.

Anderson's most interesting and unique job experience was as an *Ebony* Fashion Fair model. She had attended modeling school in San Francisco as a self-improvement project, and when the Fashion Fair came to that city she interviewed for a modeling job and was hired. Anderson had an opportunity to meet President John F. Kennedy at a White House luncheon, and she was excited to learn that he knew about the organization because of his wife's involvement with the Fashion Fair in Boston. Although Anderson gave up her modeling career to complete her college degree, she explained to *Ebony* in 1992 that she still values the experience: "It has helped me a lot subsequently to be at ease in public situations, to feel comfortable with my body and in presenting myself."

- *Anderson's*

Academic

Career Begins

Anderson began her academic career in 1969 as assistant professor of social work at her alma mater, San Diego State University, and then in 1972 moved to Grossmont College in El Cajon, California, as dean of counseling services, where she also worked with nursing students. Her next career move was to Los Angeles Harbor College in 1981 as dean of student services and later dean of students. While at Grossmont, Anderson had served as mentor to a younger female colleague, Linda G. Salter, who later became president of Skyline College in San Bruno, California. The two had promised that the first one to "make it" would reach back and help the other, and that promise was kept. Salter was instrumental in hiring Anderson in 1986 at Skyline as vice-president for instruction—a position that enabled her to gain valuable management and administrative skills and enhance her growing reputation. Her work at Skyline contributed to her being selected for the presidency at San Jose City College.

Another major factor in developing Anderson's reputation was the highly innovative Model Matriculation Program she designed and implemented at Los Angeles Harbor College. She had long been disturbed over the negative results of the revolving-door policy of California community colleges. Since eight of every ten black students in California are enrolled in community colleges, Anderson was especially concerned about the negative effects on black students, many of whom were not receiving the education they needed to compete in the job market. "I turned the corner philosophically to end the 'revolving door syndrome,'" Anderson stated. She created a new system that would enable students to succeed academically and be qualified to either transfer to four-year colleges or obtain worthwhile jobs.

Anderson's program instituted strict requirements for all prospective students at Harbor College, including orientation and placement testing. Anderson was severely criticized for raising academic standards and making the new procedures mandatory—especially by some blacks, who accused her of discriminating against black students. Because of the visible success of Anderson's program, however, the California legislature took notice and appointed a blue ribbon commission to study it. The commission later recommended passage of a state law mandating that all California community colleges implement the Model Matriculation Program.

Anderson survived a nationwide search for a president of San Jose City College and emerged as the top candidate from a field of 167 applicants. San Jose City College, a two-year public community college that was founded in 1921, has nearly 13,000 students and 390 faculty members. Unlike many other community colleges with a 100 percent commuter student population, San Jose City College provides student activities and athletics, in addition to a full array of student services. Anderson has expressed the same top priority as many other community college presidents: lowering dropout rates. She is also committed to upgrading physical facilities on the old campus and attracting young teachers to replace older faculty members nearing retirement. Anderson's sixteen-year tenure as a community college administrator, extensive networking background, and continuous development of innovative educational programs helped her move toward her goals.

Anderson •

Becomes

College

President

Anderson explained in an interview that she loves being a university president because it enables her to create opportunities to help people grow personally and professionally. She is proud of being a mentor and a frequently tough supervisor who has "carried a lot of people with her." Her belief in helping others has most assuredly carried over from the support she received when she was struggling to make ends meet and reach her educational goals. Anderson claimed that she has no specific role models, but admitted that she has always admired certain strengths and qualities of successful people, especially the schoolteachers who reached out to her when she was a young girl and recognized her drive and potential. She is quick to credit significant people who opened doors that furthered her career ambitions.

Anderson is also involved in a unique civic endeavor that enables her to help people reach their potential. As her first major political initiative, the mayor of San Jose, Susan Hammer, asked Anderson to chair Project Diversity—a policymaking body designed to promote equity among people of different race, gender, age, and physicality in city government. The group was commissioned to recruit applicants, review applications for city government commissions, and make recommendations for an approved list required by law to be used within a year. Anderson allowed no publicity about Project Diversity until the success of the plan was evident, and then the mayor could take full credit for the achievement. To date, San Jose is the only city to entrust such a project to a policymaking body, as opposed to an advisory body with no power over implementation.

Anderson has also embarked on a career as a writer. She completed a chapter on "Non-Traditional Paths to Advancement" for the book *Cracking the Wall: Women in Higher Education,* edited by Patricia Turner Mitchell, a professor at the University of San Francisco. Anderson also planned to edit a book about the changing face of community colleges for Jossey-Bass Publishers.

Seemingly tireless and possessed of an enormous amount of energy, Anderson has expressed even more professional and personal goals. In an interview, she noted that she plans to continue writing and to learn more about corporate fundraising. Buying a piano and taking piano lessons are more immediate personal goals. Anderson claimed that she is not a "social joiner" because her job entails chairing and attending meetings on a regular basis. Although she has no children from a previous sixteen-year marriage, she has always taken an interest in her nieces and nephews. Anderson is a big fan of jazz music, an avowed chocoholic, and a lover of haute couture clothes. Before career demands became so time consuming, she made most of her own clothing, and she is known by her friends as the best bargain shopper around. Reading is another favorite pastime.

Once a high-fashion model, Del Marie Anderson is now a role model for 13,000 San Jose City College students and a mentor to those she believes have the drive and potential to succeed. As Anderson pursued her own dreams, many people assisted her because they recognized her initiative and capability. Now she is returning the favor by helping others.

Profile by
Dolores Nicholson

ANITA BAKER

S *ince the appearance of her album* Rapture *in 1986, Anita Baker*

1958– •

has been recognized as a major recording star. The album won two

Grammy Awards, as did its successor, 1988's Giving You the Best That I

Singer •

Got. In the early 1990s, Baker slowed down her recording and touring

schedule and gave birth to two children. But in 1994 she released

another double Grammy Award-winning album, Rhythm of Love.

Baker's deep, sultry voice and powerful delivery have earned her the

nickname "Queen of Rhythm and Blues."

Baker was born on December 20, 1958, in Toledo, Ohio. She grew up in a foster family as the youngest of four girls. Baker was abandoned by her biological mother at the age of two, but she did not learn this until her foster parents died when she was twelve. At this time an older foster sister, who took over responsibility for her, began telling Baker about her biological family. Shortly thereafter, Baker met her mother, who had been sixteen when Baker was born. Contact between the two has continued over the years, although the relationship is still somewhat strained.

Baker grew up in Detroit, where her foster mother ran a beauty shop and managed to instill a work ethic in her daughters by requiring them to work in the shop to earn money for their clothes and makeup. Baker's foster mother also saw to it that her daughters attended a church that emphasized spontaneity and the workings of the spirit. It was the music of the church that made Baker decide to become a singer at the age of twelve. Her voice was already deep, and her idol was Mahalia Jackson, since Jackson was the only singer Baker knew about whose vocal timbre resembled hers. Until she was about sixteen, Baker sang gospel music at church and enjoyed singing rhythm-and-blues and soul with her friends. Later she became aware of jazz and found a new favorite singer, Sarah Vaughan, whom Baker still idolizes.

Baker first began singing in Detroit clubs when she was sixteen. Her family, thinking that Baker was using poor judgement, prayed for her. In 1978 Baker became the lead singer for a hard-core funk band, Chapter Eight. The popularity of the band in Detroit led to concert tours and a contract with the now-defunct Ariola Records in Los Angeles. The group recorded an album in 1980, and the single "I Just Want to Be Your Girl" was a regional hit, but the band's sound did not match the styles popular at the moment. Executives at Ariola apparently decided that Baker did not have the potential to be a star.

Discouraged, Baker returned to Detroit and stopped singing. At first she waited tables in a club, and then her speaking voice won her a job as a receptionist at a law firm. In 1982 she heard from Otis Smith, formerly with Ariola, who had established the Beverly Glen independent label. Since by this time Baker had a secure job, her own apartment, and a mother happy to see her out of the clubs, it took considerable persuasion to convince Baker to return to Los Angeles and resume a recording career. But she finally acquiesced and recorded the 1983 album *The Songstress* for Beverly Glen. The ballads Baker sang on the album filled an empty niche in the market. The album remained on the rhythm-and-blues charts for over a year, and a single, "Angel," made the top ten. Baker, however, was having difficulties with the label; she was receiving no royalties and her next album was delayed.

Baker began to look for a new record company, but Otis Smith threatened to sue. After spending a considerable amount of time in court due to an action brought by Smith, Baker was finally free to sign with a new label. She chose Elektra, which allowed her the unusual privilege (for a beginner) of acting as the executive producer of her first album for them. After much haggling with Elektra, Baker chose Michael J. Powell, former guitarist with Chapter Eight, as her producer. She then had difficulty coming up with material and eventually wrote three of her own songs to add to the five songs by other people she had chosen. A perfectionist, she also went $100,000 over budget—an expense she was glad to pay.

The album *Rapture* appeared on the Elektra label in late summer 1986. It was well-received by critics and featured two hit singles, "Sweet Love" and "You Bring Me Joy." Baker won an NAACP Image Award that year, and in 1987 she received two Grammy Awards for the album. Sales of *Rapture* had not been impressive initially, but by the end of 1988 it had sold five million copies.

Although she was recording primarily love songs, Baker was also keeping in touch with other types of music. She sang gospel at Trinity Baptist Church from time to time, and in the summer of 1988 she opened for Al Jarreau at Switzerland's Montreux Jazz Festival, singing jazz. Baker's jazz singing brought comparisons of her voice to that of Sarah Vaughan. Baker now rejects any comparison to Vaughan or to another of her favorite singers, Nancy Wilson, saying it will be years before she has trained her voice to the point where the comparison could have any real basis. In a 1988 interview quoted in *Current Biography,* Baker expressed her feelings about her musicianship in connection with her upcoming album: "It wouldn't have been good business for me to rush off and make a jazz album. But I know I've got to expand. My musicianship is limited, and the first thing on my list of things to do is to take some theory classes and learn more harmonies on the piano."

Baker's next album, *Giving You the Best That I Got,* showed more jazz influence than her previous recordings. It was very popular and sold two million copies in the first month alone. Her performance on the album earned her Grammy Awards for best female singer and best record. Critics had mixed feelings, however, generally praising Baker's voice and delivery but questioning her choice of material. Baker's 1990 album, *Compositions,* was basically recorded live in the studio with some overdubs. This album inspired Phyl Garland to write in *Stereo Review:* "She embraces you with her voice, a lustrously textured contralto that she uses like an instrument, carefully shaping the contours of each note to produce a sculptured sound. She then bends these melodic fragments into fresh forms with absolute control and amazing fluidity. And she devotes just as much thought to a song's lyrics, investing them with a mesmerizing intensity."

Baker's *Rhythm of Love* album appeared in September 1994, with a single, "Body and Soul," released in mid-August. The bulk of the album was recorded at a studio at her old home near Detroit, with Baker as executive producer. Although Baker acted as executive producer on her earlier albums for Elektra, *Rhythm of Love* was the first on which she did not work with producer Michael J. Powell.

In concert and in videos, the barely five-foot-tall Baker wears designer gowns and light makeup in a simple setting. This image contrasts sharply with that of her contemporaries Janet Jackson, Madonna, and Whitney Houston. She also contrasts sharply in the amount of publicity she generates; she keeps a very low profile for a major recording star.

Since the summer of 1987 Baker has been living in a home on Lake St. Clair in Michigan. In 1989 she married Walter Bridgforth, who once worked for IBM in the area of marketing but is now a real estate developer. Their first child, Walter Baker Bridgforth, was born in January 1993; a second, Edward Carlton Bridgforth, was born in May 1994. Her family accompanied her on a concert tour to promote *Rhythm of Love* in the spring of 1995.

Despite the four years between her latest albums, Baker retains her popularity. Upon the 1994 release of a sampler of her three previous albums for Elektra, record executive David Bither noted in the *Tennessean Showcase:* "We want to remind people of her stature and influential role in music. She introduced a specific kind of vocal style which other performers have picked up and found success with. Yet she has such a distinctive sound that there is no way she can be confused with anyone else."

**Profile by
Robert L. Johns**

KATHLEEN BATTLE

*F**rom her debut in 1972 at the Spoleto Festival of Two Worlds in*

Italy, Kathleen Battle has emerged as an internationally renowned

operatic singer possessing a light lyric coloratura voice ideal for roles of

ingenues and soubrettes. Battle respects the limitations of her voice,

which lacks the steel quality in its middle range to portray the traditional

grand opera heroines. According to Bernard Holland of the New York

Times Magazine, *Battle's voice "actually challenges the definition of*

'small'.... There is a shimmer, a gleam, above all, a heart, which together

convey the elusive 'ping'—that purity of intonation and sheer musical

caring." In addition to her performances in German and Italian, Battle

frequently includes spirituals in her recitals. She and Jessye Norman,

1948– •

Opera singer •

another African American, have been hailed as two of the nation's finest contemporary sopranos. According to Thomas H. Stahel in *America,* during a recorded concert at Carnegie Hall in March 1990, Battle and Norman "gave a performance of their people's spirituals that will live in the nation's memory, and on its videotapes, as a new standard of American excellence."

Kathleen Deanne Battle was born on August 13, 1948, in Portsmouth, a small industrial city in the southern part of Ohio. In *Current Biography Yearbook, 1984,* Battle describes her family as "wonderfully close" and the source of her strength. Battle is the youngest of seven children of Grady and Ollie Lane Battle.

Battle learned to sing by listening to her father, who was part of a gospel quartet. A sister taught her to read music, and on her own she began to experiment on the piano. She has always enjoyed performing. Attending the African Methodist Episcopal Church with her family as a child, Battle would often be placed on a table to sing at civic functions, banquets, and church activities. As she grew older, she began playing the organ and piano at summer services.

At the public schools of her hometown, Battle excelled in all subject areas. Thus her special musical talent was not immediately recognized when she began formal piano lessons at age thirteen. In high school, Battle continued to study piano and began voice lessons. Since she had a practical approach to life, she also enrolled in secretarial courses and studied typing and shorthand. Charles Varney, Battle's high-school music teacher, encouraged her to go to Cincinnati to study music and gave her her first classical music scores. Upon her graduation from Portsmouth High School in 1966, Battle received a Ford Foundation National Achievement Scholarship.

Battle originally intended to attend college and major in mathematics. However, Varney persuaded her to major in music instead. In her characteristically practical manner, Battle elected to specialize in music education rather than performance upon entering the University of Cincinnati College Conservatory of Music. Having little prior knowledge of the classical vocal repertory and not fully understanding her own capabilities, Battle immersed herself in a program of music studies, art, dance, and languages. By 1971 Battle had earned both her bachelor's and master's degrees in music education from the University of Cincinnati.

Upon completing her formal education, Battle began teaching music to fourth- through sixth-graders in inner-city Cincinnati. She spent her evenings studying second-year German at night school and taking private voice lessons, emphasizing the oratorio literature, with Franklin Bens.

After a year of private lessons, Battle auditioned for Thomas Schippers, director of the Cincinnati Symphony Orchestra and co-founder with Gian-Carlo Menotti of the Spoleto Festival of Two Worlds held annually in Italy. Schippers hired Battle to sing the soprano part in Brahms's *Ein Deutsches Requiem,* as well as several Handel arias, at the 1972 Spoleto Festival. Since she had previously sung only in local church choirs, this festival effectively launched Battle's professional career. Although she returned to the elementary school classroom in the fall of 1972, by this time Battle was certain that she wanted to be a professional singer. She spent much of her leisure time studying opera interpretation, song literature, and acting.

In 1973 Battle was introduced to pianist/conductor James Levine, who was then director of the Cincinnati May Festival. She told *Current Biography Yearbook* that Levine would become "the cornerstone of my career—my mentor, coach, adviser and friend." Not only did Levine hire Battle to appear with him at the Cincinnati and Ravinia (Illinois) festivals, he supervised her training and developed her repertory to include Mozart's *Mass in C Minor,* Haydn's *The Creation,* and Bach's *Cantata No. 202/Weichet nur* (Wedding Cantata).

In March 1974, Battle won first place in the WGN-Illinois Opera Guild Auditions of the Air. She received three thousand dollars and an appearance as featured soloist in the annual Chicago Grant Park Summer Concert Series. In April 1975, Battle's talent was further recognized when she received the top prize in the Young Artists Awards, a national competition at the Kennedy Center for the Performing Arts in Washington, D.C. Also in 1975 she won the Martha Baird Rockefeller Fund for Music Award.

Battle spent part of the summer of 1975 at the Ravinia Festival and was considering spending the next several months auditioning in Europe. But when she was offered the opportunity to understudy and eventually succeed Carmen Balthrop in the title role of *Treemonisha,* the Scott Joplin folk opera on Broadway, Battle altered her plans. When Battle eventually took over the role, her performance was described as one of rare quality.

Singing with increasing confidence, Battle appeared in operas and recitals across the United States. She made her New York City Opera debut as Susanna in Mozart's *Le Nozze di Figaro,* conducted by David Effron, in September 1976. She made her first appearance at the Metropolitan Opera as the Shepherd in a production of Wagner's

Tannhäuser. Her roles during the following season included Sophie in Jules Massenet's *Werther,* Nanetta in Verdi's *Falstaff,* and the page, Oscar, in Verdi's *Un Ballo in maschera.* In addition to singing in various operas, in January 1982 Battle performed a recital of Brahms, Schumann, and Schubert staged by James Levine at New York City's Alice Tully Hall.

Since then Battle has earned an international reputation. Perhaps her most challenging performance in the 1983–84 season was a three-concert recital series at Alice Tully Hall entitled "Kathleen Battle and Friends." Assisted by her manager, Samuel Niefeld, Battle selected music by Bach, George Gershwin, and Duke Ellington and invited pianist James Levine, trumpeter Wynton Marsalis, and flutist Hubert Laws to accompany her. She also received great acclaim that season for her performance of the roles of Solomon's Queen and Queen of Sheba in Handel's *Solomon* with the Musica Sacra Chorus and Orchestra at Avery Fischer Hall in New York City. Of this performance *New Yorker* music critic Andrew Porter wrote: "Miss Battle's singing of the two queens was so exquisitely beautiful and distinguished that one wanted to hear as much of her as possible.... I thought her account of the Queen of Sheba's 'Will the sun forget to streak Eastern skies with amber ray' the most ravishing performance of a Handel air I have ever heard."

Battle's career continued to expand internationally in the following years. During the summer of 1984, Battle went to Paris to sing the role of Susanna in *Le Nozze di Figaro* and to Salzburg to perform Despina in *Così fan tutte.* A live recording grew out of her 1988 Tokyo performance. Another high point came with the videotaped performance entitled *Kathleen Battle and Jessye Norman Sing Spirituals,* aired on PBS in December 1990 as a part of the Great Performances series.

A disciplined performer, Battle is said to exude professionalism. Bernard Holland observed that in contrast to many singers, including some celebrities, who use rehearsals to learn what they will perform, Battle arrives at her first rehearsal "scrupulously prepared." When asked by *Esquire* magazine, "Whom are you trying to please?" Battle replied: "Sometimes you try to put all thoughts out of your head and try to become closer to the music. At those moments . . . you soar with the music. Then, of course, you would be singing to the deities."

Battle's reputation changed somewhat in February 1994, when the Metropolitan Opera cancelled all of its contracts with her. Management characterized Battle as one who cancels performances and storms out of rehearsals. Battle's agent, however, released a public statement saying that she had not been told about unprofessional actions. The dispute prompted the *Washington Post* to label her a "tempestuous mega-soprano," and she was included with other difficult artists in "the world's

Battle's •

Reputation

Grows

major leagues of vocal drama." Already a diva and overbooked for performances, Battle's career is not expected to suffer and might even benefit from the notoriety.

In 1992, Battle was among the recipients of Candace awards given by the National Coalition of 100 Black Women. The award recognizes black women who embody the coalition's goal of empowering black women through programs focused upon volunteering, building leadership, role modeling, and mentoring.

Battle, an attractive woman both on- and offstage, maintains a striking figure and dresses in designer clothes. She is said to possess sensuality and sophistication uncommon among soubrettes. Though Battle may be described as somewhat reserved with strangers, she is very confident about herself and her objectives. As she explained to Bernard Holland, "I've accepted my reality. . . . I was meant to sound the way I do."

**Profile by
Dawn Cooper
Barnes**

HALLE BERRY

H *alle Berry, considered one of Hollywood's hottest black actresses*

and one of the fifty most beautiful women in the world, gained fame first

as a beauty queen, then for her roles in film and on television. Since her

film debut in 1991, she has enjoyed a high-profile rise to success. While

she may be best known for her lead role as Alex Haley's grandmother in

the television miniseries Queen, *Berry calls herself an activist for the*

integration of the film industry.

c. 1967–

Actress,

model,

activist

Berry was born around 1967 in Cleveland to a white mother and a black father. Her father, who was an alcoholic and abusive to his wife, left the family when Berry was four years old. Berry and her sister, Heidi, were raised by their mother, Judith (Judy) Berry, a registered nurse. Life in a racist society was not easy for the young, biracial child. At first Judy Berry and her daughters lived in Cleveland's inner-city neighborhood, where race was not an issue. But when they moved to the racially mixed suburban neighborhood of Bedford, such taunts as "half-breed," "mulatto," and "Oreo cookie" were often hurled at Berry, who was totally unaware of their meaning.

Berry attended the predominantly white Bedford High School, where she was constantly confronted with racial discrimination. Her schoolmates rejected her, often engaging her in fights. As she told Laura Randolph in *Ebony,* "The Black kids assumed I thought I was better than they were, and the White kids didn't like me because I was Black. And I didn't know who I felt comfortable with, Black people or White people."

She added that her mother had cleared up any uncertainty about whether she was white or black when Berry was very young. Berry paraphrased her mother's remark for Randolph: "When you look in the mirror you're going to see a Black woman. You're going to be discriminated against as a Black woman so ultimately, in this society, that's who you will be." Berry continued: "And that's made my life very easy.... I think if you're an interracial child and you're strong enough to live 'I'm neither Black nor White but in the middle,' then more power. But I *needed* to make a choice and feel part of this culture. I feel a lot of pride in being a Black woman."

Her mother's words and her early experiences helped to shape Berry's thoughts on matters of race. After she was elected prom queen in her senior year in high school, she was accused of stuffing the ballot box. Backed by the school administration, the students forced Berry to share the crown with "this White, blond, blue-eyed, all-American girl," Berry recalled to Randolph. "It made me feel like I wasn't beautiful; that they don't see *us* as beautiful."

When Berry was seventeen years old, a high school boyfriend entered her name in the Miss Teen Ohio Pageant. She won that title in 1985 as well as the Miss Ohio Pageant. The state title qualified her for competition in the 1985 Miss USA contest, in which she was named first runner-up. In 1986 she was winner of the dress competition in the Miss World Pageant.

In 1986 Berry entered Cuyahoga Community College in Cleveland, where she studied broadcast journalism. However, she left college that year, moving to Chicago to pursue modeling and to study acting. Berry auditioned for a role in Aaron Spelling's television pilot *Charlie's Angels '88,* a show that never aired. Impressed with her Los Angeles screen test, however, Spelling encouraged her to continue to pursue acting. Berry's career began to take off. She did a three-week USO tour with Bob Hope and also signed with a manager, Vincent Cirrincione. She moved to New York City and landed a role as a brainy model in ABC's situation comedy *Living Dolls,* which premiered in September 1989. When the show was canceled in December, Berry worried that people weren't taking her seriously as an actress.

Berry's big break came in 1991, when she won a leading role in Spike Lee's film *Jungle Fever*. In preparing to play Vivien, a crazed crack addict, Berry interviewed more than eighty recovering cocaine addicts and deliberately delayed taking a bath for ten days to "get into character." Berry's performance established her as a talented character actress and enabled viewers to see her as more than a pretty face.

Additional roles followed quickly. Later in 1991, Berry appeared as a sexy, aloof entertainer in *Strictly Business* and co-starred with Damon Wayans and Bruce Willis in *The Last Boy Scout*. In 1992 she appeared as Eddie Murphy's friend and lover in the film *Boomerang*. She had a recurring role in the popular nighttime soap opera *Knots Landing*, but left the show to work on Murphy's movie.

Berry gained popular attention again in 1993 when she played Alex Haley's grandmother in the television miniseries *Queen*. This role enabled Berry to get in touch with her feelings about her racial identity. "I saw a lot of the young me in *Queen*," she admitted to Randolph. "The confusion, the uncertainty, not really knowing if you should be Black or White." The film also led Berry to examine the continued oppression of blacks.

Berry has since appeared in many other movies. She played a journalist opposite Patrick Swayze in *Honor among Thieves*, and she played a college student in *The Program*, with James Caan. She won praise for her work in *Halle-lujba*. She appeared as a seductive Stone Age secretary in *The Flintstones* in 1994, having studied old tapes of Mae West to prepare for the role. After completing shooting on *Losing Isaiah* in Chicago, she was off to Morocco to play the Queen of Sheba in the film *Solomon and Sheba*. Beyond this, Berry has been studying the life of educator and activist Angela Davis, gearing up to convince the studios that Davis's work affected all Americans regardless of race. In addition, Suzanne de Passe of de Passe Entertainment approached Berry about a film on the life of Elaine Brown, who headed the Black Panther Party.

Since 1993 Berry has focused on projects "to open doors to the mainstream," as she told Lisa Jones in *Jet*. She further stated that she would like to see blacks in the film industry depart from stereotypical roles: "I'd like to see us change the picture of ourselves that we're presenting to the public. It's something that *we* have to do because the studios won't." Berry also became an AIDS activist in 1993, when she shared an apartment with Paul Kirkpatrick, a gay white male who was dying of AIDS. She explained to Randolph that their friendship gave her a new perspective on life and a new understanding of AIDS: "I've learned how short and precious life is."

Berry faced a health-related challenge of her own when she was diagnosed with diabetes after collapsing on a set. Her doctors noted that stress probably caused the disease to manifest itself early in her life. Although doctors predicted that she would be insulin-dependent the rest of her life, she has improved her health through diet, exercise, meditation, and low-stress activities. For example, she installed a state-of-the-art gym at home and hired a personal trainer to work with her when she was filming away from home.

Prior to her marriage in 1993, Berry was involved in several abusive relationships with men. She explained to Randolph that she had always wanted an honest, romantic relationship, but she allowed herself "to get in some strange relationships because I was searching for that." She had turned to men who needed to be "rescued" but in time they left her "holding all their baggage." One highly abusive relationship left her permanently damaged. "One guy hit me in the eardrum and I lost 80 percent of my hearing in my left ear," she told Randolph. Although she should wear a hearing aid, often she is too self-conscious to do so.

One of the most personally rewarding events in Berry's life was her marriage to Atlanta Braves outfielder David Justice, a native of Cincinnati. After a courtship of ten months, Justice accepted Berry's marriage proposal. Berry told Jones that proposing to Justice "was part of my taking control of my love life and relationships." The couple have similar backgrounds: both were raised by their mothers after their fathers left home when they were four years old. At their wedding, Judith Berry was maid of honor and Nettie Justice, David's mother, was "best woman." Although Berry and Justice have busy careers that require them to spend time apart, they respect each other's work. The marriage has resulted in greater calm and internal peace for Berry.

Halle Berry is constantly in the news because of her talent, her film work, and her beauty. In 1993 *People* magazine named her one of their "50 Most Beautiful People in the World." *Ebony's* Annual Readers Poll, published in the September 1993 issue, called Berry and Denzel Washington the "hottest stars in Black America." But Berry has used her fame to become an activist on behalf of a number of worthwhile causes. For example, Berry is committed to addressing the problems that destroy black communities—guns and drugs. She also protests against a color-biased film industry, trying to force the industry to stop portraying black women as nannies, prostitutes, and crackheads. As she noted to Jones, "I feel that this is *our* time to break new ground, to make statements."

**Profile by
Jessie Carney Smith**

WILLA BROWN

A pioneering aviator, Willa Brown was the first African-American

officer in the Civil Air Patrol (CAP). In 1943, she became the only

woman in the United States who simultaneously possessed a mechanic's

license and a commercial license in aviation. She was employed as

president of the National Airmen's Association, the Pioneer Branch,

located in Chicago. A tireless advocate of aviation, Brown was instru-

mental in integrating the aviation industry. She is also remembered for

training some of the most celebrated African-American pilots of World

War II. In addition, Brown became the first African-American woman

to run for a U.S. congressional seat in 1946.

Willa Beatrice Brown was born on January 22, 1906, in Glasgow,

1906–1992 •

Aviator, •

activist,

educator

Kentucky, to Eric B. Brown, a minister, and Hallie Mae Carpenter Brown. Her parents moved the family to Indianapolis, Indiana, when Brown was about six years old. They later moved to Terre Haute, Indiana, where Brown received most of her education, graduating from Sarah Scott Junior High School in 1920, and from Wiley High School in 1923.

After high school Brown attended Indiana State Teachers College, where she received a bachelor of science degree in business in 1927. Brown began to teach in Gary, Indiana, immediately after graduating from college. Five years later, she moved to Chicago and began teaching in the city's public schools. In 1934, Brown began postgraduate studies at Northwestern University. Three years later she obtained a master's degree in business administration. In addition to her various teaching positions, Brown secured numerous other jobs in Indiana and Chicago after receiving her college degree. Between 1927 and 1939, she worked as a secretary for several prominent men, held two federal civil service positions, and was employed as a social service worker and as a cashier.

Brown began to pursue her interest in aviation while attending Northwestern University in the mid-1930s. She signed up for flight lessons with Fred Schumacher, who taught at the Harlem Airport in the Oak Lawn suburb of Chicago. She also exercised her business acumen by managing Brown's Lunch Room, a small sandwich shop at the airport. She undertook additional training from Dorothy Darby and Colonel John C. Robinson and received a master mechanic's certificate in 1935 from the Aeronautical University, located in the Chicago Loop. Subsequently, she studied aviation with Lieutenant Cornelius R. Coffey (who was to become her second husband).

Brown earned her private pilot's license, which permitted her to carry passengers, on June 22, 1938—passing her examination with a grade of 96 percent. Brown then became affiliated with a flight service located at Harlem Airport, taking curious adventurers up in an airplane for ten-minute entertainment jaunts for a dollar. Her involvement with aviation soon expanded into administration and activism. Brown became a member of the Challenger Air Pilots Association, one of the first African-American pilot organizations, founded in 1931 by Colonel John C. Robinson. The pilots owned their own hangar, located at the Harlem Airport. Brown served as chairperson of the education committee for the group.

Brown, along with her husband Cornelius R. Coffey and journalist Enoc P. Waters Jr., founded the National Airmen's Association of America in 1939. That same year the association elected Brown as its national secretary, and she also began to teach aviation subjects for the Works Progress Administration (WPA) Adult Education Program. She received her Civil Aeronautics Authority (CAA) ground school instructor's rating in 1940. Also in 1940, Brown and Coffey established the Coffey School of Aeronautics. Brown was director of the school during its first two years of existence. Brown's education in business administration served her well because, in addition to teaching at the school, she handled administrative and promotional responsibilities. The Coffey School of Aeronautics closed in 1945, after World War II.

Inspired by the life of her predecessor, aviator Bessie Coleman (1896–1929), Brown enlisted the assistance of *Chicago Defender* editor Robert Abbott when she embarked upon her career as an aviation advocate. During the early 1930s Abbott was providing financial sponsorship for tours of African-American aviators to African-American colleges and universities, where they encouraged students to get involved in aviation. He was also lobbying Congress to include African Americans in federally sponsored aviation programs. At this time, the U.S. military forces were segregated; African Americans were denied enlistment in the U.S. Army Air Corps, and there was no indication that the government would award contracts for the training of African-American pilots.

Brown also promoted the efforts of Chauncey Spencer and Dale White, two licensed pilots and members of the National Airmen's Association (a black organization) who flew from Chicago to Washington in an outmoded airplane to lobby for the inclusion of African Americans in the Civilian Pilot Training Program (CPTP)—a government-funded aviation training program initiated in 1939 and designed to prepare a reserve supply of civilian pilots who could be called upon in the event of a national emergency. Brown traveled throughout the country encouraging young African Americans to take up aviation, and she also went to Washington, D.C., to persuade the federal government to award CPTP contracts for the training of African-American pilots. *Chicago Defender* city editor Enoc P. Waters Jr. covered the majority of her recruitment activities and the air shows in which she performed to stimulate the interest of prospective aviators.

During this same period, Brown taught aviation mechanics for the Chicago Board of Education and was elected president of the Chicago branch of the National Airmen's Association and vice-president of the Aeronautical Association of Negro Schools. Brown used these administrative positions to successfully petition a reluctant U.S. government to integrate African Americans into the U.S. Army Air Corps and to provide them with training through the CPTP.

Brown was widely respected in the white male-dominated field of aviation. As a testament to this fact, in 1940 she was chosen by the U.S. Army Air Corps and the Civil Aeronautics Administration to participate in an experimental program for the admission of African Americans to the U.S. Army Air Corps. Her abilities were recognized again when the U.S. government appointed her federal coordinator for two Chicago units of the CPTP. Brown achieved the rank of lieutenant in Squadron 613-6 of Illinois in 1942, making her the first African-American officer in the Civil Air Patrol. In her capacity as lieutenant in this squadron, as noted by Jesse J. Johnson in *Black Women in the Armed Forces,* "she organized more than 1,000 young people who also marched in military and civilian parades. Brown was adjutant of this squadron; Captain Coffey was commander."

The majority of the CPTP government contracts that went to blacks were awarded to black colleges between 1939 and 1945. Tuskegee Institute was the only school to train African-American officers. Brown, however, was awarded contracts to train African-American pilots at the Coffey School of Aeronautics and at Wendell Phillips High School, two non-college units. As director of the Coffey School of Aeronautics, she administered federal contracts valued between sixty and one hundred thousand dollars annually. Brown trained some of the most distinguished African-American pilots of World War II. Several of the men she trained in aviation mechanics went on to become members of the now-legendary Tuskegee Airmen of the Ninety-ninth Pursuit Squadron—the military's first African-American pilots.

From 1935—when she joined other supporters in organizing a memorial flight to pay homage to the first internationally licensed American pilot, Bessie Coleman—until her death in 1992, Brown was a prominent advocate for aviation. After the closing of the Coffey School in 1945, she established children's flight clubs to stimulate interest in careers in aviation. For many years she remained active in the National Airmen's Association, the Civil Air Patrol (Illinois wing), Women Flyers of America, the National Aviation Training Association, the International Women's Air and Space Museum, the OX-5 Pioneer Aviation Club, and the Tuskegee Airman's Association.

In addition to her other achievements, Brown was the first African-American woman to run for a U.S. congressional seat, making unsuccessful bids as a Republican in 1946, 1948, and 1950. In 1947, Brown campaigned for the position of Chicago alderman, also unsuccessfully. Remarkably, she continued to teach in the Chicago Public School System until she retired in 1971. In 1972, she was appointed to the Federal Aviation Administration's Women's Advisory Board in recognition of her contributions to aviation in the United States. Brown was proud of her accomplishments, and she clearly created opportunities for African Americans in the field through her work as an aviator, aviation instructor, and aviation activist.

Brown was married three times: first to Wilbur Hardaway, an alderman in Gary, Indiana; then to Cornelius R. Coffey, a certified flight instructor and an expert aviation and engine mechanic; and finally to the Reverend J. H. Chappell. After marrying Chappell in 1955, she became very active in the West Side Community Church in Chicago. She had no children. Brown died of a stroke at the University of Chicago's Bernard Mitchell Hospital on July 18, 1992 at the age of eighty-six.

**Profile by
Elizabeth Hadley
Freydberg**

NANNIE HELEN BURROUGHS

Nannie Helen Burroughs was a spellbinding, outspoken orator

who was a member of a network of southern black female activists who

emerged as leaders of national organizations. William Pickens, a

pioneer NAACP administrator and writer, commented that "no other

person in America has so large a hold on the loyalty and esteem of the

colored masses as Nannie H. Burroughs. She is regarded all over the

broad land as a combination of brains, courage, and incorruptibleness"

(*Pickens,* Nannie Burroughs and the School of the 3B's*).*

1879–1961 •

School founder, •

civil rights

activist

Nannie Helen Burroughs was born in Orange, Virginia, on May 2, 1879, to John Burroughs and Jennie (Poindexter) Burroughs. Her parents belonged to that small and fortunate class of ex-slaves whose energy and ability enabled them to start towards prosperity almost as soon as the war that freed them was over. Young Nannie moved with her mother to Washington, D.C., in 1883. She was educated through the high school level at the M Street High School in the nation's capital and graduated with honors in 1896. She studied business in 1902 and received an honorary A.M. degree from Eckstein-Norton University in Kentucky in 1907.

Burroughs was employed in Louisville, Kentucky, from 1898 to 1909 as bookkeeper and editorial secretary of the Foreign Mission Board of the National Baptist Convention. While in Louisville, she organized the Women's Industrial Club, which conducted domestic science and secretarial courses. She was also one of the founders of the Women's Convention, auxiliary to the National Baptist Convention USA, and served efficiently as its corresponding secretary for almost a half century (1900-1947). From 1948 until her death in 1961 she was president of the Women's Convention. The convention comprised the largest group of African-Americans in the world, and the auxiliary was a potent force in black religious groups.

Burroughs's childhood dream of establishing an industrial school for girls led her to mobilize the Women's Convention to underwrite such a venture. On October 19, 1901, the National Training School for Women and Girls opened in Washington, D.C., with Nannie Burroughs as president. By the end of its first year the school had enrolled thirty-one students. Twenty-five years later it boasted of more than two thousand women trained at the secondary and junior college level. Taking in girls from all over the United States, Africa, and the Caribbean Basin, Burroughs placed great significance in training for spiritual values. She thus dubbed her school the "School of the 3 B's—the Bible, bath, and broom." In 1934 the school was named the National Trades and Professional School for Women, but the school was inactive for a time during the Great Depression of the 1930s. Burroughs later reopened it, and she continued to direct the school until her death in 1961. In 1964 the board of trustees abandoned the old trade school curriculum and reestablished it as the Nannie Helen Burroughs School for students at the elementary school level.

Burroughs's sensitivity for the African-American working woman was expressed during her participation in the club movement during the late decades of the nineteenth century and the early decades of the twentieth century. Black women organized first on a local level and then nationally to shoulder educational, philanthropic, and welfare activities. The growing needs of the urban poor in a period of rapid industrialization, coupled with the presence of a sizeable group of educated women with leisure time, led to the emergence of a national club movement. These women's clubs proved tremendously beneficial in many communities. The dearth of social welfare institutions in many southern areas, and the recurrent exclusion of blacks from those facilities that did exist, led black women to found orphanages, day-care facilities, homes for the aged, schools, and similar services. In the case of the most prominent female founders of black educational institutions—Lucy Craft Laney, Charlotte Hawkins Brown, Mary McLeod Bethune, and Nannie Burroughs—their schools became centers for community organizations, women's activities, and a network of supporting institutions.

In the 1890s local clubs began to form federations almost simultaneously in a number of cities. In 1896 the newly formed National Association of Colored Women (NACW) united the three largest of these groups as well as more than a hundred local women's clubs. In addition to her laudable contributions to the NACW, Burroughs also founded the National Association of Wage Earners in order to draw public attention to the dilemma of Negro women. Its national board included Nannie Burroughs as president, with well-known clubwoman Mary McLeod Bethune as vice-president and banker Maggie Lena Walker as treasurer. The women placed more significance on educational forums of public interest than on trade union activities.

Nannie Burroughs and several other clubwomen contended that black women should not take a passive or subordinate position to men. While they criticized those black males who refused to support efforts toward equal rights, these reformers differed from their white sisters in that they did not define feminism as a response to male exploitation. Burroughs, a majestic, dark-skinned woman with a commanding presence and voice, was a vocal supporter of racial and sexual consciousness. An unyielding advocate of racial pride and African-American heritage, Burroughs was a long-time member of the Association for the Study of Negro Life and History. She continually urged blacks to learn and understand their history and culture.

Equal Rights •

for Black

Women

Advocated

In addition to her work on behalf of various organizations, Burroughs was a steadfast supporter of the religious and secular program advanced by Walter Henderson Brooks and the Nineteenth Street Baptist Church in the District of Columbia. Brooks was a prominent clergyman, scholar, and temperance advocate who, while capable of directing withering criticism at those who succumbed to drunkenness, gambling, fornication, and adultery, also preached and advocated the social gospel. The NACW was founded at his church in 1896. Finally, as a devout Baptist, Burroughs worked for almost fifty years with the Baptist World Alliance.

Throughout her life Burroughs fought hard for issues she believed in. Burroughs was active in antilynching campaigns and in the successful effort to memorialize the home of abolitionist Frederick Douglass (she served as secretary of the Frederick Douglass Memorial Association). She was also a member of the Women's Division of the Commission on Interracial Cooperation (CIC), although she disagreed vehemently with the views of the CIC's Association of Southern Women for the Prevention of Lynching regarding the legitimacy of federal intervention in the matter (Burroughs favored it).

Burroughs came to be regarded as one of the most stirring platform orators in the country, and her writings likewise reflected her belief in desegregation, self-help, and self-reliance. Her public pronouncements were deeply influenced by her faith in God, and she felt that racial equality was an ethical priority—a spiritual mandate from heaven. She told her readers to use "ballots and dollars" to fight racism instead of "wasting time begging the white race for mercy" and hailed the great moral, spiritual, and economic assets of the black woman (*Afro-American,* April 28, 1934). On other occasions she exhorted blacks to "chloroform your Uncle Toms," warning that "the Negro must unload the leeches and parasitic leaders who are absolutely eating the life out of the struggling, desiring mass of people" ("Fighting Woman Educator Tells What Race Needs," *Pittsburgh Courier*).

In 1944 the Baptist Woman's Auxiliary initiated a quarterly journal, *The Worker,* under the editorship of Nannie Burroughs. She also wrote several longer works of a religious nature, including *Grow: A Handy Guide for Progressive Church Women, Making Your Community Christian,* and *Words of Light and Life Found Here and There.* For a number of years she wrote a syndicated column, "Nannie Burroughs Says," which was carried by several black newspapers in a prominent position. In a lighter vein, she authored *The Slabtown District Convention: A Comedy in One Act,* which was a popular church fundraiser.

At one point the intrepid Nannie Burroughs took W. E. B. Du Bois of the NAACP to task after Du Bois suggested to black Americans that they submit to segregation. "You would think that the world is coming to an end because one man 'does not choose to fight' segregation any longer," said Burroughs in the *Afro-American* in April 1934. "Any man who is hired can quit when he pleases. A person who is getting paid to solve the Negro problem is no exception to the rule.... Du Bois is at least or at last honest. He could have kept his mouth shut and continued to draw his decreasing stipend from the NAACP.... Dr. Du Bois is tired. He has fought a good fight. It is too bad that he did not keep the faith and finish his course."

In July 1934 Nannie Burroughs launched Washington's first "Negro self-help project." A laundry, formerly owned by the training school, was turned over to the federal government by Burroughs. The Federal Emergency Relief Authority renovated the building, which included a laundry and dry cleaning plant, a barber shop, a sewing and canning center, a commissary, a garment-making and upholstery shop, and a shoe repair shop. Nationwide interest was kindled in the project, and it subsequently served as a model for other projects that were inaugurated during the Great Depression in other parts of the United States.

Nannie Helen Burroughs died of natural causes in Washington, D.C., in May 1961. Funeral rites were held in the Nineteenth Street Baptist Church with interment in Lincoln Memorial Cemetery, Suitland, Maryland. There were no immediate survivors.

**Profile by
Casper LeRoy
Jordan**

SEPTIMA CLARK

S eptima Poinsette Clark is known for her pioneering efforts to

establish equality across all social and racial lines. Her years of dedica-

tion to the cause of black literacy, black voter registration, and women's

and civil rights led others to recognize her as the "queen mother" of the

civil rights movement.

1898–1987 •

Educator, •

humanitarian

Clark was born on May 3, 1898, in Charleston, South Carolina, the second of eight children of Peter Porcher Poinsette (who was a slave until the age of eighteen) and Victoria Warren (Anderson) Poinsette. Septima was a gregarious youngster. She often gathered younger children together for outings, thus earning the nickname "Little Ma" or "Le Ma." After completing her elementary education, Clark attended Avery Normal School, a private school for educating black teachers that was operated by the American Missionary Association. After graduation her teachers encouraged her to attend Fisk University, but her parents were unable to afford the tuition.

In the early twentieth century black teachers were forbidden to teach in the public schools of Charleston. Clark was free to teach in the surrounding communities, though, and she began her teaching career at Promise Land School on Johns Island in 1916. She soon joined the National Association for the Advancement of Colored People (NAACP).

When the Charleston chapter of the NAACP fought to strike down the state law that forbade black teachers from teaching in public city schools, Clark was a leading force in the effort. The NAACP bid proved successful, and the law was changed in 1920.

On May 23, 1920, the young teacher married Nerie Clark, a sailor she met in Charleston. Clark had two babies, one who died after twenty-three days and one healthy boy named Nerie. The marriage ended with her husband's death from kidney failure about 1924. Clark never married again. Leaving the baby with her parents-in-law in Hickory, North Carolina, Clark returned to Johns Island to teach for three more years, then moved to Columbia, South Carolina. She received her bachelor's degree from Benedict College and her master's degree from Hampton Institute (now University) in Hampton, Virginia.

Active in many clubs and civic groups, Clark learned to organize programs of all kinds in an atmosphere that was more democratic than Charleston had been. Back in Charleston, the city's rigid caste patterns did not permit Clark to associate with lighter, upper-class blacks. In Columbia she worked with the NAACP to secure equal pay for black teachers. Attorney Thurgood Marshall successfully argued the case put together by the local chapter before a federal court.

In 1947 Clark returned to Charleston to care for her mother, who had suffered a stroke. During the ensuing years she taught remedial reading and worked in several civic organizations. In 1947 Julius Waties Waring, a local white judge of the federal district court, ruled that blacks must be permitted to vote in the Democratic primary. Clark, who admired this principled stand, established a friendship with Waring and his wife. The courage of Clark and the Warings was greatly tested, though, for white society ostracized the Warings, while some blacks began to shun Clark for stirring up trouble.

In 1954 a coordinated legislative attack by white southerners led the South Carolina legislature to bar teachers from belonging to the NAACP. Clark refused to deny her membership and lost her job just four years short of retirement. Unable to find employment anywhere in South Carolina, in 1956 she was named director of education for the Highlander Folk School in Tennessee, a noted planning center for both black and white community activists that had been founded by Myles Horton.

In the mid-1950s Clark directed a workshop at Highlander on the United Nations that was attended by Rosa Parks. Parks later commented that "I am always very respectful and very much in awe of the presence of Septima Clark because her life story makes the effort that I have made very minute. I only hope that there is a possible chance that some of her great courage and dignity and wisdom has rubbed off on me" (Brown, *Ready From Within*, 16-17).

Although Clark had left Johns Island, she had not forgotten the people there. In January 1957 Clark and others opened a citizenship school on the island. This school served as the prototype for similar schools all over the South. Clark coordinated the citizenship schools program from Highlander while simultaneously pushing ministers and other local leaders all over the South to establish similar programs. By the spring of 1961, eighty-two teachers who had been trained at Highlander were holding classes in Alabama, Georgia, South Carolina, and Tennessee.

A foreboding cloud descended over Clark's work, however, in the summer of 1959. Tennessee state police raided Highlander in an attempt to find evidence they could use to revoke Highlander's charter and shut it down. The state closed Highlander and in December 1961 auctioned off all its property without compensation.

Horton, however, had anticipated the closing of the school. He had negotiated with Martin Luther King Jr. to transfer the sponsorship of the citizenship program from Highlander to the Southern Christian Leadership Conference (SCLC). Undaunted by the events in Tennessee, Clark moved to Georgia and set up her training sessions at the Dorchester Cooperative Community Center. She and two other SCLC staff-members—Dorothy Cotton and Andrew Young—drove all over southern states, herding busloads of students to the center, which became an important shaper of future civil rights leaders. Clark used the practical teaching methods she had been developing for more than forty years at the center. Her great gift, however, lay in recognizing natural leaders among the poorly educated students and imparting to them her unshakable confidence and respect.

Clark Leads in •

the Women's

Movement

In 1962 the SCLC joined four other civil rights groups to form the Voter Education Project. In the next four years, ten thousand teachers were trained for citizenship schools and almost seventy thousand black voters were registered across the South. After the passage of the Voting Rights Act in 1965, registration increased rapidly, and at least one million more black people were registered by 1970. Two years later Barbara Jordan and Andrew Young were elected to the U.S. Congress, the first blacks to serve in that legislative body since Reconstruction.

Clark fought discrimination of all kinds throughout her life. Known for her civil rights work, she also defended the rights of women, encouraging women's rights activists wherever she went and criticizing some ministers of the SCLC for their arrogance toward women.

Clark was emphatic in her belief that the civil rights movement grew out of the women's movement, not the other way around, as is commonly interpreted:

> Many people think that the women's liberation movement came out of the civil rights movement, but the women's movement started quite a number of years before the civil rights movement. In stories about the movement you hear mostly about the black ministers. But if you talk to the women who were there, you'll hear another story. I think the movement would never have taken off if some women hadn't started to speak up.... It took fifty years for women, black and white, to learn to speak up. I had to learn myself, so I know what a struggle it was (Brown, *Ready from Within,* 82-83).

When Clark retired from active SCLC work in the summer of 1970, she was presented with a flurry of awards in recognition of her accomplishments, including the Martin Luther King Jr. Award "for Great Service to Humanity" and South Carolina's highest civilian award, the Order of the Palmetto, in 1982. Clark still had to fight the state for her pension and back pay, though. After her dismissal in 1956, all her retirement funds in the state pension had been canceled. By 1976, though, the National Education Association was airing her case all over the United States. Stung by the publicity, South Carolina's state legislature decided to pay her an annual pension of $3,600. In July 1981 the state, which still owed her a salary from 1956 to 1964, approved paying her back salary.

Clark celebrated her seventy-eighth birthday by winning election to the Charleston School Board; she served two terms before turning it over to younger leadership. In 1987 she received an American Book Award for her second autobiography, *Ready from Within: Septima Clark and the Civil Rights Movement.* Later that year, on December 15, 1987, Clark passed away after enduring a series of strokes.

Sometimes known as "Mother Conscience," Clark was also known and loved as the "queen mother" of the civil rights movement. At Clark's funeral many leaders testified to the enduring importance of Clark's life. Charleston Mayor Joseph P. Riley Jr. spoke for many when he remarked that "her purity is everlasting and universal; her legacy is everywhere." Reverend Joseph E. Lowery, president of the SCLC, testified: "Like Harriet Tubman, who led her people to freedom through territorial pilgrimages, Septima Clark led her people to freedom through journeys from the darkness of illiteracy to the shining light of literacy" (Blakeney, "Mourners Recall Extraordinary Life," 1). Two years later, Taylor Branch,

• *Clark Called*

"Queen Mother"

of the Civil

Rights

Movement

author of *Parting the Waters: America in the King Years 1954-1963*, wrote that Clark's character was:

> a miraculous balance between leathery zeal and infinite patience. Clark was a saint even to many of the learned critics who predicted she would fail.... She worked both sides of the gaping class divide without letting the friction ruin her spirits. (Branch, *Parting the Waters*, 264).

Profile by Cynthia Stokes Brown

ALICE COACHMAN

"I've always believed that I could do whatever I set my mind to do,"

Alice Coachman once told Essence *magazine. "I've had that strong will,*

that oneness of purpose, all my life.... I just called upon myself and the

Lord to let the best come through." That dedication and determination

guided Coachman to a station as one of the world's finest athletes, and

enabled her to become the first black woman to win an Olympic gold

medal in track and field.

1923– •

Athlete •

Coachman was born on November 9, 1923, in Albany, Georgia. She discovered her love for sports while in the Monroe Street Elementary School, when she and her friends tied strings of rope together and practiced seeing how high they could jump. After establishing herself as the kid to beat, Coachman took on the boys at a local playground who, despite their bravado about their jumping ability, were never able to defeat Coachman. Such play worried her parents, who wished their daughter was more ladylike. Coachman, though, loved the rough-and-tumble life of competition, so she paid no attention. Despite the spankings her parents occasionally administered to discourage her wild ways, Coachman kept running off to the games of the playground. "It was a rough time in my life," she told *Essence*. "It was a time when it wasn't fashionable for women to become athletes, and my life was wrapped up in sports. I was good at three things: running, jumping, and fighting."

Fortunately, Coachman's fifth-grade teacher, Cora Bailey, recognized the young athlete's potential and began to encourage it in a more formal way. When Coachman entered Madison High School in 1938, she easily made the track team under coach Harry E. Lash. Her remarkable abilities soon attracted the attention of Tuskegee Institute recruiters, and both of her former coaches encouraged her to enroll there for the coming academic year. The next summer, when she was only sixteen, she was invited to compete for Tuskegee in the women's track and field national championship. She thus represented the institution even before attending her first class there.

During her childhood, Coachman had dreamed her fame might come on the stage, for she had been strongly influenced by her two favorite entertainers—the white movie star Shirley Temple and the black jazz saxophonist Coleman Hawkins. But after she won first place in the AAU high jump in 1939, she understood she could find stardom through the sports she had so long loved and nurtured. She later recalled that this first national competition, held in Waterbury, Connecticut, was her biggest thrill: "That first medal, in Connecticut, was probably the greatest. I'd never been anywhere, and I just loved the sights along the way. It was all so new" (Albany *Herald*).

In 1940 Coachman entered Tuskegee Institute High School, where her skills could be nurtured under the guidance of women's track coach Christine Evans Petty and coach Cleve Abbitt. By the time Coachman graduated in 1943, she had already won national fame; in that year alone she won the AAU nationals in both the running high jump and the fifty-yard dash. She continued at Tuskegee Institute, working toward a trade degree in dressmaking, which she received in 1946. By that time, she held four national track and field championships in the fifty and hundred-meter dashes, the four-hundred-meter relay, and the running high jump. While at Tuskegee she also played basketball—so tenaciously, in fact, that as an all-conference guard she led her team to three straight SIAC women's basketball championships.

Coachman's six years at Tuskegee were marked by great national honors, but with World War II raging in Europe she was denied the chance to prove herself in international competition. When she transferred to Albany State College in 1947, it was to continue both her education and her athletic career in American track and field. Two years later, in August 1949, she graduated from Albany State with a bachelor's degree in home economics.

By the time she entered Albany State, Coachman was a national figure in women's track and field. She had become the one to beat during the women's national championships of 1945, where she finally overcame her chief rival, the Polish-American superstar Stella Walsh, by winning both the hundred-meter dash and the high points trophy. At the same meet Coachman again won in her specialty—the running high jump. Her success in this event was a result of her unique jumping form, which she called neither western roll nor straight jumping but rather "half and half." She did not attribute her accomplishments to her unorthodox style, however. "I trained hard," she told the Albany *Herald*. "I was sincere about my work. As I look back I wonder why I worked so hard, put so much time into it—but I guess it's just I wanted to win. And competition was very tough. You had to be in shape to win" (Albany *Herald*).

Since the last Olympiad had been held years before, in 1936, Coachman did not ponder international competition very often. The officials for the 1948 U.S. women's team, though, invited her to join the American team for the London Olympics that year. Although her back was sore and even the thought of overseas travel made her homesick, she decided to compete: "I was the country's best prospect, and I couldn't let my country down." For the five previous years she had been the only black on the All-American Women's Team, and while several other black women represented the United States in 1948 (including two-hundred-meter specialist Audrey Patterson, whose third place finish would make her the first black woman to become an Olympic medalist), Coachman remained something of a loner on the trip over.

Coachman recalled in an *Essence* magazine article that she was shocked when she arrived in England to discover "my picture was everywhere and everyone seemed to know all about me. All those people were waiting to see the American girl run, and I gave them something to remember me by."

The young woman who took the field in London was five feet, eight inches tall, weighed 130 pounds. A comely girl, she garnered praise for her warm demeanor. But as the Olympics wore on, Coachman also proved that she was a superior athlete with a fighting heart. She battled her way through the competition despite injuring her hip in the high jump preliminaries: "That was the toughest victory I ever won. Those girls from Europe jumped from odd angles. Every time I jumped a distance they came back and matched it." Finally, in the finals, on her first jump, Coachman soared over the bar set at five feet six and one-

Coachman Wins •

Olympic Medal

eighth inches. The jump was a new Olympic record and gave her the American women's team's only gold medal of the competition.

Returning to America in triumph, Coachman was introduced to President Harry S. Truman. As she told a reporter for the *Afro-American* "I felt good for my family, for my Albany, Georgia, home, for my school, and for my fellow Americans who are privileged to live in this land of opportunity" (Albany *Times,* 28 March 1979). The major American newspapers had failed to notice her achievements, but in Georgia she was given a motorcade ride from Atlanta to Macon, where she was welcomed by the chief of police, who was standing in for the mayor. She was happy to be home, and she knew that her own people, at least, appreciated her accomplishments.

The Olympics over, Coachman left athletics at the pinnacle of her career. She took up teaching high school physical education in Albany, Georgia, and married N. F. Davis (whom she later divorced). She also established the Alice Coachman Foundation, which provides aid to former Olympic athletes who are down on their luck. As the mother of two children, son Richmond and daughter Diane, she continued to coach young athletes. Many of these youngsters were probably only dimly aware of her trailblazing accomplishments, which included twenty-five AAU national titles, twelve straight years as national high jump champion, recognition as the first black female Olympic gold medalist, and induction into the National Track and Field Hall of Fame (1975).

In an era when too many American women held an ideal of femininity that was antithetical to hard work and fierce competitiveness, Coachman was different. Her athletic talent, coupled with her tremendous desire to succeed, enabled her to carve out a lasting spot in Olympic history. Today, as an educator, she continues to champion the characteristics that brought her success when speaking to students. "When the going gets tough and you feel like throwing your hands in the air, listen to that voice that tells you 'Keep going. Hang in there.' Guts and determination will pull you through" (Rhoden, *New York Times,* B14).

Profile by
William D. Piersen

CAMILLE O. COSBY

*C*amille Olivia Hanks Cosby is a philanthropist, entrepreneur, and

chief executive of Cosby Enterprises, a foundation primarily concerned

with the support of Black colleges and the education of Black youth.

Convinced of the importance of Black schools and the necessity of

education in enriching the Black community, she has challenged all

African Americans to come to the aid of Black institutions.

1944– •

Philanthropist, •

foundation

executive

Camille Hanks Cosby was born in 1944 to Guy and Catherine Hanks in Washington, D.C., the oldest of four children. Her father attended Southern University in Baton Rouge, Louisiana, for his undergraduate degree and Fisk University in Nashville, Tennessee, where he received his master's degree. Her mother attended Howard University in Washington, D.C. Camille Cosby attended parochial schools and was reared in rather genteel surroundings.

After completing high school, she studied psychology at the University of Maryland. There she was introduced to Bill Cosby on a blind date that took place at a club where he was performing. It was "love at first sight" for Bill Cosby and he proposed marriage on the second date (Norment, 150). Camille's father objected, arguing that she was too

young—she was nineteen—and insisting that she should concentrate on her studies. Despite the opposition, though, Camille accepted the proposal. They were married on January 25, 1964, at the starting point of Bill Cosby's illustrious career.

Cosby dropped out of the University of Maryland and traveled with her husband as he tried to launch his career. "Then he made an appearance on *The Tonight Show* and came to the attention of the producer of *I Spy* and the rest is history," said Camille Cosby (Oliver, 114). The Cosbys moved to California, where Bill Cosby's meteoric rise as a comedian triggered a corresponding increase in the family's income and dramatic changes in their lifestyles. Both were inexperienced in financial management and in dealing with people who asked for their financial assistance. But after irregularities in the management of their money became apparent, the Cosbys decided that the two of them would manage his career and their finances as well. After a time, Camille Cosby resumed her education as well, attaining a master's degree and a doctoral degree in education from the University of Massachusetts School of Education in 1980 and 1992, respectively.

They established a high-powered family business in Los Angeles. Camille Cosby, whom her husband describes as a shrewd business-woman and "rough to deal with when it comes to my business" (Norment, 152), managed the enterprises, which came to include television's *The Cosby Show* and *A Different World* series, movies, comedies, videos, recordings, television commercials, books, and phil-anthropic gifts. She managed all personnel, including attorneys, ac-countants, private pilots, and the clerical and maintenance staff, includ-ing those in their homes in California, Massachusetts, Pennsylvania, and New York.

As Bill Cosby became a multimillionaire and a multimedia megastar and the family enterprises prospered, the Cosbys searched for meaning-ful ways to support the Black community. "None of us can be strong unless we have the support of the community," Camille Cosby ob-served. "And unless the community is strong, it's impossible for us to be strong. No matter how big we become" (Oliver, 114).

Camille Cosby's interest in Black colleges was inspired partly because her parents had attended them and partly because of the research that she had conducted to identify the difficulties they faced. She visited eight Black colleges, interviewed their presidents, and came away troubled by the realization that all eight schools shared a common problem—their alumni were not providing support. Many of the schools were receiving first-generation college students, an indication that alumni who had college-age students were sending them to other

Helping Black •

Colleges

colleges. "It was a real eye-opener. I was stunned to know that the graduates of these institutions were not supporting them and that was because, perhaps, we as a people had bought into the idea that 'White is better'" (Johnson, "Bill and Camille Cosby," *Ebony,* 34).

Determined to make their feelings about the quality and importance of Black colleges clear, the Cosbys have donated millions of dollars to Black colleges since 1986. Their largest gift, $20 million, was given to Spelman College in Atlanta, Georgia, in 1988—the largest personal gift ever in the history of Black institutions. The funds have been used to build the Camille Olivia Hanks Cosby Academic Center, which opened in January 1996, to endow three chairs in the fine arts, social sciences, and humanities, and to support a library and archives in international African women research. Commenting on the importance of education, Camille Cosby said:

> Once you educate someone, then you are allowing them to enter the mainstream of society, which means that they can then afford decent housing. First of all, they can get a decent job. They can buy good food, but most important is that they can start another generation cycle of educated African-Americans. The cycle can continue for generations to come (Johnson, "Bill and Camille Cosby," *Ebony,* 34).

Camille Cosby has become involved in a number of philanthropic activities in recent years. More recently, she has served as a member of the board of directors of Essence Communications, the National Council of Negro Women, and the National Rainbow Coalition. She and her husband also send a number of deserving students to various, mostly-Black colleges and universities every year. Beyond the world of philanthropy, Camille Cosby has also produced albums, videos, a play, and a documentary. But while she values her philanthropic work, Camille Cosby most treasures her role as mother to four daughters and one son.

• Practicing What

They Preach

Camille and Bill Cosby sent their son Ennis to Morehouse College in Atlanta, while daughter Erinn enrolled at Spelman. As her home gradually emptied of children, she became more visible in the business affairs of the family in her position as partner in all of the Cosby enterprises.

In 1987 Cosby was recognized for her philanthropic work with an honorary doctorate from Howard University. She received another honorary doctorate from Spelman on "Camille Cosby Day," the school's May 1989 commencement day. In a spirited commencement address entitled "Victory," she said:

Despite all the [adversity] we have known in this country, we have had our victories.... Given the odds, we weren't supposed to stop being slaves. Given the opposition, we weren't supposed to have an education. Given the history, we weren't supposed to have families. Given the blues, we weren't supposed to have spirit. Given the power of the enemy, we weren't supposed to fight back. Not only have we achieved victories, we have—despite the powers against us— become our own victories" (Oliver, 64).

In the early 1990s Cosby has tackled several different projects. *No Dreams Deferred,* a documentary produced by Cosby about the relationship between an Atlanta couple with a catering business and the five youths they hire, was released in 1994. The film has since been seen on PBS. Cosby and producer Judith Rutherford James completed a successful Broadway run of *Having Our Say* where the play received three Tony nominations. The play is currently on national and university tours. A feature film based on *Having Our Say* is in the planning stages for 1997. Cosby and James are also preparing a film based on the life of Winnie Mandela .

Another 1994 project reflected Cosby's interest in television and the messages it often sends today's youth. This project, a book called *Television's Imageable Influences: The Self-Perceptions of Young African-Americans,* was inspired by her doctoral dissertation, and reflects her concerns about the medium. "The people who control television are creating and encouraging negative, stereotypical depictions of African-Americans and other cultural people," she said in an interview with the *New York Times.* "The bombardment of negative imagery is not only having a devastating effect on how African Americans, especially Black youths, view themselves, but also on how others see them.... I want to focus on our victories, not to ignore the negatives, but to show people what can be and what possibilities are out there" (Williams, *New York Times,* C8).

Described as "classy, reserved and stubborn" (Norment, 154) and "a stunning woman with an earthy personality and a ready smile" (Oliver, 114), Cosby is concerned with self-image and obedient to the laws of health, proper diet, and exercise. Faced with the issue of whether or not to allow her gray hair to go without the color rinse that she used since she started graying while in her twenties, she decided to let the beauty of nature take its course. "I began to realize how imprisoned I had been to the [dye] bottle, and how wonderful it was to

Profile by
Jessie Carney Smith

deal with my hair as it really is—and how wonderful it was to acknowledge my age" (Oliver, 114).

JULIE DASH

*J*ulie Dash claims that she never intended to become a filmmaker;

indeed, it was serendipity that led her to discover the joys and possibili-

ties inherent in cinematography. Today, she has become an indepen-

dent filmmaker acclaimed for her fine screen representations of Afri-

can-American women. With the general release of Daughters of the

Dust *in 1992, Julie Dash became the first African-American woman*

director to have a full-length general theatrical release.

1952– •

Filmmaker •

Born in New York City in 1952, Dash spent her early years in the Queensbridge Housing Projects in Long Island City. In her book *"Daughters of the Dust": The Making of an African-American Women's Film,* she explained that she discovered filmmaking by accident when she was seventeen: "I was just tagging along with a friend who had heard about a cinematography workshop (at the Studio Museum in Harlem) and thought she could learn to take still photos. We joined the workshop and became members of a group of young African Americans discovering the power of making and redefining our images on the screen."

When Dash was nineteen years old, she made her first film: *The Legend of Carl Lee DuVall*. Using pictures from *Jet* magazine attached to pipe cleaners and shooting with a super 8 camera, she created an "animated film about a pimp who goes to an African village and is beaten and dragged out of the village by the people there," she recalled in her book.

Although she loved the creative potential and the sheer fun of cinematography, Dash did not think of it in terms of a career. She intended to become a physical education teacher when she entered college; then, as an undergraduate at the City College of New York, she majored in psychology. While still a student, she discovered a special film studies program—the David Picker Film Institute—at the Leonard Davis Center for the Performing Arts. It was her successful interview for this program that permitted her to graduate from City College of New York with a degree in film production. Even before graduation, however, she was already making films: in 1974, she wrote and produced *Working Models of Success*, a promotional documentary for the New York Urban Coalition.

Armed with a bachelor of arts in film production, Dash immediately set off for the West Coast. Los Angeles was home to many black documentary filmmakers; the promise of camaraderie, mentorship, and support was appealing. She began her career by joining the crew of Larry Clark's film *Passing Through* (1973) as a sound assistant. Dash then received a fellowship to the Center for Advanced Film Studies at the Americàn Film Institute, where she studied under William Friedkin, Jan Kadar, Slavko Vorkapich, and other distinguished filmmakers.

During her two-year fellowship, Dash worked diligently and her efforts foreshadowed the quality of her later films. She completed a feature-length screenplay, *Enemy of the Sun,* and she received two auspicious awards: a Director's Guild Award in 1977 for a student film, *Diary of an African Nun;* and a Gold Medal for Women in Film at the 1978 Miami International Film Festival for *Four Women,* an experimental dance film that she conceived and directed.

Dash next worked for the Motion Picture Association of America (MPAA) in Los Angeles. As a member of the Classifications and Rating Administration, she was one of six voting board members who rated more than 350 movies each year. As part of her affiliation with the MPAA, she traveled to Europe and attended the Cannes International Film Festival in France. In 1980 she cosponsored a session at the festival comprised of several short films by black Americans.

Films Earn •

Recognition

and Awards

Dash's commitment to depicting diverse and positive images of black women in film led to a 1981 Guggenheim grant to create a series of films about black women. First in the series was 1983's *Illusions,* a thirty-four minute film set in Hollywood that explores issues of race and gender by focusing upon two African-American characters. As N. H. Goodall noted in *Black Women in America:* "Two black women occupy differing spaces in wartime (1942) Hollywood: one has become a studio executive while passing for white; the other is a behind-the-scenes singer, dubbing the voices of the white starlets on the screen. Both illustrate how the film industry specifically and society in general conspire to keep Black women both voiceless and invisible." Dash's drama was awarded the 1989 Jury Prize for Best Film of the Decade by the Black Filmmakers Foundation, was nominated for a 1988 Cable Ace Award in Art Direction, was the season opener of the Learning Channel's series on fictional works by independent filmmakers, and won the 1985 Black Cinema Society Award.

• Daughters of

the Dust *Takes*

Form

Dash's acclaimed film *Daughters of the Dust* began quite modestly in 1975; but during the 1980s, the filmmaker continued to work on this project and expand its scope. Originally, as Dash admitted in her book, she had conceived "a short silent film about the migration of an African-American family from the Sea Islands off of the South Carolina mainland to the mainland and then the North. I envisioned it as a kind of 'Last Supper' before migration and the separation of the family." The birth of her own daughter, N'zinga, in 1984, was further impetus for the *Daughters of the Dust* project. As a mother, Dash clearly and personally saw unity of the past, present, and future. N'zinga became the prototype for the unborn spirit child who moves so freely among the film's characters. The film was also, in a sense, a gift to N'zinga, since it is grounded in Dash's own family history.

In 1988, Dash founded her own company, Geechee Girls Productions, Inc., based in Atlanta. She has said that the company "brings to bear the power and the voice of the African-American female's spirit into the area of media production." *Daughters of the Dust* was a Geechee Girls production. The release of *Daughters* catapulted Dash to national attention. It won first prize in cinematography for dramatic film at the 1991 Sundance Film Festival in Utah, where it premiered, and it also was nominated for Outstanding Motion Picture of 1992 by the Beverly Hills chapter of the NAACP for the twenty-fifth annual Image Awards.

Reviewers found *Daughters* to be truly affecting. Gregory Tate stated in Dash's book that "the film works on . . . emotions in ways that have less to do with what happens in the plot than with the ways the characters personalize the broader traumas, triumphs, tragedies, and anxieties peculiar to the African-American experience." Critics noted that the work is poetic in its voice, stunning in its photography, creative in its structure, and eloquent in its vision. Centering upon a turn-of-the-century African-American community belonging to the South Carolina coast culture known as Gullah or Geechee, the film captures the tenacious, independent spirit of these people whose unique society developed in self-imposed, carefully guarded isolation. The sense of cultural unity that transcends time and place is vividly depicted through a complex interaction of character, structure, and symbol.

Despite the film's critical success, however, Dash had difficulty finding a distributor, in part because film executives were concerned that the film's attempts to recreate the Gullah dialect would be incomprehensible to moviegoers. Eventually, in July 1992, *Daughters* was nationally televised as part of the PBS American Playhouse series. Since then, appreciation among scholars has been growing. Toni Cade Bambara said in the preface to Dash's book that "currently *Daughters* is enjoying cult status. It is not unreasonable to predict that it will shortly achieve the status it deserves—classic."

Dash continued to receive important awards into the 1990s, including a Maya Deren Award from the American Film Institute in 1993, and a Candace Award from the National Coalition of 100 Black Women in 1992. Most recently, Dash received a Fulbright fellowship for work in London with Maureen Blackwood on a screenplay about the black British film collective Sankofa.

Dash's contributions lie in her achievements as an African-American woman filmmaker, in the superior quality of her work as cinematographer, and in the message she offers. Her creation of strong, positive female images, her fusion of reality and spirituality, and her holistic view of African-American identity all combine to truly enrich American filmmaking. In her book, Dash acknowledged the challenge of making twentieth-century American films that speak to the black experience: "One of the ongoing struggles of African-American filmmakers is the fight against being pushed, through financial and social pressure, into telling only one kind of story. African Americans have stories as varied as any other people in American society. As varied as any other people in the world. Our lives, our history, our present reality is no more limited to 'ghetto' stories, than Italian Americans are to the Mafia, or Jewish Americans to the Holocaust. We have so many stories to tell. It will greatly enrich American filmmaking and American culture if we tell them."

**Profile by
Margaret Duckworth**

THE DELANY SISTERS

Sadie Delany was the first African-American domestic science teacher at the high school level in the New York City public schools. Bessie Delany was the second African-American woman licensed to practice dentistry in New York City. At the age of 104, Bessie died in her sleep at her Mt. Vernon home. Sadie, at 106 years old, is the oldest surviving member of one of America's most prominent black families. In 1993 they became celebrities with the publication of their autobiography, Having Our Say, *which chronicles the first one hundred years of their lives and shares their unique perspectives on American history.*

Sadie Delany •

1889– •

Educator •

Bessie Delany •

1891–1995 •

Dentist •

Sarah Louise "Sadie" Delany, born September 19, 1889, and Annie Elizabeth "Bessie" Delany, born September 3, 1891, were the second and third of the ten children born to Henry Beard Delany and Nanny Logan Delany. Their father studied for the ministry at St. Augustine's

College in Raleigh, North Carolina, and he eventually became vice principal of the college and stayed on to raise his family there. According to Bessie in *Having Our Say,* "It was religious faith that formed the backbone of the Delany family." The sisters witnessed their parents putting into practice the family motto: "Your job is to help somebody." For instance, the family yearly distributed Thanksgiving baskets to the down-on-their-luck former slaves who lived in the neighborhood of St. Augustine's.

At five and seven years of age Bessie and Sadie were introduced to Jim Crow when they were forced to sit at the back of a segregated trolley car. Although their parents tried to shelter them from the brutalities of the southern racial caste system, the girls heard about lynchings from the whisperings of the teachers at school.

• *Delany Sisters*

Become

Educators

Upon graduating from St. Augustine's, Sadie took a job as supervisor of the domestic science curriculum in the black schools in Wake County, North Carolina, but ended up assuming the duties of the county school superintendent at no extra pay. She proudly recalls driving Booker T. Washington around to show him her schools. Bessie, who also graduated from St. Augustine's, spent two lonely years as a young, single teacher in the mill town of Boardman, North Carolina, before getting another teaching job in Brunswick, Georgia. She came close to being lynched when she rebuffed a drunken white man on a train while on her way to assume her teaching position in Brunswick. As she admits in *Having Our Say,* "I am lucky to be alive. But I would rather die than back down."

The Delany sisters moved to Harlem in their mid-twenties to further their educations. Sadie enrolled in the domestic science program at Pratt Institute in New York, then a two-year college. After graduating from Pratt, she enrolled in Columbia University's Teachers College. In 1920 she graduated from Columbia with a bachelor of science degree. Her first teaching job in New York was at a mostly black elementary school. Continuing her studies, she obtained her master's degree in education from Columbia in 1925. During the depression she landed a job at an all-white high school by being appointed to the position, skipping the required face-to-face interview (which would reveal her race), and then showing up on the first day of class. Thus she became the first black high school domestic science teacher in New York. Sadie taught in various New York high schools from 1930 to 1960, when she retired.

Bessie, who had taken some science courses at Shaw University in Raleigh, enrolled in Columbia University's dental school in 1919. She was awarded her doctor of dental surgery degree in 1923 and became the second black woman licensed to practice dentistry in New York. In her practice, located in the heart of Harlem, Bessie experienced not only discrimination from whites, who would not patronize a black dentist, but also from some blacks, who would not patronize a woman dentist. But she soon earned the reputation of taking any patient, no matter how sick, and she never turned away anyone who did not have money. When she retired in 1950, her rates were the same as when she started her practice in 1923; two dollars for a cleaning, two dollars for an extraction, five dollars for a silver filling, and ten dollars for a gold filling. As she explained in *Having Our Say,* "I never raised my rates because I was getting by OK. I was always proud of my work, and that was enough for me."

By the mid-1920s Bessie's dental office had become a meeting place for black activists. At her urging, sociologist E. Franklin Frazier, future executive director of the NAACP Walter White, and noted educator and writer W. E. B. Du Bois demonstrated at the 1925 rerelease of the movie *The Birth of a Nation,* which featured black villains, Ku Klux Klan heroes, and whites in blackface. Also in this year Bessie experienced a harrowing encounter with the Ku Klux Klan. She and a boyfriend were on an outing on Long Island when they ran into twenty white-robed Klansmen stopping and searching the cars of blacks. Bessie credits the powerful engine of her companion's Cadillac for zooming them right around the Klansmen. After this encounter with the Klan, Bessie became a staunch activist for the rights of blacks.

The Delany siblings all moved to Harlem, and by 1926 they lived together in the same apartment building. Bessie and Sadie proudly maintained in Harlem the wholesome, family-oriented lifestyle that they had in Raleigh. Their favorite pastime was having friends over for dinner, and every Sunday found them at Saint Mark's Episcopal Church. In *Having Our Say* Bessie noted, "We were proud of the Delany name, and because of our self-discipline it came to mean in Harlem what it had meant in North Carolina—that is, it stood for integrity."

Continuing •

Familial

Closeness

Bessie and Sadie's father, who in 1918 had become the first elected black Episcopal bishop, passed away in 1928 after a brief illness. The sisters then persuaded their mother to move to New York. At the age of fifty-nine Bessie retired from her dental practice to take care of their mother, who was then over ninety years old. As a special surprise for their mother, their brother Hubert—an assistant U.S. attorney in New York—arranged for her to meet Eleanor Roosevelt. In *Having Our Say* Bessie recalled, "It was pretty wonderful to see the former first lady of the United States jump up, so respectful like, to greet Mama, an old colored lady." After the death of two of the Delany brothers in quick succession, Mama Delany herself died at the age of ninety-five. Shortly afterward, in 1957, the sisters moved to Mount Vernon, New York, joining an exodus of middle-class blacks from New York City to the suburbs.

One of Bessie and Sadie's biggest regrets was not going to the March on Washington in 1963 and hearing Martin Luther King's "I Have a Dream" speech. In *Having Our Say* Bessie recalled, "The civil rights movement was a time when we thought: Maybe now it will finally happen. Maybe now our country will finally grow up, come to terms with this race mess. But it seemed like the momentum was lost when the Vietnam War happened. It was like all the energy of the young people, and the focus of the country, got shifted away from civil rights."

Bessie explained that women's rights have always been important to her as well, though in *Having Our Say* she noted that "no matter how much I had to put up with as a woman, the bigger problem was being colored. People looked at me and the first thing they saw was *Negro,* not *woman.* So racial equality, as a cause, won my heart." One of the happiest days of her life occurred back in 1920 when women finally won the right to vote. She and Sadie immediately registered and have not missed a vote since.

• *Sisters Become*

Authors of

Best-Selling

Autobiography

In 1993 the Delany sisters became celebrities with the publication of their best-selling autobiography, *Having Our Say: The Delany Sisters' First 100 Years.* The book resulted from eighteen months of interviews with Amy Hill Hearth, a free-lance writer who collaborated with them on the project. Hearth wove thousands of anecdotes into a lively, seven-part, largely chronological narrative. Before each part, she also provided a brief overview that placed the narrative in the context of black history. Camille Cosby has acquired the film, stage, and television rights to the book.

Because of the popularity of the autobiography, the sisters have been featured on a number of television shows, where they have graciously shared their secrets to a long and productive life. These include yoga exercises, eating up to seven vegetables a day, and taking daily vitamin supplements, garlic, and cod liver oil. Reading the newspaper, watching *The MacNeil/Lehrer News Hour,* and praying twice a day are also part of their routine.

In *Having Our Say* Bessie stated, "If you asked me the secret to longevity I would tell you that you have to work at taking care of your health. But a lot of it's attitude. I'm alive out of sheer determination, honey!" Bessie also attributes their longevity to having never married. In *Having Our Say* she noted, "When people ask me how we lived past one hundred, I say, 'Honey, we never had husbands to worry us to death!' . . . And why would I want to give up my freedom and independence to take care of some man? In those days, a man expected you to be in charge of a perfect household, to look after his every need. Honey, I wasn't interested! I wasn't going to be bossed around by some man!" The Delany sisters followed the success of *Having Our Say* with the publication of a second book, 1994's *The Delany Sisters' Book of Everybody Wisdom*. The American public continues to be enthralled by their spirit.

**Profile by
Phiefer L. Browne**

SUZANNE DE PASSE

*S*uzanne de Passe has become a powerful executive and one of the

dynamic forces in the entertainment industry, first in her work with the

Motown music empire and then with her own company, de Passe

Entertainment. Using her creative talent and business acumen, she

organized Berry Gordy's record and film industry into one of America's

best-known and most effective black businesses. Through her company

she has produced some of television's outstanding miniseries.

1948– •

Entertainment •

company

executive

Of West Indian heritage, Suzanne Celeste de Passe was born in 1948 in the Harlem section of New York City, where she grew up and received her early education. Although her parents divorced when she was three years old, her father remarried when she was nine, and he and his second wife provided a strong support network for her. As a child, de Passe modeled designs created by DeVera Edwards for prominent Harlem families. From early on, she pictured herself leading a glamorous life. She attended New York City's New Lincoln School, a private integrated institution. Aspiring to be a writer, she then attended Syracuse University and later transferred to Manhattan Community College, where she majored in English. In 1978 she married Paul Le Mat, an actor who played the role of Melvin in the 1980 movie *Melvin and Howard*.

Suzanne de Passe's business career reveals a pattern of steady progress. She worked briefly at several jobs, including "three days as a Bloomingdale's sales clerk, one month in New York's garment district, part-time horse riding instructor, and talent coordinator of a night club," according to Bonnie Allen in *Essence*. It was the informal work as talent coordinator that presaged de Passe's outstanding career as a business executive in the entertainment industry.

While attending college, de Passe began to observe and critique the performers appearing locally. In 1967 her observations led to a position as talent coordinator at the Cheetah Disco, a popular Manhattan discotheque. She decided the worth of auditioning performers and learned basic business skills for scheduling performers and negotiating contracts. De Passe was later employed as a talent consultant for the Howard Stein firm—a job which led to her position with Berry Gordy and Motown.

- *Named Motown*

Executive

De Passe was first introduced to Gordy by Cindy Birdsong, who later performed as one of the Supremes. De Passe described this occasion to Robert DeLeon in *Jet:* "While I was with Cindy at some affair one night, she introduced me to Berry Gordy. His limousine didn't show up to take him from there for some reason, so I offered him a ride in mine.... A friendship blossomed then, and every time he or some other Motown people would come to town, I'd take them around."

De Passe also interacted with Motown professionally in her efforts to recruit Motown performers for Howard Stein. She was often unable to schedule such performers, and on the occasion of her next meeting with Gordy, in Miami in 1968, she expressed her concern to him. Subsequent to this second meeting, Gordy offered de Passe a position as his creative assistant. From that point forward, de Passe became a dynamic part of the evolution of the Motown industry, which was at the time based in Gordy's home in Detroit, Michigan.

Upon joining Motown, de Passe helped to organize and promote the business. Following her first assignment—critiquing a Smokey Robinson performance—de Passe participated in most aspects of the company's business. Later in 1968 she moved with Motown to its new home in Los Angeles. There, as the business grew, so did de Passe's responsibilities; she advanced in the company from director to vice-president of Motown's West Coast operation's creative division, and from there to vice-president of Motown Industries. In 1981 de Passe became president of Motown Productions—the company's motion picture and film division, which had a ten million dollar budget.

Her principal activities at Motown were varied. In 1970, de Passe became involved in talent acquisition for Motown, and from then on was instrumental in signing and developing some of America's star African-American musical talent. In her first three years with Motown, not only did she travel extensively with artists such as the Jackson Five, but she also had a substantial hand in the production of the company's television specials. Her writing skills were put to the test first for "Diana," Diana Ross's 1970 solo television special, and soon afterward she served as head writer for "Goin' Back to Indiana," an ABC special featuring the Jackson Five.

In 1972, de Passe and coauthor Chris Clark wrote the screenplay for Motown's first movie, the hugely successful and critically acclaimed *Lady Sings the Blues,* starring Diana Ross and Billie Dee Williams. De Passe had a major role in the writing and production of numerous other Motown productions, including *Mahogany* and *The Wiz*—both of which were somewhat less successful than *Lady* due to problems with directing and distribution, despite being well received by black audiences nationwide.

As president of Motown Productions, de Passe's focus shifted from the broader interests in both record and film production to a concentration on the film industry, which gave her total control over and full responsibility for the division's status in theater, television, and movie production. Under de Passe's leadership, Motown Productions developed productions in all three genres. These included the successful feature "Berry Gordy's the Last Dragon" and the renowned NBC special "Motown 25: Yesterday, Today, Forever." She presented two television movies of the week on CBS, "Callie and Son," starring Lindsay Wagner, and "Happy Endings," starring John Schneider, as well as an ABC Afterschool Special, "Out of Step." She developed two theater works, *Satchmo,* a biography of Louis Armstrong, and *Daddy Goodness,* a musical proposed for the Broadway stage.

Despite the glamour of her profession, De Passe's always maintained a realistic perspective. As early as 1974—when she was twenty-six and held the position of vice-president of Motown's creative division—she held a down-to-business view of the company's focus on producing high-quality singles and albums. As she stated in *Black Enterprise:*

> It's a real fight to get to the top . . . but the biggest gift of all is staying there. Our artists have enjoyed tremen-

dous staying power. I think we are the only company in the business that can brag of eight, ten or twelve artists who have been hot for ten years or better. I think that shows the degree of concentration that is exerted on, first of all, picking the right people, those people with enough potential to have that kind of staying power, and then staying with them even through the rough spots, because it's virtually impossible to stay on fire all the time.

De Passe left Motown in 1988 and again gained national exposure by establishing her own company, de Passe Entertainment, in January 1992. One of her major triumphs came as executive producer of "Lonesome Dove," the critically acclaimed, landmark eight-hour CBS miniseries. It won Peabody, Golden Globe, and Emmy awards, and the Television Critics Association declared "Lonesome Dove" Program of the Year. De Passe was also executive producer for several other successful shows, including the celebrated "Motown on Showtime" series; "Small Sacrifices," the critically acclaimed, Peabody Award-winning, four-hour miniseries on ABC; and "Motown 30: What's Going On!," a two-hour CBS special. De Passe's most recent work as producer includes the four-hour ABC miniseries "The Jacksons: An American Dream," a sequel to "Lonesome Dove" called "Return to Lonesome Dove," and the ABC series "Sister, Sister."

Her talent and success in the entertainment industry have earned de Passe a number of awards. In 1972, she received an Academy Award nomination for *Lady Sings the Blues,* and later she received an Emmy Award and the NAACP Image Award as co-writer and executive producer of "Motown 25." De Passe won a second Emmy and a second Image Award for the celebrated NBC three-hour special "Motown Returns to the Apollo."

De Passe has received numerous other recognitions, including the Candace Award for Business from the National Coalition of 100 Black Women in 1983. In 1986, de Passe was named one of twelve Women of the Year by *Ms.* magazine for her "leadership in combining art, business and history to give us unprecedented television specials on black music as part of our national heritage and joy." She was inducted into the Black Filmmakers Hall of Fame in 1990 and the Legacy of Women in Film and Television in 1992. Active in civic and cultural affairs, de Passe is a board member of the New York City Ballet and the Academy of Television Arts and Sciences. In Los Angeles, where she lives, she is a board member of the Los Angeles Opera and a member of the Hollywood Radio and Television Society, among many other organizations.

Given de Passe's obvious success as a high-profile executive in the entertainment industry, it is clear she is one of the outstanding black professionals in the United States. She has conquered the racism and sexism that exists in the record industry and in Hollywood with energy, determination, and hard-won expertise.

**Profile by
Laura C. Jarmon**

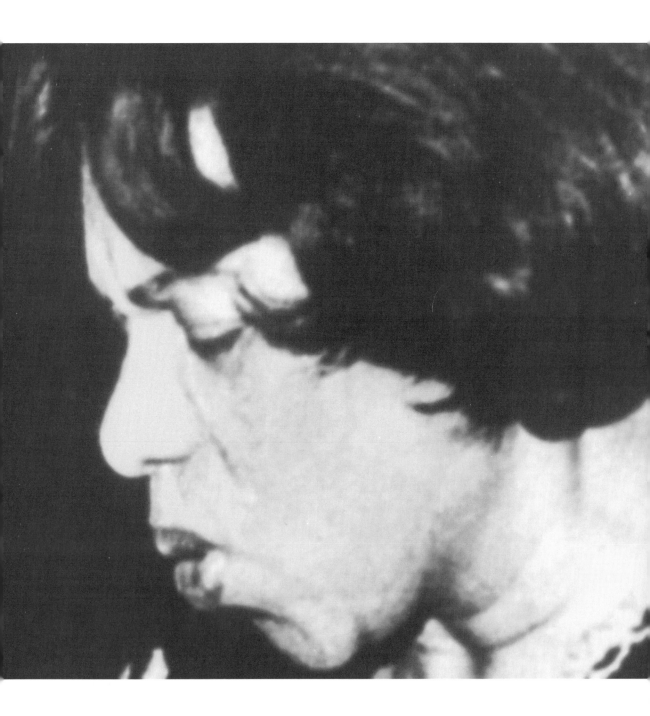

DOROTHY DONEGAN

*D*orothy Donegan is one of America's great piano virtuosos. Her

interests range from classical music, which she studies and practices

daily, to jazz performances in clubs, where her spirited piano playing as

part of a piano, drums, and bass ensemble has provided her with a

rewarding career. Although she performed the Grieg concerto in 1972

with the New Orleans Philharmonic and the Southeast Symphony in Los

Angeles, only rarely does she perform straight classical music for an

audience. Still, she is noted for borrowing from classical pieces. As New

Yorker *contributor Whitney Balliett explains, "She may flavor "The*

Man I Love," say, with bits and pieces of Chopin, Fats Waller, Rachmani-

noff, and Nathaniel Dett" (Balliett, 40). Her career has been buffeted by

1922– •

Pianist •

the trends that have affected all of jazz: the decline in interest that took place with the advent of rock and roll and the subsequent refusal of the major recording companies to record and support this music, along with the modest revival in interest in the musical form that began in the 1970s.

Donegan was born on April 6, 1922, in Chicago, the daughter of Donazell Donegan and Ella (Day) Donegan, who had been married once before. They had two children; Leon Donegan, the youngest, died around 1987. Donazell Donegan, an Alabama native, was a cook on the Chicago, Burlington, and Quincy Railroad who eventually died of a stroke in 1958. Dorothy's mother Ella died fourteen years later, in 1972.

The Donegan family lived in a large apartment during their early years together. Ella Donegan supplemented the family's income by renting out rooms. She strongly supported her daughter's early interest in music, and by the time Dorothy was eight years old she was taking piano lessons. For the first five years she studied with Alfred N. Simms, who also taught Cleo Brown. She then studied with Rudolph Gantz, the head of the Chicago Musical College, and during her high school years she practiced under the tutelage of Walter Dyett. At the age of ten, Dorothy Donegan was playing organ in a church; by the age of fourteen, she was earning money by playing in small clubs on the South Side, eventually denting the color barrier by working at Costello's Grill, a downtown venue. By this time her mother was serving as her business manager. In January 1942 Dorothy Donegan cut her first recording, *Piano Boogie.* The song was the first and only Dorothy Donegan recording to appear on the Bluebird label.

Donegan's professional concert debut was in 1943 at Orchestral Hall in Chicago; she presented Grieg and Rachmaninoff compositions in the first half of her program and jazz in the second half. She may have been the first black musician ever to perform in the hall. The concert received a front page review by Claudia Cassidy in the *Chicago Tribune,* and her reputation brought her to the attention of Art Tatum, who came to be a mentor for Donegan. A 1946 story in *Ebony* claimed that the concert was actually the result of a $1,500 bet made by Garrick Stage Bar owner Joe Sherman, who wagered that Donegan could outdraw Vladimir Horowitz at the hall: Sherman is said to have won.

In 1944 Donegan and her mother arrived on the West Coast, where Donegan appeared in a duet with Eugene Rodgers in the United Artists film *Sensations of 1945.* She appeared in clubs in Los Angeles and New York, and traveled with a Moms Mabley show for a while around this time. In the mid-1940s she cut a dozen or so records for Continental.

In 1946 Donegan appeared in the New York show *Star Time*. The following year she took a nondramatic role in a play that closed before reaching Broadway. She married John McClain in 1948; they had one son, John, born in 1954. The McClains ran their own club in Los Angeles for a year, and Dorothy Donegan recorded for several companies during the decade. In retirement when her son was born, she studied sociology at the University of Southern California. This first marriage ended in 1958, but she was to marry twice more, once to William Miles and once to Walter Eady, with whom she had another son, Donovan Eady. Looking back, she said "I married two more men after that [first marriage], and I think I've been married three times too many. Every time there were dry periods in the sixties and seventies, I'd marry again. Then, when I got work, I'd drift away" (Balliett, 40).

During the 1940s and 1950s, Dorothy Donegan spun her keyboard magic at some of the finest clubs in the nation. During this time it was not unusual for her to pull in $2,000 a week, an especially princely sum in those days. She had a long-term contract with the Embers, a posh supper club on East 54th Street, as well as arrangements at other top clubs in New York, Chicago, and Los Angeles, for Donegan's playing and showmanship were well suited to intimate clubs.

Pianist Plays at •

Top Clubs

Still, Donegan's performances had plenty of snap in them. She recalls an amusing story about how her exuberant performance style nearly proved costly during a period when a twenty percent tax on entertainment was applied if a club had dancers or singers in addition to musicians:

> I was doing a lot of wiggling then, moving my derrière around and snapping my fingers and carrying on, and the I.R.S. decided I was entertainment and put the tax on. That hurt business, so I went to the musicians' union, and the union asked, can she wiggle as long as she's playing? And they said yes, and took the tax off. A wiggle never hurt anybody (Balliett, 40).

By 1958, though, Donegan's style had evolved somewhat. "Once known for her souped-up versions of the classics," *Ebony* observed, "today she plays a modern, hard-driving style with overtones of Art Tatum. She has little respect for the current crop of male and female jazz pianists. Of the males, she says: 'I've snowed them all under except one (the late Art Tatum). Most of them play like women' ("Queen of the Keys," 84).

With the meteoric rise of rock and roll in the 1960s, Dorothy Donegan and other jazz musicians found it increasingly difficult to find work. Around the time of the breakup of her marriage to Eady in 1974, however, her career began to pick up again. During the 1980s she made sensational appearances at the "Women Blow Their Own Horns" program of the Kool Jazz Festival in New York City in 1981 and at the *Festival Der Frauen* in Hamburg in 1988. In 1992 she was made the subject of a documentary and received an American Jazz Masters' fellowship, a $20,000 prize bestowed by the National Endowment for the Arts. Shortly after she received news of the fellowship she was asked to perform at the White House, where she delivered a scintillating show. "From the outhouse to the White House—not too bad," she remarked (Reich, *Chicago Tribune*, 12).

Whitney Balliett notes that Donegan remains "an electric performer, and a transcendental clown" (Balliett, 37). Describing Donegan's current style and technique, he writes that:

> On her fast numbers she swings as hard as any pianist who ever lived, and on slow ballads she is delicate as a rose. Her technique rivals Art Tatum's. She is completely ambidextrous, her runs plummet like mercury, and she can play so fast that the individual beats merge into a kind of rhythmic glissando. She can produce thunder in her low registers and seconds later, that leggiero touch in her high registers (Balliett, 40).

Profile by Robert L. Johns

Dorothy Donegan is still an active musician. She lives in west Los Angeles. The recent issue of a compact disc, *Dorothy Romps: A Piano Retrospective 1953-1979,* available on Rosetta Records as part of its the *Foremothers* series, makes a selection of her recordings readily available.

RITA DOVE

*A*warded the Pulitzer Prize for poetry in 1987, Rita Dove is widely

1952– •

regarded as one of the finest of America's contemporary poets. In 1993

she was named the nation's youngest poet laureate ever.

Poet, writer •

Dove was born on August 28, 1952, in Akron, Ohio, the daughter of Ray Dove, a chemist, and Elvira (Hord) Dove. Influenced by such giants of poetry as T. S. Eliot and Robert Frost, young Dove became interested in writing at an early age. "When I told my parents that I wanted to be a poet," she told the *Chicago Tribune,* "they looked at me and said 'OK.' They didn't know what to make of it, but they had faith in me."

Dove graduated summa cum laude from Miami University in Oxford, Ohio, in 1973 and received an M.F.A. in creative writing from the Iowa Writers Workshop at the University of Iowa in 1977. In addition to the Pulitzer Prize, Dove has received numerous major awards, including fellowships from the National Endowment for the Arts and the Guggenheim Foundation and honorary doctorates from Miami University and Knox College in Illinois.

Rita Dove's first volume of poetry, *The Yellow House on the Corner,* was published when she was twenty-seven years old. Her second

volume, *Museum,* was published in 1983. Both collections were hailed by reviewers for their technical excellence and unusual breadth of subject matter. In 1985 she added a book of short stories, called *Fifth Sunday,* to her growing list of works.

Thomas and Beulah was published in 1986. This Pulitzer Prize-winning collection interweaves personal and social history in a series of short lyric poems. In later discussions about the work, Dove commented that the characters of Thomas and Beulah were based loosely on her grandparents' lives. The book, which spans the years 1919-1968 and takes place in Akron, Ohio, is divided into two parts. The first is written from Thomas's perspective and the second from Beulah's perspective. Although Thomas and Beulah share thirty-nine years of marriage and raise four children, their inner lives rarely intersect. Dove's powerful examination of their relationship won critical acclaim from many quarters. Reviewer Robert McDowell, for instance, praised her ability to represent "the opposing sides of conflicts she deals with," and noted that Dove's poetry "gathers the various facts of this life and presents them in ways that jar our lazy assumptions. She gives voice to many positions and many characters" (McDowell, *Callaloo,* 61).

Dove Wins •

Pulitzer Prize

Dove describes herself as committed to combining "historical occurrences with the epiphanal quality of the lyric poem" (*Contemporary Authors,* 115). If her dramatization of characters, personal relationships, and social events is powerful, observant, and affectionate, her mastery of lyrical verse is brilliant. Critic Emily Grosholz remarked that "Dove can turn her poetic sights on just about anything and make the language shimmer" (Grosholz, 160-61).

Dove typically focuses on the tragedies, joys, and dreams of "ordinary" black people in the Midwest. In her fourth collection of poetry, though, she commented on a wide range of issues and subjects. *Grace Notes,* published in 1989, contained a variety of short poems ranging in topics from intimate reflections on sexuality, motherhood, and aging to meditations on history, art, and international politics. As in her earlier poetry, Dove communicates powerfully through her incisive use of concrete details. She expresses her philosophy of poetry in the final stanza of a brief poem entitled "Ars Poetica:"

> What I want is this poem to be small,
> a ghost town
> on the larger map of wills.
> Then you can pencil me in as a hawk:
> a traveling x-marks-the-spot (*Grace Notes,* 48).

In addition to her volumes of poetry and her book of short stories, Dove has published work in dozens of magazines and anthologies, as well as a 1992 novel called *Through the Ivory Gate*. A prolific and highly-disciplined writer, she has taught creative writing for more than a decade at various universities, including Arizona State and Tuskegee. She travels widely, noting that travel is "a good way to gain different perspectives and to avoid becoming complacent" (*Contemporary Authors*, 115). Awarded a fellowship to write in Germany in 1980, she has since visited other distant lands such as Israel and southern Europe.

In 1993 Dove was chosen to serve as the United States' poet laureate. The first black poet to hold that position, she followed in the footsteps of such famous American poets as Robert Penn Warren, Richard Wilbur, and Joseph Brodsky. In announcing her selection, Librarian of Congress James H. Billington said "I take much pleasure in announcing the selection of a younger poet of distinction and versatility.... We will be pleased to have an outstanding representative of a new and richly variegated generation of American poets" (Molotsky, *New York Times*, C15). Upon learning of her selection, Dove commented that she hoped to reach young people who are currently inundated with signals that monetary rather than intellectual achievements are indications of ultimate success. "If only the sun-drenched celebrities are being noticed and worshiped, then our children are going to have a tough time seeing value in the shadows, where the thinkers, probers and scientists are who are keeping society together" (Molotsky, *New York Times*, C15).

Currently a professor of English at the University of Virginia, Dove lives in Charlottesville with her husband, Fred Viebahn (a novelist), and their daughter Aviva.

**Profile by
Kari Winter**

JOYCELYN ELDERS

J oycelyn Elders was named the first woman and first black director

of the Arkansas Department of Health in 1987, and in 1993 she became

the first woman and the first black U.S. Surgeon General. The honor

came under President Bill Clinton's administration. Elders is a crusader

for health-care reform and advocates health care for all citizens. Her

outspokenness and progressive stand on sex education in schools ulti-

mately led to her being dismissed from the federal position late in 1994.

1933– •

Former U.S. •

Surgeon

General

Joycelyn Jones Elders was born on August 13, 1933, in Schaal, Arkansas, the oldest of eight children born to indigent sharecroppers Curtis and Haller Jones. During her childhood, Elders worked with her parents and siblings as field hands in this tiny farming community. She also experienced poverty and deprivation; her family lived in inadequate housing with no plumbing. She walked miles to school, where the children studied in old, dilapidated buildings with outdated textbooks discarded by white schools. While growing up, she never saw a doctor, let alone thought seriously about becoming one.

Her family was astonished when she decided to go to college, but Elders persevered despite her lack of role models and encouragement. She even persuaded her brothers to do the same, convincing them that their lives could improve. Upon receiving a scholarship at the age of fifteen, Elders entered Philander Smith College in Little Rock, Arkansas. At first, when she found she enjoyed biology and chemistry, she decided to become a laboratory technician. But after hearing a speech by Edith Irby Jones—the first black to study at the University of Arkansas and the first black woman president of the National Medical Association—Elders became more ambitious. She received her B.S. in 1952, joined the army, and became a physical therapist. After serving from 1953 to 1956, she was admitted to the University of Arkansas School of Medicine; she was the only black woman and one of only three students of color in her class.

After graduating from medical school in 1960, Elders worked as a pediatric intern at the University of Minnesota Hospital and was a resident in pediatrics at the University of Arkansas Medical Center. Because she had a strong interest in research, she began studies for a master's degree in biochemistry at the University of Arkansas Medical Center in 1967, receiving that degree in 1971. She also taught at the medical college for several years, becoming a professor in the department of pediatrics in 1976. By this time, she had done extensive research in metabolism, growth hormones, and somatomedia in acute leukemia. Her research made her an expert in the treatment of juvenile patients with insulin-dependent diabetes.

When then-governor Bill Clinton appointed Elders to head the Department of Health in Arkansas in 1987, it marked the first time a woman or an African American had held that post. One of her main goals in this position was to lower the rate of teenage births in Arkansas, which was second-highest in the nation. She was also concerned about the state's high abortion rate, non-marital birthrate, and pregnancy rate. To address these issues she advocated wide-ranging sex education, and her views created a great deal of controversy. For example, she outraged many conservatives when she encouraged the distribution of condoms in schools.

Elders's outspoken nature also drew criticism. Although pro-choice, she discouraged abortion and instead focused on preventing unwanted pregnancies. She condemned right-to-life proponents for having undue concerns about the fetus and blamed male domination in various areas for the prevailing attitudes toward abortion. In the June 3, 1993, issue of *USA Today* she said: "Abortion foes are part of a celibate, male-

Volatile Health •

Care Issues

Addressed in

Arkansas

dominated church, a male-dominated legislature and a male-dominated medical profession."

When Elders suggested placing health clinics in schools to address issues such as venereal disease and contraception, opponents blasted her idea as little more than how-to sex clinics that led to promiscuity and the breakdown of the family. Liberals applauded her support of a woman's right to an abortion, while some conservatives felt her views threatened the moral fiber of the country. Opponents also viewed Elders as a radical doctor because she advocated the use of marijuana for medicinal purposes.

In addition to her other professional concerns, Elders also supported health-care reform, though she believed that the lack of health insurance was not the only problem. She contended that geography and transportation were also significant factors in the health-care crisis, as few doctors and hospitals were available to citizens in poor and rural areas. Elders recommended addressing the shortage of doctors by training a mix of health care providers for underserved areas and utilizing certified nurse midwives, nurse practitioners, and physician assistants.

• **Elders**

Confirmed as

Surgeon

General

President Bill Clinton nominated Elders for the position of U.S. Surgeon General in July 1993. Her nomination was confirmed by the Senate after considerable debate on September 7, and she was sworn in the following day. During the confirmation hearings, Elders explained her philosophy to *USA Today* (July 28, 1993):

> The government in the 1990s must be prepared to grapple with some very tough challenges as we focus on health care for all the people—not just the rich and privileged. Our work is not socially valuable and satisfactory until the needs of all the poor and indigent are met. We cannot be content with devising a narrowly satisfactory patch-work solution for this dilemma. We must work for a society in which people of all classes find satisfactory health care delivery a priority.

Controversy surrounded Elders's confirmation hearings. At first, some conservative senators—not realizing that Elders was not only a physician but a leading pediatric endocrinologist and noted professor—tried to block her nomination by passing legislation that would require all nominees for Surgeon General to be physicians. Elders also faced intense criticism over her advocacy of condom distribution in schools, and she was accused of a cover-up in Arkansas. Tests on four lots of the condoms purchased by the Arkansas Department of Health found a defective rate more than twelve times higher than the limit set by the Food and Drug Administration. State officials in Arkansas decided to withhold the information about possible defects rather than inform people that the condoms were unreliable. Elders concurred with her staff's decision, and her political opponents used this incident to try to prevent her confirmation.

Elders's confirmation hearings before the Senate were delayed until September 1993 as her nomination came under fire. Senate opponents raised questions about Elders's finances, and anti-abortion groups attacked her outspoken views on abortion and sex education. In addition, her husband was accused of not paying social security taxes for a nurse who attended to his mother, a victim of Alzheimer's disease. Elders, however, was backed by the American Medical Association and C. Everett Koop, the conservative former Surgeon General.

As Surgeon General, Elders spoke just as pointedly as she had before on health-care issues, sometimes igniting political controversy. For example, she came under fire in December 1993 for her comments on drug legalization. In what she later called "personal observations" based on experiences of other countries, she stated that she believed the United States should study the legalization of drugs, as legalized drugs might reduce crime. The White House press secretary announced that President Clinton did not share her views. Elders also continued her strong support of sex education in schools and abortion rights, while privately admitting she opposed abortion. She continued to arouse controversy among conservatives by stating in *USA Weekend* that the Boy Scouts and Girl Scouts should admit homosexuals. She also advocated gun control, calling violence a public health issue. In June 1994, *USA Today* reported that a drumbeat of criticism against Elders was mounting, but Elders responded by reminding the public that President Clinton never asked her to soften her rhetoric.

After Elders delivered a speech on World AIDS Day at the United Nations in December 1994, a psychologist asked Elders if she would encourage masturbation as a means of discouraging school children from becoming involved in other forms of sexual activity. According to *U.S. News & World Report,* Elders replied: "With regard to masturbation, I think that is something that is part of human sexuality and a part of something that perhaps should be taught." The next day President Clinton demanded and received Elders's resignation, explaining in the *Washington Post* that her "public statements reflecting differences with administration policy and my own convictions have made it necessary for her to tender her resignation." Although her position as Surgeon General demanded a leader who was outspoken, her blunt statements

Fired By •

President

Clinton

and controversial stands had gone too far. Elders explained in a television interview on "Nightline" that her comments had been misunderstood: "I was saying that we need to address all issues related to sexuality and teach our children what's normal behavior, not teach them masturbation.... That's not something you have to teach anybody." While Elders regretted the misunderstanding and the resulting media uproar, she told the *Washington Post,* "I don't regret what I said."

In addition to her work in state and national health care administration, Elders has been active in a number of professional associations. An author of 147 papers and monographs, Elders served as president of the Southern Society for Pediatric Research and of the scientific society Sigma Xi. Most recently, she became a member of the board of the American Civil Liberties Union. Until Elders moved to Washington, D.C., she lived in Little Rock, Arkansas, with her husband Oliver, a coach at a local high school and later a special assistant in the U.S. Education Department. They have two adult sons, Eric and Kevin.

Throughout her tenure as Surgeon General, Elders brought a serious commitment to the health-care issues of the day. Her radical stance reflects her dedication to a new approach to health issues. The principle upon which her medical philosophy is based—the dignity of the individual—carried her to the top health-care position in the federal government. Now that she has returned to her teaching position at the University of Arkansas Medical Center, she aims to continue her outspoken stance on health-care issues.

**Profile by
Joan C. Elliott**

JUSTINA L. FORD

*E*quipped with courage, determination, and a medical degree,

Justina Ford became the first black woman physician licensed to

practice medicine in Colorado. She was also the first black woman

physician in the entire Rocky Mountain West. She overcame discrimina-

tion based on her race and gender and defied those who attempted to

prevent her from practicing medicine, beginning with the licensing

examiner in Colorado and continuing with administrators of local

hospitals who denied her hospital privileges. Ford is important not only

for breaking down barriers for blacks and women in the medical field

but also for her humanitarianism: she selflessly cared for people of all

races as well as indigents, many of whom were denied treatment by

1871–1952 •

Physician, •

humanitarian

other doctors.

The seventh child in her family, Justina Laurena Carter Ford was born January 22, 1871, in Knoxville, Illinois, and grew up in Galesburg, Illinois. Little is known about her family background, though sources confirm that her mother was a nurse. Ford refused to play with her brothers and sisters unless the game was hospital, and she always insisted on assuming the role of doctor. "I didn't know the names of any medicines," she told Mark Harris for the *Negro Digest,* "so I had one standard prescription: tobacco pills." Ford's love for medicine was unfaltering. "I remember I used to like to dress chickens for dinner so I could get in there and see what the insides were like," she continued. She also tended to the needs of her ill neighbors. "I hope I didn't do them any harm," she confided.

Ford graduated from Hering Medical College in Chicago in 1899, then for two years directed a hospital and was a physician at a state school in Normal, Alabama, probably the forerunner of Alabama Agricultural and Mechanical State University. Since the Alabama community rejected Ford as a doctor on the grounds of race and gender, she decided to relocate to an area where blacks might be a more integral part of the community. Although she considered Denver still a pioneer town, she chose the city for her work. "I tell folks I came to Denver in time to help them build Pike's Peak, and it's almost the truth," she told Harris. Some sources say that she was licensed in Colorado on October 7, 1898, but it is more likely that she moved to Denver in 1902 to begin practice. As a black and a woman, Ford faced great odds and was shielded from acts of discrimination only by her determination and courage. "I fought like a tiger against those things," she stated in *Negro Digest*.

Moves Practice •

to Colorado

When Ford applied for a medical license in Colorado, the medical examiner told her, "I feel dishonest taking a fee from you. First of all you're a lady and second, you're colored," according to Ford's biographical statement from the Black American West Museum. Ford responded that she had thought it through before leaving Alabama and that Denver was where she wanted to establish her practice. Successful in the licensing examination, Ford then faced the next obstacle: building a practice in a medical community hostile to black professionals.

During the course of her practice Ford also met obstacles many physicians encounter frequently: irregular hours and pay, and long periods without sleep. It was not uncommon for her low-income patients to pay her in goods rather than cash, and one client paid Ford for delivering her daughter thirteen years after the birth. Ford's specialties—gynecology, obstetrics, and pediatrics—were unusual then for blacks and women.

Since neither Ford nor black patients had access to Denver General Hospital, Ford's practice began with health care delivery to homes, which she initially reached by horse and buggy and then later by bicycle. In time, she purchased a car and hired a relative to drive her to see her patients. Since few families had cars in those days, whenever her "big limo" pulled into a neighborhood everyone knew that someone was having a baby. Still later, Ford, who never obtained a driver's license, relied on taxicabs for transportation.

Since Denver and the surrounding counties were mountainous, access to many of her patients was limited to rugged mountain roads. Responding to those who criticized her for delivering babies at her patients' homes, she is reported to have said that the babies "were probably conceived at home, and have nowhere else to be born but at home," according to *Colorado Medicine*. Upon reaching the home, Ford removed her dress and delivered the baby in her slip to protect the infant and mother from germs on her outer clothing.

- *"The Lady*

Doctor" Earns

Acceptance

Ford had a distinguished practice for fifty years and became known as "The Lady Doctor," a title given her out of respect and affection. She delivered over seven thousand babies to parents who lived around the perimeter of an area called Five Points. Many of her patients preferred to have a woman present while they were giving birth. Her patients came from all classes and races, and Ford is especially known for treating those ignored by the conventional health-care systems of the day. The *Denver Post* quoted Ford as saying, "Folks make an appointment and whatever color they turn up, that's the color I take them." Only 15 percent of her deliveries were black. She took a particular interest in poor people, many of whom she cared for without charge. To communicate with her patients, she became fluent in somewhere between eight and eleven languages and dialects.

As racial barriers slowly eroded, Ford was admitted to practice at Denver General Hospital. She also received full membership in the Denver Medical Society, the Colorado Medical Society, and the American Medical Society, which early on had denied her membership. As recently as 1950, Colorado had only seven black doctors, with Ford still the only black woman in the group. Although Denver had a population of half a million by then, she was one of only five black physicians there.

In the *Urban Spectrum,* Magdalena Gallegos printed a statement Ford made four months before her death in which she commented on the religious beliefs that guided her work. Pointing to a baby she had just delivered, she said:

This one will be of a generation that will really see opportunity. I won't see the day, you very well may, and this one certainly will. Hard feelings between the races, my people will come up from the south, your people will see that come to pass. When all the fears, hate, and even some death is over, we will really be brothers as God intended us to be in this land. This I believe. For this I have worked all my life.

Ford received a number of awards during her lifetime, and Denver residents now recognize her as a pioneering medical doctor and humanitarian. Her home and office, once called a beacon of light during her unselfish years of practice, was relocated in 1984 just twenty-four hours before it was scheduled to be demolished. The house now serves as a memorial to her work and to other pioneer minority and women physicians in Colorado, and it appears on the National Register of Historic Places. In September 1988, a grand opening and dedication ceremony were held to recognize the home. Now established as the Black America West Museum and Heritage Center, the house contains documentation of the area's history. The office and waiting room that Ford used remain on the first floor as a permanent exhibit. Many of Ford's patients and those she delivered as babies continue to live in the area. The museum attempts to locate people who were delivered by Ford, or their relatives, in an effort to obtain an accurate record of the babies she delivered in Denver and other areas of Colorado.

Home and •

Office Becomes

Museum

Ford's legacy is also witnessed through the Dr. Justina Ford Medical Society, which was organized in 1987 as a support system for black physicians in training in Denver. Also in recognition of her career, the Warren Library in East Denver was renamed the Ford-Warren Library in 1975. The Colorado Medical Society, which denied her membership until 1950, passed a resolution in 1989 honoring Ford posthumously "as an outstanding figure in the development and furtherance of health care in Colorado."

Sometime early in her career she married a man named Ford, a minister in the Zion Baptist Church. After his death she married Alfred Allen but retained the name by which she had become known professionally. Harris described Justina Ford as a "tiny, round, gray-haired woman," while Gallegos said she was "a stern-visaged woman whose unmistakable authority was sharply defined." Gallegos also quoted one of Ford's former patients, Agneda Lopez-Stoner, who said of the doctor, "She had a spiritual quality about her and it showed through her eyes." In her later years Ford began to lose her sight. She died at her home on

October 14, 1952, at the age of eighty-one, having treated patients until just two weeks before her death.

Steadfast in her determination to be a physician, "The Lady Doctor" refused to allow her race and gender to stand in her way and defied the odds in becoming a pioneer in the medical field in Denver. Ford's contributions are memorable to blacks and women as well as to disadvantaged and underprivileged people of all races.

Profile by
Jessie Carney Smith

HAZEL B. GARLAND

A *pioneering journalist who championed the cause of the black*   **1913–1988** •

press, Hazel B. Garland was the first African-American woman to serve

as editor-in-chief of a nationally circulated newspaper chain. Her   **Journalist,** •

popular columns appeared in various editions of the Pittsburgh Courier   **editor**

for more than forty years, from 1943 to 1988. As an editor during the

1960s and 1970s, Garland made some of her most significant contribu-

tions behind the scenes, where she determined newspaper policy, shaped

staff assignments to reflect social needs, and trained those who would

carry on her torch.

Hazel Barbara Maxine Hill Garland was born on January 28, 1913, on a farm outside Terre Haute, Indiana. She was the oldest of sixteen children born to George and Hazel Hill. After the family moved to Pennsylvania in the early 1920s, her father supported his growing brood

by working as a coal miner. Garland assisted her mother in caring for her younger siblings, often amusing them by telling stories. Although Garland was a bright student who loved reading and yearned for more education, she had to drop out of high school, at her father's urging, so that a younger brother might continue. Recalling this incident in 1980, Garland told Jean E. Collins in an interview for *She Was There: Stories of Pioneering Women Journalists:*

> My father was a dear soul. I loved him dearly. But his idea was, "Why waste your money on sending a girl to college? She's going to get married. Save your money for the boys." I used to go to the library where I would read and read. They didn't have student loans for young people as they do today. I lived in libraries. I read everything. That's why I say there's no excuse for a person today not to take advantage of all the opportunities that are available. There's no excuse for ignorance.

Career in •

Journalism

Begins

On January 26, 1935, she married Percy A. Garland, a photographer and businessman, and settled down to a life as a homemaker in McKeesport, a suburb of Pittsburgh. In October of that year, she gave birth to her only child, a daughter named Phyllis. Meanwhile, she came under the influence of her mother-in-law, Janey Garland, who encouraged her to become active in local organizations. Since Garland liked to write, she usually was asked to serve as the club reporter. She was on the publicity committee of the local YWCA in 1943 when a reporter for the *Pittsburgh Courier* got lost on the way to cover a YMCA function. Since Garland had written down all the details, it was suggested that she submit the materials herself. The *Courier* editors were impressed by her eye for detail and asked her to cover events in nearby communities, working as a stringer—meaning she would be paid two dollars for each news item the paper used. She produced so much material that the editors suggested that she combine them into a column called "Tri-City News," which began appearing that year. Community columns were a common feature of black newspapers in those days, since mainstream publications included little news about African Americans and most of what they did carry was negative.

When *Courier* editors offered to train stringers who came into the office on Saturday mornings, Garland took advantage of the opportunity. Eventually she was asked to substitute when staff reporters went on vacation, and she finally joined the full-time staff of the *Pittsburgh Courier* in 1946. At that time, the name of her column was changed to "Things to Talk About." In it she covered events that highlighted the lives of her readers: marriages, births, new jobs, parties, honors, visits from friends, even tragedy when it struck. She also wrote about her own family and shared her reflections on current events or social trends. In an interview, Frank E. Bolden, who was city editor and one of her colleagues on the *Courier,* analyzed the philosophy that underscored Garland's work throughout her career:

> She would give a wedding in the housing projects the same attention she would give a wedding that occurred in the upper echelon of what was then called Negro society. When I asked her about it, she'd say, "They're all human, and as long as I'm doing this, that's the way it's going to be." The clubs relied heavily on Hazel to write about them, and the religious people, too. Family allegiance also was a hallmark of her work. She had come from a small town where life centered on the family. I think she wrote with such compassion because she had such strong feeling for her own family.

One of the high points of Garland's career came in 1952, when she was sent to a rural South Carolina community to do a story on a nurse-midwife named Maude Cullum, who often worked without pay and had delivered most of the babies, black and white, in her community. Garland was appalled by the poverty and social conditions she witnessed in Cullum's community and wrote a series of articles based on what she called "The Three I's: Ignorance, Illiteracy and Illegitimacy." *Courier* editors submitted the series to a regional journalism competition judged by the writers from the nation's leading daily newspapers. The *Courier* was the only black newspaper entering the competition. Garland later recalled for Collins:

> The entries were numbered. They didn't name the newspaper or reporter who wrote it, or mention whether the person was black or white. I won the award for the best series. The prize was awarded at the Page One Ball. Oh, I was so thrilled! And I was shocked, too, because I beat some people who had been perennial winners. One had won a Pulitzer Prize the year before and had entered a series. I said that if I don't win anything else again, I had won that.

When the *Courier* introduced a new magazine section in 1952, Garland was named associate editor. In preparation for this assignment, she took courses in magazine writing and editing at the University of

Pittsburgh. When the magazine section was phased out, she became woman's editor and in 1960 was named entertainment editor.

In 1955 she also began writing a weekly column about television, called "Video Vignettes." Though she focused on programs featuring African Americans, she also wrote about significant productions of all types, interviewing black and white producers and performers when they came to town. She commented on the way blacks were portrayed on television and waged a personal protest when relevant programs were discontinued or black performers and newscasters dismissed. To make certain her points got through to those responsible, she would send copies of her column to network and station managers. She was the first African-American journalist to initiate such a column and sustained it until a month before her death, making it one of the longest-running television columns in newspaper history.

By the mid-1960s the *Courier* was in the throes of serious financial problems due to high production costs, mistakes in management, and the mainstream press's incursion into coverage of black topics. The number of editions had been cut back and the lustre had faded from the *Courier*'s reputation. Paychecks began to bounce, but Garland held on. As she told Collins: "I loved the *Courier*. It was everything to me. I had spent the greater part of my life there, so I wanted to work even if I didn't get paid. I thought maybe we could keep on and hold it together." Eventually her commitment was credited with reviving the ailing newspaper.

In 1966 John Sengstacke, publisher of the *Chicago Defender* and owner of several other black newspapers, purchased the *Courier*'s assets and renamed it the *New Pittsburgh Courier*. At the time Garland held dual posts as women's and entertainment editor. Sengstacke broke with tradition by naming her city editor, a management-level post. In 1972 she became the paper's editor-in-chief. She worked day and night reorganizing the paper into sections, developing new beats, and emphasizing features. She changed the women's section to the Leisure and Living section, including articles about men. In 1974 Garland was named "Editor of the Year" by the National Newspaper Publisher's Association (NNPA). A tireless civic worker, she belonged to several organizations and served on many boards. Eventually the walls of her home were covered with plaques and citations.

Garland Named •

Editor-in-Chief

When Garland stepped down as editor-in-chief in late 1974 due to health problems, Sengstacke named her assistant to the publisher, relying on her advice. She continued to write her columns and played a major role in the paper's editorial operations. In 1976 the *Courier* won the NNPA's John Russwurm Award, which is given to the best black-oriented paper in the country. After she retired in 1977, Garland continued as editorial coordinator and consultant, writing her columns, contributing feature articles, and working one day a week in the office doing editing and layouts. In 1978 and 1979 she served as a juror for the Pulitzer Prize, journalism's highest honor. Garland worked up until three weeks before she died on April 5, 1988, of a heart attack following surgery for a cerebral aneurysm.

Garland received her last honor in 1988, shortly before her death, when *Renaissance Too,* a Pittsburgh magazine, established a scholarship fund for journalism students in her name and that of Mal Goode, a former *Pittsburgh Courier* staffer and the first black journalist in network television. Perhaps it is as an example that Garland made one of her most significant contributions. Many women in journalism and related communications fields consider her their role model. When asked to advise the young, Hazel Garland would say: "We must always have the three D's: Desire, Determination and Dedication. We must not let anything turn us aside. And to be truly successful, we must always reach back and try to lift someone else as we climb."

**Profile by
Phyl Garland**

ZINA LYNNA GARRISON

With two medals in the 1988 Olympics in Seoul, South Korea, as

well as strong showings in major tournaments such as Wimbledon, the

United States Open, Australian Open, French Open, Canadian Open,

and Virginia Slims, Zina Lynna Garrison is ranked among the top

tennis players of the world. Aside from her athletic records, she is well

known for her encouragement of inner-city young people interested in

careers in sports and other areas of endeavor.

1963– •

Tennis •

champion

Garrison was born on November 16, 1963, in Houston, Texas, the last of the seven children of Mary and Ulysses Garrison. To emphasize that she was their last child her parents chose the final letter of the alphabet to begin her name. Prior to Zina's first birthday, her father, a letter carrier for the Houston post office, suffered a fatal stroke. In the same year, Zina's twenty-one-year-old brother, Willie, a catcher in the Milwaukee Braves minor league system, died after being struck by a baseball. Mary Garrison raised her children as a single parent while working as an aide in a nursing home. Because Zina was the baby of the

family, born ten years after the other children, she grew up almost as an only child.

Garrison's introduction to tennis came when she was ten years old and went with her brother Rodney to MacGregor Park, a tennis facility in what was formerly the well-to-do, all-white Riverside section of Houston. She watched the resident coach, John Wilkerson, for an hour as he gave a lesson to a student. When Wilkerson saw this keen interest, he invited her to take a racket and try the game that would assume a dominant role in her life. Wilkerson became her coach, as well as friend and father figure, as he sharpened her skills. He stressed discipline and the basics of the game, once forcing Garrison to complete a practice game with the racket she had broken by throwing it to the ground in a fit of rage.

Because Garrison was such a natural player, Wilkerson began entering her in local competitions within two months. By the time she was fourteen years old, she was among the top players of her age group in the country; four years later she was rated number one of all the junior players. On the day of her graduation in 1982 from Ross S. Sterling High School in Houston, she went directly to the French Open to compete in her first professional match. In 1983, the year she turned twenty, she was ranked among the top ten women tennis players in the United States.

At the same time that Wilkerson was teaching Garrison, he had another promising MacGregor protégée, Lori McNeil, who in 1986 was ranked number fourteen in the United States. Garrison and McNeil became a formidable doubles team and best friends. They played together until 1987, when problems arose that led to the dissolution of the partnership and a change of coach by Garrison. Garrison retained the services of Willis Thomas, who was well acquainted with her rise in the world of tennis. Garrison felt that although Wilkerson had given her the basis to develop as a professional and had contributed to her rapid advancement, their strong relationship had begun to deteriorate.

The break with Wilkerson came at the time of two major disappointments in Garrison's life. She had been forced to miss both the French Open and Wimbledon because of a stress fracture in her right foot and, on a more traumatic level, she was still feeling the loss of her mother to a diabetic coma four years earlier. Garrison's mother had been her friend, her greatest supporter, and the person she could telephone to share successes and challenges. With her mother's help Garrison found it easier to adjust to the contrast between her modest upbringing and the affluence she was experiencing as a professional athlete.

Garrison •

Becomes Top

Ranked Tennis

Player

In denial over her mother's death, Garrison went into a depression that manifested itself in her overeating. After suffering a bout with bulimia, she sought professional assistance and was finally able to understand her behavior and reconcile herself to her loss. This restored order in her life, allowing her to refocus upon her career as a professional athlete.

- **Star Wins**

Olympic Medals

In the 1988 Olympics in Seoul, South Korea, Garrison won a gold medal in doubles with Pam Shriver and a bronze medal in singles. Her greatest ambition is to achieve a Grand Slam victory in the four greatest annual events in tennis: the Australian Open, the French Open, Wimbledon, and the United States Open. To date the goal has escaped her. She came close to winning at Wimbledon in 1990, having defeated both Monica Seles and Steffi Graf, but she lost to Martina Navratilova in the finals. This was the first time a black woman had reached the finals in a Grand Slam competition since Althea Gibson was victorious at Wimbledon in 1957 and 1958.

Garrison has won numerous landmark matches, defeating such luminaries as Chris Evert for the first time in 1985 and again in an emotional meeting at the 1989 U.S. Open. She has won matches in singles, doubles, and mixed doubles in numerous U.S. cities and has taken titles in Britain, Canada, Australia, Korea, and Japan. In her matches, Garrison often demonstrates an unusual degree of sportsmanship by applauding her opponents' spectacular plays.

- **Garrison**

Becomes

Community

Servant

Garrison is also well known for her community service work. She visits schools in cities where she plays to give clinics and talk to students about not only pursuing sports but making commitments to serious study as well. After winning the 1988 Olympic medals, she appeared at Public School 125 in Harlem in the midst of a blinding rainstorm. The students were surprised that a person of her status would inconvenience herself to come to see them, especially in the unfavorable weather of that day. Her reward was a packet of individually written letters filled with expressions of appreciation for her interest in them and good wishes for her career.

Since 1988, Garrison has supported youth organizations, antidrug programs, and projects designed to improve the lot of the homeless through funding from the Zina Garrison Foundation. In the summer of 1992, she opened the Zina Garrison All-Court Tennis Academy, which provides opportunities for economically disadvantaged children to increase their self-confidence through tennis. Her mission is to encourage young people who may have the talent to become tennis professionals, including African Americans and other minorities, to seek out places to learn the game, even though they may have more access to other sports. For example, she often explains that while women basketball players have limited opportunities after college, women can continue competing in tennis for years beyond graduation. Garrison's dream is to establish a shelter for the homeless and initiate additional junior tennis programs in Texas. In honor of the Zina Garrison All-Court Tennis Academy, and Garrison's other community service work, *Family Circle* magazine chose her for its 1992 Player Who Makes a Difference Award. For this occasion the magazine and Hormel Foods each donated ten thousand dollars to her chosen charities.

In September 1989, Garrison married Willard Jackson, who was an executive in an environmental management firm. The combination of her intenseness and basic shyness with Jackson's ability to offer comfort and support at just the right moment has fueled Garrison's stream of successes on the court.

In the early part of her career, Garrison was perceived as lacking the presence and personality to attract commercial contracts from large corporations. In spite of her disappointment she saw no racial prejudice involved, but considered it a reaction to her youthful looks and apparent lack of maturity. With the more sophisticated image she has developed under the direction of Avantage International, however, she has been featured as a glamorous woman in *Essence* and *Black Elegance,* has been a guest on the *Arsenio Hall Show* on two occasions, and has had much more success with endorsement contracts. Garrison has represented a fast food chain, Wilson rackets, Yonex rackets, and Reebok clothing and has appeared in a public service anti-litter announcement.

One of the top-rated and highest-paid tennis professionals in the world and the first black woman to reach the Wimbledon finals since the late 1950s, Zina Garrison can truly be classified as a trailblazer. Among the few black women to achieve success in a game dominated by whites, she appears not to be disturbed by her singular status. She believes it is her personal attributes—the talent and dedication she brings to the game—that are most important.

**Profile by
Dona L. Irvin**

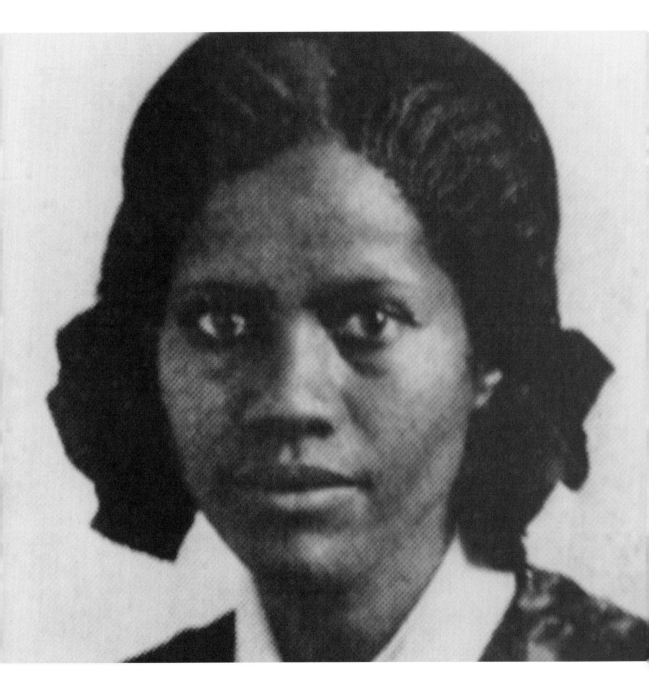

FRANCES E. W. HARPER

S cholar Nellie McKay once noted that, "in an era full of extraordi-

nary black women, Frances Watkins Harper, abolitionist and feminist,

lecturer, poet and novelist, was one of the most extraordinary among

them. If she had published nothing else, Iola Leroy *would have been*

sufficient for her to claim a place among the intellectuals of her time....

Harper takes us to the heart of the most complex problems that faced

black Americans in the post-Civil War era, and blazes a trail toward

solutions" (McKay, interview, 11 April 1991).

1825–1911 •

Writer, activist •

Frances Ellen Watkins Harper was born in 1825 in Baltimore, Maryland. Free from the yoke of slavery, she was the only child of a mother who died when she was two years old. She was reared by an aunt and educated in a private school run by her uncle, William Watkins, a minister. Harper was a lonely child given to quiet musings, and she was profoundly affected by the abolitionist teachings of the school she attended.

Unable to attend school beyond her thirteenth year, she began working as a housekeeper. The family for whom she worked owned a bookstore, so she spent her spare time reading in an effort to advance her education.

In 1850 Harper left the slave state of Maryland and settled in Ohio, where she taught at Union Seminary, an African Methodist Episcopal (AME) church near Columbus. This seminary became a part of Wilberforce University. Frances Watkins became the first black American woman instructor in vocational education at the school.

In 1852 Harper left Ohio and moved to Little York, Pennsylvania, where she taught for a brief time. Her spirits flagged, though, in part because of her increasing awareness of the atrocities of slavery. She was further devastated by Maryland's 1853 decision to forbid free blacks from entering the state. The legislation cast Harper into exile, for any attempt to return would mean risking her freedom, as the law stated that free blacks entering the state could be imprisoned or remanded into slavery.

As time passed, though, Harper's determination to battle the practice of slavery grew. A knowledgeable and articulate speaker, she became a permanent lecturer for the Maine Anti-Slavery Society and other groups. Between 1854 and 1860, Harper traveled widely and lectured often, usually two or three times a day. Harper's performances sometimes prompted disbelief from the more dimwitted members of her audience, who contended that she had to be a white person in disguise.

Often referred to as the "Bronze Muse" because of her talent for making her points through poetry, Frances Harper was a petite, dignified woman blessed with a musical voice that underscored the sincerity of her speech. She was not reluctant to extend financial support to those in need. Her friend William Still, conductor on the Underground Railroad, wrote that she was "one of the most liberal contributors, as well as one of the ablest advocates for the Underground Railroad and the slave" (Still, 755).

Frances Watkins married a young widower named Fenton Harper on November 22, 1860, in Cincinnati, Ohio. The savings from her lectures and book sales enabled her to purchase a farm near Columbus, Ohio, where she and her husband settled down to married life. During her marriage, Harper gave birth to one daughter, whom she named Mary. Married life inhibited Harper's travel, but following the death of her husband in the mid-1860s, she again emerged as an advocate, this time pushing for equal rights for newly liberated slaves.

With daughter in tow, Harper set out on a grueling self-financed speaking tour in 1867. From 1867 to 1871 she gave daily lectures throughout the war-torn South, visiting thirteen southern states. Lecturing on the needs for racial uplift, moral reform, and women's rights, she addressed Sunday school audiences, women's groups, and anyone else who would listen to her message. As women's clubs increased in popularity, Harper became a favored speaker for the women's movement.

A staunch supporter of the temperance movement, from 1875 to 1882 Harper served as superintendent of the "colored branch" of the Philadelphia and Pennsylvania chapters of the Woman's Christian Temperance Union. From 1883 to 1890, she directed the Northern United States Temperance Union. Harper was also an active member of the National Council of Women, the American Women's Suffrage Association, and the American Association of Education of Colored Youth.

As the years passed by, it was clear that Harper was unafraid to confront racism wherever it raised its ugly head. Disturbed by racist sentiments in some quarters of the women's movement, Harper and several other women charged the international gathering of women at the World's Congress of Representative Women in Chicago (1893) with indifference to the needs and concerns of black American women. Harper, an astute political analyst, declared that all women stood on the threshold of a woman's era, and that the time was at hand for them to seize political and economic power. But Harper and other black American women intellectuals, who had depended on the suffrage movement to represent their concerns, came to feel that they would have to organize themselves to achieve sexual emancipation. The National Association of Colored Women (NACW) was established as a result.

Literary Career •

Launched

Harper's first volume of poems and prose appeared in 1851. A small collection titled *Forest Leaves* but also printed as *Autumn Leaves,* it was sold in Baltimore. The book that actually launched Harper's literary career, however, was *Poems on Miscellaneous Subjects,* published in 1854 with a preface by renowned abolitionist William Lloyd Garrison. The book's popularity was unprecedented, and established Harper as the most popular black American poet of the period.

In 1859 Harper became the first black American woman to have a short story published. "The Two Offers" appeared in the *Anglo-African* in its September/October 1859 issue. In 1869 *Harper* published *Moses: A Story of the Nile,* a long narrative poem in blank verse. Other works, including an 1895 collection titled *Atlanta Offering* and a 1901 work called *Idylls of the Bible,* followed.

Unlike some of the poets of the period, who wrote sentimental verse with trite rhymes and hackneyed themes, often avoiding race and politics, Harper's literary output was decidedly political. Many of her poems focus on the atrocities of slavery in general and the cruelties towards women in particular. "The Slave Mother" was the most popular of Harper's politically conscious work. A poignant poem, it captured the traumatic separation of mother and child and recreated the terror of the auction block. "The Slave Mother" remains one of Harper's most frequently anthologized poems.

The importance of Harper's verse went unacknowledged, however, until later generations of feminist scholars and researchers delved into her work. Pointing to work such as the final stanza of "Bury Me in a Free Land," critics contend that Harper's poetry is perhaps unsurpassed in the purity of the sentiments it expresses:

> I ask no monument, proud and high,
> To arrest the gaze of the passers-by;
> All that my yearning spirit craves,
> Is bury me not in a land of slaves
> (Davis, *Calavcade,* 104).

Harper's short story "The Two Offers" reflected her interest in improving the situation for women in American society:

> But woman—the true woman—if you would render her happy, it needs more than the mere development of her affectional nature. Her conscience should be enlightened, her faith in the true and right established, and scope given to her heaven-endowed and God-given faculties. The true aim of female education should be, not a development of one or two, but all the faculties of the human soul, because no perfect womanhood is developed by imperfect culture.... To trust the whole wealth of a woman's nature on the frail bark of human love may often be like trusting a cargo of gold and precious gems to a bark that has never battled with the storm or buffeted the waves (Shockley, *Afro-American Women Writers,* 65).

Harper's lone novel, *Iola Leroy; or Shadows Uplifted,* is best appreciated within the context of its times. The novel is set in the period immediately following the conclusion of the Civil War, a time when newly-freed blacks nonetheless faced sometimes deadly obstacles to happiness. Poverty, bigotry, hatred, and violence all conspired to shackle black efforts to improve their lives. Black men were often portrayed in literature of the era as shiftless, ignorant, and violent criminals and rapists, while black women were dismissed as morally loose, unfaithful, and spreaders of sexually transmitted diseases. Harper sought to reverse these negative images while also fashioning an aesthetically pleasing work.

Iola Leroy was a novel committed to raising the social consciousness of its readers, and it reached a wide audience after its release. It tells the story of Iola, a young black woman who struggles against forbidding odds to attain happiness. Her refusal to marry in order to find happiness, her insistence upon working, and her abiding commitment to the uplift of her race take the novel beyond the boundaries of the typical sentimental novel. Ultimately, the novel concludes with Iola's marriage to Dr. Latimer, an African-American who shares the same ideals of social change. The novel was proclaimed by the *AME Church Review* as the crowning effort of Harper's life. As African-American literary aesthetics changed, however, Harper received criticism for those very aspects of her novel for which she was once acclaimed.

By 1911 *Iola Leroy* had lost its critical appeal. For the next several decades, although acknowledged as historically significant, the novel was criticized for its aesthetics, sentimentalism, and idealism, as well as its use of mulatto rather than black characters. Today, though, it is recognized as an important work that articulated the racial and gender issues and concerns of its time.

Harper herself commented in a note following *Iola Leroy* that "from threads of fact and fiction I have woven a story whose mission will not be in vain if it awakens in the hearts of our countrymen a strong sense of justice and more Christlike humanity in behalf of those whom the fortunes of war threw, homeless, ignorant and poor, upon the threshold of a new era" (Harper, *Iola Leroy,* 282).

The poem that concludes *Iola Leroy* demonstrates Harper's faith in a new day:

> There is light beyond the darkness,
> Joy beyond the present pain;
> There is hope in God's great justice
> And the negro's rising brain.
> Though the morning seems to linger
> O'er the hill-tops far away,
> Yet the shadows bear the promise
> Of a brighter coming day (Harper, *Iola Leroy,* 282).

Novel •

Articulates

Cultural

History

Profile by
Nagueyalti Warren

In 1909 Harper's daughter Mary died after a lifetime of social work and lecturing fashioned in some measure after her mother's work. Two years later, on February 20, 1911, Frances Ellen Watkins Harper died in Philadelphia, Pennsylvania, of a heart ailment at the age of eighty-seven. Funeral services were held at the First Unitarian Church, and she was buried on February 24 in Eden Cemetery in Philadelphia.

CHARLOTTE HAWKINS BROWN

A s the distinguished founder of the Palmer Memorial Institute,

1883–1961 •

Charlotte Hawkins Brown served for more than half a century as one of

the pioneering and driving forces in American preparatory education

Educator, •

for black youths. Brown was a major contributor to the effort to foster

author, civic

equality of educational opportunity in the South. Her vision for black

leader

youth spurred her determination to set high standards of educational

excellence both for her faculty and her students.

The granddaughter of slaves, Charlotte Hawkins Brown was born Lottie Hawkins on June 11, 1883, in Henderson, North Carolina. She and her brother Mingo were the children of Caroline Frances Hawkins. Raised in an attractive home on land that was part of a former plantation, Lottie Hawkins came to share the educational and cultural aspirations of her mother and grandmother.

In 1888 Lottie Hawkins moved to Cambridge, Massachusetts, with eighteen other members of her family. Her mother and a man named Nelson Willis had married, and together they operated a hand laundry

and provided a good home for the family near Harvard University. Lottie Hawkins attended nearby Allston Grammar School.

Lottie Hawkins showed an early talent for leadership and oratory, and at Cambridge English High School she proved to be an exceptional scholar. One day she met Alice Freeman Palmer, the educator, humanitarian, and second president of Wellesley College. Palmer was impressed by the girl's intelligence and desire for knowledge, and she became an enduring influence in the girl's life.

Convinced that "Lottie" sounded too ordinary to be put on her diploma, Hawkins changed her name to Charlotte Eugenia Hawkins. Inspired by Booker T. Washington to use her northern education to teach black people in the South, she negotiated with her mother to attend a two-year normal school. Palmer voluntarily paid Hawkins's expenses at the State Normal School at Salem, Massachusetts, where she enrolled in the fall of 1900.

At the beginning of her second year at Salem, though, Hawkins met a representative of the American Missionary Association, a group of white advocates in New York who financed and administered schools for blacks in the South. The representative offered Hawkins a job as a teacher at the Bethany Institute in North Carolina. Excited by the opportunity to return to her native state to teach less fortunate members of her own race, she accepted the offer and traveled to North Carolina in 1901.

On October 12, 1901, Hawkins held her first class for fifty children, who came from miles around. She used most of her salary of thirty dollars per month to buy clothes and supplies for the school children. At the end of the school year the American Missionary Association closed its one- and two-teacher schools—including Bethany—for lack of funds. The group offered her a position elsewhere, but the local community of Sedalia was anxious to have her remain there and teach. She put off her plans to further her education, choosing to stay and build a school for the town.

Charlotte Hawkins returned to Cambridge, Massachusetts, in June 1902 and discussed her plan to start a school with Alice Freeman Palmer, who promised to provide financial assistance. Hawkins spent the summer of 1902 in New England, giving recitations and musical recitals to raise money to open her school. When she returned to Sedalia, the people of the community gave fifteen acres of land for the school, and the minister of Bethany Congregational Church donated an old blacksmith shop, which she converted into a school with the money she had raised from northern philanthropists. With meager facilities but great

Alice Freeman •

Palmer

Memorial

Institute

Founded

enthusiasm, Hawkins opened her school on October 10, 1902. The school was named the Alice Freeman Palmer Institute in honor of her friend and benefactor. Palmer died that fall, before she was able to promote Hawkins's work with possible financial contributors, but Hawkins was eventually able to get financial backing from many of Palmer's acquaintances. Upon Palmer's death, Hawkins added "Memorial" to the name of the school.

In 1905 Hawkins used the money that she received from a letter-writing campaign to build Memorial Hall, the first new building on the Palmer campus. During the next several years, the school grew steadily, guided by Hawkins's steady hand. At the same time that she served as the school's principal administrator, teacher, and fundraiser, Hawkins furthered her own education. In addition to receiving a diploma from Salem Normal School in 1901, she studied at Harvard University and at Wellesley and Simmons Colleges. On November 23, 1907, the Palmer Memorial Institute was incorporated and a board was appointed. The school purchased additional land and added to their faculty and course offerings. Within a decade the school was known throughout the South.

On June 12, 1911, Hawkins married Edward Sumner Brown. He subsequently taught at Palmer Institute, where he was responsible for the boys' dormitory. After one year, however, he left Sedalia to teach at a school in South Carolina. He and his wife continued to correspond and visit, but their marriage, which had been so happy in the beginning, ended in divorce in 1915.

About this time Charlotte Hawkins Brown took the three daughters of her brother Mingo under her wing after their mother died. In addition, she accepted the responsibility for the four children of her youngest aunt. With these seven children to care for, Brown built her own home on the campus, a frame house that she called Canary Cottage. All of these children graduated from Palmer Memorial Institute and went on to well-known institutions of higher education.

In 1919 Charlotte Hawkins Brown published her first fictional work. *Mammy: An Appeal to the Heart of the South* was an indictment of southern slaveholding families who failed to reward their slaves' loyalty and left them destitute in old age.

By 1922, when the Palmer Memorial Institute graduated its first accredited high school class, Brown had built Palmer into one of the nation's leading preparatory schools for black students. After she introduced a junior-college academic program in the mid-1920s, the school began to focus on its secondary and postsecondary components, attracting students from around the country. It also developed a nationally recognized choir, the Sedalia Singers, which was often directed by Brown herself.

As the years passed, Charlotte Hawkins Brown and the Institute became ever more important to the rural Sedalia community. Brown encouraged the townspeople to improve their health knowledge, farm methods, political action, and general knowledge, and to seek independent home ownership. Believing that interracial contacts were necessary for the education of black students, she sponsored cultural exchange programs with the North Carolina State College for Women at Greensboro.

Brown's personal diplomacy and strong resolve were special strengths in advancing the understanding of black American life among people across the country. In the 1920s, she opposed racial discrimination by bringing lawsuits whenever she was insulted or forced to follow the Jim Crow laws and by speaking about these experiences at large gatherings. In 1921 the YWCA national board appointed Brown to its membership, the first such appointment for a black person. Brown also campaigned openly against lynching, a dangerous position to take in the South at the time. Her leadership on these matters combined a capacity to inspire with practical wisdom.

For her work as an educator, Brown was inducted into the North Carolina Board of Education's Hall of Fame in 1926, but her contribution to the state of North Carolina went far beyond her work at the Palmer Memorial Institute. As one of the organizers of the North Carolina State Federation of Negro Women's Clubs in 1909 (and a subsequent stint as president), she worked for the betterment of black women, including establishment of the Efland Home for Wayward Girls. When continuation of this institution became prohibitively expensive for Brown's organization, she persuaded the North Carolina General Assembly to establish a new facility, the Dobbs School for Girls, to continue its work. Her influence also spread to other areas of the country through Palmer's graduates, who carried Brown's zeal to their home communities.

In 1937 the county opened a public high school at Sedalia and the state withdrew its subsidies from the Palmer Institute, which had been educating the community children through the high school level. Brown responded by changing Palmer's curriculum to improve its students' general knowledge and to emphasize the acquisition of good manners and social graces in preparing each student to be a member of American society.

As the reputations of Charlotte Hawkins Brown and the Palmer Memorial Institute grew nationally in the 1940s, Brown was in great demand as a

Brown's •

National

Leadership

Emerges

lecturer and speaker. With the publication in 1941 of her second book, *The Correct Thing to Do, to Say and to Wear,* she became known as "The First Lady of Social Graces," and she received numerous invitations to lecture on fine manners and decorum.

• *Brown Retires*

from Palmer

Memorial

Institute

On October 5, 1952, after fifty years of service, Brown retired as president of the Palmer Memorial Institute, though she remained on campus as vice-chairman of the board of trustees and as director of finances until 1955. Suffering from diabetes, Brown died in a hospital in Greensboro, North Carolina, on January 11, 1961. She was buried on the campus of the Palmer Memorial Institute. The grave is marked by a bronze plaque that enumerates both her personal accomplishments and those related to the founding and development of the institute.

The spirit and ideals of Charlotte Hawkins Brown continued after her death to guide those charged with the administration of the Palmer Memorial Institute. The numbers of students who applied to Palmer Memorial Institute diminished, however, while financial difficulties began to beleaguer the school. The school was eventually closed, but in 1983 the Charlotte Hawkins Brown Historical Foundation was incorporated to assist the state of North Carolina in establishing the state's first historic site in honor of a black person and a woman. In 1987 the former campus was designated a state historic site, and the area now features exhibits honoring Brown and the Palmer Memorial Institute.

**Profile by
Marsha C. Vick**

The campus's special status is a fitting tribute to Brown. From the inception of the Palmer Memorial Institute in 1902, the history of the institution was inextricably tied to the life of its founder. In developing the school into one of the most important fountains of educational opportunity for blacks in the South, Charlotte Hawkins Brown combined qualities of leadership and appreciation of academic ideals with a profound understanding of national and regional needs, as well as an appreciation of local community aspirations.

ALEXIS M. HERMAN

A s Alexis M. Herman stated in Essence, *"It's important that we set*   **1947–** •

high goals for ourselves. It never occurred to me that I couldn't be

anything I wanted to be." During her career, Herman has worked in   **Government** •

politics, public relations, and with social service and women's rights   **official, women's**

groups. She has indeed achieved success in high-level—and highly   **rights advocate**

visible—positions. At the age of twenty-nine, for example, she was

sworn in as director of the Women's Bureau of the U.S. Department of

Labor, thus becoming the youngest person ever to serve in that capacity.

When President Bill Clinton was elected, Herman became an assistant

to the president and director of the White House Office of the Public

Liaison—the department responsible for building public support for

presidential priorities. Along with Maggie Williams—the first black chief of staff to a first lady—Herman plays an important role in creating support for the Democratic political agenda.

Alexis Margaret Herman was born July 16, 1947, in Mobile, Alabama, to Alex Herman and Gloria Caponis Herman. After graduating from the Heart of Mary High School in Mobile in 1965, she attended Edgewood College in Madison, Wisconsin, and Spring Hill College in Mobile. She received her B.S. degree in 1969 from Xavier University in New Orleans, and did graduate work at the University of South Alabama in Mobile through 1972.

Herman began her professional career at the local level. Between 1969 and 1972, she was a community worker for Interfaith in Mobile, a social worker for Catholic Social Services in Mobile, and an outreach worker for the Recruitment and Training Program in Pascagoula, Mississippi. In 1972, when Atlanta's Southern Regional Council wanted to determine whether a recruitment and training program designed to get blacks into the construction trades could be adapted to obtain white-collar jobs for minority women, Herman moved to Atlanta to develop the program. Two years later this project, known as the Minority Women Employment Program (MWEP), went national with Herman as its director. Through this pioneering initiative, several hundred women of color were placed in nontraditional private sector jobs.

From 1977 to 1981, Herman was director of the Women's Bureau in the Office of the Secretary of the U.S. Department of Labor. Named to the position by President Jimmy Carter, Herman advised both Carter and labor secretary Ray Marshall on economic and social concerns of women in the workplace and directed the department's program for small, developing, and disadvantaged businesses. At the time of her appointment, not only did she become the senior black woman Labor Department official, she became the youngest director ever to serve in the Women's Bureau.

Gains National •

Prominence

The Women's Bureau has traditionally been responsible for formulating policies and implementing programs that address the concerns of many diverse women's groups. Among these groups are minority women (including black, Hispanic, Native American, and Asian American), mature women (mid-life), women reentering the work force, displaced homemakers, battered women, women who have been charged with crimes, low-income women, rural women, and women business owners. As director of the Women's Bureau, Herman became acquainted with the many problems that affect women in the workplace, and she worked hard to address the questions women asked about their plight. Her goal was to push the Women's Bureau into the forefront of issues concerning women, to get directly involved in existing programs, and to develop model programs for various groups of women who needed specialized help.

Herman focused on what she viewed as the major issues facing working women in the 1970s: job discrimination based on gender, age, or race; limited marketable job skills, particularly in nontraditional career fields; rigid work schedules; and child care. These issues continue to be major problems in the 1990s. Writing about the prospects for advancement for black women within the labor market in an article published in 1979 in the *Black Collegian,* Herman stated:

> Black women must be qualified to fill some of the better paying jobs in the areas where skills will be in demand. It calls for more women to move into the nontraditional, higher paying jobs. And it calls for more affirmative action efforts to ensure that Black women do indeed have equal opportunity for training and education, and for consideration in recruitment. It calls for increased numbers of Black women among those being hired, and among those being promoted on the job. Only then will we begin to see a drastic change in where Black women now stand in the labor force.

In a later article for the *Black Collegian,* Herman noted that black women must also be aware that being qualified for a particular position is only part of the process of realizing job opportunities. Women, particularly those of color and those moving into nontraditional jobs, must be constantly vigilant to ensure that equal employment opportunity and affirmative action policies are being properly enforced. Herman published several other important articles on issues confronting women in the workplace, including: "Minority Women, Professional Work" (*Manpower,* July 1975); "Black Women in the Workplace: Are Their Options Really Open?" (*Ivy Leaf, AKA Journal,* Fall 1977); and "Equal Access to Equal Jobs for Workers" (*Operating Engineer,* December 1979).

Herman used her position with the Women's Bureau as a stepping stone to other jobs at the national level. For example, in 1989 she became chief of staff for the Democratic National Committee, and in 1991 the DNC chair, Ron Brown, appointed Herman deputy chair of the DNC. Also that year Herman was named chief executive officer of the 1992 Democratic National Convention Committee, with gave her responsibility for the overall strategic management and production of the convention.

Recognized as an expert in the field of multiculturalism and diversity management as it relates to mergers and acquisitions, Herman has traveled extensively in the United States and abroad speaking on workplace issues. She is founder and president of the Washington-based marketing and management firm A. M. Herman and Associates, which specializes in targeted marketing strategies, organizational analysis, and human resource management. She has demonstrated her ability to compete successfully in both the public and private sectors.

Herman has contributed her political and business expertise to various service, professional, and religious organizations. For example, she is a former chair of the National Commission on Working Women and a founding member of the National Consumer Cooperative Bank. She has also served on the boards of the Adams National Bank, the National Council of Negro Women, the National Democratic Institute, and the District of Columbia Economic Development Finance Corporation. During her tenure with the U.S. Labor Department, Herman was White House Representative to the Organization of Economic Cooperation and Development. She later co-chaired the president's task force to establish a Women's Business Ownership Initiative for the federal government.

Herman has also been involved with the United States Catholic Bishops Conference, the United States Catholic Conference on Social Justice, and the World Peace Commission. From 1972 to 1975, she served on the board of the Campaign for Human Development—the Catholic Church's national education and action program to combat poverty and injustice in the United States. As a member of Delta Sigma Theta Sorority, she has functioned in a wide array of leadership and group-service capacities. Herman has received numerous awards and accolades for her work and community service. For example, in 1979 she was touted among *Ebony* magazine's "50 Future Leaders," and in 1980 she was named Outstanding Young Woman of the Future by *Ladies Home Journal*.

A determined, creative, personable, and compassionate woman, Alexis Herman has used her intelligence and political savvy to make a steady climb from local community organizer to her current position as assistant to the president and director of the Office of Public Liaison. Her tireless work toward equality and social justice has broadened employment opportunities not only for black women, but also for many other traditionally underrepresented groups.

Starts •

Marketing and

Management

Firm

**Profile by
Marva L. Rudolph**

ANITA HILL

*A*nita Hill was catapulted into the limelight in the fall of 1991 when

1956– •

she testified before the U.S. Senate during the confirmation hearings for

Clarence Thomas, who had been nominated by President George Bush

Lawyer, •

for the U.S. Supreme Court seat vacated by Justice Thurgood Marshall.

educator

Hill charged that Thomas had sexually harassed her when she worked

for him at the U.S. Department of Education and at the Equal Employ-

ment Opportunity Commission. Because of these allegations, the pub-

licity surrounding the hearings was enormous. The Senate debate pitted

Republicans against Democrats, and public opinion was split along

racial and gender lines. Never before had the issue of sexual harass-

ment—its defining characteristics and the implications of such behavior—received such widespread attention. When the attention from the hearings died down, Hill returned to teaching law and became an outspoken opponent of sexual harassment in the workplace.

Anita Faye Hill was born July 30, 1956, in a farming community six miles east of Morris, Oklahoma. She was the youngest of the thirteen children of Albert and Erma Hill, who raised their family as Baptists. Anita, called Faye by family and friends, was one of four siblings to become valedictorian of Morris High School. She continued her scholastic achievements during her college years, graduating with honors from Oklahoma State University in 1977 with a B.S. in psychology. She went on to attend Yale University Law School on a NAACP scholarship, earning her law degree in 1980.

Her first position as an attorney was at the law firm of Wald, Hardraker and Ross in Washington, D.C. In 1981, she became an assistant to Clarence Thomas, a black man and fellow Yale University Law School graduate who was then assistant secretary at the U.S. Department of Education. What began as a positive working relationship between Thomas and Hill deteriorated after three months, according to Hill, when Thomas began asking her for dates and wanting to discuss sex—overtures that she refused. Nine months later, Thomas was tapped to chair the Equal Employment Opportunity Commission (EEOC), and he chose Hill to be his special assistant. Hill commented on her job at the EEOC during the Senate confirmation hearings, as quoted in *Black Scholar:* "The work itself was interesting, and at that time it appeared that the sexual overtures which had so troubled me had ended." Hill left her job in 1983, however, to teach law in her home state at Oral Roberts University. According to *Black Scholar,* she explained during the hearings that she "agreed to take the job, in large part because of my desire to escape the pressures I felt at the EEOC due to Judge Thomas."

Hill was contacted to appear before the Senate Judiciary Committee in August 1991, after an aide to Ohio Democrat Senator Howard Metzenbaum received a tip that Clarence Thomas had sexually harassed her during her employment with him in the early 1980s. Hill agreed to testify before the committee, but decided in September to prepare a personal statement about the allegations, which she was assured would be kept confidential. This statement and an FBI report were circulated to the committee members. Thomas, when informed, vehemently denied the charges.

The Judiciary Committee sent Thomas's nomination to the floor of the Senate with no recommendation, having split their vote seven to seven. During the subsequent full Senate debate, Hill's name and a portion of the FBI report were leaked to *Newsday* and National Public Radio. On October 6, 1991, both news agencies made public Hill's allegations of sexual harassment against Clarence Thomas. Public pressure to investigate these charges further pushed the Senate to reopen the hearings, which were carried live on the major television networks.

For three days, all media were focused on what would become a topic of national and international debate: defining sexual harassment and its consequences. Anita Hill became a household name as her allegations became the central issue that would determine whether Clarence Thomas was found competent to be a Supreme Court justice. Hill faced intense questioning during the hearings, and several senators were later criticized for their insensitive treatment of her. The White House launched an investigation into Hill's background, hoping to find information to impeach her character, even though she had come forward reluctantly. According to *Black Scholar,* Hill told the senators, "It is only after a great deal of agonizing consideration that I am able to talk of these unpleasant matters to anyone except my closest friends."

The public was divided over who was telling the truth: Hill or Thomas. Since the allegations referred to incidents that had occurred almost ten years before, some critics questioned why she had not come forward earlier and doubted her credibility. Public opinion seemed to favor Thomas, though the various polls reflected racial and/or gender bias. Many members of the African-American community debated whether a black woman should bring such charges against a black man since, in their opinion, prejudice against blacks was already a major factor threatening their employment prospects. After intense debate, the Senate confirmed Clarence Thomas as an associate justice of the Supreme Court on October 16, 1991, by a vote of 52 to 48, making him the second black appointed to the Supreme Court.

In a show of support along gender and racial lines, 1,603 black women issued a historic statement that appeared in the November 18, 1991, issue of the *New York Times.* Entitled "African American Women in Defense of Ourselves," the article conveyed their objections to the Thomas appointment and the Hill-Thomas hearings. Various articles sharing this sentiment appeared in other national publications. Poet and professor June Jordan stated flatly in *The Progressive:*

> Anita Hill was tricked. She was set up. She had been minding her business at the University of Oklahoma Law School when the senators asked her to describe her relationship with Clarence Thomas.... And with this televised victimization of Anita Hill, the American war

Aftermath of •

the Hearings

of violence against women moved from the streets, moved from hip-hop, moved from multimillion-dollar movies into the highest chambers of the U.S. Government.

Donna Brazile, chief aide to Congresswoman Eleanor Holmes Norton, stated in *Black Scholar:*

> Hill's plight was facing an institution that is not only hostile to the needs of Blacks, but hostile and insensitive to the needs of women. I've heard people say, "How could she?" We Black women have always been supportive of Black men.... Being supportive does not mean you have to support every single Black man, regardless.

Professor Orlando Patterson expressed a differing opinion in *Black Scholar,* however, writing:

> I am convinced that Professor Hill perfectly understood the psycho-cultural context in which Judge Thomas allegedly regaled her with his Rabelaisian humor (possibly as a way of affirming their common origins), which is precisely why she never filed a complaint against him. Raising the issue 10 years later was unfair and disingenuous.

• *Heightened*

Awareness of

Sexual

Harassment

Over time, public opinion seemed to move toward Hill's position. A *U.S. News and World Report* poll in 1992 indicated that the public was evenly divided (38 percent for Hill and 38 percent for Thomas) in their opinion about the credibility of the two, while during the hearings 60 percent of those polled believed Thomas and only 20 percent believed Hill. After the hearings, Hill returned to her duties as a law professor but began another career as an advocate against sexual harassment, speaking primarily before women's groups and corporate and government agencies concerned about sexual harassment in the workplace. When a staff writer from *Glamour* magazine—which had named Hill one of its ten Women of the Year in 1991—visited Hill in Norman, she found the law professor inundated with letters from Americans reacting to the hearings. Of the 24,377 letters and cards the writer perused, fully 98 percent expressed their support of Hill.

Hill's ordeal during the senate hearings did serve to raise awareness of the issue of sexual harassment in the workplace. Haki Madhubuti, poet and professor, commented in *Essence* on what he saw as a positive outcome of the hearings:

The fallout from this has heightened Black men's and women's awareness of sexual harassment. I hope that—as a result of this spectacle—Black men will be more conscientious about how they treat women in the workplace as well as in the home. I would also hope that women would be strong enough in the future to confront such harassment early rather than let it live in them as horror stories. I hope this event will enable us [black men] to grow and realize that our manhood does not depend on taking advantage of Black women.

For the American public in general, the hearings made sexual harassment an important issue. *Time* magazine reported in 1992 that "most women continue to fear that if they cry harassment, they will be ignored, stigmatized, even fired." The article reported that 60 percent of all individuals who complained to the EEOC were told that "they had 'no cause' to proceed," and the commission filed only a small fraction of those complaints as sexual harassment cases. Yet, according to *People,* "Corporations across the nation are stepping up their efforts to educate employees about sexual harassment, and at the Equal Employment Opportunity Commission . . . calls requesting information on the definition of harassment have increased a hundredfold."

Nobel Prize-winning author Toni Morrison edited a collection of essays entitled *Race-ing* Justice, *En-gendering* Power: Essays on Anita Hill, Clarence Thomas, and the Construction of Social Reality. Morrison stated in her introduction:

In matters of race and gender, it is now possible and necessary, as it seemed never to have been before, to speak about these matters without the barriers, the silences, the embarrassing gaps in discourse. It is clear to the most reductionist intellect that Black people think differently from one another; it is also clear that the time for undiscriminating racial unity has passed.

Chronicle of Higher Education stated in 1992 that the Senate hearings made Hill a "national icon" for the issue of sexual harassment. Though Thomas's nomination was confirmed, her testimony inspired needed discussion on the hotly contested topic of sexual harassment. Even though some people claimed that Hill's testimony was fabricated and that she did more to hurt than to help the cause of women in the workplace, Hill remains steadfast in her conviction that she did the right thing by testifying.

**Profile by
Jacqueline
Brice-Finch**

In 1992 Anita Hill took a sabbatical from teaching to explore the possibility of founding an institute for research on racism and sexism. The following year the University of Oklahoma Board of Regents approved a proposal to name a professorship after Hill that would be devoted to the study of discrimination in the workplace.

ANN HOBSON-PILOT

As principal harpist in the Boston Symphony Orchestra, Ann

Hobson-Pilot holds one of the most important positions for a harpist in

the world of music. She attained her current position in 1980, having

joined the Boston Symphony—one of the nation's "Big Three"—as

associate principal harpist in 1969, at the age of twenty-six. She now

holds the Willona Henderson Sinclair Chair.

Born November 6, 1943, in Philadelphia, Pennsylvania, Ann Stevens Hobson was the younger of two girls born to Grace Stevens Hobson and Harrison D. Hobson. Her mother taught in the Philadelphia public schools and was a concert pianist for many years, and her father was a social worker.

Hobson-Pilot began studying the piano at age six, with her mother. During her childhood, the family lived in Germany for three-and-a-half years while Harrison Hobson fulfilled a military assignment. This time overseas exposed young Ann to new cultural experiences and enabled her to receive private piano instruction from German tutors. Back in the States, piano instruction continued, though Hobson-Pilot sometimes

did not welcome interruptions from her perfectionist mother. As she told D. Antoinette Handy in a 1975 interview:

> The thought occurred to me to take up an instrument that my mother could not tell me what I was doing wrong. Philadelphia's Girls High School had a strong music program. I approached the music chairman about participating. My first choice was the flute, but there were already too many. The chairman suggested that I consider the harp, in view of my strong piano background.

From the time she took up the new instrument at age fourteen, harp and Hobson-Pilot seemed to mesh perfectly. As she explained to Robert Merritt for the *Richmond Times Dispatch* in 1978, "I decided almost immediately that it was worth all the trouble. First of all, I loved it, took to it immediately, and all the blisters, having to keep my nails cut short and lugging it around, that never bothered me. I knew it was what I wanted to do." She soon became a member of Philadelphia's All-City High School Orchestra and played with various pick-up orchestras, including the all-black Philadelphia Concert Orchestra.

Early in Hobson-Pilot's senior year of high school, Philadelphia Symphony harpist Marilyn Costello, who also taught harp in the city's schools, indicated that the young harpist was of concert caliber. But as Hobson-Pilot related in her interview with Handy, the question in her mind was, "What does the world want with a black harpist?" Women were fully accepted as harpists in symphonic circles, but blacks of either gender were not. Her parents shared this concern; nevertheless, they supported her decision to enroll at a conservatory. They insisted that she follow a music education program, however, to provide an alternative career in case she did not succeed as a performer.

For post-secondary study, Hobson-Pilot enrolled at the Philadelphia Musical Academy. Beginning in 1962, Hobson-Pilot spent the first of several summers at the Maine Harp Colony—now known as the Salzedo Harp Colony—in Camden, Maine. There she encountered the noted harpist and teacher Alice Chalifoux, a member of the Cleveland Institute of Music faculty and the Cleveland Symphony. Hobson-Pilot entered the institute at the beginning of her junior year and graduated in 1966.

Shortly after graduation, a rare opportunity presented itself when the principal harpist for the National Symphony Orchestra in Washington, D.C., injured a finger. With insufficient time for advertising and auditioning, a master harpist was needed at once to fill a one-year assignment. The orchestra's management contacted harp authority Alice Chalifoux, who recommended her star pupil, Hobson-Pilot. She was performing successfully in this position when she heard of an opening with the Boston Symphony Orchestra.

When she first auditioned for the Boston Symphony, Hobson-Pilot competed against thirty other harpists for the position of second harpist. She was the undisputed winner, and if she accepted the position she would also be principal harpist in the Boston Pops. But she faced a difficult decision: whether to trade her principal harpist position with the National Symphony for second harpist in a higher-ranked orchestra. To make her decision easier, Boston upgraded the position from second harpist to associate principal harpist. The talented twenty-six-year-old accepted the position in 1969. She would soon join the harp faculty of the prestigious New England Conservatory of Music.

In addition to her membership in the Boston Symphony, Hobson-Pilot made solo appearances with other orchestras. She always received glowing reviews, particularly for her rendition of Argentinean composer Alberto Ginastera's Concerto for Harp and Orchestra. Following an appearance with the Richmond (Virginia) Symphony, the *Richmond Times Dispatch* called her performance "extraordinary," noting that her "mastery of her instrument showed in very certain terms. She swept, with ethereal expression, over the harp's entire range."

In a review of a solo performance, the *Wichita (Kansas) Eagle* praised Hobson-Pilot as "an incredible technician, but more, she is able to tear the harp out of its traditional raiment and give it new and vital voices. Certainly, one will be convinced after hearing her, that she not only knows as a musician what the harp is capable of with its present limited repertoire, but also what it may be required to explore in the future. If so, she is the artist to take us into that future."

Hobson-Pilot organized the New England Harp Trio in 1971. Composed of three members of the Boston Symphony Orchestra (flutist, cellist, and harpist), the trio performs chamber and solo works from the baroque period to current times. In 1980, she became the principal harpist with the Boston Symphony. Also in this year, she married R. Prentice Pilot, a free-lance string bassist, teacher in the Boston public schools, and regular performer with the Boston Pops Esplanade Orchestra. Since 1988, Hobson-Pilot and her husband have conducted a concert series on the Caribbean Island of St. Maarten featuring African-American musicians and composers in programs combining classical and jazz genres. During the 1993–94 season, they added concerts on the island of St. Croix.

• *Appointed*

Principal

Harpist with

Boston

Symphony

The year 1992 was an impressive one for Hobson-Pilot: she received enthusiastic reviews following the release of her first solo compact disc by Boston Records Classical Corporation; she was honored at a concert and reception in celebration of her twenty-three years with the Boston Symphony; and she gave three performances of the Ginastera Harp Concerto with the Boston Pops Orchestra. The concert and reception were sponsored by the Boston Symphony Orchestra Committee on Cultural Diversity as part of their efforts to diversify the orchestra's audience, staff, and programming.

Recording became an active part of Hobson-Pilot's life beginning in 1991, when she recorded works by African-American composer William Grant Still (1895–1978) for New World Records. She was assisted by violist George Taylor, bassist Prentice Pilot, and baritone Robert Honeysucker—all African Americans. Shortly afterward, she showcased her virtuosity on the solo compact disc, which featured works by Bach, Debussy, Hindemith, Salzedo, Faure, Ravel, Pierne, and Malotte. The recording was made at the African Meeting House in Boston, the oldest surviving African-American church in the country, and proceeds from the sale of each compact disc were donated to the United Negro College Fund.

Works •

Recorded

Hobson-Pilot explained the impetus behind the cover design for her solo compact disc in correspondence with Handy in 1994: "I believe in role models. When I was growing up I never saw a black doing what I'm doing. That's the main reason I decided to put my face on the cover of my recording. I don't want to be anonymous. I want people to know that I'm a black musician."

Hobson-Pilot's talents and accomplishments have been recognized with awards by various groups. For example, Sigma Alpha Iota, an international music fraternity, named her their 1991 Distinguished Woman of the Year. Philadelphia College of Performing Arts (formerly the Philadelphia Musical Academy) granted her the School of Music's Alumni Achievement Award in 1992, as did the Cleveland Institute of Music in 1993. In 1988 she received an honorary doctor of music degree from Bridgewater State College.

Despite her many artistic accomplishments, Hobson-Pilot has not forgotten those less privileged than herself. During the spring of 1993, Hobson-Pilot was the featured performer in a concert benefiting Boston's String Training and Educational Program (STEP) for minority students. She was assisted by her husband, Prentice Pilot, and the Boston Symphony's newest black member, cellist Owen Young. She and her husband are co-directors of a music program in the Boston public schools, and she teaches troubadour harp at one of the city's middle schools.

Ann Hobson-Pilot has had a significant impact on the music world, not just through her symphony performances and recordings but also through her work as a teacher and role model. Formerly a private instructor at the Philadelphia Musical Academy and Temple University Music Festival at Ambler, she currently teaches at the New England Conservatory and the Tanglewood Music Center. She often conducts clinics for young harp students, recalling that it was in the public schools that she got her start.

Profile by
D. Antoinette Handy

BELL HOOKS

b *ell hooks has been praised as one of the few African-American scholars whose writings acknowledge the effects of racism and sexism in the lives of African-American women. hooks, a college professor, has written several books and essays outlining her ideas on feminist politics and contemporary culture. She views the representation of African Americans in many films and books as exploitive, and has called for the liberation of black women, men, and children by eliminating the prevailing "capitalist-patriarchal system" in the United States. Widely read in both academic and nonacademic circles, she now basks in the limelight as a writer, scholar, sought-after lecturer, and internationally known cultural critic.*

1952–

Feminist, critic, social activist, educator, writer

bell hooks was born Gloria Jean Watkins on September 25, 1952, in Hopkinsville, Kentucky. In the 1970s, when she began her writing career, she adopted the pseudonym bell hooks, which was the name of her maternal great-grandmother. hooks was one of seven children—six girls and a boy—born to Rosa Bell Watkins, a domestic worker, and Veodis Watkins, a janitor. Like many other writers, as a child she used books as an escape from her everyday world. Her particular love was poetry, especially the romantic poets and Walt Whitman. She also wrote her own poetry in secret.

Within the Watkins family, the male and female roles reflected the patriarchal values of the dominant society. This patriarchy at home had its counterpart in what she was taught about U.S. history in school. As she explained in her book of essays *Ain't I a Woman: Black Women and Feminism,* she was confronted with both "sexual imperialism in the form of patriarchy" and "racial imperialism in the form of white supremacy." Although she attended all-black public schools and grew up under a system of racial segregation, her education in the "politics of race" differed little from that of her white contemporaries. Her female, African-American sixth-grade teacher taught her to love and to be loyal to a government that was practicing segregation. As she commented in *Ain't I a Woman:* "Unknowingly [this teacher] implanted in our psyches a seed of the racial imperialism that would keep us forever in bondage. For how does one overthrow, change, or even challenge a system that you have been taught to admire, to love, to believe in?"

hooks first experienced an integrated environment when she went to Stanford University for her undergraduate studies, which she completed in 1973. She noted in *Ain't I a Woman* that her undergraduate education neither questioned the existing relationship between blacks and whites nor led to a greater understanding of "racism as a political ideology." Instead it condoned white supremacy and male patriarchy. She encountered a subtle form of racism in the attitudes of some of the undergraduate professors, who ignored their students of color. Although she was an eager participant in the women's movement on campus, study of African-American women was conspicuously absent, even in women's studies classes.

At the age of nineteen, hooks began researching *Ain't I a Woman: Black Women and Feminism* while pursuing full-time studies at Stanford University. She spent six years writing and revising the book, which was finally published in 1981. At this point the genteel southern girl Gloria Jean Watkins was transformed into the writer bell hooks, who, like her great-grandmother and namesake, gained a reputation for being outspoken.

Groundbreaking •

Work on Black

Feminism

Published

Ain't I a Woman is a fiery polemic in which hooks presents the thesis that racism and sexism have been powerful conjoined influences in the lives of African-American women. Taking a feminist perspective on African-American women's history from the period of slavery through the 1970s, she makes the controversial assertion that nineteenth-century African-American women had a stronger feminist consciousness than their twentieth-century counterparts. She castigates both the contemporary, mostly middle- and upper-class white women's liberation movement and the contemporary black liberation movement for ignoring African-American women.

In *Ain't I a Woman* hooks, who describes herself as having been on the forefront of the feminist movement for ten years, strongly condemns what she sees as the opportunism of many contemporary feminists:

> I became disillusioned as I saw the various groups of women appropriating feminism to serve their own opportunistic ends. Whether it was women university professors crying sexist oppression . . . to attract attention to their efforts to gain promotion; or women using feminism to mask their sexist attitudes; or women writers superficially exploring feminist themes to advance their own careers, it was evident that eliminating sexist oppression was not the primary concern. While their rallying cry was sexist oppression, they showed little concern about the status of women as a collective group in our society. They were primarily interested in making feminism a forum for the expression of their own self-centered needs and desires.

• *Pursues*

Academic

Career

According to hooks, the goal of the feminist movement should not just be equality with men, which women have achieved in some measure, but an overthrow of the entire "capitalist-patriarchal system."

Not surprisingly, feminist presses did not rush to publish her manuscript. Nevertheless, while giving a talk at a feminist bookstore, hooks made contacts that led her to South End Press, the publisher of *Ain't I a Woman* and all her subsequent books. *Ain't I a Woman* received harsh criticism from the academic community, but readers in other circles responded to it favorably.

hooks decided to pursue a career as a teacher at the college level, thinking that it would provide both personal fulfillment and a forum for disseminating her ideas. To that end, she obtained an M.A. from the University of Wisconsin in 1976 and a Ph.D. in English from the

University of California at Santa Cruz in 1983. The title of her dissertation is "Toni Morrison's Fiction: Keeping a Hold on Life." While obtaining her doctorate and shortly thereafter, she held a number of lectureships at various California universities. In 1985 she became an assistant professor of African-American studies and English literature at Yale University, and in 1988 an associate professor of American literature and women's studies at Oberlin College. At Oberlin her courses in African-American women's fiction and the politics of sexuality have been consistently filled with the maximum number of students. In 1993–94 she took a leave of absence from Oberlin to teach at the City College of New York.

In 1984 hooks published *Feminist Theory from Margin to Center.* The premise of the book is an idea proposed in *Ain't I a Woman:* that the feminist theory of white, middle-class women "at the center" rarely takes into account the experiences of either men or women "at the margin." She criticizes the feminist perspective of such writers as Betty Friedan, author of *The Feminine Mystique,* a classic of the women's movement. According to hooks, Friedan's disparagement of the housewife role is limited to the feminist perspective of the college-educated white woman.

Since 1989 hooks has produced several books, including *Yearning: Race, Gender, and Cultural Politics* (1990), which won the Before Columbus Foundation's American Book Award. According to Lisa Jones in *Village Voice Literary Supplement,* this book "solidified her reputation as an interrogator of postmodernism and cinema." *Breaking Bread: Insurgent Black Intellectual Life* (1991) is a compilation of lively dialogues with the scholar and social activist Cornel West. *Black Looks: Race and Representation* (1992) is a collection of essays on cultural criticism which further established hooks as an important film critic. In 1994 she published *Teaching to Transgress: Education as the Practice of Freedom,* in which she encourages minority students to become active participants in their own education, and *Outlaw Culture: Resisting Representations,* in which she applies her "astute eye and courageous spirit" to various aspects of American culture, according to Jerome Karabel in the *New York Times Book Review.*

In her interview with Jones, hooks discussed the representation of race in popular culture. She views the portrayal of African Americans in many films as a sad commentary on the progress of African Americans toward equality with whites. "And it's important to note that these representations aren't just made by white people," she commented. "But what we're seeing is black people reproducing the prevailing 'exploitive' images to create work that sells." She also laments the one-dimensionality of African-American women in film.

The portrayal of African-American women in the works of contemporary African-American female writers also disheartens hooks. For example, she sees author Terry McMillan's book *Waiting to Exhale* as furthering the stereotype of the African-American woman as the "bitchified, take-no-prisoners black." She also views some of Alice Walker's characters as feeding the stereotype of the African-American woman as victim. hooks continued in her interview with Jones, "Part of what I want to turn my life into is a testimony to the fact that we don't have to be punished. That we don't have to sacrifice our lives when we invent and realize our complex selves."

Due to the breadth of her scholarly concerns as a feminist and cultural critic, hooks has become one of the foremost contemporary African-American intellectuals. *Publishers Weekly* ranks *Ain't I a Woman* as one of the "twenty most influential women's books of the last twenty years." Through her scholarship, teaching, and activism, bell hooks works toward the vital goal of eliminating oppression.

Profile by
Phiefer L. Browne

WHITNEY HOUSTON

1963– •

W*hitney Houston will perhaps go down in history as one of black*

America's most highly acclaimed and successful musical performers.

Houston's career has been meteoric, characterized by great success as a

Singer, model, •

fashion model and as a singer. Beginning with her 1985 debut album,

actress

Whitney Houston—*which was the best-selling debut album ever for a*

solo artist—Houston has released a number of chart-topping songs

which have garnered her a host of Grammy Awards, among other

honors.

Whitney Houston was born on August 9, 1963, in Newark, New Jersey, and grew up in East Orange, New Jersey. She is one of three children of John R. Houston and Emily Drinkard Houston. Houston's whole family is involved in show business. Her father is president and chief executive officer of her management company, Nippy, which was named after her childhood nickname. Her mother, better known as Cissy, is a long-time performer. She sang with the Sweet Inspirations—a

soul group that toured and did record backup for such artists as Elvis Presley and Aretha Franklin—and was also featured in the gospel group the Drinkard Sisters, which included her nieces Dionne and Dee Dee Warwick. Houston's brother Michael is her road manager, and her brother Gary is one of her backup singers. In July 1992 Whitney Houston married Bobbi Brown, another award-winning singer, and in March 1993 she gave birth to her first child, a daughter.

In 1981 Houston graduated from Mount Saint Dominic Academy, a Catholic all-girls school in Caldwell, New Jersey. She left with a B-plus average, which was impressive since her modeling career often kept her away from home beginning at the age of sixteen. Although Houston's formal music career did not begin until she finished high school, she became familiar with the world of entertainment early in life, which eased her entry into show business. At the age of nine, Houston began singing in the choir of New Hope Baptist Church, where she performed her first solo at the age of eleven. Her mother was the choir director and had long shown an interest in developing Whitney's voice by coaching her. Houston first sang before a secular audience at the age of fifteen, performing with Cissy Houston at Carnegie Hall at a United Negro College Fund benefit concert. She also sang with Cissy Houston at area nightclubs and did background vocals for such singers as Chaka Khan and Lou Rawls.

It was her engagement at Carnegie Hall in about 1978 that got Houston started in fashion modeling. After the show, a photographer suggested that the exceptionally attractive, five-foot, eight-inch-tall Houston contact the Click modeling agency. She began her career with Click and later modeled with Wilhelmina, appearing in such popular magazines as *Vogue, Cosmopolitan, Glamour, Seventeen, Essence,* and *Harper's Bazaar.*

Given Houston's seriousness about singing and her obvious artistic ability, her parents sought to launch her formal career immediately upon her graduation from high school in 1981. They selected a management company for her, Tara Productions, through which she met her current personal manager, Gene Harvey. At first she worked with well-known performers, singing backup vocals; she also sang advertisement jingles. According to *Current Biography Yearbook, 1986,* she "was heard on albums by the Neville Brothers and the funk band Materials, and made an attention-getting contribution to the LP *Paul Jabara and Friends* (Columbia, 1983), on which she sang 'Eternal Love,' written by Jabara and Jay Asher."

This exposure culminated in Houston's first major step toward becoming a superstar. With the release of *Paul Jabara and Friends,*

Harvey and Tara Productions arranged a series of private club performances for Houston, open only to the media and recording executives. At one such club, Clive Davis, founder of Arista Records, recognized Houston's potential, and he subsequently assumed charge of her career, launching a two-year promotions campaign at a cost of a quarter million dollars. He ushered her into stardom, molding her persona and systematically positioning her within the world of popular music. According to *Current Biography,* Davis had total involvement in developing and promoting Houston's first album. She appeared on television, was heard on the radio, and was featured in special showcases and in duets with the well-known singers Jermaine Jackson and Teddy Pendergrass. She also had her own team of producers and songwriters.

• *Singer Achieves*

Superstardom

When her first album, *Whitney Houston,* was released to the public in 1985, her name became a household word. The album achieved unprecedented success, becoming the best-selling debut album for any solo artist ever. The LP prompted the release of several singles—including "How Will I Know?" "Greatest Love of All," "All at Once," and "You Give Good Love"—and also spawned videos and television performances. Houston also embarked on a national concert tour, during which her performances frequently sold out.

Whitney Houston sold thirteen million copies and remained in the top ten longer than any previous album. It won a Grammy Award and two National Music awards. Certain singles on the album were enormously successful in their own right. For example, "Greatest Love of All" was produced as a video that featured her mother, Cissy Houston; this video aired on nationwide television for the hundred-year celebration of the Statue of Liberty in 1986.

Since the meteoric success of Houston's debut album, she has been a tireless performer. Her second album, *Whitney,* was released in 1987, after being held in the wings for six months in order to accommodate the continued success of her first album. The second LP was no less dynamic, and it instantly made number one on the charts. The song "Where Do Broken Hearts Go?" broke the previous record by becoming her seventh consecutive number-one hit single. With this album, Houston had in her brief career won two Grammy awards, two Emmy awards, People's Choice awards, and twelve American Music awards. Her third album, *I'm Your Baby Tonight* (1990), went double-platinum.

Her fourth album accompanied her acting debut in the movie *The Bodyguard* (1992), in which she starred opposite Kevin Costner. Houston's music career greatly benefitted from her recording of the movie's theme song, "I Will Always Love You," written by country and western star Dolly Parton. By March 1993 the song had become rock music's longest-running number-one hit ever, was named the best female rhythm and blues single at the Soul Train Music Awards, and won a People's Choice video award. In March 1994, Houston picked up three Grammys for her *Bodyguard* soundtrack, including album of the year, song of the year for "I Will Always Love You," and best pop vocal performer (female). In 1995, she continued her acting career by winning a starring role in *Waiting to Exhale*.

Despite Houston's phenomenal success, she has not escaped criticism—ranging from African Americans who claim that her work does not express the black perspective to music critics who decry her choice of genre as beneath her artistic potential. With the release of her first album, Houston drew complaints that she was too commercialized and perhaps not as socially conscious as she might have been. For the most part, Houston's repertoire consists of ballads and dance tunes, yet she faced criticism early in her career that her performances were not soulful enough. Houston responded to charges that her music was not "black" enough in *Essence*:

> Black? Black—that bothers me.... What's Black? I've been trying to figure this out since I've been in the business.... I don't know how to sing Black—and I don't know how to sing white, either. I know how to sing. Music is not a color to me. It's an art.

Houston's third album, *I'm Your Baby Tonight*, was said to be more responsive to the black audience's expectation of showmanship and soulfulness. Although she continued to express more interest in song than in dance, she appeared to accept her fans' relish for dance tunes. As she stated in *Ebony* in May 1991, "Dancing is fun, and if that's what people want, then cool, I can give that portion of myself to them, I have no problem with that. I'm a public servant in that sense."

As a performer and businesswoman, Houston gives back to the world much of what it showers upon her. She has contributed her time and money to a number of charitable causes. In 1988, for example, she contributed a quarter million dollars to the United Negro College Fund; she considers its 1990 award to her one of her most prized honors. She established the Whitney Houston Foundation for Children in the hopes of combatting illiteracy at a fundamental level. Her mother heads this organization, and at the time of her wedding, Houston and her husband requested that all gifts be in the form of donations to the foundation. During the Desert Storm crisis, Houston's Super Bowl performance of "The Star-Spangled Banner" generated hefty compact disc and video proceeds that were directed to the Red Cross. In addition, Houston has invested in affordable housing for Newark citizens and has contributed

Critical and •

Popular

Reception

Mixed

money toward AIDS research and rehabilitation programs. In her first public appearance following the birth of her daughter, she sang "I Will Always Love You" at a benefit concert that raised a million dollars for the Saint Jude Children's Research Hospital.

A deeply religious person, Houston values her family, with whom she works closely in her businesses. She is a warm, spirited, and compassionate individual who has not allowed fame to go to her head. Her beauty and talent are matched by her generous heart.

Profile by
Laura C. Jarmon

ALBERTA HUNTER

Alberta Hunter's musical career was a remarkable one for many

reasons. A talented singer and composer, Hunter enjoyed a thirty-year

career that spanned from the 1920s to the 1950s. Then, after spending

twenty years in nursing, Hunter made an improbable return to show

business. In her last years she enjoyed an all-new level of acclaim and

recognition.

1895-1984 •

Singer, •

composer,

nurse

Hunter was born on April 1, 1895, in Memphis, Tennessee. She was the second child of Charles E. Hunter and Laura (Peterson) Hunter, a maid who worked in a brothel. Charles Hunter abandoned the family soon after Alberta Hunter's birth—she was told and believed until her death that he had died.

About 1906 or 1907, Alberta's mother married Theodore "Dode" Beatty, a violent and jealous man. This period of her life proved difficult for Alberta. She hated her stepfather and was jealous of her much younger stepsister and her own older sister, a tall girl with "good" hair and features, whom she felt her mother favored. She was also sexually molested by several adult men during her teen years. Hunter became a fiercely independent and aggressive child who nonetheless cultivated a

curiosity about the world around her. She developed an intense ambition to better herself and become somebody, and in July 1911 she fled her home, hopping a ride with one of her teachers to Chicago.

In Chicago Alberta Hunter eventually managed to secure a singing gig at a brothel. She learned on the job, since her initial repertoire consisted of two songs, one of which she had hurriedly learned after getting the job. She worked at the house until the place closed in 1913, learning new songs and avoiding the pimps. She moved on to other clubs, where she honed her abilities and became acquainted with various shady personalities of Chicago's criminal world. Hunter also became involved in lesbian relationships, an aspect of her life that she kept to herself when her mother later joined her in Chicago.

Singer's Career •

Begins Early

As time passed, Hunter's singing voice enabled her to work her way up to finer nightclubs such as the Panama Cafe and the Dreamland Ballroom. Her popularity became so great that composers paid her to introduce their songs. Hunter worked with some of the most talented musicians in the world during this period. Her socializing with her fellow musicians was limited by her reserve and her refusal to drink, smoke, or take drugs. Even Hunter's song selection, while not prudish, reflected her reserve. She drew a firm line between suggestive lyrics, which she handled with gusto, and those that were of an explicit nature, which she rejected.

Hunter was just as firm in her private life; she maintained complete discretion about her lesbian relations—in Chicago she had a long-term relationship with Carrie Mae Ward, and later, in New York, she became involved with Lottie Tyler. But while Hunter was a lesbian, she nonetheless married William Saxby Townsend in 1919. The union lasted for only two months before Hunter, who refused to have sex with him, kicked him out.

In May 1921 Hunter made a quick trip to New York to cut her first record for the Black Swan label. The following year she switched to Paramount because she believed that Black Swan was promoting Ethel Waters and neglecting her. Among her earliest recordings for Paramount was her own song "Down Hearted Blues." She also recorded for another label under an assumed name.

Hunter made a special effort to establish herself in New York in 1922. She starred with Ethel Waters in *Dumb Luck,* but the show sank like a stone. That fall, though, she returned to acclaim in Chicago. In April 1923, however, the boyfriend of singer Mae Alix became so upset about what he perceived as an overly close relationship between his girlfriend and Hunter that the latter decided that a quick and permanent removal to New York was prudent.

Once in New York, Alberta Hunter performed in a number of stage shows with mixed success. At the same time that Hunter was forced to turn to the vaudeville circuit to make a living, Bessie Smith scored a big hit with her recording of Hunter's "Down Hearted Blues." Hunter received little compensation, though. Performers and composers of the era—especially black ones—often saw little profit for their efforts. In later years, a more experienced Hunter was vigilant in her efforts to establish and maintain her copyrights. Hunter's involvement with the Keith Vaudeville Circuit continued through April 1927, though she also played occasional engagements at clubs around the state. Dropped by Paramount in 1924, Hunter began to record for Okeh. She cut fourteen issued records by September 1926.

• **Performer**

Entertains in

Europe

On August 5, 1927, Hunter sailed for Europe in the company of Lottie Tyler, ostensibly on vacation. Tyler soon fell in love with someone else and returned to the United States; this marked the end of their relationship, though not their friendship. Hunter, meanwhile, came to enjoy Europe. She ran with a fashionable crowd and, like most black Americans, she found the lack of overt racism in France refreshing. She performed at a number of clubs and theatres, and eventually landed a prestigious role on the stage. On May 3, 1928, Hunter opened in the part of Queenie in the London production of *Show Boat,* which also starred Paul Robeson. She won high praise for her performance in the show, which ran for 350 performances.

When *Show Boat* closed, Hunter journeyed back to the United States, where she found it hard to get work despite her star status in Europe. By the late 1920s the fashion-conscious Hunter was dipping her toe once again into stage performances. After living with her mother for a couple of years, Hunter returned to Europe in May 1933.

After returning to Europe, Hunter's career continued to blossom. In 1937 she was featured in a special short-wave program by NBC directed to the United States; this broadcast marked the first time her mother heard her perform. On the basis of this performance, Hunter was offered a chance to perform on radio in New York by NBC. When NBC's option expired early in 1938, she went back to Europe. She reluctantly returned to New York again in September when the State Department advised Americans to leave because of the imminent danger of war.

After returning to the United States, Hunter landed a featured role in *Mamba's Daughters* and made several records for the Decca label with Lillian Hard Armstrong on the piano. She decided to stay with the play when it began its road tour in October, even though co-star Ethel Waters, who viewed Hunter as a rival, treated her very badly.

The onset of World War II meant hard times for established black performers who, barred from performing in Europe, watched as many American nightclubs closed and a new wave of young black performers emerged. Hunter kept on working, though, composing and performing new songs and working venues around the country. From August 1944 to March 1945, Hunter was part of a small USO group that toured the Asian theatre to entertain troops. The tour featured considerable hardship and danger, and Hunter was given an Asiatic-Pacific Campaign Ribbon in recognition of her work upon her return.

After another USO tour of the Far East from May to September 1947, Hunter undertook a tour with the Veterans Hospitals Camp Shows in January 1948. This tour lasted most of the year. Touring conditions in the South for the black performers were atrocious, and it proved difficult to secure decent housing and food for the members of the tour.

Hunter continued to perform throughout the early 1950s, a period during which her songwriting indicated a greater emphasis on spiritual matters. In January 1954 Hunter's mother died, and thoughts of retirement, which had already been floating around in Hunter's mind, began to sharpen. In 1956 she turned away from the stage and toward another passion—nursing.

Alberta Hunter had begun volunteer work at the Joint Diseases Hospital in Harlem in the 1950s. After putting in nearly two thousand volunteer hours in one year, she was named Volunteer of the Year by the hospital on May 24, 1956. She passed the city's elementary school equivalency examination on December 16, 1955. Turned down by the hospital's nursing program, she turned to the YWCA and persuaded its director to accept her in its program. Hunter completed the program on August 14, 1956. After finishing a six-month internship and passing the state board examination, she received her practical nurse's license on August 7, 1957.

A New Career •

Begins

Hunter settled into a rewarding nursing career that was marked by her excellent rapport with her patients. Finally, though, after twenty years, the hospital notified her that she faced mandatory retirement since their records indicated that she would be 70 years old at her next birthday. In actuality, though, Hunter was 82, and had falsified her records long before to gain acceptance into nursing school.

Hunter returned to show business after attending a party wherein she sang two songs in front of songwriters Alec Wilder and Charles

Bourgeois. Bourgeois mentioned her name to restaurant and nightclub operator Barney Josephson, who immediately hired her to sing at his club, The Cookery.

Hunter's return to performing was a sensation. Hunter received rave reviews from critics, while television shows and national magazines trumpeted her inspiring return. This publicity assured her a celebrity status that she had never known before. Her celebrity was supported by an artistry that continued to impress her audiences.

Hunter's base of operations remained The Cookery until 1978, when she led off the opening of the Newport Jazz Festival at Carnegie Hall. She received roses and the key to the city when she returned to Memphis for the movie premiere of *Remember My Name,* for which she had performed on the sound track. Still, she boldly scolded the city at the film's gala opening for its lingering racism. Later that year she sang at the Kennedy Center and at the White House.

From the late 1970s through the early 1980s Hunter toured around the world, garnering critical and popular praise and awards wherever she went. As the decade wore on, though, her health deteriorated and she was forced to stop performing. She died on October 17, 1984, but her amazingly long and colorful career—as well as her magnificent comeback—will always be remembered by music fans.

**Profile by
Robert L. Johns**

LOUISE E. JEFFERSON

*L*ouise E. Jefferson is a professional commercial artist and was **1908–** •

formerly the art director for a publishing house, one of the first women

ever to hold such a position. Her work has reached many people, though **Graphic artist,** •

few would be likely to recognize her name. Nevertheless, she has built a **photographer**

fine body of work in the field of graphic arts and in her secondary field of

photography. Her work includes book designs, book jackets, book illus-

trations, and posters.

Louise E. Jefferson was born in 1908 in Washington, D.C., to Paul and Louise Jefferson. Her father was a calligrapher for the U.S. Treasury. She came from a musical family and had an exceptional knowledge of music: her parents were pianists, her grandmother a notable soprano, and her grandfather an organist at a church in the District of Columbia. She attended public schools in Washington, D.C., and then Howard University. She took private lessons in fine and commercial art and learned calligraphy from her father. From an early age, she followed her parents' advice, "Learn more than one thing well—learn many things," which helped her to develop the versatility she would later need in a

commercial art career. As she explained in *Opportunity* magazine in 1947: "Everything dovetails, you know. You have no idea how many kinds of information, picked up one place or another, will come in handy.... A commercial artist must have an encyclopaedic mind—for you can never tell what you will be called upon to depict or interpret."

Although Jefferson was urged to study music, she chose the graphic arts and moved to New York City to pursue her vocation. There she studied at the School of Fine Arts at Hunter College, Columbia University, and with Ralph Pearson and Riva Helford. She also came into contact with many artists and writers of the Harlem Renaissance.

In 1935 Jefferson was a founding member of the Harlem Artist's Guild, a Works Progress Administration project in which she was associated with sculptor Augusta Savage and poet Gwendolyn Bennett. For a time, beginning in 1931, she roomed with the multitalented Pauli Murray in Harlem, when both were poor and struggling. Murray would later become a noted lawyer, author, educator, and civil rights and women's movement activist. One early source of income for Jefferson were posters she did for the YWCA for seventy-five cents each—enough for the two women roommates to have the dinner special at the luncheonette across the street and to leave a nickel tip.

Free-Lance •

Artist Becomes

Art Director

Jefferson's work led to free-lance jobs for the Friendship Press, which was the publishing agent of the National Council of Churches, and in 1942 she was hired full time by the press. She eventually became art director, a job she held until 1968. Jefferson does not remember racism as an obstacle at her job, but she did not always escape the sexism of her male superiors. In her perception, she retired just before she would have been let go by men who had recently taken over the press and who were systematically firing women regardless of their experience or knowledge.

Jefferson's work with the Friendship Press allowed her to take on many other free-lance jobs for New York publishing houses, like Doubleday and Viking. Her activities were financially rewarding enough that she was able to purchase a cooperative apartment in Morningside Heights, where Thurgood Marshall was her neighbor, and also to purchase property in Connecticut in the 1950s.

Over the years, Jefferson's work has spanned a wide range of activities, from match covers to book design. An early commission, about 1937, was sixty posters for the federal government for the Texas Centennial Exposition. Her first book design achieved instant notoriety: her illustrations for *We Sing America,* a 1936 songbook, depicted black and white children playing together. Upon its publication it incurred the wrath of Georgia governor Eugene Talmadge, who ordered the book banned and burned. Besides designing and illustrating books, Jefferson prepared numerous political and cultural maps and pictograms, such as those appearing in *Twentieth Century Americans of Negro Lineage* (1969). Other work included covers for the magazines *Crisis* and *Opportunity.* For forty years she designed all of the NAACP holiday seals, and for twenty years she created the program covers for the National Urban League's Beaux Arts Ball.

Jefferson's interest in graphic arts extended to photography, although she considers this work a sideline. She developed the habit of always carrying a camera and even today there is one on a shelf by her front door. Her files contain well over five thousand photographs, including many taken of celebrated African Americans such as Charles Drew, Lena Horne, Martin Luther King, Jr., and Thurgood Marshall. She points out that free-lance work sometimes tends to pay sporadically, and recalls once having to sell two cameras to pay heating bills.

In 1960 Jefferson began a series of five trips to Africa over a ten-year period, two of them supported by grants from the Ford Foundation. These trips were the background for her book *The Decorative Arts of Africa,* published in 1973. She created almost all of the three hundred photos and drawings in the work.

* **A Busy**

"Retirement"

Upon her retirement from the Friendship Press, Jefferson set up base at a studio in her secluded home in East Litchfield, Connecticut. There she continued to work and pursue her hobbies of gardening and small carpentry. She had to give up the home in the early 1980s when her friends insisted that she was too frail to live alone. She then moved to an apartment in New Jersey, which was burglarized soon after—fortunately, her photographic equipment was overlooked. This incident, combined with a noise level that interfered with her work, led her to establish herself in a cottage in Litchfield near the town common.

Jefferson's work has been exhibited at many prominent galleries and museums, including the Schomburg Center for Research in Black Culture (New York City), the Baltimore Museum of Art, the Oliver Wolcott Library (Connecticut), the Austin Arts Center at Trinity College (Connecticut), and the CRT Craftery Gallery in Hartford, Connecticut. She is especially proud of an exhibit on Matthew Henson, the first man to plant a flag at the North Pole, which she did for the New York Bank for Savings.

Louise Jefferson is a longtime sports enthusiast, and she especially loves tennis and swimming. She first took up sports in childhood out of a determination to overcome infantile paralysis. Pauli Murray characterized her in *Song in a Weary Throat* as "one of the most agile persons I ever knew." In her younger years Jefferson taught swimming for the YWCA, including several summers as swimming instructor and crafts counselor at a YWCA camp. This physical energy has continued as she approaches her nineties, and many people observe that her "retirement" activities resemble the full-time work activities of other people. In her meticulously organized home she maintains extensive records of her long and productive career.

**Profile by
Robert L. Johns**

EVA JESSYE

*T*he multi-talented Eva Jessye has been called "the dean of black female musicians." As a woman who lived for nearly a century, Jessye had the rare privilege not only of looking back on a remarkable sketch of history, but of knowing that she shaped a part of it.

1895–1992 •

Musician, •

educator,

actress

Jessye was born in Coffeyville, Kansas, on January 20, 1895, to Al Jessye and Julia (Buckner) Jessye. When she was three years old, her parents were separated, and Eva Jessye lived most of her childhood with her mother's sisters and her grandmother. Her mother moved to Seattle to work, and her father had little to do with her upbringing.

Eva Jessye had strong, positive memories about her Buckner-Knight family relatives. Some of her earliest recollections are of her great-grandmother Hill, who would come to visit from the "Nation," as Oklahoma was called before statehood. Jessye attended public schools in Coffeyville and Iola, Kansas; St. Louis, Missouri; and Seattle, Washington.

At age nine, Jessye had an experience that she often indicated was the most powerful influence in her life. While recovering from typhoid, she had a dream or vision in which she was a bannister of a staircase that led upward. Two hands—one of which was beautiful and glowing—were on the bannister. When she reached out to touch the hand, she heard a voice explaining that she was not yet worthy and that she must understand that there is something higher than the intellect. Jessye interpreted her vision to mean that, while she would spend the rest of her life developing her brilliant mind and talent, she must never forget her humanity and her obligation to help others. This became a mandate that she lived by.

Jessye was accepted by Western University in Quindaro, Kansas, a suburb of Kansas City, when she was thirteen years old. The school waived the usual admission age of fourteen, since public high schools in Coffeyville did not accept black students. While at Western, the precocious student was given many opportunities to work with the chorus and develop her writing skills.

After her graduation from the university in 1914, Jessye attended Langston University in Oklahoma for three summers. At Langston, she received a lifetime teaching certificate. During the time of her attendance at the school she became a protégée of the legendary Will Marion Cook, and she later studied with master theorist Percy Goetschius.

Jessye was eager to embark on her teaching career, and she taught in Oklahoma schools for several years. In 1920 she was named director of the music department at Morgan State College in Baltimore, and in 1925 she took a position as a reporter for the weekly *Baltimore Afro-American.* A year later Jessye moved to New York, where she established her outstanding fifty-year career as a choral director, composer, performer, writer, actress, educator, and lecturer. She performed with many of the greatest musicians of the time, including maestros Leopold Stokowski, Eugene Ormandy, and Dimitri Mitropoulos.

Soon after her arrival in New York, Jessye joined a group called the Dixie Jubilee Singers. This ensemble eventually became the internationally-known Eva Jessye Choir. From 1926 to 1929, the choir performed regularly at the Capitol Theatre in New York, and in 1929 Jessye went to Hollywood to direct her choir in King Vidor's *Hallelujah,* a landmark motion picture that was the first black musical. The choir continued to thrill audiences throughout America and Europe, and in 1934 Jessye was asked to become choral director for the experimental opera *Four Saints in Three Acts,* by Virgil Thompson and Gertrude Stein.

As her career continued to blossom, Jessye became known as someone who demanded the best from those with whom she worked, for she demanded no less from herself. Charming, intelligent, and warm, she could also be unpredictable, a trait that added to her multi-faceted personality.

Early in 1935, George Gershwin selected Jessye as the choral director of his new folk opera, *Porgy and Bess*. The Eva Jessye Choir performed on the opera's opening night on October 10, 1935. As a result, she is forever associated with the story of *Porgy and Bess*—or more accurately, the many stories of rehearsals, performances, opening nights, and revivals in this country and abroad. Most of the great black singers of the day appeared in *Porgy and Bess* at one time or another. But Jessye had become known as the "Guardian of the Score." Indeed, she kept a copy of the original 1935 score, with handwritten instructions by Gershwin.

After the success of the opera, Jessye briefly returned to teaching, serving as the choral director at Claflin College in Orangeburg, South Carolina. Later, however, she returned to her choir, and the group performed at the 1939 New York World's Fair. During World War II, Jessye helped with the war fund-raising effort with her Victory Concert tour. In 1944 she wrote the theme and directed the choir for the American-Soviet Friendship Day ceremonies held at Madison Square Garden in New York and the Watergate Theater in Washington, D.C. Years later, in 1963, Jessye directed the official choir for Martin Luther King Jr.'s March on Washington.

In addition to her musical appearances, Jessye took on several acting roles on stage and screen in New York and Hollywood. In addition to her regular appearances in *Porgy and Bess,* she appeared on the stage in and in several movies, including *Slaves* and *Black Like Me*.

Jessye returned to the university campus in 1974 when she went to the University of Michigan. There she established the Eva Jessye Collection of Afro-American Music. In 1979 she went to Pittsburg State University in Kansas, where the remainder of her memorabilia is located. While in her beloved Kansas, she did much of her composing. Her outstanding *Chronicle of Job* and her oratorio, *Paradise Lost and Regained,* were both performed there, along with smaller works. During this time she was named one of the six most outstanding women in Kansas history, and in 1978 the state's governor proclaimed a "Eva Jessye Day" throughout the state.

Jessye left Kansas to return to Michigan, though she spent a semester as artist-in-residence at Clark College in Atlanta, Georgia. She was given honorary doctorates from a number of educational institutions, including the University of Michigan, Eastern Michigan University, and Wilberforce University, in recognition of her cultural contributions. Jessye also received numerous citations from government, educational, and musical organizations. She was named to the Senior Hall of Fame in Everett, Washington, and named Kansas Ambassador of the Arts. In

Famed Choral •

Conductor

Directs **Porgy**

and Bess

addition, she was honored for her contributions to the theater and to music when the historic Apollo Theatre in New York City reopened in 1985.

Until a short time before her death, Jessye maintained a busy schedule of lecturing, composing, directing, writing, and making public appearances. She remained a knowledgeable and inspiring source of information about many aspects of America's history and development. Personally acquainted with countless black writers, musicians, artists, and actors over the course of her lifetime, she was a leading expert on the Harlem Renaissance, in which she participated. Her long list of friends—including Langston Hughes, Hall Johnson, Augusta Savage, and many others—were synonymous with artistic achievement, and she discovered and assisted countless young black artists whose names became household words. In her latter years she concentrated on her poetry. She saw a poem in many daily life experiences, and her poetry was frequently witty and usually featured a moral. One of her best-known poems is "A Bag of Peanuts," a reminiscence of her childhood with her mother in Seattle many years ago.

**Profile by
Florence Robinson**

Deeply religious, Jessye was a lifelong member of the African Methodist Episcopal church. She was also a member of ASCAP, the Songwriters Hall of Fame, and the Actors Guild. On February 21, 1992, Jessye died in her sleep at a nursing home in Ypsilanti, Michigan.

QUEEN LATIFAH

*Q*ueen Latifah is one of the few women to make a mark in the male-

dominated field of rap music, and she has done so not by simply

imitating the men. Instead, she has established a reputation as rap's first

feminist. As a result, she is the first person in the field to have made a

breakthrough into the over twenty-four-year-old market. Not content

with just making records and videos, she has formed a record and

management company specializing in rap artists. Her popularity and

striking appearance have also led to a career as an actress in movies and

television series.

1970– •

Rap artist, •

actress, business

executive

Queen Latifah was born Dana Owens in 1970 in Newark, New Jersey, the second child of Lance and Rita Owens. Her mother was eighteen years old when she gave birth to Dana. Her father was a policeman who sympathized with the Black Panthers. In *New York*

magazine, Queen Latifah described him as "a supporter of self-defense and lifting the race." Her parents' marriage was troubled, and the couple parted for good in 1978, though her father kept in touch with the children. Queen Latifah's brother, Lance Jr., became a policeman like their father. He died in a motorcycle accident in 1992, an event which devastated her.

Rita Owens and the children moved to the High Court project in East Newark. A strong woman, Rita Owens set two goals for herself: to get the children out of the project and to attend college. She managed to hold down a full-time job and a part-time job while attending Kean Community College, and she accomplished her goals in two years. In 1980 she became an art teacher at Irvington High School.

When Queen Latifah was classified as intellectually gifted in the second grade, her mother scraped together the tuition to give her child a better education at a parochial school. Dana Owens became Latifah when she was about eight. A Muslim cousin gave her the nickname, which means "delicate" and "sensitive" in Arabic. Queen was Latifah's own addition later.

The family established itself on Littleton Avenue in Newark. Queen Latifah sang in the choir of the Shiloh Baptist Church in Bloomfield, New Jersey. She had her first public singing triumph when she sang a version of "Home" as one of the two Dorothys in a production of *The Wiz* at Saint Anne's parochial school. She had the voice but not the look for the role, since she was already tall.

This height was an advantage when Queen Latifah entered Irvington High School, where her mother taught. She became a power forward on the basketball team, and during the time she was there the team won two state championships. She made her mark in high school, becoming the only senior to win four awards: Most Popular, Best All Round, Most Comical, and Best Dancer. The fall after her graduation, she entered the Borough of Manhattan Community College. She was considering a career in broadcast journalism, but her college plans were quickly sidelined because of other developments in her life.

As a sophomore in high school, Queen Latifah began informally singing and rapping in the restrooms and locker rooms. In her junior year she formed a rap group, Ladies Fresh, with her friends Tangy B and Landy D in response to the formation of another young women's group. Queen Latifah wrote her first rap to "take out" this other group at an Irvington High School talent show. Soon Ladies Fresh was making appearances wherever they could. Rita Owens was a catalyst; she was in touch with the students and the music. She invited Mark James, a local disk jockey known as "D.J. Mark the 45 King," to appear at a school dance. Shortly afterward, Queen Latifah and her friends began hanging out in the basement of James's parents' house in East Orange, which was equipped with electronic and recording equipment. At this point they began to call themselves the Flavor Unit.

James was beginning a career as a producer and made a demo record of Queen Latifah's rap "Princess of the Posse." He gave the demo to Fred "Fab 5 Freddy" Braithwaite, host of *Yo! MTV Raps*, who in turn played it for Dante Ross, an employee of Tommy Boy Music. Tommy Boy signed Queen Latifah and in 1988 issued her first single, "Wrath of My Madness" and "Princess of the Posse," and then her second, "Dance for Me" and "Inside Out." Both sold about 40,000 copies without the support of a video. In the spring of 1989 Queen Latifah made her first European tour and her first appearance at the Apollo, which was quite successful. Her first video, "Dance for Me," was made in June 1989. In October 1989 the album *All Hail the Queen* appeared, most of which was produced by Mark James. In a review for *New York* magazine, Dinitia Smith described it as "a novel blend of hip-hop, house reggae, and jazz, it touches on themes of poverty, apartheid, homelessness, and women. Latifah raps *and* sings on the album, unusual for a rap artist." The New Music Seminar of Manhattan named Queen Latifah Best New Artist of 1990, and the album reached sales of over a million.

Even as Queen Latifah was just beginning to earn money through her music, she displayed an interest in investment, putting money into a delicatessen and a video store on the ground floor of the apartment in which she was living. She soon came to realize that there was an opening for her in record production. While she was making her own deals and making money in the process, many of her fellow rap artists were making disadvantageous recording arrangements. She organized and became chief executive officer of Flavor Unit Records and Management Company, headquartered in Jersey City. By late 1993 the company had signed seventeen rap groups, including the very successful Naughty by Nature. Distribution of Flavor Unit's records was being handled by Motown, which was pressing her to move the operation to Los Angeles.

Queen Latifah's own career flourished as she released two more albums, *Nature of a Sista'* in 1991 and *Black Reign* in 1993. Her fame and presence translated into film appearances, including roles in *Juice*, *Jungle Fever*, and *House Party 2*, and television appearances on such shows as *Fresh Prince of Bel-Air*. In these early acting efforts she almost always wore her trademark homemade crown, which she has now given up, and the parts hewed closely to her public image. In 1993, however, she demonstrated her flair for comedy with a role in the Fox sitcom

Living Single, which earned strong ratings. In the 1994 film *My Life,* she further demonstrated her versatility by playing a nurse to a patient dying of cancer.

Although her television work requires her to live in Los Angeles, Queen Latifah still maintains roots in New Jersey, where her mother lives, and she owns a home in Wayne. Her mother, Rita Owens, remains a definite influence in her life. Owens serves as art director of her daughter's company, and eight years ago she also founded her high school's nonprofit antidrug organization, SAC (Students Against Crack). It is because of her mother's influence that Queen Latifah avoids strong language. The major area of difference between the two women concerns smoking: Owens disapproves, and Queen Latifah is allowed to smoke only in her bedroom of the New Jersey home.

As a woman in the mostly male world of rap, Queen Latifah was celebrated by feminists. In *New York* magazine, however, she explained that initially she was not too happy with the label: "I have a fear of feminism. To me, feminists were usually white women who hated men. A lot seemed to be gay. They were always fightin'. I didn't want to be that.... I don't want to be classified with them. What I have is common sense. I don't want chivalry to be dead. I want to have a man who will pull the chair out for me. I want to grow old with somebody." Instead, Queen Latifah stated that she believes in "womanism—feminism for black women, to be natural, to have her sisterhood." Eventually, as she met more feminists, she found that they shared more common ground than she had first thought.

Queen Latifah's position as a defender of women against the slurs common in rap was challenged when she produced Apache's "Gangsta Bitch." She recognized its potential to be a hit but did not foresee the controversy the lyrics would cause. In *Essence* she defended herself by saying, "I wish people would leave rappers alone. We aren't the problem. We simply reflect what is going on in our society. Plus, if I believe in an artist and I sign them, [then] I don't feel it's my place to tell them how to make their music."

In her relatively brief career, Queen Latifah has emerged as the major feminine voice in rap, become a prosperous businesswoman, and demonstrated potential as an actress. She has already shown that she possesses the talent, intelligence, and drive to find continued success.

**Profile by
Robert L. Johns**

EDMONIA LEWIS "WILDFIRE"

*T**he duel heritage and accomplished marble sculptures of Edmonia*

Lewis distinguished her as the first major sculptor of black American

and Native American heritage. Accounts of her early life are sketchy at

best. Although Lewis claimed 1854 as her birthdate, it is more likely that

she was born in 1843 or 1845. Various sources, including the artist

herself, have noted Greenhigh, Ohio, and Greenbush, New York, as well

as the vicinity of Albany, New York, as her birthplace, but none of these

locales can be verified.

1845?–? •

Sculptor •

Lewis's father was a black American employed as a gentleman's servant, while her mother was a Chippewa Indian. It was she who presumably named her daughter "Wildfire." Lewis apparently spent little if any time with her father, and instead lived with her mother's tribe. Orphaned before she was five, Lewis remained with the Chippewas until she was about twelve years old. As Wildfire, she learned to fish, swim, make baskets, and embroider moccasins.

During the 1850s Lewis left the Chippewas because her brother "Sunrise," a California gold miner, had arranged for her schooling near Albany, New York. Adapting to her new circumstances proved difficult, but her brother persisted in efforts to educate her. In 1859, with his financial assistance, Lewis entered Oberlin College in Oberlin, Ohio. This event triggered her name change to Mary Edmonia Lewis. Her correspondence and the signatures on her sculptures, however, indicate that she rarely used her adopted first name at any time in her life.

Lewis was a moderately successful student, completing the preparatory department's high school courses and pursuing the college department's liberal arts program. Her only extant drawing, "The Muse Urania," still in the Oberlin College Archives, was done in 1862 as a wedding present for her classmate Clara Steele Norton. Later in life she recalled that "I had always wanted to make the form of things; and while at school I tried to make drawings of people and things" (Child, "Edmonia Lewis," 25).

Although Oberlin College and its namesake village actively promoted racial harmony, Lewis became the focus of a racially-motivated controversy in 1862, when two white female students accused her of poisoning them; Lewis was subsequently beaten by vigilantes. John Mercer Langston, a prominent lawyer who was also of African and Native American heritage, came to her defense, and she was exonerated because of insufficient evidence. A year later she was accused of stealing art supplies. Although she was again acquitted, the college refused to allow her to graduate.

Shortly thereafter, Lewis moved to Boston, in part because her brother believed that the city's resources could support her interest in becoming a sculptor. Upon her arrival, she was greatly inspired by Richard Greenough's life-size statue of Benjamin Franklin at City Hall. Using letters of introduction from Oberlin College, Lewis met William Lloyd Garrison, the abolitionist writer. He introduced her to Edward Brackett, a well-known portrait sculptor at that time. Brackett lent Lewis fragments of sculptures to copy in clay and critiqued her early efforts, a customary alternative to academic training at the time.

Despite this limited preparation, Lewis began to establish herself as a sculptor. According to Boston's business directories, she worked in the Studio Building, where the black American painter Edward Mitchell Bannister and other artists maintained studios during the 1860s. To date, however, the extent of her interaction with the members of this artistic community has not been established.

Exposure to Edward Brackett's sculpture and the impact of the Civil War combined to determine Lewis's first sculptures—medallion portraits of white antislavery leaders and Civil War heroes, which she modeled in plaster and clay. She also attempted her first portrait bust during this period. Its subject was Colonel Robert Gould Shaw, the young Boston Brahmin who was killed as he led his all-black battalion in battle against Confederate forces. Lewis's bust of Shaw, as well as most of her other early efforts, remain lost.

Lewis established a studio in Rome during the winter of 1865-66. Her decision to settle in Rome was an understandable one. Since the 1820s, American sculptors, led by the example of Horatio Greenough, had been attracted by Italy's venerable artistic traditions, abundant marble supply, and cheap artisan labor. Moreover, women artists and writers considered Rome particularly congenial because it disregarded the sexist restrictions of their Anglo-American world.

Settled into a large studio near the Piazza Barberini, Lewis quickly learned to carve in marble and experiment with the greater challenge of creating full-length figures. Seeking to hone her skills, she followed the common practice of copying classical sculptures in public collections. Proving adept at this, Lewis made copies of classical statuary which she regularly sold to American tourists.

Lewis and other American women artists and writers in Rome gathered around the neoclassical sculptor Harriet Hosmer and actress Charlotte Cushman. Both women welcomed Lewis to Rome, and it is widely believed that their influential circle greatly benefitted her. Lewis, however, shunned other customs of the art community, for she avoided instruction or criticism from her peers and also refused to hire native artisans to enlarge her small clay and plaster models and to carve the final marbles. Fierce pride in her heritage and the desire to achieve legitimacy as a sculptor led her to believe that her sculptures would not be considered original if she did not execute them herself. This viewpoint limited her output, and only forty-six different Lewis compositions·have been identified to date, with the whereabouts of most of the actual works still unknown.

Commissions for small portrait busts in terra cotta and marble became Lewis's most reliable means of support. Patrons in Boston, primarily prominent white abolitionists and social reformers, were her regular clients. She also recognized the American market for "conceits" or "fancy pieces"—sculptures that used mythological children to convey emotional, often sentimental, themes. "Poor Cupid" (or "Love Ensnared") of 1876 (National Museum of American Art collection) is probably her best-known effort in this vein.

Financial security, however, was not Lewis's principal concern. Slavery and racial oppression were the central issues of her sculptures, a focus greatly facilitated by her distance from America. This focus also distinguished Lewis from her fellow sculptors in Italy, who derived their ideas and images from classical literature, history, and art. Between 1866 and 1883, Lewis created at least six major figurative groups featuring either black Americans or Native Americans. "The Freed Woman and Her Child" of 1866 (location unknown) and "Forever Free" of 1867 (Howard University collection), for example, both capture the powerful emotion of emancipation.

Lewis's exploration of the black figure eventually reached as far as the African continent. In 1868 she sculpted "Hagar," a marble work also known as "Hagar in the Wilderness" (National Museum of American Art collection). Egyptians such as Hagar, the biblical maidservant to Abraham, were considered black by the nineteenth-century Western world; in this sculpture, Lewis included the issues of gender and women's rights in her interpretation of oppression.

Lewis also reacted against the period's negative stereotypes of Native Americans as murderous savages and a dying, primitive race. Unlike the direct social commentary and ethnographic accuracy of her black figures, however, Lewis took a more literary, sentimental approach when carving her small-scale Indian groups such as "Old Arrow Maker" of 1872, also known as "The Old Arrow Maker and His Daughter" (National Museum of American Art collection). Lewis was greatly influenced by "The Song of Hiawatha" (1855) by Henry Wadsworth Longfellow, whose portrait bust she began carving in Rome in 1869 and finished in 1871 (Harvard University Portrait Collection).

During the height of her popularity in the late 1860s and 1870s, Lewis's studio was a frequent stop for those who visited American artists abroad. Admirers often cited the emotional, naturalistic qualities of her sculptures. She was also well-received during several return visits to the United States between 1870 and 1876, when she exhibited works in Chicago, California, Boston, and Philadelphia. Perhaps the high point of her American career came in 1876, when her ambitious sculpture "The Death of Cleopatra" (Forest Park Historical Society collection) was exhibited and awarded a medal at the Centennial Exposition in Philadelphia.

From the outset, however, Lewis was considered "an interesting novelty . . . in a city [Rome] where all our surroundings are the olden Time" (Wreford, "A Negro Sculptress," 2001). Dressed in her rakish red cap and mannish costumes, Lewis captivated both Europeans and Americans, who often described her as childlike and charming. But while she had long insisted that her work not be praised solely because of her background, some clients and reviewers did precisely that. Some of the encouragement she received could be traced to a sincere belief in her talents, but others encouraged her out of a sense of well-meant but misguided indulgence.

Equally diverse, if not confused, are the descriptions of Lewis's appearance. Some described her hair as being black and straight like an Indian's and associated her complexion with her mother's ancestry, while others believed that her facial features and hair reflected her father's background.

In 1883 Lewis received her last major commission, "Adoration of the Magi," (location unknown) for a church in Baltimore, no doubt a reflection of her conversion to Catholicism in Rome in 1868. After 1883 demand for her work declined, as it did for neoclassical sculpture in general. Her presence in Rome was reported in 1911, but the activities of her final decades are barely documented and the date and place of her death are unknown even today.

Profile by Lynda Roscoe Hartigan

JACKIE "MOMS" MABLEY

S tand-up comedienne Jackie "Moms" Mabley played the part of a

cantankerous, spicy, raucous old lady with shabby wardrobe and

broad, toothless smile in black nightclubs and vaudeville for half a

century. After years of relative obscurity, she enjoyed a surge in popu-

larity in the mid-1960s, buoyed by her recordings and television

appearances. Veteran observers of the entertainment industry were

pleased for her, for while her comedy act was typically bulging with

insults toward old men, it was her generosity and compassion for all of

her fellow performers that had earned her the sobriquet "Moms." In the

late 1980s, more than a decade after her death, the life of Moms Mabley

was revisited in an off-Broadway act by Clarice Taylor and a play by

1894–1975 •

Dancer, singer, •

comedienne

Alice Childress that was designed to honor the talent of the comedienne and her influence on humor.

Jackie "Moms" Mabley was born Loretta Mary Aiken in Brevard, North Carolina, in 1894. Accounts of her younger years are sketchy and often contradictory, but a hazy portrait can be drawn. Loretta Aiken was one of twelve children. Jim Aiken, her father, owned several different businesses, including the local grocery store. He was also a volunteer fireman, and he died when the truck in which he was riding exploded. Harriet Smith, a former slave who was Loretta Aiken's great-grandmother, helped inspire young Loretta's religious beliefs.

By the time Loretta Aiken was eleven years old, she had been raped by an older black man. Two years later she was raped again by the white town sheriff. Both rapes resulted in children. With two children to support and a stepfather she could not abide, she prayed to God for deliverance. She left Brevard to escape her hated stepfather, leaving her children in the care of two women, and moved to Cleveland at the age of fourteen. In Cleveland she lived with a minister and his family, and soon became acquainted with a show business performer named Bonnie Belle Drew. Struck by the teenager's beauty, Drew encouraged her to give show business a try. (Aiken later named her fifth child after Bonnie.)

Loretta Aiken felt her prayers had been answered when Bonnie Drew invited her to accompany her to Pittsburgh the next day. Later that night, Aiken threw her clothes over the fence and joined Bonnie Drew and some other entertainers. Loretta Aiken did her first show that night, dancing, singing, and even trying her hand at some comedy routines. During these early days on the road she met Jack Mabley, also an entertainer, and they became close friends. Looking back on those days, she noted that "he took a lot off me, the least I could do was take his name" (*New York*). Thus was Jackie Mabley born.

• *Mabley Rises*

on the Chitlin'

Circuit

Mabley suffered two cruel blows around this time. The two women who were taking care of her children disappeared with the toddlers. She did not see her children again until they were adults. Soon thereafter Mabley's mother was hit by a truck and killed on her way home from church on Christmas day.

Jackie Mabley's entertainment career continued to grow in modest fashion. She traveled throughout the country to venues that catered to black artists, a series of stops known as the chitlin' circuit. She started at twelve dollars a week. The routine was very difficult, especially in the South, where she did two performances a night—one for blacks and one for whites. One never knew when the racism that was so prevalent in that era might rise up and strike you down. In an interview with the *Washington Post,* Mabley remarked:

> All those white men had black mistresses, you know what I mean. But in the public they made like they didn't know. And one time, I can't forget this, we were going in a Jim Crow-car and we were travelling from Dallas to San Antone. And the train stops in Paris, Texas, and I look out and see this man tied to a stake. They were gonna burn him. So I pulled down that shade. Ignorance. Just ignorance, I say (*Washington Post,* 4 October 1974, B-1).

Jackie Mabley became pregnant again, and although it is unclear whether she was legally married, she gave birth to her third child. Determined to establish a career in entertainment, though, Mabley returned to show business almost immediately.

During the 1920s Jackie Mabley continued to develop her act. Over time she became especially known for her comic talents, though she also danced and sang. She developed the character of the dirty old lady with a penchant for younger men. Mabley typically appeared on stage dressed in baggy dresses, oversized shoes, a hat, and droopy stockings. Her trademarks became her bulging eyes, rubbery face, gravelly voice, and later, her toothless grin. She took to referring to the members of her audience as children, and described her character as a good woman with an eye for shady dealings. Mabley envisioned her character as her granny—the most beautiful woman she ever knew.

On the black vaudeville circuit, Jackie Mabley appeared on bills with such diverse talents as Pigmeat Markham, Cootie Williams, Tim "Kingfish" Moore, Bill "Bojangles" Robinson, Dusty "Open The Door, Richard" Fletcher, Peg Leg Bates, and John "Spider Bruce" Mason. In the mid-1920s Jackie Mabley was discovered by the dance team of Butterbeans and Suzie. They later brought Mabley to New York, where she made her debut at Connie's Inn. The appearance galvanized her career, and soon she was playing at notable venues such as the Cotton Club in Harlem and Club Harlem in Atlantic City, appearing on bills with such luminaries as Louis Armstrong, Cab Calloway, Duke Ellington, and Count Basie.

Moms Rules the

Apollo

In 1939 Jackie Mabley became a regular at the Apollo Theatre in Harlem, playing fifteen-week engagements at a time. Mabley appeared at the Apollo Theatre more often than any other act in the history of the theatre. She constantly changed her act to maintain her popularity, and noticed after a time that many white comedians ventured up to the

Apollo, notebooks in hand, to see her show. Mabley said that, with the exception of Jack Benny and Redd Foxx, every comedian stole her material. She was calm about such thefts, though, because she felt that God always gave her more to draw from.

Mabley became a well-known fixture at the Apollo, both in front of and behind the stage. Colleagues commented on her love for card-playing, as well as her propensity for cheating. Louis Armstrong, Duke Ellington, and Sophie Tucker noted Mabley's compassion for her co-workers and her willingness to help them in times of need; they named her Moms in honor of this maternal quality, and the nickname stuck.

While Mabley's stints at the Apollo were long, she still had the opportunity to display her talents elsewhere. She played Broadway in such shows as *Fast and Furious, Swinging the Dream,* and *Blackbirds.* She was also a regular on the radio show *Swingtime at the Savoy.* In the 1960s the white audience discovered her. She cut a record album, entitled *Moms Mabley—The Funniest Woman in the World,* for Chess Records, and in 1966 she moved to Mercury Records, where she recorded *Now Hear This* and other recordings. Mabley then appeared on television, debuting on "A Time For Laughter," an all-black comedy special produced by Harry Belafonte in 1967. Mabley's star continued to ascend, and soon she was a guest star on a number of popular television shows, appearing as a guest on shows hosted by Ed Sullivan, Merv Griffin, the Smothers Brothers, Mike Douglas, Bill Cosby, and Flip Wilson. "The only difference I found when I started doing TV," Moms said, "was that instead of looking at the audience as my children I looked at the world as my children" (*Current Biography,* 263).

Mabley's fortunes soared as a result of the increased television exposure, and the demand for her talent grew at such top venues as the Copacabana in New York City, the Kennedy Center in Washington, D.C., and Carnegie Hall in New York City. Moms rode her popularity to a starring role in the movie *Amazing Grace.* During the filming she had a heart attack, and a pacemaker was implanted. She recovered and returned to filming.

After more than sixty years in the entertainment business, Mabley died of natural causes on May 23, 1975, in White Plains Hospital. She was presumed to be eighty-one. Mabley was survived by her three daughters—Bonnie, with whom she lived in later years, Christine, and Yvonne—and a son, Charles, as well as five grandchildren.

In 1986 Alice Childress honored Moms Mabley with *Moms: A Praise for a Black Comedienne.* The play was based on Mabley's life, with music and lyrics by Childress and her husband, Nathan Woodard. It was first produced by Green Plays at Art Awareness in 1986, then off-Broadway at Hudson Guild Theatre on February 4, 1987.

**Profile by
Richelle B. Curl**

MARY MAHONEY

M ary Eliza Mahoney was the first black professional nurse in

America, but her fine career made her an example for nurses of all

races. She provided more than forty years of expert nursing service while

at the same time serving as a champion of civil and women's rights.

During the course of her lifetime, Mahoney made important contribu-

tions to the effort to secure acceptance of black women in the nursing

profession and to improve the status of the black professional nurse.

1845–1926 •

Nurse, civil rights •

activist,

suffragist

Mahoney was born in Dorchester, a part of Boston, Massachusetts, on May 7, 1845, to Charles Mahoney and Mary Jane (Steward) Mahoney. There were three children in the family; Mahoney, who was the oldest, also had a younger sister and brother. She grew up in Roxbury, and at the age of eighteen began to show an interest in nursing as a career. Between the ages of eighteen and thirty-three, Mahoney worked at the New England Hospital for Women and Children, where she was employed to cook, wash, and scrub. In 1878, at the age of thirty-three, she was accepted as a student nurse.

The school in which Mahoney enrolled was a demanding one. Of the forty-two students who entered in 1878, only four students graduated. Mahoney was one of these few who persevered, and she graduated on August 1, 1879.

The New England Hospital for Women and Children was progressive in its philosophy and took pride in its racially mixed patient population. This philosophy flowed to the School of Nursing, and by 1899 there were five other black graduates of the hospital's school of nursing.

After graduation, Mahoney registered with the Nurses Directory at the Massachusetts Medical Library in Boston for work as a private-duty nurse. This directory—organized in 1873, it was the first directory of its kind in the United States—provided a nurse's name and reference upon request for those seeking a private-duty nurse.

Mahoney's references specified that she was "colored," but any misgivings that white families might have had about her abilities were quickly squelched. Families who employed Mahoney were eager to employ her again, for her well-known calm and quiet efficiency instilled confidence and trust and in many instances were sufficient to neutralize the racial barrier. Her reputation spread, and she was called to nurse patients in New Jersey, Washington, D.C., and North Carolina.

Mahoney, who viewed herself as a professional caregiver, objected to the domestic work also assigned to the nurse. Still, she performed these domestic tasks with her usual dignity. Rather than eat in the kitchen with the household help, though, she chose to eat in the kitchen alone.

• *Rights of Black*

Nurses

Emphasized

Through her alumni association, Mahoney became a member of the Nurses Associated Alumnae of the United States and Canada, organized in 1896, which later became the American Nurses Association (ANA). She was one of the few early black members of the ANA.

By 1908 Mahoney had become convinced that if black nurses were to have the same privileges that white nurses were granted, they would have to organize. She enthusiastically welcomed and supported the organization of the National Association of Colored Graduate Nurses (NACGN), founded by Martha Franklin in 1908. At the first annual convention of the NACGN in Boston in August 1909, Mahoney delivered the welcoming address. Through this national endeavor, Mahoney developed a professional bond and friendship with Franklin and Adah Thoms.

In 1911 Mahoney was awarded life membership in the NACGN and was elected the national chaplain. As chaplain she was responsible for the opening prayers and the induction of new officers, as well as instructing them in their new duties and responsibilities. She rarely missed a national nursing meeting and her local and national involvements were extensive. She also proved to be a strong force in convincing other nurses to join the NACGN.

A religious woman, Mahoney regularly attended the People's Baptist Church, a historic black church in Roxbury. An enthusiastic and talented cook, she often cooked for her patients as well as her family. Mahoney had dark brown skin and stood less than five feet tall and weighed under one hundred pounds. She never married. "She enjoyed being alone at times, valued her privacy, and enjoyed her own company," her great-nephew Frederick Saunders explained in an interview. Yet she knew many people and had ties with Boston's black medical circle as a result of her friendship with prominent physician John B. Hall and his wife.

In 1911 Mahoney relocated to New York to take charge of the Howard Orphan Asylum for Black Children in Kings Park, Long Island. She held this position for more than a year, retiring in 1912.

Throughout her life, Mahoney acted on her concerns about the progress of women as citizens, working diligently to secure equal status for women. A strong supporter of the women's suffrage movement, the seventy-six-year-old Mahoney was among the first women in her city to register to vote in 1921.

Mahoney became ill in 1923, struck down by metastatic cancer of the breast. She died on January 4, 1926, at the age of eighty-one, and was buried in Woodlawn Cemetery in Everett, Massachusetts. Since then her grave has been made into a shrine by the Chi Eta Phi nursing sorority and the American Nurses Association, and national pilgrimages are made to her grave.

Among many honors, several local affiliates of the NACGN were named in honor of Mahoney. In 1936 the NACGN established an award in her name to honor her active participation in nursing organizations and her efforts to raise the status of black nurses in the profession. When the NACGN dissolved in 1951, the award was continued by the American Nurses Association. The Dimock Community Health Center, previously the New England Hospital for Women and Children, the institution where she launched her nursing career, houses the Mary Mahoney Health Care Clinic, a comprehensive health care center.

**Profile by
Althea T. Davis**

185 •

JULIANNE MALVEAUX

W ith her combined careers as journalist, economist, and television host, Julianne Malveaux has become a successful and highly visible figure of national reputation. Since her teenage years she has been committed to women's rights, civil rights, and the African-American struggle, working continuously through a variety of channels to bring about change.

1953– •

Columnist, •

television host,

activist

Julianne Marie Malveaux was born September 22, 1953, in San Francisco, the oldest of five children. While both parents were educators, her father, Paul Warren Malveaux, was also a realtor, and her mother, Protcone Alexandria Malveaux, a social worker.

Malveaux studied economics at Boston College, graduating magna cum laude in 1974 with a bachelor's degree and completing a master's degree in 1975. Continuing her studies in that field, she graduated from Massachusetts Institute of Technology in 1980 with a doctor of philosophy degree.

An academic scholar from 1980 through 1991, Malveaux was most recently a visiting faculty member in the African American Studies

Department at the University of California, Berkeley (1987–91). She has been a staff member of the Council of Economic Advisors (1977–78), the Rockefeller Foundation (1978–80), the New School for Social Research (1980–81), and San Francisco State University (1981–85). In addition, from 1987 to 1989 she was affiliated with Stanford University's Institute for Study of Research on Women and Gender.

Her talent as a writer was noticed early on. Malveaux was first published in the late 1960s, when she was a teenager, contributing a poem to the *Journal of Black Poetry*. Between her high school and college years, Malveaux published a review of the book *Blake, or the Huts of America*, by Martin Delany, in *Black Scholar*. While in college she won an *Essence* magazine contest with her poem "Black love is a bitter / sweetness" and her work was published again in a later issue of the magazine. Her popular and academic writings have appeared in other magazines, newspapers, and professional journals.

Now a syndicated columnist, Malveaux's weekly column has appeared nationally since 1990 in about twenty newspapers through the King Features Syndicate. She has written the "Left Coast" column for *Emerge,* as well as the column "Economics and You," published in *Essence* magazine. She has written on a variety of themes such as women's issues, racism, and reading, as well as on prominent topics in the news such as U.S. intervention in Haiti, the crime bill supported by President Bill Clinton, and gender-based exclusion within the NAACP. She has contributed regularly to *Ms.* magazine, *USA Today,* and the *San Francisco Sun Reporter.*

In her feature "Women's Silence Is Indefensible," syndicated in August 1994, Malveaux examined the disintegration of the NAACP as a result of the activities of former executive Benjamin Chavis and the charges of sexual harassment against him. The internal strife within the NAACP troubled Malveaux deeply, as she had been a member of the organization most of her life and an officer in the San Francisco branch. For Malveaux, the circumstances involved two areas of her longstanding concern: a civil rights organization and the matter of women's rights. Although women comprise the majority of the NAACP membership, the elected board is heavily populated with male members. As Malveaux explained in her article, "Part of the problem is the absence of women's voices at the leadership level. This whole situation has become a 'men's thing' with few women weighing in on executive decisions." She noted the NAACP's problematic record on women's leadership, which dates back to 1983. In that year former board chairwoman Margaret Bush Wilson risked, and ultimately lost, her leadership role when she challenged former executive director Benjamin Hooks.

In addition to her writings, Malveaux is a regular commentator on sociopolitical issues on radio and television, especially on CNN's *CNN and Company*. She also was a panelist on the PBS show *To the Contrary* and occasionally served as fill-in talk show host on San Francisco's news-talk station KGO. She left San Francisco in September 1994 for a new program, "Malveaux in the Morning," which is aired on station WPFW-FM, 89.3, in Washington, D.C.

Malveaux frequently serves as a consultant to institutions and organizations. She has consulted for numerous women's and civil rights organizations, including the National Organization of Women's Legal Defense and Education Fund and the National Coalition of 100 Black Women. Her academic publications include *Slipping through the Cracks: The Status of Black Women,* which she co-edited with Margaret Simms in 1986. She has completed a manuscript on the status of black women in the labor market. She also published a collection of her newspaper columns under the title *Sex Lies and Stereotypes: Perspectives of a Mad Economist* in 1994. Her ongoing research focuses on the labor market and public policy and the impact of such policy on women and minorities.

Malveaux believes she is a born activist, and in fact she became involved in several causes by the time she was a teenager. Her college years began at the time campuses across the nation were settling down from the protests of the sixties. Malveaux also became involved in community work in San Francisco. She tried her hand in the political arena for a while, and in 1984 ran an unsuccessful campaign for a seat on the San Francisco Board of Supervisors. That same year she sponsored the ballot initiative called Proposition J that divested over $300 million of city pension funds from companies doing business with South Africa. In 1986 she worked to keep local playgrounds open.

Malveaux's memberships and organizational affiliations are numerous, and she has held or currently holds leadership positions in civic, civil rights, political, and women's organizations. She was president of the San Francisco Business and Professional Women's Club from 1987 to 1989, for example, and of the local Black Leadership Forum from 1989 to 1990. She has also served as vice president of the San Francisco NAACP. On the national scene, Malveaux is vice president of the National Child Labor Committee and a board member of the Center for Policy Alternatives. Currently, she is first national vice president of the National Association of Negro Business and Professional Women's Clubs.

In recognition of the diversity of her interests and activities, Malveaux admitted in an August 1994 interview, "I can't be categorized." At times Malveaux's devotion to activism caused her to be "looked on as an

Profile by
Jessie Carney Smith

oddball," she said. Many of her black sisters are career women, a position she endorses, and Malveaux contended that "struggle and career go together." As an activist, her longstanding commitment has been to women's rights, civil rights, and the African-American struggle.

OSEOLA MCCARTY

A laundry woman from Mississippi found herself in the company of

1908– •

Monica Seles, John F. Kennedy, Jr., Jim Carrey, Dr. Rick Nelson, Ted

Turner, Newt Gingrich, Christopher Reeve, Courtney Love, and retired

Laundress, •

general Colin Powell on Barbara Walter's special The Ten Most Fasci-

philanthropist

nating People of 1995. *How she got there and why she has unwittingly*

become 1995's "most talked about philanthropist" (Barbara Walters

Presents The Ten Most Fascinating People of 1995*), is an inspiring story*

that will continue to benefit students at the University of Southern

Mississippi for generations to come.

Oseola McCarty was born in Wayne County, Mississippi, on March 7, 1908. Her mother Lucy worked as a cook and sold candy to support the family. When McCarty was in sixth grade, she had to quit school to take care of an aunt who could not walk. Despite her aunt's recovery a

year later, McCarty never returned to school, but instead, "got up with the sun, started the washing and ironing and stopped when the sun went down" (Plummer, *People*). McCarty saved her money, living her life quietly, without a husband or children, a car, or expensive hobbies. The payments she received for bundles of clean laundry went into savings accounts. She eventually invested in certificates of deposits and mutual funds, following the advice of bank personnel. Her frugal lifestyle allowed her to accumulate about a quarter of a million dollars.

When arthritis forced her to retire in December of 1994, McCarty met with Paul Laughlin of Trustmark Bank to discuss her finances and what she wanted to do with her money in the event of her death. After setting aside money for her church, family members, and living expenses, she gave $150,000 to the University of Southern Mississippi, a college in her hometown. This donation has since been established as the Oseola McCarty Scholarship, for African-American students who demonstrate a financial need. When asked why she would leave her money to a college she has never visited, she "thought it would be nice, if she could 'help someone else's child to get an education'"(Smith, *Newsweek*). Inspired by her gift, local businesses have pledged to match the $150,000 contribution. About this, McCarty remarked, ". . . the locals weren't about to let some wash-and-iron woman show them all up" (*Barbara Walters Presents The Ten Most Fascinating People of 1995*). Four years from now, McCarty hopes to watch the first recipient of her scholarship, Stephanie Bullock, graduate from USM. Bullock now visits McCarty regularly, helping her with errands, and providing companionship. Bullock says "she feels a little pressure, . . . not to fail the woman who helped her" (Bragg, *New York Times*).

The story of McCarty's gift has received international attention, and the woman whose only travels had included a trip to Niagara Falls, has been boarding trains to New York City and Washington, D.C., to receive awards and recognition. President Clinton presented McCarty with the Presidential Citizens Medal, the nation's second highest civilian honor. Following the ceremony, McCarty was the President's guest at a dinner held by the Congressional Black Caucus. In a letter President Clinton wrote, "Hillary and I were moved by your gift to the University of Southern Mississippi. Your unselfish deed is a remarkable example of the spirit and ingenuity that made America great" (University of Southern Mississippi, The Oseola McCarty File). Other awards McCarty has received include the UNESCO's Avicenna Medal, presented by Jorge Werthein, United Nations' representative and director of UNESCO's New York office; the Living Legacy Award from the National Caucus and Center on Black Aged, Inc.; the Premier Black Woman of Courage Award from the National Federation of Black Women Business Owners;

A Lifetime of •

Savings

Becomes a

Living Gift

the Wallenberg Humanitarian Award and the Equal Opportunity Award from the National Urban League; a gold medal from the National Institute of Social Sciences, Union League Club, honorary membership in the USM's Institute for Learning in Retirement; and honors from the National Society of Fundraising Executives.

Despite the awards and recognition, McCarty maintains her modest lifestyle, walking to the store, reading her worn family copy of The Bible, and turning on her recently acquired air-conditioner—but only for company. "Ms. McCarty, . . . is living proof to impatient young people that dignity and reward in work is what you make of it. She exemplifies donors who struggled to achieve a measure of success in one generation and then reach forward to help the next generation" ("The Gift of a Lifetime." *New York Times*).

Profile by
Leslie A. Norback

ROSALIE "ROSE" MCCLENDON

R osalie Virginia Scott McClendon's voyage from Greenville, North

1884–1936 •

Carolina, to Broadway stardom took place at an unlikely time in her

life. She was about forty-six years old when she appeared in Deep River,

Actress •

the first work in which her performance made a vivid impression on New

York critics. After that appearance, though, she emerged as a highly

respected actress on the stage, as well as a champion of black theater,

actors, and playwrights.

Named Rosalie Virginia at her birth on August 27, 1884, to Sandy Scott and Tena (Jenkins) Scott, details about McClendon's early years are scanty. The family moved from Greenville to New York City about 1890. Her father worked as a coachman and her mother as a housekeeper for a wealthy family. McClendon attended public school and became active at Saint Mark's Methodist Episcopal Church.

On October 27, 1904, Rose Scott married Henry Pruden McClendon, a Pullman porter for the Pennsylvania Railroad. Both St. Mark's Church and the McClendons joined the black migration north to Harlem, where

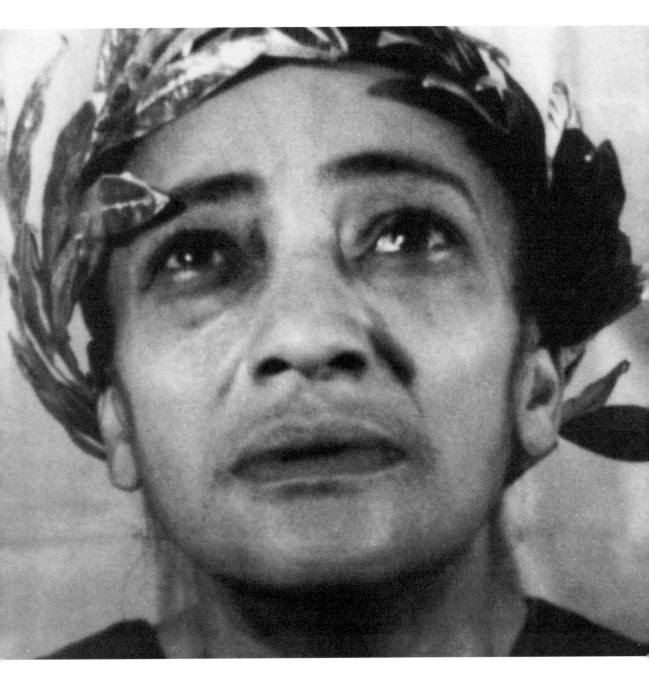

the McClendons built a happy but childless marriage. Other than her activities on behalf of the church, Rose McClendon settled into a quiet life.

Around 1916, though, McClendon was offered a scholarship at the American Academy of Dramatic Art, housed in Carnegie Hall. She accepted the offer in part to teach the children in church to be better actors. She studied at the academy with Franklin Sargent for three years and during the 1919-1920 season was given a leading role—one of two for black actors—in the Bramhall Players' production of Butler Davenport's *Justice*.

In early 1924 McClendon worked in a production by the Lafayette Players in Harlem, starring in a revival of *Roseanne*. The play, which had previously enjoyed a long run at the Greenwich Village Theater with white actors in blackface, told the story of the seduction of a young girl by a preacher entrusted with her education. While other actors were not as fortunate, McClendon was lauded for her performance.

On October 4, 1926, McClendon appeared on Broadway in a supporting role that made her a legend. The production was a "native opera," *Deep River*. It presented the rivalry between two Kentuckians and a Creole over the selection of a mistress from the "débutantes" at the quadroon ball. The feud eventually ends in the death of all three men. McClendon played an aging mulatto, the hostess of the ball. While the production only gave thirty-two performances, critics raved about McClendon's stage presence and noted the tragic dignity with which McClendon infused her character.

On December 30, 1926, McClendon opened in a starring role in Paul Green's play, *In Abraham's Bosom,* in which Abraham, a black worker in eastern North Carolina, dreams of establishing a school. McClendon's performance as a suffering wife and mother was a memorable one. The play did not attract the public in large numbers initially, but after it received the Pulitzer Prize, the audience for the production swelled.

McClendon's next role was that of Serena in *Porgy,* which opened on October 10, 1927. A huge hit in New York, the play toured successfully for another season in the United States and abroad. The play was based on Du Bose Heyward's novel *Catfish Row* and served as a basis for George Gershwin's opera *Porgy and Bess.* At the time, some black critics objected to the use of heavy black dialect and what they perceived as the excessively negative picture of black life written by Heyward, a white South Carolina aristocrat. Nonetheless, the spectacle of a very large cast of black actors presenting a nonmusical hit play about black life was a major breakthrough in 1927. In 1931 another play by Paul Green, *The House of Connelly,* opened September 28 on Broadway. McClendon took a supporting role in the play.

After appearing in *Never No More* in January 1932, McClendon moved on to Annie Nathan Myer's *Black Souls* on March 30, 1932, a play that examined the lust of a white senator for the wife of the president of a black college. McClendon then took a lead part in a radio program, *John Henry, Black River Giant,* in 1933. When Paul Green brought a new play, *Roll Sweet Chariot,* to Broadway on October 2, 1934, McClendon and Frank Wilson took the lead roles. In November 1934 McClendon appeared in *Brainsweat,* which also managed only a brief run.

In 1935 a new major project was developed to showcase McClendon's talents. John Houseman had just launched his career with the remarkable success of Virgil Thompson's opera *Four Saints in Three Acts,* which was presented, as the composer stipulated, with an all-black cast of singers. At the suggestion of James Light and with the aid of Countee Cullen, Houseman began work on a production of Euripedes' *Medea* in which McClendon would star. The project fell apart, though, stricken by McClendon's illness and set designer Chick Austin's financial problems.

It is important to note that these plays in which McClendon appeared were by white Americans writing about black life. Produced by whites, and largely patronized on Broadway by white audiences, the presence of black actors nonetheless marked a step forward from the days in which blacks were portrayed by whites in blackface.

McClendon was well aware of the need to develop black talent in all facets of the theater. She served on the board of the Theatre Union, which ran the Civic Repertory Theatre, and directed plays for the Harlem Experimental Theatre. She also joined forces with Dick Campbell to organize the Negro People's Theatre, which merged into the Works Progress Administration's (WPA) Negro Theatre Project towards the end of 1935. As time passed, she emerged as a focal figure in the black theatre community. "Rose McClendon is a perfect culinary artist in her home," noted biographer Robert Lewis. "Her house in Harlem is meeting place for the most prominent as well as the most promising artists of the day" (Lewis, "Rose McClendon," 200).

The last play in which Rose McClendon appeared on Broadway was Langston Hughes's *Mulatto,* which was the first full-length play by a black author to be produced on Broadway. McClendon played the part of a mother whose son has been sent to the North to be educated. Rejected by his father upon his return, the son finally murders him. The play opened October 24, 1935, at the Vanderbilt Theatre and ran for 270 performances, although McClendon was forced to withdraw from the production due to illness. Despite the show's popularity, the play's run was a difficult one for Hughes in several respects. He was thrilled that his friend McClendon had agreed to act in the play, but he was alarmed by the nature of script rewrites made by producer Martin Jones. Of greater consequence was Jones's attitude upon learning that Hughes was black. Jones sought to cheat Hughes out of his rightful royalties and generally treated the author very badly.

The last service McClendon undertook for black theater was to become co-head of the Negro Theatre Project. The organization had been founded in late 1935 to address the pressing plight of unemployed theatrical personnel. The situation of black artists and actors, living even more precariously than their white counterparts, was desperate. It was quickly decided to set up black branches of the project in major cities. According to John Houseman, there were three factions involved in selecting the project head in New York. The first comprised the Lafayette Players, who felt the project director should be black and one of their number. The second was the Harlem intelligentsia, who tended to look down on performers. Given the social and political climate, they felt the director should be a well-known white with national reputation and connections. Naturally, such a person would need black advisors, roles for which they felt themselves well qualified. The black theatre performers were the third group. They were torn between black pride, which called for a black director, and their perception of the realities of the social structure, which they shared with the intelligentsia.

All groups, though, agreed that Rose McClendon would perform admirably. She in turn accepted the offer, but with the proviso that since she felt she was primarily a performer, a white codirector with equal authority be appointed. When her position was accepted, she nominated Houseman, who became co-head of the project. By this time, though, McClendon had become quite ill, and the collaboration became one wherein all that Houseman could do was visit her on her sick bed and try to give her a sense of participation. McClendon's illness finally became so grave that she resigned.

McClendon died on July 2, 1935. Her death certificate lists the cause of death as pneumonia, but Houseman stated that the disease that ravaged her was cancer. As a tribute to her work for black theater, her old collaborator Dick Campbell named a theatrical group he founded in 1937 in her honor. The Rose McClendon Players, Campbell noted, would carry forward her vision of training the community in all aspects of the theater.

Negro Theatre •

Project

Promoted

**Profile by
Robert L. Johns**

GAY JOHNSON MCDOUGALL

G ay Johnson McDougall is director of the Southern Africa Project of

the Lawyers Committee for Civil Rights under Law, which provides legal

services to victims of apartheid, and founder and director of the

Commission on Independence for Namibia. With worldwide attention

focused on recent changes in South Africa—Nelson Mandela ascending

to power and blacks gaining the right to vote and participate in the

governance of their country—McDougall is being recognized as a

major player on the international scene. Her expertise in international

law led to her selection as the lone American on the sixteen-member

Independent Electoral Commission (IEC). This group monitored the

implementation of the democratic process in South Africa; specifically,

1947– •

Lawyer, social •

activist,

administrator

201 •

the first elections held in the country that were open to all races. Upon receiving notification of her IEC confirmation, McDougall told the *Washington Post,* "My God . . . for nearly 15 years I'm denied a visa to the country, and now I'm going to run the election!"

Gay Johnson McDougall is a native Georgian who grew up in Dixie Hills, a northwest Atlanta neighborhood. She was born on August 13, 1947, to Louis Johnson, a hospital cook, and Inez Gay Johnson, a high school mathematics teacher. McDougall graduated from Booker T. Washington High School in 1965. She cites her mother and aunts as primary influences during her younger years. McDougall's aunts were social workers who, along with their sister, were well known for their social activism and compassion for the needy.

In the *Washington Post,* McDougall explained the origin of her name, Gay, which is her mother's maiden name and the name of a Georgia town. McDougall's ancestors were enslaved in Gay, a place she described as "a sort of Faulkneresque Southern white town that had their, you know, 'colored people.'" Her great-grandfather, the Reverend Jordan Reese Gay, had been a circuit-riding AME minister and presiding elder in the town of Gay.

McDougall was faced with a formidable challenge in the spring of 1965. Out of all the black female high school graduates in Atlanta, she alone was admitted to Agnes Scott College, an all-white women's college in Decatur, Georgia. For some years, it had been a pro forma act to submit the application of a qualified black female just to test the admissions office. Since she had not considered it a viable possibility, McDougall was quite surprised to be accepted. McDougall's days at Agnes Scott were very stressful, partly due to the ordinary stress of making the transition to college, but also due to her adjustment to being in an all-white situation at a school where former plantation owners sent their daughters for a finishing school education.

• *Practice of Law*

After two years, McDougall transferred to Bennington College in Vermont, which she described in an interview with Dolores Nicholson as "an avant garde, free-floating place that was ideal for self-starters and one where I could be comfortable and set my own agenda." During the required winter work term, she enjoyed working at the *Boston Globe* as a city room reporter and in Washington, D.C., at the U.S. Commission on Civil Rights General Counsel Office. McDougall received a bachelor of arts degree from Bennington in 1969. She gravitated towards a career in law, having worked in voter registration drives and civil rights campaigns. In 1972, she graduated from Yale Law School with a doctor of jurisprudence degree and was hired by a New York corporate law firm.

In the *Washington Post,* she discussed her reasons for joining Debevore, Plimpton, Lyons and Gates:

> I was really there to learn to be the best professional that I could be . . . because I thought that the issues I cared about deserve that. Our side ought to be as good as their side. My thought was to go to their side and get trained. So that's what I did. And after a little over two years, I decided I had gotten as much as I could from them at that time.

In 1975 McDougall began a one-year stint as an unpaid general counsel with the National Conference of Black Lawyers (NCBL). This position enabled McDougall to use her professional talents to advance her African interests. She began to focus on African liberation movements and was the United Nations representative for the NCBL. McDougall's next position was as a staff attorney for the Minimum Standards Unit of the New York City Board of Corrections. This unit was one important outcome of the 1971 Attica prison riot, and in 1977 it was still dealing with the need to legislate basic human rights for prisoners.

In 1977, McDougall enrolled in the London School of Economics and Political Science. She completed her studies in 1978 and earned a master of laws degree with a concentration in public international law. At this time, future African leaders from Zimbabwe, Namibia, and South Africa were in London formulating plans to gain control of their respective countries. In addition, the school was known as a testing ground for political activists interested in social justice issues. McDougall described it as a heady experience, being associated with people who inspired her and provided insight into the issues African Americans faced in the South during the 1950s and 1960s.

In 1980 McDougall became director of the Southern Africa Project of the Lawyer's Committee for Civil Rights under Law. Under McDougall's leadership, the project increased both its budget and the number of pro bono lawyers who represented political prisoners and handled court proceedings dealing with the effects of apartheid. Speaking about the effectiveness of the project, McDougall told the *Washington Post:*

McDougall •

Becomes Active

in African

Affairs

> I would say we have been responsible for getting literally thousands of people out of jail. We helped to mount cases that challenged a lot of apartheid laws and caused many of them to be overturned.... We helped communities who were being forcibly removed to get legal counsel to resist, and a lot of them won.

As director of the Southern Africa Project, McDougall testified before Congress and the United Nations; raised over a million dollars annually to finance South-African trials; organized and financed the defense preparations of political prisoners in South Africa and Namibia; organized six international conferences in South Africa that focused on governance after apartheid; produced an annual series of briefing papers on the state of affairs in South Africa and Namibia; recruited and coordinated pro bono services of lawyers; and lectured on South-African issues across the country. McDougall's most ambitious project was establishing the Commission on Independence for Namibia, a bipartisan group of thirty-one Americans who monitored the United Nations-supervised, year-long process leading to elections in Namibia.

• McDougall Becomes Part of History

In early 1994, McDougall learned that she had been named to the sixteen-member Independent Electoral Commission (IEC) in South Africa; she was one of only five non-South Africans selected and the only American. This agency was charged with running South Africa's first all-race elections and overseeing the implementation of a new South African democracy. According to *USA Today,* "McDougall's reputation for fairness and thoroughness in constitution-writing seminars she ran for South Africa's political parties won her a spot on the electoral commission." McDougall's selection was also tinged with irony; she recalled having been spied upon by South African officials who had a full dossier on her legal and anti-apartheid activities.

Some South Africans reacted negatively to McDougall's high visibility. As she told the *Washington Post,* she was criticized as being "abrasive in her passion to achieve goals." McDougall realized that the comment was applicable to Americans in general, who are often perceived as being "blunt compared to South Africans. We tend to press points more." In comparison to other election observers, however, McDougall kept a fairly low profile. Her important role in the South Africa elections was attested by the August 1994 issue of *Ebony,* which features a photograph of Nelson Mandela casting his first ballot with McDougall standing at his side.

In addition to her success as an attorney and activist, McDougall is the author of numerous articles dealing with apartheid, U.S. policy proposals, Namibian independence, and international law issues, which have appeared in leading newspapers and law journals. McDougall serves on the board of directors of CARE, Africa Watch, the International Human Rights Law Group, and the Robert F. Kennedy Memorial Foundation. In September 1994 McDougall became executive director of the International Human Rights Group, a Washington, D.C.-based organization that deals with human rights projects abroad.

McDougall has been married since 1991 to John Payton; a first marriage ended in divorce in 1978. Payton is a partner in the law firm of Wilmer, Cutler and Pickering and a litigator who has argued civil rights cases before the U.S. Supreme Court. McDougall described her husband in the *Washington Post:* "I have met one hell of a lot of incredible people in my work in all these years and I don't think I've met anybody who is more committed to equal rights and social justice and issues of that sort than John Payton."

During her limited leisure time, McDougall enjoys the company of friends, movies, and beach holidays. In reviewing her life and accomplishments, it is quite clear that McDougall has never expended her energies on superfluous matters. She has used her talents to achieve the same goals she ascribed to her mother and aunts in the *Washington Post:* "Caring about the way people [live] . . . trying to find a way to reorder the world so that everybody lives a decent life."

**Profile by
Dolores Nicholson**

PATRICIA CARWELL MCKISSACK

*P*atricia McKissack is a prolific writer of books for children and

young adults, primarily historical fiction and biography. The approxi-

mately one hundred works she has published address a wide range of

subjects and are known for their clarity and appeal to readers. She

writes to build bridges of understanding through books. Her childhood

experiences listening to storytelling in her family spurred her to become

a successful storyteller as well.

1944– •

Children's •

author,

educator

Patricia McKissack, who prefers to be called "Pat," was born August 9, 1944, in Smyrna, Tennessee, a small town near Nashville, to Robert and Erma Carwell, who were civil servants. When she was three years old, her family moved to St. Louis. Her parents divorced later and her mother relocated to Nashville with McKissack's brother and sister. McKissack remained with her paternal grandparents in St. Louis for several years then joined her mother and maternal grandparents in Tennessee. She attended Tennessee State University in Nashville, graduating with a B.A. degree in English in 1964. In 1975 she received her M.A.

in early childhood literature and media programming from Webster University in St. Louis.

At Tennessee State University, McKissack became reacquainted with Fredrick McKissack, who had begun his college career after a three-year stay in the Marine Corps. In *Something about the Author,* she recalled:

> I had known him practically all my life. We grew up in the same town, where every family knew every other family, but [Fred] was five years older and you just didn't date boys who were five years older than you. When I was fifteen and he was twenty dating was forbidden. But when I was twenty and he twenty-five it was perfectly okay.

Fred McKissack proposed to Pat Carwell on their second date, and she accepted. Four months later, on December 12, 1964, they were married. Although both their families and friends felt they had made a foolish mistake, the couple knew they were right for each other. Since then they have reared three sons, co-authored many books, and built successful businesses together.

McKissack's love for reading developed when she was about seven years old. She also had an early interest in writing. After she had married and had children, she began to spend more time in the library. In this quiet, peaceful atmosphere she identified reading interest levels in literature from beginning readers to adult books. To expand her knowledge of children's materials, she read publisher's catalogs, writer's magazines, and book reviews and attended workshops and seminars. Although she did not publish during this time, she honed her skills as a writer and at the same time helped her sons to become excellent readers and writers.

While working on her master's degree at Webster University in the mid-1970s, McKissack wrote for the preschool series "L Is for Listening," broadcast by KWMU-Radio, and also wrote radio and television scripts. In addition, she contributed articles and short stories to such magazines as *Friend, Happy Times,* and *Evangelizing Today's Child.* McKissack taught English at a junior high school and at Forest Park College in St. Louis from 1969 to 1975, and a course called "Writing for Children" at the University of Missouri from 1976 to 1982. She served as children's book editor at Concordia Publishing House, a publishing arm of the Lutheran Church-Missouri Synod, from 1976 to 1981. She left to become a freelance writer, editor, and teacher of writing. Today Pat McKissack is co-owner with her husband of All-Writing Services. Together they conduct educational workshops, lecture at universities, and speak at educational meetings and seminars on the subject of minority literature for children. In addition to works bearing her name, Pat McKissack has published a number of works—now out of print—under the name L'Ann Carwell. McKissack is also active in the storytelling community and in 1992 was elected a board member of the National Storytelling Association.

McKissack's writing career began in 1971 in Kirkwood, Missouri, where she was teaching English to eighth graders. She wanted to introduce her students to Paul Laurence Dunbar, a well-known African-American poet. When she found no juvenile biography of Dunbar in the library, she decided to write one herself. "I spent the whole summer working on the Dunbar manuscript," she told Jessie Carney Smith. "It was the first time I had disciplined myself to write a book—beginning, middle, and end. The idea of sharing it with real readers was scary, too." When she did share her first efforts, her eighth graders were brutally honest: they said the manuscript was boring! McKissack recalled that she "rewrote the Dunbar manuscript at least five times before my students' responses to it changed for the better."

After having written nearly one hundred successful books, McKissack is still concerned about the readability of her material, especially her nonfiction. "My students taught me a lesson that has been the corner-stone of my career as a writer," she told Smith. "Keep the material interesting, fast-moving, and up-beat; keep the reader involved and tell a good story, and kids won't have time to be bored."

A major influence in the lives of the McKissacks was the civil rights movement of the 1960s. As McKissack explained to Smith, "Martin Luther King, Jr. was—and still is—my hero. He helped change a system that was politically and morally corrupt without violence." The McKissacks also found the Vietnam War and the television coverage of American soldiers in combat very disturbing. Explaining to today's children just how difficult—but yet how exciting—those times were motivated the McKissacks to write *The Civil Rights Movement in America from 1865 to Present*. Fred McKissack, who participated in the Nashville sit-ins, told *Something about the Author* that "The reason we write for children is to tell them about these things and to get them to internalize the information, to feel just a little of the hurt, the tremendous hurt and sadness that racism and discrimination cause for all people, regardless of race."

The McKissacks' nonfiction works helped fill a void in literature about African and African American contributions and their struggles for freedom and justice for readers in kindergarten through high school. But McKissack also writes fiction, because she feels it fills yet another void in

Writing Fills •

Void in

Literature

literature for children, as she explained to Smith: "When children don't see themselves in books, they aren't motivated to read. If children don't read often they usually don't read well. And soon that translates into failure. I don't want that to happen, so I try to create characters children enjoy reading about. The hope is they will then read more and thus read better."

Several of McKissack's fictional characters are warmly recognized by schoolchildren everywhere. *Flossie and the Fox, Mirandy and Brother Wind, Messy Bessey,* and *Nettie Jo's Friends* are on required reading lists in school districts all over the country. These books have received many positive reviews, especially *Flossie and the Fox.* According to McKissack's 1995 biographical statement, *Kirkus Reviews* called it "a perfect book." In 1991, McKissack collaborated with author Mavis Jukes and wrote her first movie script. The movie, produced by Disney Educational Productions under the title *Who Owns the Sun,* won several major film awards.

"Writing is a kind of freedom," McKissack said in *Something about the Author.* "Writing allows us to reach far more children than ever imagined. We try to enlighten, to change attitudes, to set goals—to build bridges with books." Pat and Fred McKissack encourage other African Americans to write: "It's a big world and we are just two writers. We cannot possibly represent 30 million African American experiences. We shouldn't have to either. There's room for many points of view." Their hope for more African Americans to accept the challenge of writing was realized when their oldest son, Fredrick McKissack, Jr., became a journalist. In 1994 he co-authored *Black Diamond, The Story of the Negro Baseball Leagues* with his mother.

McKissack's writings have brought her wide recognition. For example, among many other awards, she received the Jane Addams Children's Book Award from the Women's International League for Peace and Freedom, and the Coretta Scott King Award from the American Library Association, for *A Long Hard Journey: The Story of the Pullman Porter* in 1989. She also won the Newbery Honor Award and another Coretta Scott King Award in 1993 for *The Dark-Thirty: Southern Tales of the Supernatural* and again in 1995 for *Christmas in the Big House-Christmas in the Quarters.* Pat and Fred McKissack have also received an Image Award from the NAACP for their work in children's literature. In 1993 they were named Tennessee Authors of the Year by the *Nashville Banner,* and they were jointly honored again in 1994 with an honorary doctorate degree from the University of Missouri, St. Louis.

McKissack spends her free time relaxing in her renovated home near St. Louis, working in the family garden, or "junking," which is her term for visiting antique shops. The McKissacks enjoy plays and films, particularly art films, as well as horseback riding, boating, and outdoor activities.

Well known for her work as children's author, editor, consultant, and storyteller, Pat McKissack has enriched the lives of thousands of young people and their mentors across the nation. While she has been rewarded for her work with many honors and awards, the compelling stories she writes and tells have been equally rewarding to young readers and listeners. She and her husband Fredrick McKissack have become ambassadors of understanding and good will.

**Profile by
Jessie Carney Smith
and Phyllis Wood**

TERRY L. MCMILLAN

1951– •

A relative newcomer to the list of best-selling authors, Terry McMillan is

an exciting and vibrant novelist who examines African-American life

Writer, •

and relationships. Her novels are realistic stories about the contempo-

educator,

rary African-American experience. Her best-known work, 1992's

editor

Waiting to Exhale, *was adapted into a much-awaited motion picture in*

1995.

Terry L. McMillan was born on October 18, 1951, in Port Huron, Michigan, a factory town approximately sixty miles northeast of Detroit. She was the oldest of five children born to Edward Lewis McMillan and Madeline Washington Tillman. Her mother worked at auto plants and, at one time, a pickle factory, and her father was a blue-collar worker. Her father was also an alcoholic who beat his wife frequently, and as a result McMillan's parents were divorced in 1964; three years later her father died.

The only books available to McMillan in her home were the Bible and the required reading for school. It was not until she acquired a job shelving books in a local library at age sixteen that she began to read for pleasure. African-American authors were not included in any textbooks

McMillan used in high school, and until she discovered a book by James Baldwin in the library she was not aware that any existed. McMillan later immersed herself in classic African-American literature when she enrolled in a class at Los Angeles City College. She explained in the introduction to *Breaking Ice: An Anthology of African-American Fiction:*

> I couldn't believe the rush I felt over and over once I discovered Countee Cullen, Langston Hughes, Ann Petry, Zora Neale Hurston, Ralph Ellison, Jean Toomer, Richard Wright, and rediscovered and read James Baldwin, to name just a few. I'm surprised I didn't need glasses by the end of the semester. My world opened up.

McMillan's writing career began at age twenty with a poem she wrote in reaction to having her heart broken during a love affair. She did not intend to write a poem, but like magic it appeared on the page, lightening and lessening the pain. Later a friend discovered the poem on her kitchen table and asked to publish it in a new black literary magazine he had just started at the college. Writing then became an outlet for her dissatisfaction and a way to explore personally what she did not understand.

At age twenty-two, upon transferring to the University of California, Berkeley, McMillan thought first of becoming a social worker but decided instead to major in journalism. After receiving her B.A. degree, she left California for New York City, where she enrolled in a master's degree program in screenwriting at Columbia University. She soon dropped out, however, attributing her decision to discontinue her studies to the racism she faced at the school. McMillan then took a word processing job in a law firm in Manhattan, and her personal life took a turn for the worse. Living with a boyfriend, Leonard Welch, who had lost his job and turned to dealing cocaine to support himself, McMillan began drinking and using drugs. In the early 1980s, according to *Current Biography,* "she recognized in herself the seeds of the alcoholism that had consumed her father and resolved to overcome her addiction. Since then she has been drug-free and sober." McMillan's relationship with Welch lasted three years and produced a son, Solomon, born in 1984.

Ishmael Reed, novelist and founder of the Before Columbus Foundation, published McMillan's first short story, "The End," in 1976 while she was a student at the University of California, Berkeley. She also submitted a collection of short stories to Houghton Mifflin at this time. Although the publisher rejected the stories, they did express an interest in the novel she mentioned in her letter to them.

McMillan's first novel started out as a short story. On the advice of the Harlem Writer's Guild, she spent six weeks expanding it into a novel of over four hundred pages. Houghton Mifflin accepted *Mama* for publication in 1987. McMillan decided to promote the novel herself, as her publishers limited its exposure to press releases and galleys. She sent out over three thousand letters to bookstores and colleges, which gained her several reading engagements. Launching her own publicity campaign and scheduling her own book tour, she generated thousands of sales even before the official publication date of *Mama*. In a 1992 interview with Wendy Smith for *Publisher's Weekly*, McMillan noted that "My editors called and said, 'Terry, we don't think this would have happened if you had not done all this.'"

Mama earned McMillan critical praise as an important contemporary novelist. Valerie Sayers of the *New York Times Book Review* called it "original in concept and style, a runaway narrative pulling a crowded cast of funny, earthy characters." The novel recounts Mildred Peacock's struggle to raise her five children and defend herself against an abusive, alcoholic husband. Mildred is not always likable, but regardless of her weaknesses and failures, she does love her family and finds in them a source of strength.

In 1987 McMillan accepted a teaching position at the University of Wyoming in Laramie, and in 1988 she was awarded a National Endowment for the Arts fellowship. The following year McMillan moved with her son to Tucson, Arizona, to begin teaching at the University of Arizona. Also in 1989, McMillan published her second novel, *Disappearing Acts*. McMillan used her three-year association with Welch as inspiration for this story, which explores the deteriorating relationships between African-American men and women. The main characters are Zora Banks, an aspiring songwriter, and Franklin Swift, an often unemployed contractor. The two fall in love, but their prospects for lasting togetherness are thwarted by their inner frustrations, their past love affairs, and their different backgrounds. The novel is lively, sparking with electricity, and yet at the same time McMillan shows great sympathy for her characters, creating in the reader compassion for what they went through in their lives.

The appeal of the novel led MGM to acquire the movie rights, and they commissioned McMillan to write the screenplay. As McMillan enjoyed the success of *Disappearing Acts,* however, a defamation of character suit was filed by Leonard Welch, her former lover and the father of her child. Welch charged that McMillan had divulged the intimacies of their relationship and used him as a model for Franklin. He claimed that the novel was written out of malice and revenge. The New York Supreme Court ruled in McMillan's favor in April 1991.

As McMillan read anthologies for her students to use, she realized that African-American writers were rarely included. This omission led her to compile *Breaking Ice: An Anthology of African-American Fiction.* The anthology includes not just well-established authors, but also writers who had not yet been published or whose work had not yet been recognized. McMillan received nearly three hundred submissions, fifty-seven of which appear in the anthology. Many of the stories are excerpts from novels, and all reflect the varied and distinct voices of a new generation of African-American writers.

• **Waiting to**

Exhale *Hits*

Best-Seller List

Shortly after *Disappearing Acts* was published, McMillan already had an idea for her third novel. She told her editor at Viking that she planned to write about "some black women who were having trouble finding men. They were educated, smart, attractive—and they were alone," according to Audrey Edwards in *Essence. Waiting to Exhale* appeared in 1992, reaching the *New York Times* best-seller list at the same time as the works of two of America's most renowned African-American women writers, Toni Morrison and Alice Walker. McMillan was disappointed that neither writer acknowledged her work or its tremendous success, as she explained to Edwards: "I've dropped them notes over the years congratulating them when their books have come out, and it hurts that they've never done the same for me."

Nonetheless, McMillan received $2.64 million for paperback rights to *Waiting to Exhale,* which sold over 700,000 hardcover copies by the end of 1992, outselling Walker's *Possessing the Secret Joy* and Morrison's *Jazz* by three to one. Readers of McMillan's novel were of varied ethnicity, attesting to the fact that her stories were realistic enough to reach far beyond the boundaries of race and class.

The four main characters in *Waiting to Exhale* are Savannah Jackson, a smart and successful television producer; Robin Stokes, an insurance company executive hooked on a "lying, sneaky, whorish Pisces"; Bernadine Harrison, Savannah's college roommate who, after eleven years of marriage to a successful businessman, is betrayed and must start all over after a divorce; and Gloria Matthews, a hair salon owner who is overweight and afraid to get involved with a man. The women discuss honestly and candidly all the "knots" (issues) in their lives and relationships. McMillan shows how these characters develop strength as they begin to appreciate what they have. They decide not to give men authority over their lives and instead become empowered by their own inner resources and beauty. A major motion picture adaptation of *Waiting to Exhale,* starring Whitney Houston and Angela Bassett, was released in 1995.

McMillan lives in a five-bedroom, southwestern-style home in Danville, California, in the San Francisco Bay area. She exhibits much of the sass and style displayed by the characters she creates. Responding to critics who objected to her heavy use of profanity and male-bashing, for example, McMillan retorted in *Publisher's Weekly,* "That's the way we talk. And I want to know why I've never read a review where they complain about the language that male writers use!" McMillan has made it her mission to write about the real world in the language and tone that real people use when they are not trying to impress or stand as role models for their race.

**Profile by
Brenda Robinson
Shaw**

CAROL E. MOSELEY-BRAUN

O n March 17, 1992, at her campaign headquarters in downtown

Chicago, Carol Moseley-Braun lifted her hands, swayed from side to

side, and broke into her familiar infectious smile as she moved to the

music of "Ain't No Stopping Us Now" and "We Are Family." Having just

defeated longtime Democratic Senator Alan Dixon in the Illinois prima-

ry, she was on the most important path in her life: the one leading to the

United States Senate. Running as a Democrat, Moseley-Braun won the

senatorial election the following November. The first black woman in the

U.S. Senate, Moseley-Braun, quoted in Jet magazine, told her cheering

supporters: "We have won a great victory tonight.... You have made

history. And as much to the point of history making you are showing the

1947– •

Lawyer, •

politician, radio

host

way for our entire country to the future."

Carol E. Moseley-Braun was born on August 16, 1947, in Chicago, Illinois, the eldest child of Joseph Moseley, a policeman, and Edna A. Davie Moseley, a medical technician. The comfortable, middle-class setting of Moseley-Braun's early life was far from ideal, however, for her father, a frustrated musician, sometimes took out his personal disappointments on Moseley-Braun by beating her. When she was sixteen, Moseley-Braun's parents divorced, her father moved to California, and she and her siblings, along with Edna Moseley, settled in with their maternal grandmother for two years in a black neighborhood nicknamed the Bucket of Blood, a violent and poverty-stricken area.

Moseley-Braun's exposure to the darker aspects of urban life instilled in her a belief in public service. As she indicated in the *Washington Post,* "when you get a chance to see people who are really trapped and don't have options and you've got all these blessings, you've got to be a pretty ungrateful person not to want to do something" ("Senate Bows to Braun," *Washington Post*). The blessings Moseley-Braun referred to included her education at the University of Illinois at Chicago, from which she graduated in 1967, and at the University of Chicago Law School, from which she obtained a J.D. degree in 1972. It was at the University of Chicago law school that she met Michael Braun, a white fellow student, whom she married in 1973; he is the father of her only child, Matthew.

• Political Career

Begins

Moseley-Braun's public life started with her work as an assistant U.S. attorney from 1974–77. Prior to this, she worked at a private firm. The U.S. attorney position was pivotal to her career; as Moseley-Braun noted in the *Chicago Reader,* "it opened up for me the way [federal] government interfaces with local and state government, how policy is made, and what opportunities there are for changing things via the courts" (Levinsohn, *Chicago Reader*). In 1977, running as a Democrat, she won a seat in the Illinois House of Representatives, serving the Hyde Park area near the University of Chicago, a liberal and racially integrated neighborhood.

Moseley-Braun proved to be a bold and effective member of the Illinois legislature. Her performance gained her public notice and the respect of her colleagues, both of which were integral to her future career in Illinois politics. Moseley-Braun was a member of the Illinois House of Representatives until 1988. During these years she championed educational reform and redistricting efforts to create fairer legislative districts. In addition, she worked against investing in South Africa and discrimination by private clubs. She was recognized for her performance on a number of occasions, and received the Best Legislator Award in 1980 and 1982 from the Independent Voters of Illinois. Moseley-Braun also found time to write newspaper articles for the *Hyde Park Herald* and the *South Shore Scene*. In addition, she was a radio talk show host for WXOL in Chicago.

Chicago's first black mayor, Democrat Harold Washington, admired Moseley-Braun's energy. In 1983 he designated her his floor leader in the House, even though she was not the senior legislator. Apparently her relationship with Washington was not without conflict, however. According to the *Washington Post,* he blocked her bid for the lieutenant governorship in 1986.

That year was devastating for Moseley-Braun for other reasons as well. Her mother was seriously ill and had a leg amputated, and one of her brothers died as a result of his drug and alcohol abuse. Her marriage ended as well. When she later ran for the U.S. Senate, however, Michael Braun worked on her campaign.

This low period in Moseley-Braun's life was brief. She successfully campaigned for the office of Recorder of Deeds and in 1988 became the first black elected to an executive office in the history of Cook County government. Managing a staff of three hundred people and a budget of eight million dollars, Moseley-Braun, according to the *Chicago Reader,* "dramatically reorganized" the recorder's office.

Moseley-Braun's personality and appearance have always been counted as pluses in her political career, contributing to her broad appeal. The *National Review,* however, commented that Moseley-Braun was fond of pointing out a sign in the restroom of her Chicago office that read, "I'm 51 per cent sweetheart, 49 per cent bitch. Don't push it." She acknowledges that there have been times when she's had to put away her winning smile and battle in the trenches, and she points to her difficult ascension to the Senate as an example. "In light of the fact that women and minorities are not generally put on the track to access the higher level position in government, or anything else for that matter, the only way that you can move into these circles is to go for it" (*Jet,* September 7, 1992).

Moseley-Braun was inspired to run for the U.S. Senate after watching Senator Alan Dixon vote to confirm Clarence Thomas as a Supreme Court justice in 1991. Thomas's confirmation hearings garnered an unusual amount of attention when a former colleague of Thomas, law professor Anita Hill, accused him of sexual harassment. Moseley-Braun was outraged at Dixon's vote and the treatment that Hill received from the middle-aged white men who made up the confirmation committee. Defining herself in her Senate campaign as an agent of

Politician •

Becomes

Activist in U.S.

Senate

change, Moseley-Braun tapped into an anti-incumbent grassroots sentiment that ultimately carried her to a primary victory over an opponent who had not lost an election in 42 years.

Moseley-Braun followed up her primary victory with a triumph over her Republican opponent, Richard Williamson. She thus became the first black woman in U.S. history to serve in the Senate. Since taking her seat, Moseley-Braun has been an outspoken and visible member despite the heavy pressure she carries. As Senator Dianne Feinstein noted in the *Washington Post,* Moseley-Braun "has been pulled and tugged and torn. There's a period of testing that goes on—whether it's the first woman, the first black, the first Asian." The daily grind of elected office, combined with the demands of motherhood, have taken their toll as well at times. The *Washington Post* noted in 1994 that "compounding her weariness is an embarrassing string of controversies. Questions about her campaign finances, her love life, her actions as a state legislator, staff shake-ups and staff screw-ups, have slowed her down" (Merida, *Washington Post*).

Moseley-Braun has had her triumphs, too, though. She has been an outspoken presence on the Senate floor on many issues, and has shown a determination to vote on issues based on her beliefs rather than opinion polls or party dogma. Although regarded as a liberal Democrat in many respects, Moseley-Braun "has parted company with her traditional allies by supporting the North American Free Trade Agreement (NAFTA), the General Agreement on Tariffs and Trade (GATT) and the balanced-budget amendment" (Greenburg, *Chicago Tribune*). She also secured a seat on the important Senate Finance Committee, where she makes sure that her voice is heard.

And, noted the *Washington Post,* sometimes Moseley-Braun's "successes are so magnified they take on a folkloric quality—like when she shamed the Senate into killing Jesse Helms's proposal to renew the patent on the United Daughters of the Confederacy's flag insignia. African Americans applauded her as if she were Joe Louis after delivering a knockout punch" (Merida, *Washington Post*). This mesmerizing event took place on July 22, 1993. Before a final vote on whether to approve the renewal of the patent, an eloquent and angry Moseley-Braun, speaking on behalf of African Americans everywhere, made her case for voting against Helms:

> The issue is whether or not Americans such as myself who believe in the promise of this country . . . will have to suffer the indignity of being reminded time and time again that one point in this country's history we were human chattel. We were property. We could be traded,

bought, and sold.... This vote is about race . . . and the single most painful episode in American history.... [The Confederate flag] has no place in our modern time . . . no place in this body . . . no place in our society.

Senator Edward Kennedy later marveled at Moseley-Braun's impassioned words. "That was an extraordinary day," he recalled, "really unique in the time I have been here. She reserves her special kind of force for things she is really moved by" (Merida, *Washington Post*).

In 1994 Moseley-Braun announced that she intended to defend her Senate seat in 1998 against all comers. She acknowledges that the political life can be a rocky one, but she has proven to be a resilient and eloquent senator, qualities that will no doubt serve her well in the coming years.

**Profile by
Margaret Perry**

JEANNE MOUTOUSSAMY-ASHE

*J*eanne Moutoussamy-Ashe has made her mark on America through

1951– •

___

her photography and her work on behalf of AIDS victims. A photojournalist

___

who has been published extensively in books and magazines, she wrote

Photographer, •

___

Viewfinders: Black Women Photographers, *a groundbreaking histori-*

writer, AIDS

___

cal guide to black women photographers.

activist

___

Jeanne Marie Moutoussamy-Ashe, the youngest of three children, was born in 1951 to John Warren and Elizabeth Rose (Hunt) Moutoussamy. Moutoussamy-Ashe, a third generation African American, is of mixed heritage. Her paternal grandfather, who was born in Saint François, Guadeloupe, came to America and married the daughter of a slave from Louisiana. The name Moutoussamy is the English version of his East Indian name "Moutou-swami." Her maternal grandfather was of Cherokee ancestry.

Both of Moutoussamy-Ashe's parents cultivated professional careers during her childhood— her father was an architect and her mother was an interior designer. She grew up in Chicago, nurtured by her parents in an atmosphere that emphasized the visual arts. She began taking drawing and painting lessons at the age of eight at the Art Institute of Chicago, and continued to paint throughout her teen years. At one time she also modeled and appeared in a commercial for the product Mr. Clean.

In 1971 Moutoussamy-Ashe enrolled in the College of New Rochelle, New York, where she took her first photography course. She was overwhelmed when she encountered the work of Roy DeCarava, a photographer of Harlem life. DeCarava's work stimulated Moutoussamy-Ashe's interest in pursuing photography as her life's work. After one year in New Rochelle, she transferred to the prestigious Cooper Union School of Art in New York City. During her junior year she received a fellowship which allowed her to tour West Africa for a semester. She toured seven West African countries, photographing the people, their lives, and their customs. From this experience, she produced three photographic studies. Armed with an impressive color portfolio and numerous hours of hands-on experience, she felt confident enough to seek and secure a full-time position with NBC as a television photojournalist. Juggling her job and schoolwork, she continued her program of study, graduating with a B.F.A. in photography in 1975.

In 1976 Jeanne Moutoussamy met her future husband, tennis star Arthur Ashe. Even before they met, she jokingly told a friend that she was going to marry him. In his book *Days of Grace,* which includes photographs by Moutoussamy-Ashe, Ashe discussed her effect on him the moment he met her at a benefit for the United Negro College Fund on October 16, 1976. Ashe was one of the celebrities in attendance at the event to promote the scholarship program, while Moutoussamy-Ashe was photographing the activities for NBC. Ashe said that, while she was photographing him, he "took a mental picture of her as maybe, just maybe, what my heart desired." The couple went on their first date a few days later and were married four months after that on February 20, 1977. Andrew Young, who was then ambassador to the United Nations, officiated the ceremony.

Moutoussamy-Ashe has always been an independent woman with a sense of self-worth and purpose. This did not change after her marriage. Instead, she and her husband established a mutually supportive relationship that was kept fresh by their shared interest in the world around them. In a 1981 interview with *Sepia* magazine, Moutoussamy-Ashe remarked that the three most important experiences in her life were her marriage, her trip to West Africa while in art school, and three trips that she made to South Africa. The first two trips were undertaken with her husband, and featured some of the comfortable trappings that accompany the stardom that Ashe enjoyed. On her third visit, though, she did not travel as an American celebrity wife. Instead, she went alone and experienced firsthand the injustice of apartheid in South Africa. At one point, in fact, she was nearly arrested.

Being the wife of a sports star afforded Moutoussamy-Ashe the opportunity to pursue personal goals without concerning herself with financial gain. She has had the freedom to develop her work based on her feelings and her inner spirit. As a result, her work documents the overwhelming concern she holds for black people and their lives, whether in America, South Africa, or elsewhere. This is evident in her photographic work on the culture of the people of Daufuskie Island off the coast of South Carolina, published in 1982 as *Daufuskie Island: A Photographic Essay.* Her experiences as a black woman in the field of photography, which has been historically dominated by white males, led her to explore the history of African American women in the profession. The result of that research was her much acclaimed 1986 book, *Viewfinders: Black Women Photographers,* which documents the work and lives of black women photographers from 1839 to 1985.

Over the course of her career, Moutoussamy-Ashe has had her work displayed in numerous individual and group exhibitions in cities around the world, including Chicago, New York City, Boston, Washington, D.C., Los Angeles, Detroit, Paris, London, and Florence. In 1978 she participated in a traveling exhibit which toured the Soviet Union. A contributor of photographs to numerous magazines and newspapers, including *Ebony, Black Enterprise, New York Times, Essence, Life, Smithsonian, World Tennis, Self,* and *Sports Illustrated,* Moutoussamy-Ashe also worked as a photo-commentator for the television show *PM Magazine.* In addition, she provided photographs for Arthur Ashe's book *Getting Started in Tennis* (1977) and *Songs of My People: African Americans, A Self Portrait,* edited by Erin Easter (1991).

Maintains a •

Thriving Career

In the late 1970s Moutoussamy-Ashe was commissioned by President Jimmy Carter's administration to provide official photo-portraits of U.S. cabinet members. Her work has also become a part of the permanent collections of the Schomburg Center for Research in Black Culture, the Studio Museum in Harlem, the New York Public Library, and the Columbia Museum of Art and Science in Columbia, South Carolina.

In describing Moutoussamy-Ashe's work, art dealer and photographer Frank Stewart told Judith Wilson that she uses a "strong sense of people, especially black people with a classical simplicity of design to produce images that make powerfully direct visual statements" (Wilson, *Essence*). Her best friend, obstetrician Machelle Allen, described her in the October 1993 issue of *Ebony* as a "woman of tremendous poise and internal strength."

For her part, Moutoussamy-Ashe pointed to the affirming relationship she enjoyed with her husband before his death as central to her success. Ashe, she said, "taught me a greater love of myself. He brought out so many things in me that I didn't know I had inside" (Randolph, *Ebony*). Arthur Ashe died February 6, 1993, of complications related to AIDS, which he had contracted from a tainted blood transfusion following a heart attack in 1979.

Moutoussamy-Ashe told Laura B. Randolph for *Ebony* that her book *Daddy and Me,* published in the early 1990s, was a family project designed "to help other children understand you can live with illness and help people who are sick." The book contains Moutoussamy-Ashe's photographs of routine family activities during the last year of her husband's life. The text is written in their daughter Camera's words, making it easy for other young children to identify with and understand.

In addition to her work as a photographer, Moutoussamy-Ashe remains busy with projects to help others in her community. She is one of the founders of the Black Family Cultural Exchange, which is comprised of African-American women in New York City and Connecticut who provide a series of book fairs for black youth. The profits from these fairs provide scholarships and books for local community centers. Since her husband's death, Moutoussamy-Ashe has also emerged as a spokesperson for AIDS education and research.

**Profile by
Karen Cotton
McDaniel**

GLORIA NAYLOR

*T*o explore a range of characters united in their quest for wholeness, to seek a causal connection between desperation and violence, and to celebrate the endurance of the human spirit: these are the touchstones of Gloria Naylor's fiction. Her four novels—The Women of Brewster Place *(1982),* Linden Hills *(1985),* Mama Day *(1988), and* Bailey's Cafe *(1992)—grapple with moral and emotional crises, and in all of Naylor's fiction (which includes short stories and plays) she challenges the reader to respond to basic human needs and emerge with a better sense of self. Although many of her characters reside on the periphery of society, their relentless quest for dignity remains undiminished.*

Gloria Naylor was born on January 25, 1950, to Roosevelt Naylor, a

1950– •

Novelist, short •

story writer,

playwright

transit worker, and Alberta McAlpin Naylor, a telephone operator, in Robinsonville, Mississippi. Naylor's early years in the South would later provide fertile soil from which to mold a variety of her fictional characters. The Naylor family's eventual migration to the North was typical of African Americans in pursuit of economic stability and better educational opportunities for their children.

Before choosing writing as a primary career, Naylor worked as a Jehovah's Witness missionary, serving New York, North Carolina, and Florida from 1968 to 1975. Horrified by the assassination of Martin Luther King Jr. while she was in high school, Naylor believed that changing the world meant finding a "solution to the chaos" by evangelizing to the populace (Donahue, *Washington Post*).

Naylor, though, became dissatisfied with the restrictive nature of the Jehovah's Witness organization. She committed herself to completing her education and enrolled in college. It was during a sophomore creative writing seminar at Brooklyn College that Naylor read Toni Morrison's *The Bluest Eye*. The experience proved to be a defining one. In a conversation with Toni Morrison published in *Southern Review*, Naylor remembers the dramatic moment well:

> It said to a young poet, struggling to break into prose, that the barriers were flexible; at the core of it all is language, and if you're skilled enough with that, you can create your own genre. And it said to a young black woman, struggling to find a mirror to her worth in this society, not only is your story worth telling but it can be told in words so painstakingly eloquent that it becomes a song.

Naylor recognized that one did not have to be white or a male to create memorable literature. Moreover, the revelation that black women were capable of penning great works opened a new world for Naylor, and she immersed herself in the writings of African Americans. She came to feel that writing might provide her with an outlet for the feelings and thoughts that she had repressed for so long.

While an undergraduate at Brooklyn College, Naylor decided to test the waters. She published her first short story in a 1980 issue of *Essence* magazine. The story, entitled "A Life on Beekman Place," was revised in the final draft and included as part of *The Women of Brewster Place*, published two years later. Naylor earned a bachelor's degree in English from Brooklyn College in 1981 and a master's degree in African American Studies from Yale University in 1983. Since the early 1980s, she has taught and conducted workshops at George Washington University, New York University, Boston University, Princeton, the University of Pennsylvania, Brandeis University, and Cornell University.

• *Depicts Reality*

of Black

American

Women

Naylor's first novel, *The Women of Brewster Place* (1982), won the American Book Award for First Fiction in 1983, and it established her as an accomplished writer. She opens the work by showing how geography determines character. Through the clandestine deliberations of a white alderman and a realty company owner, Brewster Place becomes the "bastard child" of an urban ghetto, literally and figuratively cut off from the rest of the city. People who live there can live nowhere else. Seven strong-willed women who live there—Mattie, Etta Mae, Kiswana, Ciel, Cora Lee, Lorraine, and Theresa—form a microcosm of diversity in terms of background, age, marital status, political persuasion, and sexual preference. Poor, disinherited, flawed, and vulnerable, all of these women single-handedly consolidate their strengths to form a vibrant community. Mattie Michael, resident matriarch and dream keeper of Brewster Place, becomes emblematic of what it is to be black and female in America. Miss Mattie's dream of a block party to fund improvements on Brewster Place unites the women. They dismantle the wall that ultimately isolates them from "respectable folk."

A lyrical and powerful work, Naylor's first novel garnered praise from many corners. Critic Deirdre Donahue hailed *The Women of Brewster Place*, writing that "Naylor is not afraid to grapple with life's big subjects: sex, birth, love, death, grief. Her women feel deeply, and she unflinchingly transcribes their emotions.... Vibrating with undisguised emotion, *The Women of Brewster Place* springs from the same roots that produced the blues. Like them, her book sings of sorrows proudly borne by black women in America" (Donahue, *Washington Post*).

In 1985, two years after receiving her M.A. degree from Yale, Naylor published her second novel, *Linden Hills*. This sequel to *The Women of Brewster Place* chronicles the Luther Needed family history through four generations and examines the promise of the American dream gone wrong in Linden Hills. Although successful, upper-middle-class blacks with material wealth, the Needed patriarchs oppress women. The Needed wives—Luwana Packerville, Evelyn Creton, Priscilla McGuire, and Willa Prescott—find their lives defined only in relation to their spouses. As babymakers who perpetuate the family name, the Needed wives become marginalized at the hands of both their spouses and offspring. In the character of Willa Prescott, though, Naylor brings to life a voice that speaks movingly for the Needed wives.

African religious folk traditions serve as the context for Naylor's third novel, *Mama Day* (1988), written with the aid of a grant from the National Endowment for the Arts. Within the closed community of

Willow Springs, located between Georgia and South Carolina, Naylor empowers another matriarch in the tradition of Mattie Michael and Willa Prescott Needed. A conjurer and a descendant of the island's mythic founder, Sapphira Wade, Mama (Miranda) Day awaits the opportunity to pass the family heritage to her great-niece, Ophelia.

The first half of the narrative focuses on Ophelia's return to Willow Springs from New York City with her new husband, George. However, the action reaches a climax when Ophelia, known as Cocoa on the island, becomes ill due to the "hoodoo" magic of Ruby, a jealous rival. A hurricane, characterized by Mama Day as a "storm born in hell," destroys the only bridge to the mainland. The hurricane, which functions as an organizing principle for the concluding chapter, sets the stage for healing to occur.

In her fourth novel, *Bailey's Cafe* (1992), Naylor continued to examine the themes of female bonding and survival in a hostile urban environment. Naylor sets the tone by using the blues as a unifying metaphor in the epigraph:

> hush now can you hear it can't be far away/
> needing the blues to get there/ look and you
> can hear it/ look and you can hear/ the blues
> open/ a place never closing: Bailey's Cafe.

Bailey is the maestro who conducts a symphony of disharmonies referred to in more familiar terms as the blues. In the rhythmic prelude, Bailey explains that the customers "don't come for the food and they don't come for the atmosphere;" they come to find answers within themselves. Like choral voices, the cafe patrons—Sadie, Eve, Sweet Esther, Mary, Jesse Bell, and Mariam—enter and inform the narrative with tales of everyday circumstances in song. In addition, the lives of less frequent visitors to Bailey's Cafe serve as variations from the melodic line of life, but they too are inextricably bound to play their roles in the symphony.

In *Bailey's Cafe* and other work, Naylor studies the notion that to be a woman of color means relinquishing autonomy and following the prescribed dictates of a patriarchal society. By evoking the ritual of memory as a catalyst for action, Naylor involves the reader and the characters simultaneously. Together they recreate the present and its impact on the future. The characters of Mattie, Willa, Miranda, and Eve break down traditional barriers of exclusion to empower themselves.

Essays and screenplays are part of Naylor's repertoire, but they receive less attention than her novels. Best known for her novel *The*

Women of Brewster Place, Naylor scripted both a mini- and weekly series about ghetto life in the 1960s. Although the mini-series garnered an audience of 40 million viewers in 1989, the weekly series based on *The Women of Brewster Place* did not fare as well. Armed with strong financial backing from Oprah Winfrey's Harpo Productions, the future appeared bright in 1990. Winfrey portrayed Mattie Michael, and Olivia Cole appeared in the role of Miss Sophia. It was given one of ABC's best prime-time placements, coupled with a guarantee of thirteen episodes, but the show was eventually canceled. At the same time, Naylor became the founder and president of One Way Productions, an independent film company established to bring *Mama Day* and other projects to the screen.

Profile by Sharynn Owens Etheridge

HAZEL O'LEARY

*T**he first woman to become U.S. Secretary of Energy, Hazel O'Leary*

1937– •

is a confident and determined leader in President Bill Clinton's cabinet.

She has seen many sides of the energy world as a consultant, federal

U.S. Secretary of •

regulator, lobbyist, and corporate executive. She now heads the agency

Energy

that determines the direction of energy development in this country, and

she has emerged as one of the most powerful women in the world.

Hazel Rollins O'Leary was born on May 17, 1937, in Newport News, Virginia, the daughter of Russell E. Reid, a physician. O'Leary and her older sister, Edna Reid McCollum, were raised by their father and stepmother, Hazel Palleman Reid. O'Leary told Richette L. Haywood in *Ebony* that her family stressed the importance of helping other people. She learned this lesson by observation at home as well as through her teachers at school. For example, her grandmother kept clean clothes arranged by size in a box on her back porch and distributed them to others as the need arose. Her grandmother was also a founder of the black public library in her community. "I grew up in a family and an environment where opening the doors for others and literally opening your front door to others was not only expected but was a practice," she said.

O'Leary spent the first eight years of school in the racially segregated public schools of Newport News. Determined to encourage the talent that they saw in their daughters, the Reids arranged to send them to Essex County, New Jersey, where they lived with an aunt and attended Arts High School, a school for artistically gifted youth. In high school O'Leary studied voice and alto horn. She received a bachelor of arts degree cum laude from Fisk University in Nashville, Tennessee, in 1959. Although she was interested in pursuing a law degree after completing her undergraduate work, she postponed her studies and married Carl Rollins, a physician, with whom she had a son. She returned to school and received a J.D. degree from Rutgers University School of Law in 1966.

After passing the New Jersey Bar, O'Leary became assistant prosecutor in Essex County, New Jersey, in 1967. She was subsequently named assistant attorney general in the state. By now divorced, she moved to Washington, D.C., where she became a partner in the accounting firm of Coopers and Lybrand.

O'Leary's work in public service and energy policy began during the Ford administration and continued under three presidents. She joined the Federal Energy Administration (FEA) during Ford's presidency and from 1974 to 1976 was director of the Office of Consumer Affairs/ Special Impact. This office managed many of the antipoverty programs initiated during the Great Society years of the 1960s and O'Leary became known as an advocate for the poor. From 1976 to 1977 she was general counsel for the Community Services Administration. She was assistant administrator for conservation and environment with the FEA from May 1977 until the following October, when the FEA became part of the new Department of Energy (DOE). From 1978 to 1980, during President Jimmy Carter's presidency, she was chief of the DOE's Economic Regulatory Administration. Under both the Ford and Carter administrations O'Leary was a part of the effort to regulate the petroleum, natural gas, and electric industries and the federal government's conservation and environment programs. She supervised more than 2,000 lawyers, accountants, and engineers.

O'Leary received praise as well as criticism for her work. She was often called a fair administrator, and some environmentalists and energy executives cheered her innovative conservation programs, including underwriting the cost of insulating homes for low-income families. But critics attacked some of her policies, specifically the Fuel Use Act. Detractors insisted that the legislation punished energy supplies such as nuclear power, coal, and oil in favor of cleaner but more problematic energy options like natural gas.

In 1980 Hazel O'Leary married John F. O'Leary, who was deputy energy secretary under President Carter. The couple set up their own energy consulting firm, specializing in the preparation of expert testimony, project financing, and the development of independent power plants. It also lobbied Congress and state legislatures and advised clients on issues involving the energy industry.

John O'Leary died in 1987. Two years later O'Leary closed their firm and became director of Applied Energy Services, an independent power producer, and director of NRG Energy, the major unregulated subsidiary of Minnesota-based Northern States Power Company. She then served for three years as an executive vice president at Northern States Power Company, where she was in charge of environmental affairs, public relations, and lobbying. On January 1, 1993, she was promoted to president of the company.

Under O'Leary's direction, the Northern States Power Company developed into a leading and progressive utilities company. The company's treatment of nuclear waste concerned environmentalists, though. In 1989 O'Leary helped plan for the temporary above ground storage of spent radioactive fuel at Northern States Power Company's Prairie Island Nuclear Plant in Minnesota, located in close proximity to homes on the Mdewakanton Sioux reservation. Many residents of the area contended that Northern States Power acted tyrannically in its dealings with state agencies and the legislature. The company was subsequently accused of squelching public debate about the storage sites on television stations in Minneapolis. During her tenure there, though, O'Leary also became known as a savvy negotiator with an open and progressive outlook on issues.

- *First Woman*

Secretary of

Energy Named

When President-elect Bill Clinton announced his intention to nominate O'Leary to serve as the seventh Secretary of Energy, all observers knew that she faced a daunting task. In past years the Department of Energy (DOE) had become known as a plodding bureaucracy with a "reputation for secrecy and arrogance," according to *Nation* contributor David Corn. Many observers praised Clinton's selection, though. An executive for the Solar Energy Industries Association commented, "I'm generally bullish on Mrs. O'Leary. She's frankly one of the first energy secretaries we've ever had with a background in energy" (Pendleton, *Christian Science Monitor*). On January 21, 1993, O'Leary was confirmed by the U.S. Senate.

Once in place at the top of the DOE, O'Leary immediately called for changes in a number of areas, including reliance on foreign oil, environmental cleanup, and natural gas use. "The health and quality of our environment and economic performance are linked to our energy policy decisions," she noted. She called for a continuation of nuclear testing and modified production of armaments. Praising the national energy laboratories as "jewels," she stressed their contributions to national security in the form of new technology for industrial, medical, and communications communities.

During the first months of O'Leary's tenure, President Clinton wrote in his *100 Day Report* on the DOE's accomplishments that she was "acting decisively . . . to help America create good jobs, compete in the global marketplace, protect the environment, and reinvent the government while maintaining national security." Indeed, O'Leary made a quick and noticeable splash across the nation after taking the reins. The O'Leary-led DOE disclosed information about shocking radiation experiments that the U.S. government made on unsuspecting Americans after World War II. These experiments primarily took place during the 1940s and early 1950s, but some occurred as recently as the 1980s. Eleven thousand documents reviewed disclosed that in at least forty-eight experiments humans were given radioactive isotopes, generally without their consent, to determine the effects of radiation on the body.

Releases •

Formerly

Classified

Documents

O'Leary offered a heartfelt apology to the victims and their families on behalf of the United States, and commented that openness in government "is an affirmative obligation of the government, not simply a limitation on secrecy" (Corn, *Nation*). O'Leary also spearheaded efforts in other areas of the Department of Energy. Engaged in an ongoing battle to secure adequate funding for conservation and alternative energy programs (and to keep the department alive in the face of Republican efforts to shut it down), O'Leary has also "ended decades of secrecy about nuclear-bomb production, tackled a huge fissile-material cleanup problem, and tried to bring the efficiency of the private sector to government," noted Amy Kaslow in the *Christian Science Monitor*.

In 1995, though, O'Leary was buffeted by several news reports. The first indicated that she had used taxpayer money to "grade" the tone of reports produced by various members of the media. O'Leary insisted that the initiative had only been intended to determine whether the DOE's efforts were being adequately disseminated to the public, but she put a halt to the practice.

Later in the year it was disclosed that O'Leary spent significantly more money on travel expenses than any other member of President Clinton's cabinet. Again critics pounced, arguing that she was pampering herself on the trips and being wasteful with taxpayer money. The Department of Energy pointed out, though, that her varied responsibilities require a great deal of travel. In addition to supervising the DOE's many sites in the western United States, she "has led high-profile overseas trade missions to India, Pakistan, and China, where U.S. energy firms signed deals that the Energy Department said were worth at least $19.2 billion" (Miller, *Los Angeles Times*).

Hazel O'Leary has admitted to mistakes, but she continues to hold her head high. A pioneer, she has succeeded as an expert in a field where women are rarely found. During her tenure as energy secretary, she has gained the support of many people who initially questioned her commitment. She continues with her efforts to promote openness, create safe and environmentally-sound methods of energy consumption, and reduce the nation's dependency on foreign energy sources.

Profile by
Joan C. Elliott

JENNIE R. PATRICK

J ennie Patrick is the first African-American female to earn a Ph.D.

in chemical engineering in the United States. Encouraged by caring

parents and nurturing black teachers who instructed her during her

early years of schooling, she was blessed by emotional, mental, and

intellectual capabilities that enabled her to pursue her challenging

career path without flinching. Her strong commitment to scientific

excellence is matched by an equally strong commitment to improving

the lives of disadvantaged black youth in the United States.

1949– •

Chemical •

engineer,

educator

The fourth of five children, Jennie R. Patrick was born in Gadsden, Alabama, on January 1, 1949. Patrick spent her early years in segregated schools in her hometown. Her parents, James and Elizabeth Patrick, had no education beyond the sixth grade and lived modestly, but they were determined to launch their children on to successful lives, and encouraged them to strive for excellence in all their endeavors. Their difficult life prompted Patrick's early obsession with independence. "As a child,"

she told *U.S. Black Engineer,* "the thing that struck me the most was the hardness of my parents' life. They always talked constantly about using the mind as a way out of poverty" (Bradby, *U.S. Black Engineer*).

As a child, Patrick enjoyed a nurturing environment not only at home but also at school. She had several helpful black teachers who made a lasting impression on her by challenging her to search for knowledge and to pursue her dreams in any area. In 1964 Patrick entered the newly integrated Gadsden High School. The academic setting there was different in many ways. While Gadsden was equipped with much better teaching resources than Patrick had seen at her segregated school, it also had a very small minority enrollment, and the black kids were faced with the ugly specter of racism. The love and nurturing that Patrick had received as a child served her in good stead as she faced violence and harassment at the hands of white students. Academic, emotional, psychological, and physical survival became her greatest challenge. She followed through on her commitment to succeed, though, and graduated with honors.

Patrick's interest in science was born early. "As a kid, I wasn't sure what engineers did, but there seemed to be an awe about them. People admired them and considered them hardcore technical people," she told Bradby. She entered Tuskegee Institute (now Tuskegee University) in 1967, where she remained for three years. When the program in chemical engineering, which she had selected for a major, was discontinued at Tuskegee, she transferred to the University of California at Berkeley. She worked a year to obtain money for her education at Berkeley, then received her bachelor of science degree in chemical engineering in 1973. While in school, Patrick worked as an assistant engineer for Dow Chemical Company (1972) and Stouffer Chemical Company (1973).

In graduate school at the Massachusetts Institute of Technology (MIT), as at Berkeley, Patrick not only had the demanding schedule required of all students, but the greater challenge of overcoming racial prejudice. At MIT from 1973 to 1979, she concentrated in thermodynamics, homogeneous nucleation, and heat and mass transfer. She worked as a research assistant while pursuing a doctorate. In 1979 she earned her Ph.D. in chemical engineering, becoming the first black woman in the United States to do so. Her dissertation was titled "Superheat-Limit Temperature for Nonideal-Liquid Mixtures and Pure Components." During her years at MIT, Patrick also worked as a Chevron research engineer and an Arthur D. Little engineer.

After obtaining her Ph.D. degree, Patrick went to work for General Electric Research in Schenectady, New York, where she stayed for more

Patrick Earns •

Chemical

Engineering

Degree

than three years. Here she developed a research program in supercritical fluid technology—an area then in its infancy. In 1983 she switched to Phillip Morris in Richmond, Virginia, where she designed a state-of-the-art research plot plant in super critical extraction. In 1985 she moved to Rohm and Haas Company Research Laboratory in Bristol, Pennsylvania, working in emulsion technology and polymer science as she supervised other employees. Five years later Patrick became assistant to the executive vice president of Southern Company Services. She then returned to Tuskegee to the Department of Chemical Engineering, which closed during her studies there but had since been reestablished. A professor of chemical engineering at Tuskegee, Patrick is recognized as one of the university's brightest stars.

Science and

Survival

Promoted

Though she has received many honors and other attention for her technical accomplishments, Patrick's recent emphasis has been on promoting the progress of young black people in U.S. society. Although she spoke to predominantly black audiences at colleges and schools across the country during the 1980s, her schedule prevented her from devoting as much time to such activities as she would have liked. She eventually settled on pursuing a speaking project wherein she could make a permanent and lasting impression on young people:

> I started devoting considerable thought to various approaches to this project. The focus will be to teach young African Americans survival tactics in hostile environments. However, these strategies are valuable to everyone. The desired outcome is to provide psychological, emotional, and mental tools that allow African Americans to establish values, goals, standards, independence, and awareness. These tools are essential if we are to have our destiny in our own hands. This project will focus on historical contributions of Blacks worldwide, as well as highlight the subtle but intentional psychological and mental weapons that are used against us daily. By using some of my personal experiences, I hope to provide insight on the power of an independent thought process which ensures survival accompanied by happiness and self-assurance (Patrick, *Sage*).

Perhaps if others in her profession had been more forthcoming with Patrick, she could have avoided the unfortunate experiences that changed the course of her life and spurred her to devote her energy to examining hazards in the workplace and the community. She noted in correspondence to Jessie Carney Smith that:

I would have never imagined that I could have selected a profession that would destroy the normality of my life by exposing me to thousands of industrial chemicals in the work place. In all professions there are probably health hazards. Depending on the profession these hazards will be greater or less. What we must understand as individuals is that our lives and health are our responsibility. Total hazard-free work environments are not the norm.... I have developed a health problem that most people will never understand or appreciate, known as "multiple chemical sensitivity." This condition has made me become extremely allergic to many, many common substances such as perfume, cologne, hair spray, and cleaning agents. This condition has taken away the normality of my life. I urge young people to recognize the importance of not viewing an employer as the protector of your health. Police the environments in which you work or live to make sure it is safe for you and your family.

Patrick is a member of the prestigious scientific organization Sigma Xi and the American Institute of Chemical Engineers. She has received several honors, including the National Organization of Black Chemists and Chemical Engineers Outstanding Women in Science and Engineering Award in 1980, and she was a subject in the Exceptional Black Scientists Poster Program in 1983.

Patrick is married to Benjamin Glover; they have no children. Physical fitness is a central part of her life—she jogs, and she walks three miles each day. She is also an avid flower and vegetable gardener. She continues her work at Tuskegee, where she pushes to instill in young African Americans the sense of history and the sense of self that she believes are necessary for them to reach their goals.

Profile by
Vivian O. Sammons
and
Jessie Carney Smith

BILLIE GOODSON PIERCE

B illie Goodson Pierce was a spirited blues and jazz pianist, singer,

1907–1974 •

and dancer who, with her trumpeter and cornetist husband, DeDe

Pierce, led the New Orleans Preservation Hall Jazz Band during the

Jazz and blues •

1960s. During that time both she and her husband gained internation-

pianist,

al renown for the unique Creole flavor of their brand of blues, boogie-

singer

woogie piano, and jazz. In fact, the Pierce husband and wife duo are

hailed as one of the primary contributors to the revival or "Second

Coming" of New Orleans jazz in the 1960s.

Pierce endured and flourished in a musical genre that was almost completely male-dominated. Linda Dahl, who interviewed Pierce for *Stormy Weather: The Music and Lives of a Century of Jazzwomen,* notes that "a woman musician attempting to break into jazz needed more than musical talent; she needed great self-confidence, a tough, no-nonsense attitude and the skills of a diplomat." Pierce certainly possessed all of these qualities. When asked about her start as a pianist in the 1920s, she replied, "I don't know if it was rough or not. I was rough along with it."

Wilhemina Goodson Pierce was born on June 8, 1907, in Marianna, Florida. She came from a large, music-loving family that included seven children. Her parents, Madison H. Goodson and Sarah Jenkins Goodson, were both musicians, as were her six sisters—all of whom were pianists. Pierce spent her childhood years in Pensacola, Florida.

Pierce's musical career began at a very early age. She taught herself to play the piano when she was about seven years old and became an accomplished player, although she never had any formal training and never learned to read music. Instead, she acquired the basics from her Baptist parents, who were fond of singing hymns. Indeed, many of Pierce's childhood memories concern the family's passion for music:

> Most all of my days I've been playing music. I started playing the blues. My mother and father you know, were very religious people. Me and my sisters would get around the piano and have a good time playing ragtime and singing the blues. Somebody watched out for daddy and when he'd come, we'd break into, "What a Friend We Have in Jesus." He never knew the difference (Handy, *Black Women in American Bands and Orchestras*).

Pierce was also greatly influenced by the music of the local bands in Pensacola, as well as by the many New Orleans groups that toured the South in the early 1900s. On many nights one or more of the Goodson girls would sneak out of the house at night to go listen to the bands play. Billie recalled that "whenever a show at the Belmont Theater would get in a pinch for a piano player . . . the manager would send for a Goodson girl, not caring which one he got" (Handy, *Stormy Weather*).

● *Show Business*

Career Begins

Pierce's show business career really took off in 1922 at the age of fifteen, when she left home to play professionally as a traveling performer. When Clarence Williams, the regular accompanist for singer Bessie Smith, became ill, Pierce was offered the position and a chance to tour with Smith's show, working theaters throughout Florida. She gladly accepted the offer to serve as accompanist for Smith, who was known as the "Empress of the Blues."

For nearly ten years Pierce worked with various bands in her hometown state, as well as throughout the South. From 1922 to 1927, she toured the Gulf Coast with her sister Edna Goodson in the all-black Mighty Wiggle Carnival Show, where she did triple-duty as a singer, dancer, and pianist. During the late 1920s, she played with Slim Hunter's Orchestra, the Douglas Orchestra, the Joe Jesse Orchestra, and the Nighthawks Orchestra in local clubs. Pierce also frequently worked as an accompanist for Gertrude "Ma" Rainey, Mary Mack, and Ida Cox. Cox, along with Bessie Smith, emerged as major influences on Pierce's music. As time passed, Pierce soaked herself in the music that was all around her. Increasing numbers of listeners recognized that a talented new blues pianist and singer was in their midst.

In 1929 Pierce went to New Orleans as a temporary replacement for her older sister Sadie Goodson, a highly regarded professional musician who was then playing in Buddy Petit's legendary band. Petit's band was performing on the *SS Madison* on Lake Ponchartrain. Pierce immediately felt comfortable in the Crescent City. She decided to settle there in 1930.

Pierce spent the years of the Great Depression earning a dollar a night working in the rough waterfront taverns and honky-tonks along Decatur Street. It was at one of these establishments that she met DeDe Pierce (born Joseph de Lacrois), who later joined Billie's four-piece band. On March 28, 1935, having known each other for only three short weeks, Billie and DeDe were married. Thus began a lifetime partnership of marriage and music.

After Billie and DeDe married, the couple worked primarily at the popular weekend club Luthjen's, a small neighborhood dance hall on Marais Street. DeDe Pierce's New Orleans upbringing and Creole, French-speaking ancestry helped to enliven their repertoire, which included such famous blues tunes as "Sallee Dame" and "Eh La Bas."

During the late 1930s the Pierces played, together or separately, in clubs along Decatur Street and in little French Quarter spots such as Kingfish's, Pig Pen's, The Cat and The Fiddle, and Popeye's. They played with many of New Orleans' finest musicians, among them Alphonse Picou, Big Eye Louis, and Emile and Paul Barnes. It was not long before Billie and DeDe had themselves become big names in the city.

In 1951 the Pierces made a recording for Bill Russell's American Music label and were included in an anthology compiled by Sam Charters. During the late 1950s, though, the couple's musical career was sidetracked by illness. DeDe was stricken with glaucoma, which caused him to go blind, while Billie suffered from a stroke that left her paralyzed for months. She was determined to recover so that she could devote herself to DeDe's care, and over time, both Billie and DeDe made splendid recoveries. DeDe adjusted to his disability and soon the couple was able to continue playing together.

New Orleans •

Offers

Opportunity

and Fame

During the 1960s the Pierces staged a remarkable comeback, achieving international fame. Their success was due in part to the rebirth of New Orleans jazz and the founding of Preservation Hall in 1961 by Sandra and Allen Jaffre. The Pierces became leading figures and principal attractions in the Preservation Hall Jazz Band, along with William Humphrey (clarinet), Cie Frazier (drums), Jim Robinson (trombone), and Allen Jaffre (tuba).

The duo's popularity was due in part to their success in combining Billie's classic blues and ragtime jazz style with the Creole and folk influences of DeDe to form a unique blend of jazz that perfectly symbolized the South. In fact, the Jaffres had opened Preservation Hall on their hunch that interest in this unique southern style of jazz—now commonly called Dixieland—would remain healthy. As Billie and DeDe Pierce became established as the mainstay of the Hall during the 1960s and early 1970s, it was clear that the Jaffres had been correct.

The couple kept their classic blues style alive by combining tasteful and sensitive low-keyed variations. Billie Pierce was described as a musician with a rough and earthy style and a moving singing voice. She wrote and sang songs such as "Get a Working Man," "Panama Rag," "Freight Train Moanin Blues," "Going Back to Florida," "Good Tonk Blues," "In the Racket," and "Billie's Gumbo Blues."

DeDe Pierce was influenced not only by his French Creole culture but also by the New Orleans marching brass bands. His trumpet playing was described as clear and syncopated, and he was instrumental in helping to make the song "Eh! La Bas" famous. Some of his other songs included "I Got Rhythm," "Yeah Man," and "Pork Chops."

The fame and recognition that resulted from the Pierces' involvement with the Preservation Hall Band led to work on many recording labels, including Atlantic and Riverside. Their tours were popular as well, and the duo spent many months on the road, playing at college jazz festivals, concert halls, and nightclubs.

Billie and DeDe made appearances on television and radio programs from coast to coast. In 1967 the Pierces toured Europe and the Orient with the Preservation Hall Jazz Band, and the band made several appearances at Philharmonic Hall in Lincoln Center in the late 1960s and 1970s. The Pierces spirited brand of jazz and blues struck a chord with younger music lovers, too, and they toured with the Grateful Dead, Jefferson Airplane, and other rock groups.

The Pierces enjoyed their time in the limelight until 1973, when DeDe fell seriously ill with cancer of the larynx and related problems. He died on November 23, 1973. Billie Pierce was inconsolable after the death of her husband. Less than a year after DeDe's death, Pierce entered Sara Mayo Hospital, where she died of natural causes at the age of 67. She is buried at the Saint Louis Cemetery in New Orleans. According to Paige Van Vorst of *Downbeat* magazine, "DeDe's death . . . broke up a team of forty years' standing, and Billie never returned to full-time playing. Her death further reduces the number of authentic traditional jazz musicians."

Billie Pierce's life was one filled with adventure and excitement, as well as hardship and struggle. Although the rough life of the jazz musician is not one that many women chose, her choice has been applauded by jazz and blues enthusiasts all over the world.

**Profile by
Tanty R. Avant**

SARAH FORTEN PURVIS

S arah Louisa Forten Purvis was a noted poet and abolitionist who *c. 1811–1898?* •

did not allow her own personal good fortune to blind her to the

inequities and cruelties of slavery. She was born in Philadelphia in 1811 **Poet, activist** •

or 1812 to the wealthy freeborn businessman James Forten and his

second wife, Charlotte Vandine Forten. She was the third of eight

children, and grew up in a warm and supportive atmosphere.

Like her brothers and sisters, Sarah Forten Purvis received a private education. Unhappy with the quality of the schools available to his children, and prevented from sending them to private academies because of their race, James Forten joined forces with other wealthy free black parents to establish a private school for their children. This formal education was supplemented by tutoring at home. A refined and accomplished young woman, Sarah Forten Purvis pursued her pleasure in music and literature with zeal.

Her family's wealth and status did not blind Sarah Forten Purvis to the evils of racial prejudice or the shadow of slavery. She was acutely aware that her father's wealth insulated her from the worst effects of racial injustice. Even so, racism remained a fact of life, as she noted in an

1837 letter to abolitionist Angelina Grimké: "For our own family—we have to thank a kind Providence for placing us in a situation that has hitherto prevented us from falling under the weight of this evil. We feel it but in a slight degree compared with many others.... We are not disturbed in our social relations—we never travel far from home and seldom go to public places unless quite sure that admission is free to all—therefore, we meet with none of the mortifications which might otherwise ensue (Purvis to Angelina Grimké, April 15, 1837, *Letters of Theodore Dwight Weld*).

Purvis was taught from earliest childhood to loathe slavery, to work for its eradication, and to reject the notion that her freeborn status somehow divorced her from those held in bondage in the South. Still, she credited Garrisonian abolitionism with awakening her "from apathy and indifference, [and] shedding light into a Mind which has been too long wrapped in selfish darkness" (Purvis to Angelina Grimké, *Letters of Theodore Dwight Weld*, 380).

• *Writes*

Antislavery

Verse as "Ada"

Using the penname "Ada," Purvis began writing antislavery verse for William Lloyd Garrison's abolitionist journal the *Liberator* in 1831, at the age of nineteen or twenty. Purvis maintained her association with the journal for years, publishing many of her poems in its pages. After two of her early poems had been published, James Forten revealed the true identity of "Ada" to Garrison.

Other poems followed. In "The Slave Girl's Address to Her Mother" and "Prayer" she spoke of religion as affording consolation to the slave, but she was no apologist for slavery. Purvis often referred to her belief that America had abandoned its revolutionary principles because of its continued embrace of slavery. The daughter of a man who had fought for the independence of his country and suffered imprisonment in the defense of liberty, Purvis found it bitterly ironic that so many of her fellow citizens espoused liberty while simultaneously sanctioning slavery. She comments on this hypocrisy in "The Slave":

> Oh! speak not of heathenish darkness again,
> Nor tell me of lands in error's dread chain!
> Where—where is the nation so erring as we,
> Who claim the proud name of the 'HOME OF
> THE FREE'? . . .
> Speak not of 'my country,' unless she shall be,
> In truth, the bright home of the 'brave and the
> free.'
> Till the dark stain of slavery is washed from her
> hand,
> A tribute of homage she cannot command

(Purvis, "The Slave," *Liberator*, 4 January 1834).

Purvis's message was equally forceful when she forsook poetry for prose. In the spring of 1831, in a letter signed "Magawisca," she addressed the theme of "The Abuse of Liberty." She pointed out that the enjoyment of life, liberty, and property was confined to white men, and expressed pity for the slaveholder, even as she condemned him for his injustice and prayed that he might see the error of his ways. "[T]here is no state of life so anxious as his . . . he is in constant dread lest they, who he unjustly condemns to bondage, will burst their fetters and become oppressors in their turn." She ended with a warning about the inevitability of divine retribution. "[C]an you think . . . He, who made the sun to shine on the black man as well as the white, will always allow you to rest tranquil on your downy couches? No,—He is just, and his anger will not always slumber. He will wipe the tears from Ethiopia's eye; He will shake the tree of liberty, and its blossoms shall spread over the earth" (Purvis, "The Abuse of Liberty," *Liberator*, 26 March 1831).

In December 1833 abolitionists from around the country converged on Philadelphia to found the American Anti-Slavery Society. The organization was strongly supported by the Forten household, which invited many of the travelers to dine in the home. That same year, William Lloyd Garrison left for Britain to spread his abolitionist message. Purvis shared the fervent admiration for Garrison that was so often expressed by her father and other members of her family, and she was moved to comment on Garrison's work in her poem "Hibernia."

"An Appeal to Woman," which is perhaps Purvis's best known work, was published in the *Liberator* on February 1, 1834, after first appearing in the Lowell *Observer*. In this poem she called upon white women to support their black sisters and to "nobly dare to act a Christian's part":

> Dare to be good, as thou canst dare be great,
> Despise the taunts of envy, scorn and hate;
> Our 'skins may differ,' but from thee we claim
> A sister's privilege, in a sister's name.
> (Purvis, "An Appeal to Woman," *Liberator*, February 1,
>   1834)

Purvis did not confine her antislavery activism to writing poetry and prose. Almost all of her activities were concerned with the fight against slavery. With her older sisters, Harriet and Margaretta, she signed the charter incorporating the Philadelphia Female Anti-Slavery Society in December 1833. Serving several terms on the society's board of managers in the 1830s, she took part in a number of varied abolitionist campaigns. She remained active in the work of the Philadelphia Female Anti-Slavery Society until her marriage and her departure from the city.

On January 7, 1838, Sarah Forten married Joseph Purvis, the younger brother of her sister's husband. Joseph Purvis was the youngest son of William Purvis (1762-1826), an English immigrant who had amassed great wealth as a cotton merchant in South Carolina, and his mistress, Harriet Judah. William Purvis acknowledged the children, though, and, after making generous provision for their mother, he left his estate to be divided among them.

Joseph Purvis was thus a man of means, and he used his share of his inheritance to establish himself as a farmer in Bucks County. In 1838 he moved his bride there, to a life markedly different from the one she had known in the city. Over the course of twelve years, Sarah Forten Purvis gave birth to eight children. Raising a family and helping to manage a farm left Sarah Purvis little time to pursue her interest in abolitionist work and antislavery verse. (Poems by a writer who signed herself "Ada" continued to appear in antislavery periodicals during this period. However, Sarah Forten Purvis was almost certainly not their author: the writer refers to growing up in New England and favors the Quaker style of dating her work.)

Joseph Purvis may have been too rash with some of his investments, though. A heavy investor in farm machinery, livestock, and real estate, Purvis was in the midst of a series of complicated land deals when he died suddenly on January 17, 1857. Purvis left no will, and all of his eight children were minors at the time of his death. The Bucks County Orphans' Court stepped in, and it was soon apparent that his reserves of cash were "not sufficient for the payment of his debts," in part because loans that Purvis had made to other area farmers were not repaid. Portions of his property were ordered to be sold off. The property holdings were considerable, but in 1857 the nation was gripped by a financial panic that made the divestment more difficult.

Sarah Purvis and her children were not immediately faced with ruin, but the descent into genteel poverty proved inevitable. By 1871 Joseph Purvis's once considerable estate had dwindled to three small properties comprising forty acres and two houses. It was by no means a negligible holding, but it was not much to divide among his surviving children and his widow. Sarah Purvis was eventually obliged to declare bankruptcy in 1875.

In addition to her financial woes, Sarah Purvis also endured the loss of three of her children in less than a decade. Two more of her children left Pennsylvania to join the exodus of black settlers to Kansas. Sarah Purvis subsequently returned with two of her children to the childhood home she had left almost four decades earlier. She died in the late 1890s and was buried in a lot owned by William Forten in an Episcopal church cemetery. Her grave is unmarked.

Profile by Julie Winch

CHARLOTTA GORDON PYLES

C *harlotta Gordon Pyles had no formal education, yet she stands as*

one of the most effective abolitionists of her time, dedicated to educating

others about the evil of slavery. Her zealous quest for freedom for her

family and other enslaved blacks impelled her to leave Iowa in 1854 to

speak against slavery in Pennsylvania, New York, and the New England

states. In Philadelphia, where she was welcomed and entertained by

Quaker families, Pyles had the privilege of speaking in Independence

Hall. Several times during her lecture tour she met with and confided in

the great abolitionist and journalist Frederick Douglass. It is evident that

he admired this woman's courage, for he honored her with a poem in the

December 12, 1855, Frederick Douglass Paper. *Although Douglass*

c. 1806–1880 •

Abolitionist, •

lecturer

259 •

misspelled Pyles's name, entitling the poem "Charlotte Piles," his description of her leaves no doubt who the subject of the poem is: "A noble woman, now travelling in the free States, soliciting aid for the redemption of part of her family from Republican slavery."

Little is known of the early life of Charlotta Gordon Pyles. Born a slave around 1806, she was of mixed ancestry. Her father was of German and black ancestry, while her mother was a full-blooded Seminole Indian. Their daughter was described in adulthood as "tall and straight as a pine, with high cheekbones, copper-colored hue, and straight, glossy black hair" (Jones, *Palimpsest*).

According to Mrs. Laurence C. Jones, a granddaughter of Pyles, social reformers marveled at the resolute nature of this unlettered woman. They wrote letters of recommendation, easing her reception during her varied travels. Jones wrote that "the most precious heirlooms among her descendants today are the photos and letters of these men and women, given to Charlotta Pyles as personal reminders of their association with her in a noble cause" (Jones, *Palimpsest*).

<table>
<tr><td>• The Difficult</td></tr>
<tr><td>Road to</td></tr>
<tr><td>Freedom</td></tr>
</table>

Before ever being freed, Pyles had come to understand the complexities of slavery through her own experience. In Bardstown, Kentucky, she had been the slave of Frances Gordon, who inherited Pyles and her children from her father. On his deathbed, though, Mr. Gordon made his daughter Frances promise to free the Pyles family according to Wesleyan Methodist rules for the manumission of slaves. In 1853 Frances undertook an arduous journey to take the family's slaves north to freedom.

Frances Gordon's brothers, however, were envious of their sister's "possessions." They kidnapped Benjamin Pyles, Charlotta's second-oldest son, and sold him to a slave driver in Mississippi. This act caused Frances Gordon to take legal action to establish her possession of the Pyles so she could ensure the safety of the rest of the family. She moved the family to Springfield, Kentucky, and at one point had them jailed as a safety precaution.

In addition to Charlotta Pyles and Frances Gordon, the traveling group included Charlotta's husband, Harry MacHenry Pyles, and their children, Emily, Barney, Paulina, Sarah Ann, Mary Ellen, Henry, Charlotta, Elizabeth, and Mary Agnes. The group also included several other families.

Unlike his wife, Harry MacHenry Pyles was a free black, the son of William MacHenry, who was from Scotland, and his light-colored maid. With his blue eyes and fair complexion, Harry resembled his father. In order to feel less guilty about his mulatto son, William MacHenry declared Harry free, thus allowing Harry to travel where he wanted without being bothered. He could thus visit Charlotta and the children at any time, but he could not have charge of his family despite his free status; slavery rules declared that children of a free Negro and a slave inherited the status of the mother. Harry, though, was trained in harness and shoe mending and had a shop where he could ply his trade. The shop allowed Harry to provide support to his wife and eleven children.

Since Harry MacHenry Pyles was a free black, he was able to travel with his wife and children and Frances Gordon on their long road northward. The party left Bardstown, Kentucky, in early fall 1853, and traveled by wagon to Louisville, Kentucky, where Gordon had to validate her right to remove her slaves from the state. To insure their safety from her brothers as well as from slave hunters, Frances Gordon hired a white minister, Reverend Claycome, to accompany the Pyles family. After attending to the legal matters, the party took a steamboat to St. Louis via Cincinnati.

Once in St. Louis, a white man named Nat Stone offered to guide the group to Minnesota for a fee of one hundred dollars. A few days into the trip, though, Stone demanded another fifty dollars. Gordon agreed, fearful of their vulnerability in Missouri, a slave state. As time passed, the cold winter of the Midwest forced the group to abort their plans to reach Minnesota. They settled at Keokuk, a trading post.

After settling her family in Keokuk, Iowa, Pyles felt compelled to launch a lecture tour in the East, mindful that she needed to raise $1,500 for each of her enslaved sons-in-law. This lecture tour, a thousand miles away in strange territory, was a difficult task for a poor woman who had never had a day's schooling in her life. Her efforts were effective, though, and in six months she had raised $3,000. She went back to Kentucky, where she bought freedom for the two men and returned them to their families in Iowa. Word of her efforts reached the kidnapped Benjamin, who was still in Mississippi. He sent correspondence in which he pleaded with her to buy his freedom, suggesting that he use her money to free him rather than one of her brothers-in-law. Pyles replied that since he had neither a wife nor children he could find the wherewithal to free himself.

Purchases •

Freedom for

Enslaved

Relatives

Once the Pyles became settled in Keokuk, Iowa, their home became a haven for runaway slaves. Many slaves from the state of Kentucky, where Pyles and her children had previously been enslaved, as well as those she met on her travels through Tennessee and Missouri, fled to her home. Once there, Pyles and her white friends helped them escape to Canada.

Even after Frances Gordon freed the Pyles, she lived under their roof as a member of the family. Gordon was like a doting grandmother to the children. Young Mary Ellen Pyles, who was a particular favorite of Miss Gordon, inherited her mother's courageous and industrious spirit. According to *Homespun Heroines,* she was seventeen when the family arrived in Iowa and had never attended school, but once in Keokuk, she hired out to a Quaker family in Salem in exchange for room and board and a chance to go to school. Mary Ellen then encouraged her sister Mary Agnes to join her. After four terms of school, Mary Agnes returned home, but Mary Ellen stayed the full limit of time afforded her as a colored girl.

The Pyles were zealous in their quest for education. Their efforts to secure a quality education for their children eventually resulted in integration of the Keokuk High School; Charlotta Pyles's grandson became one of the first colored high school graduates in the state of Iowa in 1880. This effort spurred an enduring passion for education in the Pyles family, for future generations served as educators down in Mississippi. "And so the spirit of a noble woman, Charlotta Pyles, goes marching on in the efforts of her grandchildren to educate the negro race in the Southland" (Jones, *Palimpsest*).

In the early 1870s Frances Gordon died at the Pyles home in Iowa. Pyles herself died from heart disease several years later, on January 19, 1880, at the age of seventy-four. The same pallbearers from the First Baptist Church of Keokuk who had carried the remains of Frances Gordon to her rest carried those of Pyles. A well-liked and respected figure in the community, two Iowa newspapers, the *Burlington Hawkeye* and the *Keokuk Daily,* carried notices of her death.

**Profile by
Margaret Ann Reid**

Former slave, abolitionist, and lecturer, Charlotta Pyles possessed an indomitable spirit in her fight against slavery. She taught her children and grandchildren that with faith and education they could overcome the evils of racism.

MA RAINEY

1886–1939 •

M *a Rainey, known by music fans as the "Mother of the Blues," is*

regarded as the first great blues vocalist. Rainey's ability to belt out the

Blues singer •

blues in her own uniquely gritty, powerful way set a high standard that

few other musical artists have been able to approach, let alone match.

Rainey was born Gertrude Malissa Nix Pridgett on April 26, 1886, in Columbus, Georgia, to Thomas and Ella (Allen) Pridgett, both Alabamians. She was the second of five children. Little is known about the singer's early and formative years, although it has been determined that her mother was employed by Central Railway of Georgia after the death of Thomas Pridgett in 1896.

Gertrude Pridgett made her first public appearance at the age of fourteen in a local talent revue. Shortly after this stage debut, she began to perform in tent shows, and is reported to have started singing the blues as early as 1902.

On February 23, 1904, at the age of eighteen, Gertrude Pridgett married Will Rainey, a comedy singer who was purportedly performing with one of the minstrel shows that passed through Columbus when he and Gertrude met and fell in love. Travelling with the Rabbit Foot Minstrels to circuses, minstrel shows, and black variety circuits, the couple did a song-and-dance routine as "Ma" and "Pa" Rainey, "Assassinators of the Blues."

Gertrude and Will Rainey adopted a son, Little Danny Rainey, who performed as a dancer with the troupe and was billed as "the world's greatest juvenile stepper." He was one of several children for whom Ma Rainey was a foster mother. Some years later, Gertrude and Will Rainey separated. She later married a younger man not involved with show business.

Ma and Pa continued to tour in the South with such companies as the Rabbit Foot Minstrels, the George Smart Set, the Florida Cotton Blossoms, and Shufflin' Sam from Alabam'. Her popularity grew to such an extent that she eventually got separate billing as "Madame Gertrude Rainey." Reputed to be one of the first singers to add blues to her selections in minstrel shows, Rainey's fame grew at the same time as the spread of interest in the blues.

Influence of •

Minstrelsy and

Vaudeville

Demonstrated

Ma Rainey sang what is called classic blues, which, according to Sandra Lieb, "emerged partly from black minstrelsy and vaudeville and partly from the work of anonymous male folk blues singers whose songs appeared most prolifically in the East Texas and Mississippi Delta regions after 1890" (Lieb, *Mother of the Blues*, 58). Ma Rainey sang what came to be known as the classic blues in a decidedly down-home style. Her southern audiences, largely black and rural, grew to love Rainey's performances, which typically touched on "the drudgery, pain, and joys of her folk" (Stewart-Baxter, *Ma Rainey and the Classic Blues Singers*). According to Lieb, the blues singer spoke to the "poverty, suffering, heartbreak, and pain, as well as humor, fortitude, strength, and endurance" characteristic of the black experience (Lieb, *Mother of the Blues*, 82). "Her great theme is the intense sexual love between men and women, and her secondary themes concern the sensual, earthy, and often rough side of life: music and dancing, drunkenness and superstition, lesbianism and homosexuality, women in prison, jealousy and murder."

Compassionate and tender, Ma Rainey was a big, short woman with a taste for flashy dressing. "A warm-hearted, generous human being, wrapped up in the world of the theatre, the vaudeville stage with its songs, and the blues of her race were very much part of her. All the toughness of her life and character is there in her singing" (Stewart-Baxter, *Ma Rainey and the Classic Blues Singers*, 42).

Rainey became very popular with white audiences, but she had a special bond with members of the black community. Sandra Lieb commented on the nature of this bond:

> Ma Rainey's itinerant life and the development of her career in many ways paralleled the growth of an important segment of black consciousness, from roughly 1900 to 1930—from rural folk culture to modern urban metropolis; from privation in the South to opportunity and cultural chaos in the North.... For her audience, Ma Rainey was a folk figure who reached her greatest popularity at the same time that black writers like Jean Toomer, Zora Neale Hurston, Langston Hughes, and Sterling Brown were all celebrating the Southern folk experience in novels, poems, essays, and plays (Lieb, *Mother of the Blues*, 168-69).

• *Rainey Makes*

Her Mark

Another important figure to whom Rainey was no doubt an inspiration was Bessie Smith, whose career would eventually receive even greater acclaim than Ma Rainey's. The two women met sometime between 1912 and 1916 and, though the exact nature of their relationship has been the subject of considerable speculation—people have suggested everything from bitter rivalry to lesbian encounters—it is safe to say that they recognized the scintillating talent that each of them possessed.

Ma Rainey extended her audience with her recordings at Paramount Records in Chicago in December 1923. These records reached a northern audience previously unaware of Rainey's gutty style, but music critics bemoan the poor acoustical quality of the recordings. The lack of representative recordings, along with the white critical community's failure to wholly recognize her talent at the time, are often blamed for her relative obscurity in the northern states. Still, some of the recordings are priceless nuggets that provide the listener with a glimmer of understanding of the power and grace that marked Rainey's singing. Her classic recordings included such songs as "Honey Where You Been So Long," "Those Dogs of Mine," "Barrel House Blues," "Lawd Send Me a Man Blues," "Memphis Bound Blues," "Blame It On the Blues," and "Big Feeling Blues."

From 1923 to 1928, Ma Rainey, who performed a mix of original and traditional material, made ninety-two recordings. While these recordings extended Rainey's audiences, her bookings around 1924 through the Theater Owner's Booking Association (TOBA) circuit also expanded her audience and contributed to her ascension. Though the white-controlled TOBA had a mixed reputation among black performers, it was nonetheless a viable showcase for black talent.

The climate of the entertainment industry changed in the latter part of the 1920s, though. Rainey made her last recording with Paramount in 1928, while TOBA collapsed in 1931. Critic Daphne Harrison noted that the demise of TOBA had a significant impact on the careers of Rainey and other blues artists:

> TOBA was instrumental in the development and expansion of the black entertainment industry from 1907 until its destruction by the economic forces of the Depression. It could not compete with the competition from "talkie" movies, radio programs and dance music as opposed to vaudeville and minstrel acts.... Fortunately for some of the blues women, there were opportunities in brief roles in the movies; for others the radio weekly shows kept them singing for a while; and those who could adjust their style and repertoire were able to continue as cabaret or revue performers.... But none of these activities brought them the fame and fortune that were theirs in the heyday of the 1920s. Like the TOBA, the blues women lost in a market that disappeared (Harrison, *Black Pearls*, 40-41).

After the death of her sister in 1935, Ma Rainey went back to the family home she had built with her earnings. Months later the blues singer's mother died. No longer performing by this time, Ma Rainey operated two theaters that she owned—the Lyric in Columbus and the Airdome in Rome, Georgia. She later joined the Friendship Baptist Church.

Ma Rainey, the earliest professional blues singer, died December 22, 1939, at the age of fifty-three of heart disease. She was buried in the family plot at Porterdale Cemetery in Columbus, Georgia.

**Profile by
Vanessa D.
Dickerson**

FLORENCE SPEARING RANDOLPH

Florence Spearing Randolph's achievements as a civic, religious,

1866–1951 •

and cultural leader rank with those of some of the most celebrated

Americans in history. Yet, as important as her contributions were and as

Minister, •

well known as she was, she faded into a measure of obscurity less than a

suffragist

decade after her death.

Florence Spearing Randolph was born in Charleston, South Carolina, on August 9, 1866, the seventh child of John Spearing and Anna Smith Spearing. She was born into a family of privilege and culture, whose free black lineage stretched back almost two generations before the Civil War. The daughter of a prosperous cabinetmaker, she was educated at local public schools and graduated from Avery Normal Institute in Charleston.

In 1885, at the age of nineteen, Randolph moved to New Jersey, taking up residence with an older sister in Jersey City and establishing herself as a dressmaker. Jersey City proved to be a beneficial environment for several reasons. She earned higher wages there than she was able to in the South, and was heartened by the greater sense of freedom that she felt in the northern city. Jersey City was also the place that she met and married Hugh Randolph of Richmond, Virginia, who worked on the railroad as a cook. The Randolphs had one child, a daughter named Leah Viola, who was born in February 1887. Hugh Randolph died in 1913.

In 1886 Florence Spearing Randolph became a member of the Monmouth Street African Methodist Episcopal (AME) Zion Church, where she was appointed Sunday school teacher and class leader for the young people. As a child in Charleston, she had frequently accompanied her blind grandmother on house visits to pray with the sick and to explain the Scriptures. This experience left a deep impression on the young Randolph, who eventually decided to pursue a career in the ministry. In the late 1880s she began studying the Bible under the tutelage of a Greek and Hebrew scholar.

• Begins
Temperance
and Church
Work

Throughout the late 1880s and early 1890s, Randolph operated a flourishing dressmaking business from her home, located in downtown Jersey City. It was during this period that she began to exhort, giving rousing speeches designed to sway listeners about the importance of faith and the evils of alcohol. Her views about the latter spurred her membership in the Women's Christian Temperance Union (WCTU).

During the unexpected illness of R. R. Baldwin, the pastor of the Jersey City AME Zion Church, Randolph was given permission to take on a more visible role in the church. As a result, she spurred one of the greatest revivals in the history of the church. Randolph's youth and gender attracted large crowds to church gatherings, which helped to increase the membership of her church and others in the vicinity. Local press coverage and word-of-mouth revelations about Randolph increased her visibility and popularity. Invitations to speak and conduct revivals came from small churches and missions. Congregations of white worshippers sought her out as well.

As Randolph's popularity continued to grow, though, she also became more controversial. Granted head preacher status in 1897, she was admitted to the New Jersey Conference of the AME Zion Church a year later. Her licensing as a preacher came only after a lengthy and somewhat bitter debate. The presiding bishop was opposed to Randolph's appointment, and this set the tone for disaffection among fellow ministers who were opposed to elevating women to positions of authority in the church. This episode marked the first of many instances wherein Randolph struggled to be accepted and treated as an equal in the AME Zion ministry.

Once admitted to the New Jersey Conference, Randolph became conference evangelist. At the May 1900 AME Zion Church conference meeting in Atlantic City she was ordained a deacon, and in August of that year she was named a delegate to the Ecumenical Conference meeting in London, England. During this trip she also traveled to Scotland, France, and Belgium, speaking and lecturing.

Between 1897 and 1901, the Reverend Florence Randolph pastored several churches in New York and New Jersey, usually toiling without benefit of a salary. The churches to which she was assigned were small, poor, and struggling. Once the churches became solvent, she was reassigned to another problem church. Her last difficult experience in her ministerial career was at Wallace Chapel in Summit, New Jersey. She served as pastor of this church from 1925 until her retirement in 1946.

Randolph's work with the WCTU against liquor and other alcohol influenced her ministerial thought and style. Her lectures and organizing work on behalf of the WCTU, which she continued until the repeal of the Eighteenth Amendment in 1933, reflected the fiery zeal of the WCTU reformers. Her speeches frequently attacked racism, colonialism, and sexism. Even though her public posture was forceful and she spoke and worked on behalf of women's suffrage, she was accepted and supported by a number of men because of her feminine demeanor.

Racism, Sexism, •

and Colonialism

Attacked

Very early in her career, Randolph became identified with educational and religious movements that were supportive of interests on the African continent. In 1921 and 1922 she traveled in Africa, working as a missionary in Liberia and spending more than a year on the Gold Coast, where she lectured, preached, and studied conditions in the region. She became well known in Africa for her work on behalf of the Quittah AME Zion Mission Sunday School and Varick Christian Endeavor Society. Randolph served in Africa for thirteen months. She paid her own traveling expenses, for she did not receive a salary. After her return to the United States, she conducted a series of lectures designed to educate Americans about conditions on the continent.

Randolph's concern for the cause of foreign missions—and her unparalleled ability to raise money for them—led to her appointment as AME Zion Secretary of the Bureau in 1912. In 1916 she was elected president of the Women's Home and Foreign Missionary Society of the AME Zion Church, a post she held for twenty-five years.

Randolph's work in the AME Zion Church was singular and distinguished. In many ways she was a pioneer who expanded opportunities for women in the church through her achievements. In 1933 Livingstone College in Salisbury, North Carolina, bestowed upon her the honorary degree of doctor of divinity. She was the first woman of the AME Zion denomination to receive this honor from the college.

Randolph's work as a minister, missionary, and temperance worker never overshadowed her work as an organizer. One of Randolph's most important contributions was her organization of the New Jersey Federation of Colored Women's Clubs in 1915. Like most of her endeavors, the founding of the federation was influenced by her temperance work. In this instance, the federation developed as a result of the efforts of thirty WCTU organizations to arouse greater interest in the temperance movement among African Americans in New Jersey.

Randolph's philosophy had a great impact on the work of the federation in its early years. As its founder and first president (from 1915 to 1927), and in later roles as president emeritus and board of trustees member, she continued to influence the organization's structure and policies. Moreover, Randolph's position as the national chaplain of the National Association of Colored Women (NACW) provided her with added leverage and clout. Finally, she also served for a number of years as state president of the Temperance Union League, an organization that included both black and white women.

Randolph skillfully used politics to effect change. The New Jersey federation established contacts and made known its concerns to elected state and national officials. It conducted studies of legislation pertinent to race and gender issues, and its members were encouraged to seek appointments to key boards and commissions where they could influence policy-making. Letters and appeals articulating the federation's concerns were sent to key political figures, and the press was adeptly used to publicize its activities and causes.

The New Jersey federation became involved in a number of other activities during Randolph's tenure as well. The organization launched fundraising for student scholarships, established homes for underprivileged girls, demanded greater media coverage about African Americans, appealed to Congress to enforce the Fourteenth and Fifteenth amendments, and lobbied the attorney general and the Department of Justice to abolish peonage (a system wherein debtors are bound in servitude to their creditors until their debts are paid).

Randolph's feminist leadership displayed itself in her work as a suffragist for the passage of the Nineteenth Amendment and in other diverse efforts to elevate the status of women, particularly African-American women. For years she served as a member of the executive board of the New Jersey State Suffrage Association. A key player in securing ratification of the suffrage amendment, Randolph spoke before the state legislature on its behalf.

- *Randolph*

Works for

Women's

Suffrage

An ardent believer in the importance of learning black history, Randolph actively supported the Association for the Study of Negro Life and History. The New Jersey federation was among the first of the New Jersey organizations to champion the significance of African American history and to sponsor programs during Negro History Week.

Outspoken in her beliefs about racism and sexism, and untiring in her efforts to help the needy, Florence Spearing Randolph was a major figure in the early twentieth century. Her unflagging commitment to ideals of equality and temperance greatly influenced the lives of blacks—and all Americans.

**Profile by
Bettye
Collier-Thomas**

SYLVIA M. RHONE

If it were not for a rigid dress code that Sylvia Rhone encountered

early in her professional career, she might never have reached her

station as a powerful record company executive. Sylvia Rhone initially

dreamed of becoming a financial high roller. Armed with a degree in

economics from Wharton School of Finance and Commerce at the

University of Pennsylvania, Rhone had no trouble securing a marketing

specialist position at Bankers Trust of New York. She lasted only nine

months, though, because her preference for casual dress caused a

problem. As she told Ebony, "I wore pants to work and all eyebrows

turned up. No one actually said anything but they made it clear that

what I'd done was unacceptable" (Norment, Ebony, 14).

1952– •

Record •

company

executive

The trust company's position hastened Rhone's departure from the world of high finance and her entry into the field of commercial music, a move that seemed a reckless venture to many who knew Rhone. Taking a drastic pay cut, Rhone secured an entry-level position at a well-known record company. The position enabled her to get hands-on experience in the promotional end of the music business. From this lowly start, Rhone rapidly moved up the ladder, becoming a top administrator at three leading record companies. In 1994 Rhone was promoted to the position of chairperson of the new Elektra/EastWest Company, thus becoming the first black woman to be appointed head of a major record label.

A native of Philadelphia, Sylvia M. Rhone was born on March 11, 1952, to James and Marie Christmas Rhone. While growing up in Harlem, she was an avid music fan who spent many youthful hours singing Aretha Franklin hits into her hairbrush. She graduated from college in 1974.

After discovering that she did not want banking to be her life's work, Rhone made a career decision based in part on her passionate love for music. She took a fifteen-thousand-dollar pay cut to start at the bottom of the record industry. Rhone accepted a secretarial position at Buddah Records, an independent company that once had distribution arrangements with such companies as Arista and Curtom. Buddah also boasted notable recording artists at one time or another, including the Edwin Hawkins Singers, Phyllis Hyman, Melba Moore, Gladys Knight and the Pips, the Isley Brothers, and—after a shake-up at the Motown label—the gifted writer and musician team of Holland-Dozier-Holland. As a marketing specialist, Rhone could have secured a much higher-level job, but she decided that the experience would be worth the financial sacrifice.

In a *Black Enterprise* interview, Rhone commented that "from the moment I sat in my new chair, I knew I was cut out for this business" (Baskerville, *Black Enterprise,* 76). Because she was attentive to the inner workings of the record company, Rhone was soon able to utilize her education in ways beneficial to Buddah. Within a year she was elevated to the position of promotions coordinator, which led to a more prestigious job. She became the national promotions director for a small, independent label. Although the label soon folded, Rhone gained valuable experience there that enabled her to become a regional promoter for other independent labels. Her uncanny ability to discover and mold new black talent came to the notice of Atlantic Records, which had once been a giant in the record industry with such stars as Aretha Franklin and Otis Redding under contract.

Atlantic's star was on the wane, though, and its black music division had fallen into woeful condition. A money-loser for several years, the division's once stellar roster of black stars had also disintegrated into a sad shadow of its former stature. Despite many warnings from her industry peers, Rhone accepted the offer to become director of Atlantic's Black Music in 1985. The impetus for her decision was her memory of the company's heyday when, as a Harlem teenager, she was an Aretha "wannabe."

Rhone was determined to restore the division to its former glory. Those who doubted Rhone's ability to meet such a challenge were soon silenced as she launched her quest to make Atlantic and black music once again synonymous. She began by changing the way the company marketed its acts and by developing new and exciting acts.

Within the year, Rhone was named vice-president and general manager of Atlantic's black music operations. Shortly thereafter, she was promoted to senior vice-president of the company. Atlantic's chairman, Ahmet Ertegun, explained her rapid rise in the November 1988 *Ebony:* "Under her expert guidance, our commitment to Black music has seen a revitalization marked by innovation, imagination and freshness. This is a well-deserved promotion for a most gifted woman" (Randolph, *Ebony*).

Rhone became senior vice-president in 1986, and in 1987, Atlantic's black music division showed a profit. In 1988 the records of two of Rhone's protégés were number one: Gerald Albright saw his first LP, *So Amazing,* go to number one on the jazz charts, while a new group called Troop saw its first single go to number one.

In 1991 Rhone's trailblazing achievements were rewarded when she was named co-president and chief executive officer of her own label under the auspices of Atlantic. At EastWest Records America she oversaw her label's recruitment, marketing, and promotion of recording artists with the assistance of a forty-seven-person staff. In *Black Enterprise,* she described the new label as being "very similar to a boutique label . . . [where] we want to keep the register down to a manageable size of 25 to 30 releases per year" (Baskerville, *Black Enterprise,* 76). That same year Rhone became chairperson and chief executive officer of the newly formed Atco-EastWest label, which encompassed rock, pop, R&B, jazz, and rap. The new position added forty acts, black and white, to her artist roster.

Rhone Heads •

Her Own

Record Label

At the "Jack the Ripper" fifteenth annual convention and reunion, an August 1991 Atlanta event, Rhone was honored as one of four black heads of major record labels owned by America's leading record companies. The other award winners were men: Jheryl Busby (Motown),

Ed Eckstine (Mercury), and Ernie Singleton (MCA). During her acceptance speech, Rhone took note of their stature: "It shows that African-Americans can not only create music, but control it as well. The world is watching us" (Vaughn, *Black Enterprise*).

Rhone not only oversaw the development of artists who recorded for her label, she participated as well in corporate ventures designed to showcase the contributions of black musicians in new and innovative ways. Atlantic Records, EastWest Records, and the Warner Music Group initiated a lecture series entitled "Our Roots Run Deep" in honor of Black History Month.

This innovative marketing scheme, designed to highlight and publicize black music, showed another facet of the savvy of Rhone, who was promoted again—to chairperson of Elektra/EastWest—during the summer of 1994. As the head of the new Elektra/EastWest Company, Rhone assumed sole responsibility for the recording businesses of Elektra, Asylum, EastWest, and their associated labels. These labels hold contracts with nearly two hundred acts and report annual revenues in the hundreds of millions of dollars.

Over the course of twenty years Rhone has made an astonishing transition from secretary to corporate executive officer. But as Rhone recalled in *Rolling Stone,* the journey was not all champagne and roses:

**Profile by
Dolores Nicholson**

> A glass ceiling definitely still exists, but I think it's being shattered everyday.... Those of us as minorities who break through the glass ceiling do get some scratches along the way . . . but I think there is definitely social change and headway being made. Some companies may hold out for a time, maintaining that archaic view of women as unsuitable executive material, but those old philosophies are changing drastically (Ali, *Rolling Stone*).

LINDA JOHNSON RICE

1958– •

*L*inda Johnson Rice is president and chief operating officer of

Johnson Publishing Company in Chicago. One of the few black women

publishing company executives in America, she has over sixteen years **Publishing** •

experience with her father's thriving $306 million company, which is **company**

the parent corporation for such popular publications as Ebony and Jet **executive**

magazines. Determined to show America the first-rate character of the

Chicago-based, family-owned Johnson Publishing, Rice has indicated

that the company plans to continue to add new life to its magazines as it

also investigates expansion of its cosmetics and broadcasting interests. A

tireless proponent of the business, Rice is excited about the prospect of

guiding the company in the twenty-first century as

its future chief executive officer.

Linda Johnson Rice was born on March 22, 1958. Her father, John H. Johnson, started his company in 1942 with an investment of $500 that he secured from mortgaging his mother's furniture. He used the sum to launch the publication of *Negro Digest*. From this humble start, Johnson built "an empire in publishing, broadcasting, cosmetics, hair care, and, in a separate company, life insurance" (Therrien, *Business Week*, 40). Johnson's wife Eunice serves as *Ebony*'s fashion editor as well as director of their traveling fashion show, *Ebony* Fashion Fair.

Rice's older brother, John, died of sickle-cell anemia at age twenty-five, leaving his sister as sole heir to the Johnson empire. *Working Woman*'s Renee Edelman says that he was "never a rival for a role in the company," for he preferred photography and sports to publishing.

Rice entered the family business with enthusiasm. Her apprenticeship with the company began with frequent visits to the office from the time she was six years old. As she grew, her mother began to take her to fashion shows in Paris, and these trips continued throughout Rice's teenage and college days. Rice worked as a summer intern during her undergraduate years and completed a bachelor's degree in journalism from the University of Southern California. At age twenty-three she went overseas to choose clothes for *Ebony* Fashion Fair, this time alone. As she later told *Working Woman*, that solo journey was an important one for her self-confidence: "That was a turning point.... I saw I could do it" (Edelman, *Working Woman*).

Rice's first full-time position with Johnson Publishing Company was vice-president and fashion coordinator. Later, as her title was changed to vice-president and assistant to the publisher, Rice was able to use and enhance skills that she had acquired as an intern. Learning directly from her CEO father and mentor, she became familiar with all aspects of his empire. To enhance her hands-on experience in the office, she enrolled at Northwestern University's J. L. Kellogg Graduate School of Management. The MBA program taught her how to tackle business problems from an analytical point of view and to create innovative solutions for them. She graduated in 1987 and was promoted to president and chief operating officer of Johnson Publishing Company on June 20 of that year.

As president, one of Rice's favorite duties is attending editorial meetings. "It is the creative process that I find stimulating, sitting down and letting the ideas flow among the different groups. I love the interaction with people. To me that's the best part. I'm a people-oriented person" (Norment, *Ebony*). She stresses the importance of

Becomes •

Publishing

Company

Executive

bringing fresh young talent to the company and seeking new ideas for the business world, particularly for black-owned companies. "In regards to Black people, we have a treasure trove of information that nobody else really has. And we haven't really capitalized on that enough" (Norment, *Ebony*).

Rice-inspired initiatives in recent years have included a decision to highlight international opportunities for the company. The Fashion Fair Cosmetics line, for example, with its overseas offices in London and Paris, is a means to tap the international market of black women. Rice believes that the company's cosmetics business will grow into a major global player in the industry. Her frequent business trips to Europe with her mother gave Rice the ability to see such new horizons of untapped opportunity. Rice has also been instrumental in the development of Eboné Cosmetics for the mass market and "E-Style" Catalog, a joint venture with the Spiegel company.

Rice's work has attracted notice from the corporate boards of Bausch and Lomb, the Dial Corporation, and Kimberly Clark. Her interaction with other corporate leaders has helped her to see her own work in a broader perspective. Her mother's advice—to have a sense of humor about herself—has also helped Rice over the years. She does not merely limit her work to the boardroom and executive offices; she once worked behind the counter to promote Fashion Fair products. As she noted to *Business Week,* "sales skyrocketed during her one-hour stint at a Chicago store" (Therrien, *Business Week,* 40).

Rice long ago recognized that the image she conveyed would be an important element in the ultimate success that she and the Johnson Publishing Company enjoyed: "Every time I make an appearance somewhere, every time I make a speech, I'm selling the image of Johnson Publishing Co. I'm selling the image of Fashion Fair cosmetics, I'm selling the image of the Ebony Fashion Fair. I am constantly selling" (Norment, *Ebony*).

The "constant selling" has not been in vain. Known as a vibrant, energetic worker, who, influenced by European fashion, "eschews gray pinstripes for bright colors, polka dots, and slacks" (Therrien, *Business Week,* 40), Rice admits to being a "clothes horse," and her fashion sense reflects her management style: individual, creative, and eye-catching.

**Profile by
Erica L. Griffin**

KAY GEORGE ROBERTS

*K*ay Roberts is one of a select group of black symphony orchestra

1950– •

conductors. The first woman and second black to earn the doctor of

musical arts degree in conducting from Yale University School of Music,

Conductor, •

Roberts is equally well-trained and experienced as a violinist. While her

violinist,

professional conducting assignments have increased, she has contin-

educator

ued her responsibilities as professor of music and conductor of the

University Orchestra at the University of Massachusetts at Lowell, a

position she has held since 1978.

Journalists have often written about Roberts's success against all odds. But as she explained in *Emerge* magazine, "I feel confident enough that my background and my education and my skills, and what I bring to the performance, are accomplished; that I've earned it.... It's not usual to have a woman conducting. [But] I don't think about being in the minority; I just try to get my job done" (Grant, *Emerge*).

Kay George Roberts was born on September 16, 1950, in Nashville, Tennessee. Her father, S. Oliver Roberts, was a founder and chairperson of Fisk University's Department of Psychology. Her mother, Marion Pearl Taylor Roberts, was a librarian at Tennessee State and Fisk universities.

Music was a constant companion during Roberts's childhood. Her mother played the piano, and Tennessee State and Fisk universities offered the community the best of music with their Lyceum Series. It was in the segregated Nashville elementary public schools that Roberts encountered Robert Holmes, a public school teacher who convinced the Nashville public school music supervisor that black children deserved an opportunity to enjoy the experience of making music on string instruments, an experience readily available to children of other racial and ethnic groups. Since no string ensemble opportunities were available to black youngsters, Holmes organized the Cremona Strings for black youth in 1958. Violin study for Roberts began when she was in the fourth grade; she showed tremendous potential, and Holmes soon brought her into the ensemble.

With the arrival of Nashville Symphony music director Thor Johnson, the doors of the Nashville Youth Symphony were opened to blacks in 1964. Roberts's successful audition gained her admittance. In 1967 and 1968, during her senior year in high school, Roberts was invited to join the parent ensemble, the Nashville Symphony. She remained with this organization throughout her college years at Fisk University.

In 1971 maestro Arthur Fiedler of the Boston Pops Orchestra organized the World Symphony Orchestra, and Roberts represented the Nashville Symphony upon the recommendation of Thor Johnson. She continued her music studies during this period as well, and the World Symphony Orchestra appearance proved to be only the first of many subsequent concert performances over the next several years.

Although she was a cum laude graduate in music from Fisk University in 1972, Roberts entered Fisk as a mathematics major, changing to music only upon entering her junior year. In 1972 she entered the Yale University School of Music in pursuit of the master of music degree in violin performance, which she received in 1975. During her second year of residency, she enrolled in her first conducting class. It soon became clear that she had a flair with the conductor's baton. This early success represented the beginning of a shift in her career direction.

From Performing •

to Conducting

Between the years 1973 and 1978, Roberts received several prestigious grants and fellowships. In 1976 she received master of musical arts recognition in both conducting and violin performance from Yale.

During the 1975–76 season, Yale conducting instructor Otto-Werner Mueller gave Roberts the opportunity to rehearse both the Atlanta and Nashville symphony orchestras in Gustav Mahler's Symphony No. 1. The same season, Roberts made a successful professional conducting debut as guest conductor of her hometown orchestra, the Nashville Symphony.

Prior to receiving the D.M.A. in 1986, Roberts set out to further "demonstrate her qualifications through distinguished achievement." She became an active participant in conducting workshops and seminars and choral institutes. She studied conducting with Murry Sidlin, Gustav Meier, and Margaret Hillis, and participated in master classes with Seiji Ozawa, Andre Previn, Leonard Bernstein, Edo de Waart, and the African American Denis de Coteau of the San Francisco Ballet.

Roberts accepted a position of assistant professor of music and conductor of the university orchestra at the University of Lowell (now the University of Massachusetts at Lowell) in 1978. During this time she also served as assistant conductor of the Mystic Valley Chamber Orchestra (1983–84) and the Greater Boston Youth Symphony Orchestra (1984–85), and she made several guest conductor appearances elsewhere as well. In 1982 she assumed the leadership of the New Hampshire Philharmonic Orchestra, remaining at the helm until 1987. Utilizing her administrative skills, she also served as executive director of Boston's Project STEP (String Training and Educational Program for Minority Students), sponsored by several area symphonies, from 1984 to 1985.

With the doctor of musical arts degree in hand in May 1986, Roberts's conducting activities accelerated, and she was promoted to full professor at Lowell in 1987. Roberts was also selected for the position of music director and conductor of the Cape Ann (Massachusetts) Symphony in 1986. Both orchestras, being community organizations, presented tremendous challenges to their artistic leader. Roberts, though, was up to the task, and she remained at the helm of the Cape Ann Symphony through the 1987–88 season.

Roberts also was offered an opportunity to conduct the Bangkok Symphony Orchestra in Thailand during the summer of 1986. She thus became the first woman and first black to conduct the four-year-old Bangkok Symphony, consisting primarily of musicians from the Royal Thai Navy. Roberts was invited back to conduct the same orchestra in 1987. The concert honored the King of Thailand on his sixtieth birthday. Entitled "From Classical Favorites to Jazz," the celebration was publicized as one of the most important cultural events of the year. The *Bangkok Press* commented: "The concert was one of the best of its kind in a long time and there was little doubt that conductor Kay George

Roberts was behind the success, drawing life out of an orchestra not always known to perform with spirit."

In July 1987 Roberts made her New York City debut, conducting the New York City Housing Authority Symphony Orchestra in Damrosch Park. She conducted the orchestra on several subsequent occasions, including performances at Alice Tully Hall, Lincoln Center in New York City, and Klein Memorial Hall in Bridgeport, Connecticut.

In 1989 Roberts conducted the Detroit Symphony and its "A Celebration of African-American Sacred Music" program. She returned to Detroit during the summer of 1989 to conduct the orchestra in a park concert. During the same year, Roberts conducted a chamber ensemble in a performance of Gloria Coates's "Voices of Women in Wartime" as a part of the American Women Composers Fourth Annual Marathon in Watertown, Massachusetts.

Roberts spent the 1989–90 academic year on sabbatical in Germany, where she was appointed conductor of the Artemis Ensemble, an ensemble that performs and records works by women composers. She also founded Ensemble Americana, a professional chamber group that performs and promotes contemporary American music in Germany. She continues to maintain a relationship with Ensemble Americana today.

The Black Music Repertory Ensemble, organized in 1988, was formed "to promote appreciation for the black musical heritage written between 1800 and the present." It made its New York City debut in September 1990, with Roberts at the podium. The following day, she appeared with the group on national television, making an appearance on the *Today Show*.

As she had done throughout her career, Roberts was actively involved in youth music programs during the late 1980s and early 1990s. She contributed to the music programs of numerous orchestras and organizations, excited to be able to share her passion for music with younger people.

Conducts •

Cleveland

Symphony

Orchestra

The year 1993 provided more opportunities and achievements for Roberts. She continued her work in Germany, and accepted another invitation to conduct the Nashville Symphony. She also led the Cleveland Symphony Orchestra—one of the premier orchestras in the country—in its Annual Martin Luther King Jr. Concert in January 1993. As the concert unfolded, it was clear that the audience's initial enthusiastic reception for Roberts was not premature, for she led the symphony through a masterful performance.

In 1994 Roberts was invited to join the conducting roster of Shaw Concerts of New York City, the management agency that handles the career of international superstar soprano Jessye Norman. She also made January 1994 and April 1994 appearances with the Cleveland Orchestra, conducted the orchestra at the Cleveland Institute of Music, and wielded the baton for the Savannah Symphony Orchestra.

Roberts has been the recipient of many prestigious awards and honors over the years, although it is often stated that a conductor's career does not really bloom until he or she reaches age forty. Having reached the magic number, Roberts seems guaranteed greater achievements, although minority women often seem to be the last to be considered when an opening develops at an orchestral podium. European and American white men, and even white women, seem to enjoy more immediate consideration. Roberts, though, "a minority within a minority," remains unphased by this imbalance. Committed to the music of black and women composers, as well as contemporary American music, she is equally committed to the standard orchestral repertoire. Her guest conducting appearances are generally preceded by a focus on her racial and gender identity, but she seeks to be remembered simply as a qualified conductor who brings a new look to the podium and a different perspective to the music.

**Profile by
D. Antoinette
Handy**

LEAH J. SEARS-COLLINS

eah J. Sears-Collins is the youngest person and the first woman to

sit on the Georgia Supreme Court. The first black woman trial lawyer in

Georgia, she won election to the Fulton County Superior Court prior to

her state supreme court appointment, making her the first black woman

to win a statewide election in Georgia. Her career has served as a

powerful symbol of the evolution of the Georgia Supreme Court and the

state as a whole.

1955– •

Lawyer, judge, •

state supreme

court justice

Born in Heidelberg, Germany, on June 13, 1955, to Onnye Jean Roundtree Sears, an elementary school teacher, and Thomas Sears, an army colonel, Leah J. Sears-Collins was the second child in a family with three children. After Leah's birth, her father's career in the military necessitated frequent family moves to various places in the United States and around the world. Eventually they settled in Savannah, Georgia, where her father was stationed when he retired.

The inequities in American society became apparent to Sears-Collins at an early age. In a *National Law Journal* article she recalled

riding through Harlem at the age of four and wondering, "Why do the brown people here live so poorly? That was the moment I came to realize there was such a problem with race in this world. That one scene has always replayed in my mind" (Curriden, *National Law Journal*, 27).

At five years old Sears-Collins enrolled in the public school system of northern California. In 1960 Monterey Elementary School's student body was almost entirely white, as were most of the other schools she and her brothers attended. The one exception occurred when the family moved to Washington, D.C. As a third grader she attended an all-black school because her parents wanted her to experience her own culture.

The Sears family moved to Savannah, Georgia, in 1968, when Leah was in eighth grade. She attended Bartlett Junior High School and later transferred to Wilder. Sears-Collins recalls no particularly unpleasant experiences at either of these schools even though they were mostly white, southern, and newly integrated. Because she was accepted, loved, and encouraged by her family, Sears-Collins had the self-confidence to expect success whatever the circumstances. This attitude led her to academic achievement and active participation in school activities.

When Sears-Collins transferred to Savannah High School she became the school's first African-American cheerleader. She recalls that her experiences in the mostly white high school were difficult in ways she was then too young to comprehend. Her activities inevitably brought added pressure, for she was sometimes forced to confront racism without the support of other blacks. Even when all appeared well on the surface, there were subtle and unspoken challenges to her intelligence based on skin color. Despite these obstacles, she maintained excellent grades and graduated in May 1972.

When it was time for college, Sears-Collins confesses that she wanted to spread her wings and go as far away from home as she possibly could. Swayed by the full-tuition scholarship offered by Cornell, Sears-Collins headed north for four years of undergraduate education. At Cornell she was one of about 1,500 other African-American students. While still a minority of the school's student population, the number of black students was still far greater than she had been used to.

As a student Sears-Collins wrote poetry, became involved in the black and women's studies movements on campus, and decided to major in human development and family studies. Although her mother had been a member of Alpha Kappa Alpha Sorority, she refused to join the historically black sorority at the time because she thought Alpha

Kappa Alpha was not black enough and that it was not politically correct to be "Greek." To please her mother, however, she later pledged a graduate chapter of the sorority.

In June 1976, Sears-Collins graduated with honors from Cornell. On July 3 she married Love Collins III, a young cadet she met at Cornell when he came to run track for West Point, where he was enrolled. Leah and Love exchanged wedding vows and names, with her taking her husband's name and keeping her family's and him keeping his family name and adding hers to it. Love Sears-Collins was stationed in Columbus, Georgia, but at the end of August, Leah Sears-Collins departed for Duke University Law School in North Carolina. This time she found herself too far from home. After only five weeks at Duke, the newlywed dropped out and returned to Columbus to join her husband.

Sears-Collins became a feature writer for the *Columbus Ledger* for a year. In August 1977 she entered Emory University Law School in Atlanta, a school with no African-American professors or administrators in the law school. Her experience at Emory proved unpleasant. In addition to the long hours she spent studying, she was frustrated by the distance she and her husband had to commute to see each other on the weekends. They made the sacrifice, however, and Sears-Collins graduated from Emory University Law School in 1980. Admitted to practice law in Georgia in 1980, at the age of twenty-five, Sears-Collins faced a future full of promise.

• Lawyer

Becomes

Superior Court

Judge

Sears-Collins joined the large and prestigious Atlanta law firm of Alston and Bird in 1980, where she practiced business and intellectual-property law. Her time with the firm, though, was less than scintillating. As she later told *Barrister Magazine*, her position involved "too much paperwork, not enough people work" (Curriden, *Barrister Magazine*, 20). In 1982 she quit this job in order to take a much lower-paying position as a traffic judge in Atlanta city court.

In the 1980s Sears-Collins devoted a lot of her energy toward home. In June 1983 her son Addison Sears-Collins was born, and in December 1986 she gave birth to a daughter, Brennan, named for U.S. Supreme Court Justice William Brennan. She continued to build her career as well, though, and in 1988 Sears-Collins decided to run for a seat on the Fulton County Superior Court.

In a close three-way race, Sears-Collins emerged the winner, replacing a judge who had retired. She thus became the youngest person ever elected to a superior court judgeship in Georgia and the first African-American woman in the history of the Georgia superior court. During her term, Sears-Collins established herself as an energetic, hardworking, scholarly, and caring judge who did not "flip-flop on issues just because of the political whims of the times" (Sears-Collins, interview).

Sears-Collins legal articles during this time illustrated her dislike for complicated legal language. Her own articles, which have appeared in the *National Law Journal, Court Review,* and the *Atlanta Lawyer,* are clear and concise, and illustrate her feeling that lawyers have an obligation to be sure their clients understand legal documents.

Politically, Sears-Collins has been described as both moderate and conservative, while the judge views herself as a political moderate. A supporter of the presidency of Ronald Reagan, she nonetheless considers herself a Democrat. Not morally opposed to capital punishment, Sears-Collins is concerned about the apparent role race plays in the prosecutor's decision to seek the death penalty.

On Monday morning, February 17, 1992, Sears-Collins was in her office at the superior court when she received a telephone call from Georgia's governor, Zell Miller. He announced that he was appointing her to the Georgia Supreme Court. Sears-Collins thus became, at age thirty-six, the youngest person and the first woman ever to sit on Georgia's highest court. In a press release that accompanied Miller's announcement, the governor indicated that he chose Leah Sears-Collins "because she possesses in abundance the qualities an outstanding jurist should have: intellect, temperament and energy." She was sworn in on March 6, 1992. As an African American, a woman, and a young mother of two children, Sears-Collins brought diversity to Georgia's highest court.

Governor's Call •

Leads to

Supreme Court

With a career that demands hard work and long hours, Sears-Collins's life as a judge, mother, and wife is one of juggling priorities and time schedules and relying on frozen foods. Sears-Collins notes that she is no superwoman. Instead, she muddles along like most working women, balancing the needs of her family with the time-consuming responsibilities of her job.

Over the course of her professional life, Sears-Collins has received numerous legal and civic awards. She also holds membership in numerous professional and civic organizations. She and her family are members of Ebenezer Baptist Church in Atlanta. Her hobbies include writing, and her favorite book is *Little House on the Prairie.*

Leah Sears-Collins's moderate political philosophy garners her support from a cross section of Georgia citizens. Although she may not want to be known as a black judge or a woman judge, she acknowledges that she "had to work harder, think faster, be more involved in bar issues, just to prove I belong on this court" (Sears-Collins, telephone interview). She is thus proud of her accomplishments, and cognizant of its meaning for many Americans. "I want my appointment to stand for what America should be. America is a wonderful combination of people from every race and every ethnic background, both genders, all moving ahead, working together, and I want this country to get over this separation; you know, being a woman is an alien kind of thing, as being black is."

**Profile by
Nagueyalti Warren**

BETTY SHABAZZ

W idow of the preeminent civil rights fighter Malcolm X (El Hajji

Malik Shabazz), Betty Shabazz was the mother of four girls and

pregnant with two more when she witnessed the assassination of her

husband on February 21, 1965, in the Audubon Ballroom in New York

City. A remarkable woman who possesses great strength and determina-

tion, Shabazz successfully raised her six daughters while continuing her

education (she received a Ph.D. degree in 1975). She has been instru-

mental in perpetuating the true legacy and memory of Malcolm X, and

has been an inspiration to the countless young people who want to carry

on the struggle against the oppression of black people.

1936–

Educator, nurse,

community

activist

Betty Shabazz was born in 1936. She was reared in Detroit, Michi-

gan, by foster parents who apparently adopted her, and attended Northern High School. During her childhood and young adulthood she seldom thought about the outside world and her relationship to it. As she told *Essence* magazine in 1992, "I was not that exposed at the time I met Malcolm, nor did I have a lot of experience in the challenges that women face. Pick a week out of my life. If you understood that week, you understood my life. I went to school from Monday to Friday. On Friday I went to the movies. On Saturday I was at my parents' store. On Sunday I went to church" (Shabazz, *Essence*).

Shabazz attended Tuskegee Institute in Alabama, which was her father's alma mater. She left Tuskegee, though, to go to nursing school in New York City. She disliked Tuskegee because she experienced hostility in Alabama from whites, an issue her parents did not want to deal with; they thought her departure was her own fault.

Shabazz met Malcolm X in her junior year when she was invited by a friend to attend a lecture at Temple Seven in Harlem. The first time Shabazz saw Malcolm X, she was immediately impressed with his clean-cut, no-nonsense, and focused demeanor. At the time, she felt that somehow she knew him: "I felt that somewhere in life I had met this energy before" (Shabazz, *Essence*).

As time passed, the relationship between Shabazz and Malcolm X grew stronger. She began to teach a women's class at Temple Seven, and Malcolm X advised her on what matters to stress. She typed and corrected papers for him as well. Shabazz recalled that "he would actively seek me out, ask me questions. He was different. He was refreshing, but I never suspected that he thought of me in any way other than as a sister who was interested in the Movement.... There were too many people in line for his attention (Shabazz, *Essence*).

Begins Work •

with Malcolm X

at Temple Seven

Shabazz eventually discovered, though, that Malcolm X was very attracted to her. She later recollected, "I knew he loved me for my clear brown skin—it was very smooth. He liked my clear eyes. He liked my gleaming dark hair. I was very thin then, and he liked my Black beauty, my mind. He just liked me." They had an unusual courtship; Shabazz, a Methodist, never "dated" Malcolm X, a Muslim, because at the time single men and women of the Muslim faith did not "fraternize," as they called it. Men and women always went out in groups.

Even with such restrictions in place, though, their attraction to one another grew. One night Malcolm X called Shabazz from Detroit, their hometown, and proposed to her. While her parents liked Malcolm X and thought he was a nice young man, they objected to the marriage because he was older and belonged to a different religion. Shabazz defied her parents and eloped. At some point after her marriage, Shabazz converted to Islam.

In retrospect, Shabazz describes her seven years of marriage to Malcolm X as hectic, holistic, beautiful, and unforgettable. He was a good husband and father to their daughters, and they had "the kind of life that one reads about, plans for or wishes for between a man and a woman.... I was destined to be with Malcolm. And I think that Malcolm probably needed me more than I needed him—to support his life's mission" (Shabazz, *Essence*).

Shabazz was unable to sleep for three weeks following her husband's assassination. She traveled to Mecca, where she sought solace and looked for meaning in her shattered life.

> I really don't know where I'd be today if I had not gone to Mecca to make Hajj [a pilgrimmage] shortly after Malcolm was assassinated.... Going to Mecca, making Hajj, was very good for me because it made me think of all the people in the world who loved me and were for me, who prayed that I would get my life back together. I stopped focusing on the people who were trying to tear me and my family apart (Shabazz, *Essence*).

After the death of Malcolm X, Shabazz devoted virtually all of her time and energy to raising their six daughters (Attallah, Quibilah, Illyasah, Gamilah, Malaak, and Malikah) according to their father's principles and ideas. She gave them a well-rounded education and sought to instill in them a sense of ethnic responsibility for themselves, their people, and the broader society. For example, they studied Arabic and French and attended ballet classes in addition to taking black history courses. She also encouraged them to travel so they could learn more about Africa, the West Indies, and the Middle East.

• Activist

Becomes

National Figure

Shabazz received an R.N. degree from the Brooklyn State Hospital School of Nursing, a B.A. in public health education from Jersey City State College, and became a certified school nurse. In 1975 she earned her Ph.D. in school administration and curriculum development from the University of Massachusetts at Amherst. She is now a professor of health administration at Medgar Evers College, Brooklyn, New York, and serves as the college's director of institutional advancement and public relations.

Even though Shabazz is essentially a private person and considers herself a follower rather than a leader, she has become a national figure. She is in constant demand for speaking engagements across the country, and has received many honors, tributes, and prestigious awards, including the Congressional Record Award for her community service. A one-time radio talk show host, she has also made guest appearances on a number of radio and television shows. In addition, Shabazz works with Columbia Medical School on the Malcolm X Medical Scholarship Program for African-American students.

Shabazz has become an inspiration to young people as well as an advocate for their proper development. She challenges parents to be good role models for their children and to provide them with guidelines. A strong believer that parents should take chief responsibility for passing on black cultural traditions to their children, Shabazz also contends that parents have a spiritual and moral duty to teach their children to help oppressed people. In a speech before the National Urban League in 1990, for instance, Shabazz urged the audience to "sponsor our children . . . call newspapers and TV stations to complain about the way African-American children are portrayed.... We have to give them pride in their own culture, their roots, but we must make these decisions for children, not let them make too many careless ones on their own" (Connors, *Amsterdam News*).

Shabazz emphasizes to parents and educators the importance of teaching young people in such a way that they understand that the twenty-first century will be a century of self-sufficiency. In Shabazz's view, young people need to learn that they have to make things happen for themselves. Like Malcolm X, Shabazz cares deeply about the struggle of people of African descent in the United States:

> We have been in this country so long and have made such a vast contribution, not only with our lives but in terms of development, invention and contributions. Other ethnic groups have come to America and are automatically treated as citizens with all rights and privileges, and somehow, African descendants still are struggling. Other ethnic groups can receive money for reparations, and yet, with our several hundred years of free labor and the additional years of unfair compensation for our labor, we have not received the rights and privileges of other ethnic groups.... However, I don't know of an ethnic group that is more powerful, that has made such contributions, that has been as tolerant and that still is willing to share and to do and to be.... We're a good people (Mandulor, *City Sun*).

Shabazz also firmly believes that black women have had an immeasurably positive impact on America. "Given our resources and limited opportunities and options, Black women in America . . . are functioning at a remarkable high level, and compete on any level with women of the world," she told the *City Sun*. "She tries very hard to be her own best friend and advise others to do the same.... Love yourself, appreciate yourself, see the good in you, see the God in you and respect yourself (Mandulor, *City Sun*).

As Shabazz continues her activist efforts on behalf of the black community, she maintains her connection to the energy of the universe around her. "And then, too, there's Malcolm's energy and his spirit," she said. "I don't feel sad. I feel fortunate. I feel very blessed spiritually. My soul is at peace. My heart is full of concern and love, and I understand the meaning of my own life and the lives of others. So, no, no, I'm never alone. I'm never cut off (Mandulor, *City Sun*)."

Profile by
Bobbie T. Pollard

JEANNE C. SINKFORD

*J*eanne C. Sinkford, dean emeritus of the Howard University College

of Dentistry, is a distinguished administrator, educator, researcher,

lecturer, and clinician who broke race and gender barriers in her rise to

the top of her profession. The first woman dean of an American dental

school, Sinkford has reached out and responded in full to the demands

of her profession, striving to meet the needs of her patients and students

as well as those of various dental research associations and government

and community groups devoted to dental education and study. Sinkford

has also been widely praised for her efforts to recruit women and

minority students to the dental profession and her other community

efforts.

1933– •

Dentist, •

college

administrator

One of four daughters of Richard E. Craig and Geneva Jefferson Craig, Jeanne Frances Craig Sinkford was born on January 30, 1933, in Washington, D.C. Education was very important to the Craig family, and young Jeanne Sinkford studied ballet and dance for eight years. As she honed her talent, she received a scholarship offer for extended training in New York City, but her parents responded with a firm refusal when she told them of her plans to quit high school and leave for New York. At sixteen years of age, Jeanne Sinkford finished Washington's Dunbar High School. Recalling her childhood, Sinkford noted that:

> I grew up in a loving home where religion was synonymous with life. My beliefs, therefore, centered around strong relationships among family members that have formed the basis for loving and concerned actions throughout my life. Dreams are a part of my early existence. My dreams later became desires for achievement and actions which demanded a life of order and discipline. Being a minority and a woman required a strong work ethic, a sense of morality and decency, a willingness to "turn the other cheek" and a sincere motivation to help those who are less fortunate and underprivileged (Sinkford, "Choose the High Road," *Legacy, the Dental Profession*).

Sinkford's family was not financially well off, but they worked out a "family plan" whereby the older girl would help the next in line upon finishing college. Sinkford's education took eight years, though, and her younger sister wound up helping her instead, even though Sinkford was awarded scholarships all the way through Howard University and worked during the summer. Sinkford majored in psychology and chemistry as a Phi Beta Kappa undergraduate at Howard University. When she was eighteen years old and a junior in college, she met and married a young medical student, Stanley M. Sinkford.

Jeanne Sinkford initially spurned medical school, fearing that she would be forced to compete with her husband. She considered graduate work in psychology or dental hygiene, but her family dentist convinced her that she had the perfect background for pursuing a doctor of dental surgery degree. Sinkford received her bachelor of science degree from Howard University in 1953 and her doctorate in dental surgery from the Howard University College of Dentistry in 1958, graduating first in her class. She stayed at Howard University and taught crown and bridge prosthodontics for two years before undertaking graduate study at Northwestern University in Chicago. Sinkford received the Louise C. Ball Graduate Fellowship Fund for Graduate Study in Dentistry, which supported her postdoctoral studies at Northwestern University. After her husband completed his military service in 1960, they moved to Chicago so she could begin her studies.

Sinkford studied under Stanley C. Harris at Northwestern's dental school, completing a master of science degree in 1962 and a Ph.D. in physiology in 1963. Sinkford taught for one year at Northwestern while her husband studied at the University of Chicago.

• *Few Women*

Seen in

Dentistry

When Sinkford entered dental school, only 1.2 percent of dental students in the United States were women. However, the women's liberation movement helped to open doors for women in dentistry, and changing funding and admission practices in the 1970s encouraged other women to enter the field.

Sinkford touts dentistry as a perfect career for women because of their sense of aesthetics and beauty, their ability to be sympathetic, and their small hands, which are helpful when working in delicate areas such as the mouth. Not surprisingly, she has actively recruited women and minorities to the profession. "Dr. Sinkford has been quite an inspiration," Renee McCoy-Collins, the first woman graduate from Howard's oral surgery program, emphasized in *Atlanta Daily World*. "The dean has been a perfect example of women's ability in dentistry" ("Women on the Rise in Dentistry," *Atlanta Daily World*).

Sinkford returned to Howard University in 1964 as chair of prosthodontics, the College of Dentistry's largest department. She was the first woman head of such a department in the country. Russell Dixon, the school's long-time dean of the College of Dentistry, selected her for the administrative post because of the leadership abilities he had seen in her. Sinkford then served as associate dean from 1967 to 1974 under Dean Joseph L. Henry.

On August 24, 1972, Sinkford was named to a nine-member panel to study a U.S. Public Health Service experiment that had begun in 1932. In this experiment, known as the Tuskegee Syphilis Study, four hundred African American men with syphilis went without medical aid for forty years in order to determine the effects of the disease on the human body. Sinkford has also served on numerous other review boards and has frequently answered the community's call for her expertise.

Sinkford was inducted into the International College of Dentists on November 9, 1974. She was the first African-American woman dentist inducted into the U.S.A. section of the college. At the time of her induction, Sinkford was on sabbatical leave pursuing a special program in pedodontics at Children's Hospital National Medical Center in Washington, D.C., where she worked on a patient-oriented treatment philosophy for the adolescent-age patient.

On July 1, 1975, Jeanne Sinkford was appointed dean of Howard University's College of Dentistry. Sinkford was the first woman to be appointed dean of any dental school in the nation. Her selection was still another indication that she was at the top of her profession, though she had long been aware of issues that sometimes arise when a professional woman is successful. "It takes a lot for a woman to be in a top position, particularly in a male profession," she said in 1968. "You have to be better to be accepted as equal. Once your colleagues accept you as a competent person, they don't mind your being there. But men are resentful at first because they feel a woman has been selected for a position they might have taken" ("Howard's First Lady of Dentistry," *Ebony*).

Sinkford served sixteen years as dean at Howard University. On July 1, 1991, she was named professor and dean emeritus of the Howard University College of Dentistry in recognition of her fine work. During her tenure, she often spoke and wrote about the crises and challenges of dental education. She also maintained an almost breathtakingly busy schedule. Her stint as dean included service on some seventeen university committees, ten local committees, twenty national or international committees, participation in eighteen professional and scientific societies, several honors and awards, and attendance at ten professional conferences.

On November 4, 1991, Sinkford became director of the Office of Women and Minority Affairs, American Association of Dental Schools, Washington, D.C. She also maintained her interest in writing, a talent that has resulted in several significant works, including a manual for fixed prosthodontics for undergraduate students and scores of professional articles. Her most significant contribution to dental education, however, was the nationally acclaimed background document for the Graduate Education Workshop, cosponsored by the American Dental Association and the American Association of Dental Schools.

Sinkford is a member of dozens of professional organizations and societies, including the American Prosthodontic Society, the International Association of Dental Research, Omicron Kappa Upsilon, the Institute of Medicine of the National Academy of Sciences, and the National Medical Association. She has served on the Council of Dental Education of the American Prosthodontic Society and worked for the American Association for the Advancement of Science. Finally, Sinkford holds fellowships in the American College of Dentists and the International College of Dentists.

As the years have passed, accolades for Sinkford's stellar career have proliferated. Schools, civic organizations, and dental and medical associations have all hailed her contributions to her profession and her community. Sinkford commented on the recognition that she has received over the years in *Legacy, the Dental Profession*:

> History has taught us that the great leaders of the world stirred the consciousness of men and thereby created monumental changes that the world would come to respect and to revere. I have been called a "black pioneer," a "renaissance woman," and a modern "Candace" for I have given many years of my life in dedication to the cause that social, cultural and educational inequities in our society can be overcome by forceful leadership and constant support for equal opportunity and civil liberty (Sinkford, *Legacy, the Dental Profession*).

After Sinkford's retirement, she became active in Jack and Jill of America and with her children's activities. She also turned her attention to the needs of a growing segment of the population, geriatric dental patients. Stanley Sinkford, her husband, continued as chief of pediatrics at D.C. General Hospital and professor of pediatrics at Howard University's College of Medicine.

**Profile by
Kathleen E. Bethel**

NORMA MERRICK SKLAREK

*"T*hings that are worthwhile and from which one receives great

satisfaction are never easy but require perseverance and hard work."

That wisdom, which came from her parents, has guided Norma Merrick

Sklarek throughout her life. The first black woman to be licensed as an

architect in New York and in California, Sklarek is a trailblazer. A

highly respected architect, she has built a distinguished career in which

she has overcome longstanding barriers to women and blacks.

1928– •

Architect •

Norma Merrick Sklarek was born on April 15, 1928, in New York City, to Walter Merrick and Amy (Willoughby) Merrick. Sklarek obtained her training in architecture at Barnard College of Columbia University, where she received a bachelor of architecture degree in 1950. Recalling her years at Barnard, she notes in *I Dream a World* that "I had never seen a T-square or a triangle before I entered the School of Architecture at Columbia University. I found throughout my experiences that if something is tough initially, after I work at it, I not only catch up but move on ahead" (Lanker, *I Dream a World,* 40).

After passing the rigorous four-day licensing examination in New York on her first attempt in 1954, Sklarek was hired in 1955 to work for the prestigious New York City architectural firm of Skidmore, Owens, Merrill, where she remained for five years. While in New York she gained experience in handling complicated detail work on major projects. This growth, combined with her design expertise, enabled her to move to Gruen and Associates in Los Angeles in 1960. Sklarek stayed with Gruen and Associates for the next twenty years. After six years there, she became the first woman to occupy the position of director of architecture, a title which called for her to manage twenty to fifty architects.

The magnitude of Sklarek's accomplishments early in her career are underscored by the fact that, while she became a licensed architect in California in 1962, twenty more years passed before that achievement was repeated by another black woman. Sklarek opened new paths for black women in other areas as well. While working at Gruen in 1966, Sklarek became the first woman to be honored with a fellowship in the American Institute of Architects. Although she was the first woman in the long history of the Los Angeles chapter of that association to be so highly recognized, at the time she was still not a partner at Gruen. Sklarek later became vice-president of the California chapter of the American Institute of Architects.

In 1980 Sklarek left Gruen and Associates to become project director for Weldon, Becket, and Associates in Santa Monica, California. Sklarek took on an even greater role as a leader in her field in 1985 when she formed her own architectural firm. She proudly describes Siegel, Sklarek, Diamond as the largest totally woman-owned architectural firm in the United States. Since 1989 she has served as a principal in the Jerde Partnership in Venice, California.

Sklarek feels strongly that architecture should be appealing, functional, and, most important, pleasing for the persons for whom it is designed, "not just in the image of the architect's ego" (Lanker, *I Dream a World*, 40). Although she has been tremendously successful in the field, she has nevertheless been at times frustrated in her efforts to realize her goals, not only because of the restrictions placed on her by her clients, but also because of the difficulty of obtaining projects for which many established male firms also complete. She explains:

> Projects don't just come to us. Most of our projects are not in the public sector, government projects. Even though there is an affirmative-action policy with government work, we still have to do an enormous marketing job and spend an awful lot of money in order to

Forms Largest •

Woman-Owned

Architectural

Firm

get it, to prove that we're not just equal to, but better than any of the male firms (Lanker, *I Dream a World,* 40).

The principal works credited to Sklarek include the American Embassy in Tokyo, Japan; the Pacific Design Center in Los Angeles; the Courthouse Center, located in Columbus, Indiana; San Francisco's Fox Plaza; the city hall for San Bernardino, California; and Terminal One at Los Angeles International Airport.

Sklarek has served as a role model not only because of her professional success but also through her community service and work as an educator. She has taught at New York City College and at the University of California at Los Angeles. She has also served, since 1970, as commissioner on the California State Board of Architectural Examiners, and from 1984 to 1987 she was director of the University of Southern California Architects Guild. She has also served on the Design Grading Jury in California.

Profile by Carolyn Hodges

Sklarek has been married twice. She was first married in 1967 to Rolf Sklarek, who died in 1984. In 1985 she married Cornelius Welch, a physician. Her children are Gregory Ranson and David Fairweather from the first marriage, and Susan from her marriage to Welch.

ELLEN STEWART

c. 1920– •

*N*o one could have predicted that Ellen Stewart would emerge as a

major force in the international theatre world. As a young African-

American girl growing up in pre-World War II America, Stewart may

have wondered if even her modest ambition to become a clothes designer

was a realistic one. Yet Stewart, blessed with qualities of talent, persever-

ance, and devotion, launched a designing career that eventually

resulted in her creation of the La Mama Experimental Theater Club, a

major force in world theater for more than forty years.

Stage producer, •

fashion

designer

Little is known about Ellen Stewart's background. Her birthplace is sometimes given as Alexandria, Louisiana, but Chicago has been mentioned as a birth site as well. Stewart has stated without elaboration that some of her family members were in vaudeville and burlesque, and it was the experiences of her foster brother, Frederick Lights, in the New York theater that inspired her to create her own theatrical group.

Stewart became interested in the theater at an early age, in part because of Lights's efforts to gain a foothold in New York theatrical circles. His struggles became an important incentive for Stewart when she made her own daring forays into theatre. As a youth, though, Stewart targeted fashion designing as a profession. This was unthinkable as a field of study in the South at the time, so she studied education at Arkansas State University.

In 1950 Stewart arrived in New York City with the aim of studying at the Traphagen School of Design. Shortly after her arrival she secured a job at Saks Fifth Avenue department store. Traveling on the subway and visiting neighborhoods proved a cheap diversion for Stewart. While on one of these excursions, she struck up a friendship with an old Jewish merchant, Abraham Diamond, who encouraged her ambition to design and supplied her with fabrics. The clothes Stewart sewed at home and wore to work soon landed her a job as a designer at Saks. She held this job until about 1957, when she had to have surgery. Upon her recovery, Stewart became a freelance designer. Her interest in the theater remained high, though, despite Lights's frustrated attempts to establish himself.

In 1961 Stewart's life changed dramatically. Conversations with Theresa Klein, a friend she met during a vacation in Tangiers, stirred Stewart's interest in pursuing her dreams of the theater. Shortly thereafter, she was humiliated when a midtown shop refused to look at her design sketches, convinced that she could not possible be a designer.

It was during this time that Stewart discovered a basement apartment for rent at 321 East Ninth Street. She leased the space for fifty dollars a month and pondered a way in which she could help struggling theatrical neophytes and experimentalists such as her brother and simultaneously pursue her own interest in the theater world. She set up a business that was to be a dress boutique by day and a coffeehouse theater by night.

Around the same period, a sympathetic city health inspector—a retired actor—made it possible for her to get a restaurant license. Paul Foster tossed up Stewart's nickname, Mama, as a basis for the restaurant's name. That suggestion was adopted, although Stewart added "La" to the name to give it a fancier sound. Thus was Cafe La Mama born.

Cafe La Mama opened modestly in July 1962 with an adaptation of a Tennessee Williams short story, *One Arm*. The space inside was very small, with room for some twenty-five spectators and a playing area about as big as a single bed. Still, the fledgling venue stayed alive. In August 1962 La Mama put on its first original play, Michael Locasio's *In a*

Experimental •

Theater

Founded

Corner of the Morning. In November La Mama presented the first New York production of a Harold Pinter play, and before long, Cafe La Mama and a few other places, such as Cafe Cino, were launching what became known as the off-off-Broadway movement.

The city put difficulties in the way of the fledgling organization. A zoning ordinance forced it to move in 1963. Six months later the city found additional violations of building ordinances and forced a move to 122 Second Avenue, where there was room for seventy-four spectators. Stewart's resilience and ability to improvise a solution was on call at this time. For example, prior to one move, Stewart asked the last audience to pick up something and carry it to the new venue as they left.

Hassles with restaurant regulations resulted in the formation of a private, nonprofit club, La Mama Experimental Theater Club. The net effect of this was that the patron purchased a short-term club membership rather than a theater ticket. Another roadblock appeared in Stewart's path in 1966, when the Actor's Equity union forbade its members from giving free performances in area coffeehouses. Stewart was able to persuade the union to waive its rule for La Mama on the basis of its status as a private club.

In 1967 La Mama, which had been operating mostly on money Stewart had earned from swimsuit and clothing designs, received a much needed infusion of outside cash. It became fashionable for major foundations to give grants in support of the arts, and she persuaded the Rockefeller, Ford, and Kaplan foundations and the National Endowment for the Arts to provide her theater club with monetary aid. Armed with these funds, Stewart bought a building on East Fourth Street that came to include a 144-seat theater on the first floor, another acting space and work and storage rooms on the second floor, and an apartment for herself on the top floor.

The company opened in its new home on April 3, 1969. The acquisition of a building by no means assured La Mama's continuing physical existence, though. Its entire history has been marked by the search for funds to stay afloat. As Ellen Stewart noted in *Backstage* in 1990,

> Certainly, we have much more monies than we had in the beginning.... But for the scope of our activities and what we attempt to do, and what we *do* do, we don't nearly have the monies. And on occasion, I do lament a light that I wish we had, or a sound system that I wish we had, or things like that. But that doesn't stop the show, honey.

A charismatic woman who was fiercely proud of her theater, Stewart established a tradition of appearing in front of the audience before every performance to ring a cowbell, greet those in attendance, and hail the playwright whose work would be featured that evening. This attention to playwrights enabled Stewart and Cafe La Mama to carve out an important place for itself over the years. In its first four and a half years of existence the organization mounted more than two hundred new plays. On occasion the play being presented was a miserable failure. At other times, though, the mandate of the theater—to provide promising new playwrights, actors, and directors with a forum to show their work—enabled Cafe La Mama to unveil exciting new talent. Tom O'Horgan directed some forty plays during La Mama's first four years before going on to direct *Hair* and *Jesus Christ Superstar* on Broadway, while Sam Shepard is only one of a group of well-known playwrights whose first production was at La Mama. *Viet Rock* and *Godspell* originated there, as did the more recent *Torch Song Trilogy* of Harvey Fierstein.

In the 1970s Stewart built up ensemble companies and took steps to help playwrights seeking to get their plays published. American publishers would not accept plays that had not been reviewed, and reviewers did not cover off-off-Broadway. The situation was different in some European capitals, where all plays presented were reviewed. Stewart thus sent a troupe abroad in 1965 for the first of La Mama's international tours. The glowing reviews that resulted led to publication for twelve of the twenty-one productions sent to Europe, including *Chicago* by Sam Shepard and *Black Mass* by Adrienne Kennedy.

The success of the first tour led Stewart to establish traveling companies as a permanent feature of La Mama. The organization became an agent through which American avant-garde theater reached the world. In turn, the international connections that were made led to La Mama's involvement in bringing foreign theater companies to this country.

The continuing international influence of La Mama was manifest in 1990, when Romanian exile Andrei Serban was invited to take charge of the country's National Theater after the overthrow of the communist regime. Upon his return, Serban stunned audiences with an audacious project that he had begun at La Mama in 1972 and continued to work on there for the ensuing seventeen years.

Ellen Stewart's life has centered on La Mama. She has been recognized for her work in many ways, including the American Theater Association/International Theater Institute Award in 1975, a wave of other awards, and ten honorary doctorates. Even so, La Mama has continued to face monetary woes. In 1992, for instance, La Mama faced an accumulated deficit of $340,000 at the same time that the New York State Arts Council and the National Endowment for the Arts had cut their grants. Stewart's personal finances deteriorated, and La Mama endured a period when it could neither pay its staff or its bills. Somehow, though, this crisis, like previous ones, was overcome.

Ellen Stewart's contribution to theater is immense. The creator, leader, exponent, and defender of La Mama, she has concentrated her efforts on the company and given it a longevity that is extraordinary among groups of its kind. Her efforts gave some of today's most famous playwrights their first start and served as an important agent for international cultural exchange.

**Profile by
Robert L. Johns**

MARIA W. STEWART

*I*n 1832 Frances Maria Miller W. Stewart became the first American-

born woman to speak publicly on political themes to a mixed audience

of both men and women. She was also likely the first African-American

woman to lecture in defense of women's rights. Although her public

speaking lasted less than two years, she stands at the forefront of the

black female activist and literary tradition. A reader, writer, and

student of texts, she spoke and wrote on the importance of education, the

need for black unity and collective action toward liberation, and the

special responsibilities and rights of women. These beliefs were reflected

in her own activism, for while her roots were in the abolitionist move-

ment, she opposed all manner of political, racial, gender, and economic

1803–1879 •

Women's rights •

activist,

journalist

exploitation. Stewart's unqualified militancy and willingness to accept armed struggle if necessary set her apart from most abolitionists and was indicative of her single-minded dedication to her beliefs. According to biographer Marilyn Richardson, "Her calling was not merely reformist, it was subversive" (Richardson, *Maria Stewart*, 26).

Stewart was born in 1803 in Hartford, Connecticut, to a free black family. Orphaned at the age of five, she lived with the family of a clergyman until the age of fifteen. Between the ages of fifteen and twenty she developed her religious education and literacy in Sabbath schools while working as a domestic servant.

On August 10, 1826, at the age of twenty-three, she was married in Boston, Massachusetts, to James W. Stewart, an independent shipping agent. They were married at Boston's African Baptist Church, a focal point of Boston's black community that was known for its support of social and political causes.

The newlyweds settled in as members of Boston's small black middle class, but enjoyed only three years of marriage until James Stewart's death from a "severe illness" on December 17, 1829. They had no children. After his death, the executors of the estate, a group of white businessmen, used shameless legal maneuvers to defraud Maria Stewart out of a substantial inheritance.

In 1830, anguish over her husband's death as well as the death of David Walker, an important black activist in the antislavery movement, led Stewart to reassess the place of religion in her life, and she underwent a dramatic religious awakening. She wrote that her new commitment made her a "warrior" and potential martyr for "the cause of oppressed Africa," and a "strong advocate for the cause of God and for the cause of freedom" (Richardson, *Maria Stewart*, 8). Stewart's religious vision became intrinsically connected to her political agenda:

> From the moment I experienced the change I felt a strong desire . . . to devote the remainder of my days to piety and virtue and now possess that spirit of independence that, were I called upon, I would willingly sacrifice my life for the cause of God and my brethren. All the nations of the earth are crying out for liberty and equality. Away, away with tyranny and oppression! (Richardson, *Maria Stewart*, 9).

In the fall of 1831, Maria Stewart learned that the editors of the *Liberator* wanted to recruit black women writers. Founded by William

Lloyd Garrison and Isaac Knapp, the *Liberator* was a weekly paper based in Boston that emerged as a major voice of the abolitionist movement. Stewart's *Religion and the Pure Principles of Morality, the Sure Foundation On Which We Must Build* was published by Garrison and Knapp as a twelve-page pamphlet in 1831 (with Stewart's name misspelled as Steward). Published two months after Nat Turner's famous slave revolt in Virginia, the militant essay urged the black community to "sue for your rights and privileges" and warned whites that "our souls are fired with the . . . love of liberty and independence" (Loewenberg, *Black Women in Nineteenth Century American Life,* 189-91). The publication of the essay began an important friendship and professional affiliation between Stewart and Garrison. Over the next two years, Garrison published several other works by Stewart, including the texts of her speeches, in the *Liberator.*

Stewart's brief public speaking career began in the spring of 1832, when she addressed the Afric-American Female Intelligence Society of America. Her second public lecture took place on September 21, 1832. It was the first public lecture by an American-born woman before an audience of both men and women. (The Grimké sisters are often cited as the first American women to speak in public, but Stewart preceded them by five years.) Stewart's third lecture was delivered at the African Masonic Hall on February 27, 1833. Seven months later, in Boston, she made her last public speaking appearance, on September 21, 1833.

Stewart's activism mirrored a philosophical change in the abolition movement centered in the North in the 1820s. Progressing from the conciliatory, moralistic approach that was evident in the first two decades of the century, a new spirit of militancy and political action emerged.

The views espoused by Stewart were borne out of a black protest and abolitionist tradition that was independent of the later white and integrated groups. She was particularly influenced by David Walker (1785-1830), author of *Walker's Appeal,* an 1829 denunciation of slavery that argued for the overthrow of white supremacy, by violent means if necessary.

Stewart's contact with the abolitionist movement and her early years in the home of a clergyman, combined with her command of sophisticated rhetorical flourishes, gave Stewart's speeches a religious, sermon-like quality. She spoke "as a writer under siege," challenging and pushing her audiences to action, and blazed a trail for other black

Abolitionist •

Garrison

Recruits

Stewart

Stewart's Fiery •

Brand of

Activism

public speakers such as Sojourner Truth, Frances E. W. Harper, and Frederick Douglass.

References to religion were interspersed throughout Stewart's rhetoric, and much of the language and themes she used came from the Old Testament. Citing scripture from the Book of Revelations and other fertile sources of material, Stewart warned whites about God's coming judgment for their slavekeeping ways. Religion, however, did not stand alone in Stewart's analysis; it was interconnected with social justice and a politically pragmatic world view.

Stewart had a wide and varied political agenda and spoke of abolition issues in an international context. She also spoke out against those who would today be labeled "armchair activists." Some blacks, she said, were "abundantly capable" but "talk, without effort, is nothing . . . and this gross neglect, on your part, causes my blood to boil within me!" (O'Connor, *Pioneer Women Orators,* 146). Finally, she had little patience for those who dismissed her opinions because of her gender. Instead she insisted that women were obligated to speak and act in the struggle against oppression and exploitation.

In her address to the Afric-American Female Intelligence Society in 1832, Stewart put forth the unique responsibilities of women in the black community:

> O woman, woman! Upon you I call; for upon your exertions almost entirely depends whether the rising generation shall be any thing more than we have been or not. O woman, woman! Your example is powerful, your influence great; it extends over your husbands and over your children, and throughout the circle of your acquaintance (Richardson, *Maria Stewart,* 55).

Stewart cited education as a cornerstone of future growth for the black community on several occasions. She urged black women to instill excitement for knowledge in their children, and exhorted them to activism: "It is of no use for us to sit with our hands folded, hanging our heads like bulrushes, lamenting our wretched condition; but let us make a mighty effort, and arise" (Loewenberg, *Black Women,* 189). Yet Stewart exhorted black and white women alike to aspire to positions of greater status in the world. She urged her contemporaries to take note of the achievements of women throughout history and accept and encourage public activism in the present.

Maria Stewart's September 1833 address in Boston suggested an uncharacteristic serenity that implied that she had made a decision to end her public career. She cited disfavor on the part of the black community, and alluded to a "hissing and a reproach among the people" concerning some of her behavior. Stewart, however, remained unapologetic:

> Having God for my friend and portion, what have I to fear? As long as it is the will of God, I rejoice that I am as I am; for man, in his best estate, is altogether vanity. Men of eminence have mostly risen from obscurity; nor will I, although a female of darker hue, and far more obscure than they, bend my head or hang my harp upon the willows (Loewenberg, *Black Women,* 200).

Stewart moved to New York City in 1833. Two years later, Garrison published *Productions of Mrs. Maria W. Stewart,* which consisted of texts of her four public speeches, some biographical facts, and several essays and poems. Once in New York, Stewart joined a circle of black intellectuals and became a member of one of the city's two black female literary societies. Stewart also worked for the North Star Association and attended the American Women's Anti-Slavery convention in 1837, but she maintained her absence from the speaker's podium.

During the 1830s Stewart became a teacher in the public schools in Manhattan and Brooklyn. In 1852 she lost her school post for unknown reasons, and a year later she moved to Baltimore, Maryland, where she served as a private tutor to individual pupils.

Sometime between 1861 and 1863 Stewart moved to Washington, D.C., where she was to spend the remainder of her life. She taught in the public school system during the Civil War and became friends with Elizabeth Keckley, the seamstress to Mary Todd Lincoln, the president's wife. In 1871 Stewart established a Sunday school for all children in the neighborhood, including the poor and destitute.

Stewart also worked at the Freedmen's Hospital, affiliated with Howard University, and in the early 1870s she was appointed head of housekeeping services. By 1877 the hospital, which had served as a virtual refugee camp for former slaves at the end of the Civil War, received all classes of patients without distinction of sex or color.

In the late 1870s, Stewart learned of the passage of a pension law covering veterans of the War of 1812. In March 1879 she received a pension of eight dollars a month, retroactive to the date of the law's

**Profile by
Lisa Studier with
Adrienne Lash Jones**

passage. She used this money to finance the publication of *Meditations From the Pen of Mrs. Maria W. Stewart* in 1879. The work consisted of a reprint of her earlier book supplemented by several additional sections. Stewart died on December 17, 1879, at the age of seventy-six.

ALETHIA BROWNING TANNER

17??–18?? •

Slave, gardener •

*D*etermined not to spend her life in bondage, the ambitious,

enterprising, and selfless Alethia Tanner earned enough money work-

ing as a hired-out slave to buy her freedom. Amazingly, she also

purchased the freedom of seventeen other family members and several

friends. She made it possible for her family to settle in the Washington,

D.C., area, where they emerged as community leaders. Tanner also

became known as the mother of the African Methodist Episcopal Church,

and was co-owner of a mortgage on her church.

Alethia Browning Tanner and her sisters Sophia and Laurena Browning were slaves on Rachel Bell Pratt's plantation in Prince George's County, Maryland. Sophia married George F. Bell (Beall), a black man who was a slave in the home of Anthony Addison near the eastern boundary of the District of Columbia. In 1807 he and two other black men launched the first school in Washington, D.C., for black children. Two years later, Bell purchased his wife Sophia's freedom from Rachel

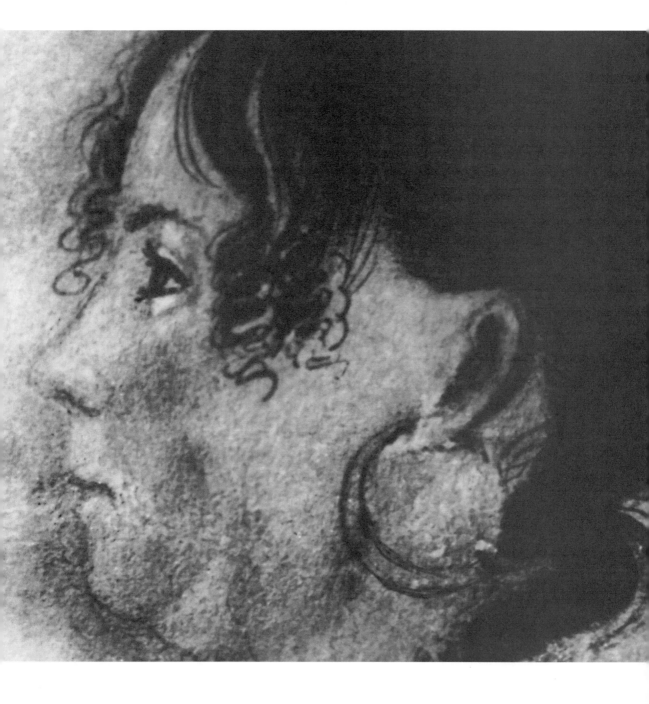

Pratt. Sophia subsequently worked as a truck gardener and saved enough money to purchase his freedom.

Alethia Tanner was one of the most foresighted and enterprising women of her time. She worked as a hired-out slave and opened a vegetable market at Lafayette Square, where her customers included Thomas Jefferson. By 1810 she had saved $1,400, enough to buy her freedom. In 1826 Tanner purchased the freedom of her older sister Laurena Browning Cook for $800. She also purchased the freedom of five of Cook's children (four sons and one daughter) that year, paying an average of $300 for each child. One of the children was John Frances Cook Sr., who was fifteen years old when freed. In 1828 Tanner is said to have purchased the other Cook children and their offspring, including Hannah Ferguson and her four children, Annette and her child, and Aletha Cook and one child.

Anxious to earn enough money to reimburse his aunt Alethia Tanner for purchasing his freedom, John Cook Sr. drew upon the trade he had learned in his childhood. For five years after gaining his freedom he served as an apprenticed shoemaker. With Tanner's assistance, he received an education from the Columbia (or Columbian) Institute and became a successful educator, minister, and community leader before the Civil War.

By about August 1834 Cook was put in charge of the Columbian Institute, an institution that Henry Smothers had built in 1822. Cook, who renamed the school Union Seminary, became the institution's third schoolmaster in its history. He conducted the school for more than twenty years before he died. He also helped establish two black churches in the District of Columbia—Union Bethel Church (1838), now known as the Metropolitan AME Church, and the First Colored Presbyterian Church (1841), later known as the Fifteenth Street Presbyterian Church. The Cook family became one of the most prominent and wealthy families in the District of Columbia, and family members were known throughout the nineteenth century for their contributions to education, politics, and community service.

Altogether, Tanner purchased the freedom of ten Cook children and seven grandchildren and, including herself and her sister, was responsible for the freedom of nineteen family members. After 1836, when all family members and their children had been freed by purchase, Tanner turned her attention to her neighbors. She purchased the freedom of Lotty Riggs and her four children; John Butler, who later became a Methodist minister; and Charlotte Davis.

According to *Alexander's Magazine*, Tanner then extended her purchasing power elsewhere:

> Having apparently smashed the slave market, and seeing no more bargains in that direction she turned her attention to buying churches, and when the first Bethel church on Capitol Hill was sold out by the bank which held a mortgage against it, she with her brother-in-law, George Bell, bought it and gave it in and gave the society time to pay for it (Joyner, *Alexander's Magazine*).

At some point Alethia either married or changed her name to Tanner. She continued to live in the Washington, D.C., area, where she became well-established as a "remarkable Christian woman" (Wayman, *Cyclopedia of African Methodism*), in part because of her reputation as the mother of the African Methodist Episcopal Church. When she died, she was a member of Union Bethel Church, which her nephew John Frances Cook Sr. had helped to establish. According to *Alexander's Magazine*, "she left a handsome property at her death. There is no telling what a woman like this might have accomplished if she could have lived long enough" (Joyner, *Alexander's Magazine*).

Profile by
Jessie Carney Smith

DEBI THOMAS

"*I guess I'm a pioneer, because I'm the first Black to make the world team,*" said Debi Thomas in the March 19, 1986, issue of Jet *after winning the United States National Women's Figure Skating Champion-*

ship in 1986. A top American contender in international figure skating competitions during the 1980s, Thomas is no stranger to pioneer roles.

She made history at the 1983 Criterium International du Sucre contest in France when she became the first African American ever to win a international senior-level singles competition. And at the age of nineteen, Thomas captured the 1986 United States International Figure Skating Championship "with a dazzling display of jumps bigger than many of the men's and a personal exuberance that won the crowds....

She made skating look fun" (Engeler, *Rolling Stone*). One month later, in March 1986, Thomas won the World Championship in Geneva, Switzerland, upsetting the reigning Olympic champion, Katarina Witt of East Germany. She then went on to win the bronze medal at the 1988 Olympics. Not only did Thomas become the first black woman ever to make the United States Olympic figure-skating team, she was also the first champion in thirty years to balance full-time university studies with competition.

Born in Poughkeepsie, New York, on March 25, 1967, Debi Thomas is the youngest of two children of Janice Thomas. She grew up in San Jose, California, where she and her brother, Rick, were raised by their mother after her divorce from Debi's father, McKinley Thomas. Exposing her children to opera, ballet, and ice shows, Janice Thomas encouraged her daughter's interest in figure skating, which was sparked at age four when Debi attended an Ice Follies performance. She began taking skating lessons at age five and quickly demonstrated her natural talent for the sport.

Thomas soon caught the attention of Janet Signorello, owner of the Redwood City Ice Lodge, who urged Janice Thomas to get Debi a professional coach. She took part in her first competition at age nine, winning with a routine choreographed to "Matchmaker," from *Fiddler on the Roof.* "From then on I was hooked on competing," said Thomas. "To this day, I skate because I'm very competitive" (Kort, *Ms.*). By ten years of age, Thomas was studying with coach Alex McGowan, with whom she worked closely for many years. Initially skeptical of her ability, Thomas's talent, determination, and love for the sport eventually changed his mind.

Rigorous •

Thomas began a rigorous training program under the tutelage of McGowan at the Redwood City Ice Lodge. The grueling training schedule was terribly time-consuming for Janice Thomas and her daughter, but by the time she was fourteen, Thomas had passed the United States Figure Skating Association's required tests. Thomas soon became a formidable competitor at local, national, and world skating meets. She skated in sixteen competitions from 1986 to 1989, winning eight and placing second in three. But preparation and training were a financial burden for her family, and at times Thomas was forced to break training for a few months for financial reasons. It was not unusual for her skates to be completely worn out before her mother was able to buy her a new pair. Although her father helped, it was her mother and her brother who paid the bulk of the bills—about $25,000 a year.

Preparation

In 1986 Thomas entered Stanford University, which was a further drain on the family's resources. Only after the 1986 Denver Nationals was Thomas able to secure a sponsor other than her family. Coach McGowan charged that it was ridiculous that Thomas, the top U.S. athlete in her sport, had no sponsor, while her international competitors were sponsored by their governments. Soon after this pronouncement, a cosmetic company offered to sponsor Thomas, and other companies and organizations called her with proposals for her to represent their products. (In 1988 Thomas became the first member of the U.S. Skating Association to receive corporate sponsors when she signed with an agent of the International Management Group in New York.)

As a freshman at Stanford in 1986, Thomas was advised to drop out of school and concentrate solely on skating until after the 1988 Olympics, but she refused. "I'm not going to make a choice between school and skating, they are both on an equal basis for me. I don't want to pursue one without the other" (Norment, *Ebony*). A fiercely competitive skater who was serious about her amateur career, but she did not let it dominate her life, even as she recognized its positive influence on her life: "Skating has given me self-discipline and a lot of drive. It's taught me how to work for things, to know what needs to be done to accomplish what I want, like getting the grades to be accepted by Stanford.... I know medical school will be hard, and skating has prepared me for that" (Slate, *Essence*).

• Thomas Wins

Skating Crowns

Thomas was blessed with tremendous ability, but her scores were lower than they should have been during her first years of national competition. McGowan commented that "because Debi was the first black skater, there may have been some doubt in the minds of the U.S. judges whether the international judges would accept her," said McGowan in *Ms.* in 1987. Instead, he noted, "she won international acceptance before she was accepted here."

Between 1985 and 1986, Thomas scored her first successes and greatly improved her standing. She moved from second place in the nation and fifth in the world to first place in each of three competitions—the National Sports Festival, the St. Ivel Competition, and Skate America 85—the last two of which took place during her freshman year as a student at Stanford.

In 1985–86, what *Vogue* called "her year of miracles," she captured the crown in both the U.S. Nationals and World Championship. Thomas's free-skate performance at the Nationals was particularly memorable, in part because it included an extraordinary five triple jumps:

> In the opening dramatic interlude, she landed all three
> triples as if she had never missed one in her life. From

then on she skated with a grin from ear to ear. The crowd loved her, and Thomas seemed to grow in stature with each new pass around the ice. She was having a ball, totally in command, urged on by the adoration of the crowd and McGowan's cheerleading.

Thomas unleashed her dazzling performance despite the duel pressures of competition and school, as well as speculation about the impact of her skin color on judges' scores. As *Ms.* noted, though, "watch her skate for a few minutes and you quickly forget about color or academics" (Kort, *Ms.*). Thomas's spectacular display of skating placed her above former champion Tiffany Chin as the United States Women's champion.

At the 1986 World Championship competition a month later in Geneva, Switzerland, she added yet another gold crown to her victories when she upset the reigning Olympic champion, East Germany's Katarina Witt. Thomas, at eighteen, had captured the World Championship. *Sports Illustrated* described her win in its March 31, 1986, issue:

> With grace as usual, starting slowly, her first two triples were a bit jolting—Thomas relaxed as she landed her third and fourth while her teammates screamed encouragement.... But, with the guts of a burglar, she suddenly and spontaneously improvised a triple-double combination in place of the four triples.... She was having fun, right up until the double axel at the end— the same one that troubled her at the U.S. Nationals last month—and when she nailed that, it became clear to everyone that they were applauding the gold medal winner.

After the World Championship competition, Thomas experienced a rigorous round of interviews, award ceremonies, and exhibitions. She participated in Sport Aid in England and the Goodwill Games in Moscow. She lost the U.S. National title to Jill Trenary in 1987 and, although she skated a rousing long program, was runner-up to Witt at the World Competition.

Taking a leave from Stanford in the fall of 1987, she moved to Boulder, Colorado, to prepare for the 1988 Winter Olympics in Calgary, Alberta. That summer, she worked to strengthen the artistic element of her program by consulting with dancer Mikhail Baryshnikov, who gave her tips and assigned his assistant choreographer, George de la Pena, to work with her.

The 1988 •

Winter Olympic

Games

The Olympic competition among the world's leading female figure skaters was intense. In compulsory figures, Thomas finished second, Witt third, and Elizabeth Manley fourth. The following night, Thomas and Witt both posted high scores, Witt on the strength of an engaging and stylish closing dance routine, Thomas on the strength of her technical presentation. In the final stage of the competition, the United States contingent—Debi Thomas, Jill Trenary, and Caryn Kaday—did not fare well. Trenary finished fourth, while Kaday had to withdraw because of the flu. Thomas faltered as well, missing three triple jumps, and Manley edged her out of the silver medal. Thomas won the bronze medal, thus becoming the first black woman athlete to win a medal in the Winter Olympic Games.

Obviously disappointed yet undaunted, she competed in the World Championship in Budapest, where she also won a bronze medal. After the competition, Thomas announced she had secretly married Brian Vander Hogen in Boulder, Colorado (they later divorced). Thomas retired from skating after the Olympics and resumed her studies at Stanford University.

In 1994 Thomas began her first year of medical school at Northwestern. Although she did some skating with the Ice Capades in the early 1990s, she has left her skating career behind in favor of new dreams of a medical career.

Profile by
Jacquelyn L. Jackson

WILLIE MAE THORNTON

inger Willie Mae "Big Mama" Thornton was one of the true giants

of blues music. Known for her earthy voice, outspoken lyrics, and

eccentric lifestyle, she was a gifted musician who also performed on

harmonica, drums, and guitar. She left behind a legacy of seminal

recordings, many of which influenced better-known recording stars

such as Elvis Presley and Janis Joplin.

1926–1984 •

Blues singer, •

songwriter

Willie Mae Thornton was born on December 11, 1926, in a rural area outside Montgomery, Alabama. She was one of seven children. Her earliest musical experiences took place in the church where her father served as minister and her mother sang in the choir. She learned to play harmonica and drums at an early age and performed as a teenager throughout the Montgomery area in a variety of blues styles.

At age fourteen, following the death of her mother, Thornton went to work in a local saloon, washing floors to help support her family. It was here that she got her first opportunity to perform blues in public. One evening she was asked to substitute on short notice for the tavern's regular singer. A short time later she won first prize in a local amateur

music contest and attracted the attention of Atlanta promoter Sammy Green.

Green engaged her to tour with his show, *The Hot Harlem Revue,* and by the early 1940s, Thornton was singing and dancing throughout the southeastern United States. Mindful of her powerful voice and mature interpretation, the revue initially billed Thornton as "the new Bessie Smith" or "Bessie Smith's younger sister." But while Thornton was undoubtedly influenced by Smith, her authoritative stage persona was already uniquely her own and not subject to manipulation by promoters.

Thornton later recalled her difficult start in the music business with authors Anthony Connor and Robert Neff:

> I had a hard way to go when I come up. Sometimes had to go to somebody's back door and ask for bread or something cool to drink. "Mister, could I have a drink of your water?" Sometimes they said no. I just kept on walking. I just made myself happy. People didn't know I was worried a lot of times. I always kept a smile on my face: I always be round friends, buy drinks, laugh. But they didn't know it. I was smiling. Didn't have nowhere to stay. They didn't know that. I slept in all-night restaurants and barrooms. Course it don't make no difference now. It's all the past. Anyway, I couldn't express what I went through. It don't make no sense to people today (Connor and Neff, *Blues*).

Thornton's style reflected her humble rural upbringing. "My singing comes from my experience," she once said. "My own experience. My own thing. I got my feelin's for everything. I never had no one teach me nothin'. I never went to school for music or nothin'. I taught myself to sing and to blow harmonica and even to play drums by watchin' other people. I can't read music but I know what I'm singing. I don't sing like nobody but myself" (Shaw, *The World of Soul*). Nonetheless, Thornton did, at times, acknowledge the influence of Ma Rainey, Bessie Smith, Junior Parker, and Memphis Minnie. Likewise, her style inspired a new generation of singers, including Elvis Presley, Janis Joplin, and Angela Strehli.

Recording •

Career Begins

In 1948 the *Hot Harlem Revue* arrived in Houston, Texas, where Thornton signed a five-year exclusive contract as a nightclub entertainer under the entrepreneurship of Don Robey. Thornton's recording debut came in 1951, when Robey arranged for her to work with Joe

Scott's band for the Peacock label. Six feet tall and already approaching 350 pounds, she celebrated the recent acquisition of her nickname "Big Mama" in an early recording session with her song "They Call Me Big Mama."

In 1952 Johnny Otis, the "Godfather of Rhythm and Blues," negotiated a contract to make a record with his band. He sent the master tapes to Robey, who added Thornton's voice and distributed the final pressing on his Peacock label. Among these recordings was Thornton's version of "Hound Dog"—the song later immortalized by Elvis Presley. Usually attributed to the Jerry Leiber-Mike Stoller songwriting team, this classic rock 'n' roll tune may actually have been written by Otis and Thornton. In fact, Otis is listed as cowriter with Lieber and Stoller on Thornton's first pressing, though not on Presley's version, which is attributed only to Lieber and Stoller. Thornton maintained, however, that she did not write "Hound Dog." "Lieber and Stoller wrote it," she said in Shaw's *The World of Soul.* "They were just a couple of kids then and they had this song written on the back of a brown paper bag. So I started to sing the words and put in some of my own. All that talkin' and hollerin'—that's my own."

A nearly perfect vehicle for Thornton, "Hound Dog" was released in 1953 and hit number one on the rhythm and blues charts in 1955. Author Ian Whitcomb described a Thornton performance of "Hound Dog" in *Repercussions:* "When Big Mama sings 'Hound Dog' she's slow and easy and also menacing, smiling like a sabre-tooth tiger, her black diamond eyes glinting fiercely. Then, with the band in full roar, she leaves her chair to ambulate off in a swaying promenade that has a certain military regality, and the whole house cheers like royal subjects." The song was Thornton's biggest studio success, selling over 500,000 copies. Still, Thornton often expressed bitterness over the credit Presley received for his recording. "That song [Presley's version] sold over two million records. I got one check for $500 and never saw another" ("Heart Attack Claims 'Big Mama' Thornton," *Jet*).

Thornton continued to perform with Otis until 1955, after which time she returned to Houston to record with Bill Harvey and his band. In 1956 her contract with Robey expired and she moved to San Francisco to tour with Gatemouth Brown. As time passed, Thornton's career stalled; she had no regular back-up band, no recording contract, and only sporadic playing engagements. The blues revival of the 1960s brought renewed interest in her work, and she was invited by Horst Lippmann to appear with the American Folk Blues Festival, which embarked on a European tour in 1965. While in England, Chris Strachwitz, representing Arhoolie records, produced an album, "Big Mama in Europe," which featured Thornton and a peerless back-up band of Buddy Guy, Walter Horton, and Freddy Below.

While the authorship of "Hound Dog" has always been debatable, no one ever attempted to deny Thornton credit for the classic "Ball and Chain." A hit for Janis Joplin in 1969, Thornton first recorded the tune in 1967. Whitcomb recounted in *Repercussions* that "whereas Joplin's performance was always cultivated and labored, Thornton's is straight from the heart with a punch to the belly. From out of the chaos of messy real life she fashions a beautifully structured and controlled performance that always contains an element of danger: whatever will she do next? It's a cliffhanger."

"Ball and •

Chain" Record

a Hit

In her later years, Thornton's appetite for whiskey and corn moonshine began to take its toll. Several years before her death she was diagnosed as having cirrhosis of the liver. She continued to perform, but often had to be helped on stage and then remained seated while singing. In 1979 she appeared at the San Francisco Blues Festival:

> Big Mama Thornton had to be led to the bandstand. She'd been ill for some time and has a difficult time keeping her music together. The standing ovation that greeted Big Mama touched something deep in her and with tears in her eyes she thanked everyone for being there and thanked God for letting her come. In the next 50 minutes, she gave one of her best performances in recent years. While it sounded good at the festival, it was only when I listened to the tapes later that the stunning nature of her show became apparent (Cohen, *Living Blues*).

As Thornton's health deteriorated, she lost a great deal of weight, plunging from 350 to an emaciated 95 pounds. Refusing to cease performing altogether, Thornton disguised her frailness by cultivating two new stage "looks": one for which she wore a voluminous African robe, and for the other, an oversized man's business suit, cowboy boots, and a Stetson hat. In 1981 Thornton was in a serious auto accident and was forced to undergo major surgery for her injuries.

In the latter part of her career, Thornton was able to look back on a fabulous career. In addition to "Ball and Chain" and "They Call Me Big Mama," Thornton wrote twenty other blues songs. She also recorded dozens of blues classics on such labels as Arhoolie, Baytone, Kent, Mercury, and Vanguard. She made a number of television appearances, and recorded portions of the sound track for the Hollywood film *Vanishing Point*. She also appeared at numerous jazz and blues festivals and on many college and university campuses over the course of her long career.

On July 25, 1984, Thornton died in her home in Los Angeles of a heart attack and complications from cirrhosis of the liver. She had been largely inactive professionally for a number of months. The funeral was held in Los Angeles and, at Thornton's request, presided over by Reverend Johnny Otis. Jimmy Witherspoon and Margie Evans sang spirituals, and Tina Mayfield, wife of songwriter Percy Mayfield, read the obituary. A special benefit concert, scheduled to take place a week after the funeral to pay for funeral expenses, was organized by the Southern California Blues Society. Thornton, who never married and had no children, was survived by her sister, Mattie (Thornton) Fields of Los Angeles, California.

**Profile by
Juanita Karpf**

ROSINA TUCKER

1881–1987 •

Labor organizer, •

activist,

educator

A s founder and secretary-treasurer of the International Ladies' Auxiliary and a major force in the establishment of its parent organization, the Brotherhood of Sleeping Car Porters, Rosina Tucker helped to improve the economic fortunes of large numbers of black people in the United States and Canada. She organized porters' wives in activities to support the auxiliary and the union, and their efforts helped to ensure that porters received adequate pay, decent working conditions, and new benefits. The brotherhood also focused on battling racism and, with Tucker's assistance, organized civil rights marches in 1941 and 1963.

Rosina Budd Harvey Corrothers Tucker, one of nine children, was born on November 4, 1881, on Fourth Street in northwest Washington, D.C. Her parents, Lee Roy and Henrietta Harvey, had been slaves in Virginia before they relocated to Washington after their emancipation.

As was the case with many former slaves, they found the brutal memories of bondage painful to recount.

Although raised as a slave, Lee Roy Harvey taught himself to read and write. As a freeman he worked as a shoemaker and surrounded himself with the books he loved, developing a particular affection for history books. Harvey was protective of his children and prevented them from working as service employees or in white people's kitchens.

Rosina Tucker had pleasant memories of her early childhood, which was marked by musical training and her father's teachings. In 1897, while still in her junior year of high school, Tucker visited an aunt in Yonkers, New York, and met James D. Corrothers, a guest minister. A graduate of Northwestern University, Corrothers became known as a poet and writer of short stories, and his sketches on black humor and folklore garnered special attention.

Rosina Harvey and James Corrothers married on December 2, 1899. The couple had one son, Henry Harvey Corrothers, who later became a fine athlete and a physical education instructor at Wilberforce University. Rosina and James Corrothers also raised a son from his previous marriage.

After marrying, the couple lived first in New York City and Michigan. James Corrothers continued to practice his ministry and to write and publish poetry. Rosina occupied herself by teaching music to some thirty students. The family moved to Washington, D.C., in 1904, when James Corrothers took a position with the National Baptist Convention. Rosina, meanwhile, became the organist for Liberty Baptist Church in the Foggy Bottom section of the District. Two years later James Corrothers became pastor of the First Baptist Church in Lexington, Virginia. During their years in Lexington, First Baptist worship services were often spiced with James's storytelling and poetry reading and Rosina's classical piano pieces. About this time she composed "The Rio Grande Waltz."

After James Corrothers died in 1917, Rosina returned to Washington, D.C., where she worked as a file clerk with the federal government and became involved in civic activities. There she met Berthea J. Tucker, known as B. J., who worked as a Pullman car porter. They married on Thanksgiving eve in 1918 and moved into a two-story brick house on Seventh Street near Gallaudet College. She lived at the house for the rest of her life.

In the 1920s the Pullman Company had a virtual monopoly on railroad sleeping-car facilities throughout the United States. The company was a major employer of black men, and those who had jobs as

Pullman porters were held in considerable esteem in the black community. Porters, whose responsibilities included working the sleeping coaches, making beds, and shining shoes, collected hefty tips. "To be a Pullman porter in those days meant respect, prestige, social status and prominence," recalled Tucker ("Still Vocal and Active at Age 103," *Washington Post*). Nonetheless, porters were poorly paid, and charges for any damage to Pullman equipment were deducted from their small salaries. They were required to work long hours without overtime pay, sometimes working up to four hundred hours a month with "deadheading" and "doubling out" responsibilities. In the absence of a union to protect the men's rights, the company took full advantage of its black labor force.

In 1909 the porters formulated their grievances and made their first efforts to organize. While the attempt was unsuccessful, the Pullman Company made small gestures to address some of the men's concerns. Driven by the continued abuse of the black Pullman workers, Ashley Totten, a militant New York porter, made a bold move in 1925. He engaged A. Philip Randolph, a radical journalist and social theoretician who was later prominent in the civil rights movement, to organize a porters' union. On August 25 of that year, the Brotherhood of Sleeping Car Porters was launched and Randolph began what was to be a long tenure as president. The union also established the Women's Economic Councils, an organization through which women could work for the rights of the brotherhood. To protect the workers who could be fired for their connection with the union and their criticisms of the Pullman Company, Randolph handled all aspects of the first meeting himself. The next day some two hundred porters came to his office, the brotherhood's headquarters, to join the union.

Randolph and Totten tried to establish a meeting with porters and their wives in Washington, D.C., but many porters were reluctant to join for fear of losing their jobs. B. J. Tucker joined the union immediately—in time he became a member of the executive board—and he and Rosina subsequently took up the union's cause in the District.

The long hours demanded of porters left them little time for union activities. As a result, their wives tackled much of the union's work themselves, even holding secret meetings so that the men's employment would not be threatened. When Rosina Tucker met with Randolph and Totten, they did so in secrecy so that informers would be unable to report on the sessions to the company. To organize unions in the South, Tucker visited the homes of some three hundred porters who lived in the Washington area, distributed literature, discussed the organization with prospective members and their wives, and collected dues.

The next step for Tucker was to organize the local Ladies' Auxiliary. From the very beginning, the women raised a great deal of money by hosting parties, dances, dinners, and other activities. Tucker called upon her church and social service background to help families experiencing illnesses and other difficulties, including loss of employment.

In time the Pullman Company learned about Tucker's work on behalf of the fledgling union. They fired her husband in retribution, an action that aroused her anger. She marched into the company's offices and demanded to see her husband's supervisor. She strolled triumphantly out of his office several minutes later. B. J. Tucker was rehired.

The 1937 agreement between the porters and the Pullman Company marked the first formal agreement between a union of black workers and a major American corporation. The next year Rosina Tucker attended the union's national convention in Chicago and chaired the Constitution and Rules Committee. Immediately after the brotherhood's convention, the International Ladies' Auxiliary was established.

Over the years, the Brotherhood of Sleeping Car Porters and the Ladies' Auxiliary became more powerful. Through its official presence in the House of Labor, a speaking platform for the workers, the union was able to focus on the evils of racism, the need for civil rights legislation, the protection of minority voting rights, and the preservation of dignity on the job. The auxiliary remained a consistent part of the effort.

Some sources report that, although the brotherhood is generally given credit for the work, Tucker helped the group organize its first March on Washington, scheduled to occur in 1941. The march was called off when A. Philip Randolph convinced President Franklin D. Roosevelt to issue Executive Order 8802, which addressed fair employment practices and discrimination in government offices and defense plants. In 1963, again with Tucker's assistance, Randolph and the brotherhood organized another March on Washington. As the years passed, however, technological advances and declining demand for rail passenger service undermined the union. In 1978 the Brotherhood of Sleeping Car Porters merged with the Brotherhood of Railway and Airline Clerks.

In 1981 an award-winning documentary, *Miles of Smiles, Years of Struggle,* was released. The film recounted the story of the work of the porter's union and the auxiliary, as well as Tucker's pivotal role in their creation. The documentary even included footage of Tucker singing "Marching Together," which she wrote in 1939 in honor of the Pullman porters.

International •

Ladies'

Auxiliary

Formed

Tucker's interest in civil rights never wavered. Over the years Tucker testified before Senate and House committees on education, day care, labor, and voting rights for the District. She lobbied Congress for legislation on labor and education and helped organize unions for laundry workers and domestics. When she was 102 years old, she testified before a Senate Labor and Human Resources subcommittee on aging. In 1986, when she was 104 years old, Tucker was still giving lectures across the country. She also completed a book-length manuscript about her life entitled *Life As I Have Lived It*.

Rosina Tucker was honored on many occasions for her union work and her civil rights leadership. Organizations recognizing her achievements included the Leadership Conference on Civil Rights, the National Coalition of 100 Black Women, the Coalition of Labor Union Women, and the District of Columbia Hall of Fame.

Even in her latter years Tucker remained an iron-willed, robust, and witty personality, and a woman who appreciated the life she led and her part in improving the status of black people. As she indicated in her autobiography, "today is my day as it is your day. Although I live far removed from the time I was born I do not feel that my heart should dwell in the past. It is in the future. Each day for over a century added to another has culminated in growth that has led to my present experience and has made the person I am today and will be tomorrow.... While I live let not my life be in vain. And when I depart may there be remembrance of me and my life as I have lived it" (Pitts, *Washington Living*). Rosina Tucker died on March 3, 1987, at the age of 105.

Profile by
Jessie Carney Smith

TINA TURNER

*T*ina Turner remains one of the most amazing success stories in the

1939– •

history of the music business. Now in her fifties, Turner still electrifies

audiences all over the world with her stellar performing abilities. A

Singer, actress •

survivor of a difficult, nomadic childhood and an abusive marriage,

Turner's talents and determination have enabled her to carve out a

substantial place in pop music history.

Tina Turner began life as Anna Mae Bullock on November 26, 1939, in Brownsville, Tennessee. Her early life was spent with her mother, Zelma, and her father, Floyd Richard Bullock, a Baptist deacon who worked as the resident overseer of a local farm. Her sister Alline was her primary childhood companion. Turner's half-sister Evelyn lived with Zelma's parents, the Curries, while Turner's paternal grandparents, Alex and Roxanna Bullock, lived just up the highway. "Mama Roxanna was a big, fine, church-centered woman of sober demeanor and harsh, starchy virtues" (Turner, *I, Tina*, 13).

Turner felt unwanted by her parents. Born into a union already full of disagreements and lacking in marital affection, she and her older sister Alline seemed to be yet another negative force in the tenuous

relationship between her parents. But while the marriage was full of "wall banger" arguments and anger, her parents were able to find time for Alline. Young Turner, however, often felt left out. She later reflected that, "my mother wasn't mean to me, but she wasn't warm, she wasn't close, the way she was with Alline. She just didn't want me. But she was my mother and I loved her" (Turner, *I, Tina*, 17).

When the United States entered World War II in 1941, Zelma and Floyd Bullock sought work in the defense industries in Knoxville. The two daughters were left behind—Alline in the warm family comfort of the Curries and Turner with Mama Roxanna. During the two years the Bullocks worked in the city, the girls were allowed one short visit to see their parents. While in Knoxville, Turner got her first taste of worship in the Sanctified Church, which was marked by a celebratory, expressive atmosphere that was light years from the rather constrained worship setting at Mama Roxanna's Baptist church. She developed a love for singing at around this time as well.

After the Bullocks returned from Knoxville, the family moved on, eventually settling in Spring Hill. Turner sang in the Spring Hill Baptist Church Choir. The youngest member of the choir, she nevertheless took the lead on all of the upbeat songs.

In 1950 the Bullock family broke up and Turner was handed off from one family member to another for a period of several years. In 1956 her mother finally took Turner with her to St. Louis, where Alline had already relocated.

Turner's time in St. Louis was a pivotal one. United with the sister she idolized, she learned about life in the city. Though she was only sixteen, she began to wear makeup and go to East Saint Louis nightclubs with Alline and her girlfriends. Their destination was often the Club Manhattan, where all the women were buzzing about the band that was playing there. The Kings of Rhythm were the hottest band on the chitlin' circuit, in large measure because of Ike Turner, the group's diminutive but charismatic lead musician.

Young Anna Mae Bullock struck up friendships with several of the bandmembers, while Alline dated Gene Washington, the group's drummer. After weeks of listening and singing along, Turner seized an opportunity to sing on stage with the band. She bowled both the audience and the band members over as she belted out a B. B. King song. Ike Turner was so impressed that he immediately negotiated with her mother to include her in the band's act. Turner first performed under the name of Little Ann.

Singer Makes •

Stage Debut

347 •

During her first year of performance Turner became close to Raymond Hill, the band's saxophone player, and she gave birth to his son, Raymond Craig, in 1958. For some time the relationship between Ike Turner and Anna Bullock remained platonic, with Ike Turner exhibiting a protective, mentoring attitude toward his newest singer.

A short while after her high school graduation, however, Turner fell in love with Ike, who had been married once before. Aware of his ugly reputation for violence, she nonetheless moved into Ike's house and some time later became his lover. In 1960 she gave birth to his son, Ronald Renelle. The couple later entered into a questionable marriage in Tijuana, Mexico. Ike Turner would later admit that he had not divorced his previous wife until 1974.

Their debut song, "A Fool in Love," was released in summer 1960. After hearing the demo version of the song with Anna Mae Bullock listed as lead vocalist, Henry "Juggy" Murray contracted with Ike Turner to press and sell the record and advised Turner to build the group around Tina. The record was released under the names Ike and Tina Turner. Although Turner felt apprehensive about being named for a woman from one of Ike's jungle fantasies, she wanted to support him in his quest for success. The song reached number two on the rhythm and blues charts.

The Ike and Tina Turner Revue debuted on a bill with Jackie Wilson. With Tina Turner's "soul-drenched quaking, pleading and shaking" (*Current Biography Yearbook*, 411), the energetic backup of the Ikettes, and Ike's musical skills and direction, the group became one of the hottest acts of its time. Recordings such as "It's Going to Work Out Fine," "I Pity the Fool," "I Idolize You," "Poor Fool," and "Tra La La La La" further solidified the band's popularity, though monetary disputes within the band and with record producers cast a shadow over the group.

The mini-skirted Tina Turner and the Ikettes proved to be a provocative combination. In 1965 well-known record producer Phil Spector took notice of Tina Turner's voice during a club date. A year later he asked Tina Turner to record a song he had just cowritten with Jeff Barry and Ellie Greenwich. The deal, however, stipulated that Ike Turner not be involved. The result of the studio recording—"River Deep, Mountain High"—was a huge success in Britain, but flopped in the United States.

The popularity of "River Deep, Mountain High" in Great Britain launched the group's success in Europe. As the opening act for the Rolling Stones 1966 European tour, the Ike and Tina Turner Revue gathered a large following. Purveying the band's trademark sound of hard-driving rhythm and blues with Tina Turner's unforgettable voice and mien, a new level of crossover was achieved, and the band toured throughout the 1960s and early 1970s. By 1971 their successful combination of pop/rock and rhythm and blues resulted in a Grammy Award for their cover version of "Proud Mary."

As the group reached new heights of popularity, Ike and Tina Turner's relationship went into a tailspin. Concerns about her husband's autocratic business style left her feeling stymied creatively. At the same time, Ike became increasingly abusive, and Tina was forced to sing through badly swollen lips on more than one occasion. As *Time* contributor Richard Corliss commented, the concert stage became the place "where she could release, through her primal art, all the anguish inside her. It was also the cage Ike kept her in, shackled by duty, love, and fear. Tina had a right to sing the blues" (Corliss, "Aye, Tina," *Time,* 65.

Gradually, though, the combination of Tina's emerging self and Ike's abuse proved to be a powerful catalyst for change. During their 1976 tour, a drug-addled Ike turned violent against his wife once again, but she fought back for the first time. Weary of the beatings, she left the group in Dallas on July 1 and started over. Drawing strength from the practice of Buddhism, she took a year off to settle her personal affairs. A key step was her divorce from Turner, who continued his descent into drugs and legal trouble after the breakup. She returned to show business slowly.

Turner's early performances were on the cabaret circuit. By 1978 she had recorded an album, *Rough,* which received little commercial success or critical acclaim. Still able to draw on her European success, though, she performed there frequently. The Rolling Stones then asked her to join their 1981 United States tour. Recognition from that tour rekindled interest, and independent bookings followed. She also made artistic changes in her show, returning to her blues roots for some selections and incorporating reggae influences into other compositions.

Her career once again on track, Tina Turner performed on a record-breaking 1983-1984 European tour and achieved special-guest billing on Lionel Richie's 1984 United States tour. That same year she returned to the recording studio and recorded *Private Dancer,* the culmination of her astounding comeback. The album was a huge hit, eventually selling more than eleven million copies worldwide. It also garnered four Grammy Awards, including Record of the Year recognition for "What's Love Got to Do with It?"

Tina Turner •

Returns

The next year Tina Turner returned to the big screen. (She had played the Acid Queen in the 1975 movie *Tommy*.) She won a role as Aunty Entity in the Mel Gibson film *Mad Max: Beyond Thunderdome*. The film also produced a hit song, "We Don't Need Another Hero," recorded by Turner.

Tina Turner's 1986 album *Break Every Rule* went multiplatinum and firmly established her as "rock n' roll's queen diva." Her 1990 tour took her to every continent. Turner's raw, powerful voice and overwhelming stage presence enabled her to sell out every venue on the tour schedule. On January 11, 1991, Tina Turner was inducted into the Rock and Roll Hall of Fame.

Profile by Sarah Crest

In 1993 a critically-acclaimed film of Turner's life, called *What's Love Got to Do with It?*, was released. The film starred Angela Bassett as Tina and Laurence Fishburne as Ike. Turner was honored by the warm reception the film received from audiences. "A movie of my life, imagine that?" she said in the *Chicago Tribune*. "How often does that happen? For black people, not very often" (Kot, *Chicago Tribune*, 4).

CICELY TYSON

1942– •

Actress •

Talent, drive, and determination have all been hallmarks of the career of award-winning actress Cicely Tyson. Early in her life, Tyson tapped into an inner drive to triumph over the impoverished circumstances of her childhood. The result was a gradual rise to film stardom and a body of work of which any actress could be proud. Moreover, Tyson's career on stage, screen, and television has been marked by the actress's commitment to the honest and dignified portrayal of black Americans.

The youngest of three children, Tyson was born December 19, 1942, in the east Harlem section of New York City. Her parents, William and Theodosia (or Frederika) Tyson, were immigrants from the West Indies. Both of Tyson's parents worked hard to provide for their children, but poverty was a constant companion.

Even as a child, though, Cicely Tyson "refused to accept the poverty of the Harlem ghetto as the totality of existence" (Klemesrud, *New York Times,* 35). She spent many childhood hours wandering the city's bus and subway systems, reaffirming her belief that another world existed to which she could aspire.

Tyson was raised in a strict household. Reminiscing with *Ebony* contributor Louie Robinson, Tyson noted that:

> Mother watched me like a hawk. Mother, who left my father when I was ten years old, said I was Daddy's baby. She seemed to resent that I adored him so much and that I had been his favorite.... I suppose I understand why. She knew if anything happened to me, I mean, if I "went wrong," my father would never forgive her . . . so my mother watched me like a hawk (Robinson, *Ebony,* 35).

Theodosia Tyson dedicated her life to her children, especially after their father died in 1962. Religion was a dominant force in Tyson's childhood, and she spent a lot of her time at Saint John's Episcopal Church. Tyson's activities, as well as those of her sister and brother, were restricted to the church, which their mother felt was the safest place for them to be. Tyson sang in the choir and played the piano and the organ. Her musical talent soon became apparent, and before long she was giving recitals at many of New York's concert halls.

Educated in the public schools of New York City, Tyson received her high school diploma from Charles Evans High School in Manhattan. At the age of eighteen, while working as a secretary for the American Red Cross, Tyson decided that she was destined for a more challenging life. The actress recalled her feelings at the time in a *New York Times* profile: "I know God did not put me on the face of this earth to bang on a typewriter for the rest of my life. I don't know what it is or where it is, but I am certainly going to find it" (Klemesrud, *New York Times,* 35). Tyson gradually developed a modeling career, although she continued to work for the Red Cross. She enrolled in the Barbara Watson Modeling School and used her lunch hour and weekends to fulfill her modeling engagements.

Tyson's modeling career blossomed and she became one of the top ten black models in the United States, earning as much as sixty-five dollars an hour in the mid-1950s. In 1956 she appeared on the cover of *Harper's Bazaar* and *Vogue,* two of America's leading fashion magazines.

Tyson's Career •

Progresses

353 •

Tyson's acting career, however, began tentatively. Her first role was a part in *The Spectrum*, an independent black film that was being shot by Warren Coleman in New York. Exhilarated by the experience, Tyson followed the advice of her friends and took up acting studies.

> When I decided to become an actress I never had any doubt that I would be successful. Once I began to study, I was in it totally. My mother had always instilled into us that whatever you try to do, do it as best you possibly can and if you are good at what you're doing, then success will come to you. I was never preoccupied with whether or not I was going to be successful, I was preoccupied with doing whatever I was doing the best possible way (Salaam, *Black Collegian*, 90).

Tyson's first role in a major motion picture was in the movie *Twelve Angry Men*, produced by United Artists in 1957 and starring Henry Fonda. In 1959 she played in *Odds Against Tomorrow*, another United Artists production. That same year she tackled her first theatrical role, playing Barbara Allen in Carroll's off-Broadway revival of the musical *The Dark of the Moon*. Several other parts quickly followed, including a role as a young African woman in "Between Yesterday and Today" for *Camera Three*, a CBS cultural series. It was in the amateur production of *The Dark of the Moon* that Tyson's mother saw her perform for the first time. After watching her daughter's performance as a prostitute in the role of Virtue—a performance for which Tyson received a Vernon Rice Award—she walked backstage and covered Tyson with her coat.

Television work in series, soap operas, and dramatic specials came along gradually. Impressed by Tyson's work, George C. Scott recruited her for a leading part in *East Side/West Side*, a 1963 CBS-TV series about social workers. Tyson thus became the first black actress ever to have a continuing role in a dramatic television series.

From 1962 to 1969 Tyson sparkled in a wide range of acting roles. A popular guest star on a number of television series, she maintained a vital theatre career as well, performing in such productions as *Moon on a Rainbow* (for which she won another Rice Award), *Tiger, Tiger, Burning Bright, The Blue Boy in Black, Trumpets of the Lord,* and *Carry Me Back to Morningside Heights.* Tyson also maintained a healthy motion picture career, appearing in a number of films.

Tyson's career reached new heights with her portrayal of Rebecca Morgan in *Sounder.* Released by Twentieth Century Fox in 1972, *Sounder* was based on a novel by William H. Armstrong that won the Newbery Medal Award in 1970. Tyson played Rebecca, a strong, dignified, loving wife of a sharecropper, played by Paul Winfield. Set in the South during the Depression years, the film was a powerful work, in large part because of Tyson's superb performance. In 1972 the National Society of Film Critics awarded her work on the film with best-actress recognition during the Atlanta Film Festival. Tyson received a five-minute standing ovation during the presentation. "My knees went to water," she later confided. "I just stood there, so astonished. Finally, I turned around and hugged Marty (Martin Ritt, the film's director)" (Klemesrud, *New York Times,* 13).

Discussing the film, Tyson called the character of Rebecca the first positive portrayal of a black woman on the screen, and noted that "*Sounder* really is significant for the black woman. She has always been the strength of our race, and she has always had to carry the ball" (Klemesrud, *New York Times,* 13). The character of Rebecca, Tyson remarked, is one with characteristics of warmth, beauty, love, and understanding, aspects of black people that are too rarely seen on film.

After her magnificent performance in *Sounder,* Tyson went on to star in several other films, but it was her depiction of another remarkable black woman that established her as a woman of truly uncommon acting ability.

Television audiences around the nation watched Tyson's next major performance with utter amazement. *The Autobiography of Miss Jane Pittman* featured Tyson in the title role. The show required the actress to portray the life of the character from the age of nineteen to her death at the age of 110. Directed by John Korty, the story was based on a prize-winning novel by Ernest J. Gaines. Aired by CBS in January 1974, the film provided a warm yet uncompromising look at the life of an ex-slave in the deep South, from the post-Civil War years to the 1960s civil rights movement.

Tyson Wins •

Emmy

Critics heaped well-deserved praise on Tyson for her magnificent performance. Movie critic Pauline Kael called Tyson "as tough-minded and honorable in her methods as any we've got.... I'm comparing Tyson to the highest, because that's the comparison she invites and has earned" (Kael, *New Yorker*). Reviewer Rex Reed concurred, calling her portrait of Pittman a masterful tour de force and one of the most brilliant performances he had ever seen from any actress.

On Tuesday, May 28, 1974, Tyson stood before family, friends, and fans to receive the coveted Emmy Award as actress of the year for television. During her acceptance speech she smiled and said "'You see, Mom, it really wasn't all a den of iniquity after all.' She said that with a smile, and she was referring to Mrs. Tyson's long-standing opposition to what she called Cicely's 'foolishness work'—her decision to be an actress" (Sanders, *Ebony*, 30).

In the aftermath of *The Autobiography of Miss Jane Pittman,* Tyson was entrenched as one of television's brightest stars. Between 1976 and 1978 she appeared in several television specials. In 1976 she portrayed Harriet Tubman, the Maryland slave who led three hundred other slaves to freedom on the Underground Railroad, in *A Woman Called Moses.* In the television adaptation of Alex Haley's powerful saga *Roots* (1977), she played Kunta Kinte's mother. In *King* (1978), she played the part of Coretta Scott King, wife of the slain civil rights leader Martin Luther King Jr.

Profile by Felicia H. (Felder) Hoehne and Barbara Lynne Ivey Yarn

On November 26, 1981, Tyson married jazz trumpeter Miles Davis in Amherst, Massachusetts. After her marriage she continued with her career, taking on a wide range of roles, including another Emmy-winning performance in *The Oldest Living Confederate Widow Tells All* in 1994. Tyson's long and distinguished body of work has brought her numerous awards and other forms of recognition, ranging from honorary doctorates to acting prizes. The actress is a member of several civic organizations, and served as a cofounder of the Dance Theatre of Harlem, a group dedicated to discovering and nurturing new talent.

SUSAN PAUL VASHON

A relief organizer and an educator, Susan Paul Smith Vashon **1838–1912** •

proved a vital member of the Civil-War era effort to comfort blacks and

wounded soldiers. Her family background and education also enabled **Civil War relief** •

her to serve as an important figure in efforts to organize black women. **organizer**

Vashon was born in Boston in 1838 to one of the city's leading black families. Her mother, Anne Paul Smith, was the eldest daughter of Thomas Paul, a Baptist clergyman and arguably the most influential black man in the city. The Reverend Paul was pastor of Boston's foremost black congregation, which met in the three-story African Baptist Church, the first church in the city constructed entirely by black laborers. Paul also sponsored the African school, which met in the church's basement, to educate black youngsters denied schooling in Boston's public schools.

The Reverend Paul's work in uplifting former slaves soon involved him in the growing abolitionist movement, and his interest in the nationalist emigration plans of the era resulted in his leadership of the first Baptist mission to Haiti in 1823, where he was warmly received by President Jean Pierre Boyer. Paul and his friend David C. Walker later

became general agents for the abolitionist *Freedom's Journal* when it was first published by John Russwurm and Samuel Cornish.

Anne Paul Smith died when Susan was still very young, but the activities of the Paul family remained formative because Susan was taken in by her maternal grandmother, Katherine Paul. In the Paul household the young Susan doubtless fell under the influence of her aunt Susan Paul, for whom she had been named. Susan Paul was a teacher and abolitionist who also served as secretary for Boston's all-black temperance organization and a speaker for women's rights.

Less is known about Susan Paul Smith's father, Elijah W. Smith. He probably met his wife-to-be at one of the fashionable concerts held at her father's church, for the Boston headwaiter was noted for his skills as a poet, cornetist, and composer. Later his music would take him to London, where in 1850 he played in concert at Windsor Castle at the command of Queen Victoria.

At about the same period as Elijah Smith's European tour, his daughter Susan entered Miss O'Mears Seminary in Somerville, Massachusetts (three miles northwest of Boston). The only black pupil in her class, she graduated from the school in 1854 as its valedictorian. Her attendance at a private school was probably due to increasing black resistance to the segregation of public education in Boston, which had reached a fever pitch in 1849. Influenced by complaints and boycotts, Boston eventually became the first large American city to integrate its schools, establishing requirements for racial integration in public education in 1855.

After graduation from the seminary, Susan moved to Pittsburgh, Pennsylvania, where her father had relocated. She took a teaching post in the segregated local school system under principal George Boyer Vashon, a man fourteen years her senior, whom she married in 1857.

Susan Vashon's new husband had a family and personal history very much like her own. Vashon had been born into an active abolitionist family that resided in Pittsburgh, Pennsylvania, during his youth. At age sixteen Vashon went west to Oberlin College, emerging as its first black graduate in 1844. He began a career in education by teaching school in Chillicothe, Ohio, during college, and after graduation he studied law in Pittsburgh. In 1848, after taking the bar examination in New York, Vashon became the first black lawyer to practice in the state; he had originally intended to take the bar examination in Pennsylvania but had been denied the privilege because of his African ancestry.

Frustrated and angry with American racial discrimination, Vashon left for Haiti that same year. His decision to leave may have been motivated by his father's interest in an emigration plan popular in Philadelphia during 1824, the year of his birth. Haiti's president, Jean Pierre Boyer, the same leader who had welcomed the missionary Thomas Paul in 1823, had sent agents to Pennsylvania to recruit free blacks to emigrate to Haiti, where their skills would help develop the island and where they could be free of the virulent racism that was so commonplace in the United States.

Whatever his motives, Vashon spent the years 1848-1850 in Haiti teaching in Port-au-Prince. He then returned to practice law in Syracuse, New York (where he wrote his great epic poem, "Vincent Ogé," about the Haitian revolution). He subsequently became a professor of belle-lettres and mathematics at New York Central College. In 1857 Vashon moved back to Pittsburgh to take a position as principal and teacher in the city's "colored" public schools.

Susan Paul Vashon and her husband, then, each had families that were active in fostering black education and the abolition movement. In addition, both families were connected to the black republic of Haiti. Moreover, Susan and George Vashon had both struggled for their educations in schools where black students were a rarity, and both had succeeded with high honors. That both also became teachers is reflective of the professional opportunities available in that era. In the course of their marriage the well-matched Vashons had seven children.

• **Soldiers and**

Refugees

Receive Care

It is highly probable that the newly-married Vashons were active participants in the Underground Railroad prior to the Civil War. Both George and his father, John Bethune Vashon, were known to have been conductors of runaway slaves in Pittsburgh. Susan Vashon carried on the same tradition during the Civil War. She cared for sick and wounded soldiers, but also organized a series of sanitary relief bazaars in 1864-65 that raised thousands of dollars in funds to house black refugees. Such charitable activities had long been undertaken by the wealthier blacks of Philadelphia and Boston; Vashon's nursing and her work with former slaves carried on well-established traditions.

In 1867 the Vashons moved to Washington, D.C., where George Boyer Vashon became the first black instructor at Howard University (1867-1868) teaching in the evening school. He subsequently took a position as a solicitor for the Freedmen's Bureau. Susan Vashon, meanwhile, began teaching in the "colored" public schools of Washington in 1872. She remained active in that capacity for the next eight years before becoming the principal of the Thaddeus Stevens School. In 1874 George Boyer Vashon returned to college teaching, taking a teaching position at the new Alcorn University in Rodney, Mississippi, just three years after its founding. He died there in 1878.

Susan Vashon moved with her four surviving children to St. Louis in 1882. She lived there with her son John B. Vashon, who, like his parents, was a highly respected educator. Her other three children also established themselves in the city. George Boyer Vashon worked as a clerk in St. Louis City Hall, while Emma Vashon Gossin taught at Sumner High School and Frank C. Vashon took up service as a postal worker.

Throughout her years in St. Louis, Vashon remained true to the Paul and Vashon family traditions of community service. She worked for the All Saints Episcopal Church, the Book Lover's Club, the Mother's Club (an organization that guided young women) and the Women's Federation until her death in 1912.

Vashon's work to foster the women's club movement in Missouri is especially noteworthy. She helped organize the Missouri Association of Colored Women's Clubs in 1900, and in 1902 she served as president of the Missouri State Federation of Colored Women's Clubs of the National Association of Colored Women (NACW), working to unify the efforts of the state's first black women's association. She was instrumental in forming the Saint Louis Association of Colored Women's Clubs, and persuaded the NACW to hold their national convention in St. Louis during the great World's Fair in 1904.

Vashon High School in St. Louis was named in honor of the Vashon family's many achievements. Susan Paul Vashon is buried in the city's Bellfontaine Cemetery.

**Profile by
William D. Piersen**

ORA WASHINGTON

Ora Washington was one of America's most versatile and talented

1898–1971 •

black female athletes. Her high standards of performance and longevity

in tennis led some to compare her early achievements to those of Althea

Tennis player, •

Gibson, one of the greatest tennis players of her time, but Washington

basketball

was also an excellent basketball player for many years. According to

player

Marianna Davis in Contributions of Black Women to America, *Ora*

Washington "earned lasting recognition as one of the greatest pioneer-

ing inspirations for black women athletes."

Washington began playing tennis when a YWCA instructor in Germantown, Pennsylvania, where she lived, encouraged her to take up a sport. The instructor felt that Washington, grief-stricken over the recent death of a sister, needed an outlet to occupy her attention. Washington's gift for tennis was soon apparent. In 1924 she entered the African American National Tennis Tournament, held every year in Baltimore, Maryland, since 1917. She won the tournament championship, defeating Dorothy Radcliffe. For the next twelve years, Washington was undefeated among players of the American Tennis Association (ATA) and the African American National Tennis Organization, founded in 1916. She won her first women's singles trophy when she defeated Lula Ballard, a teacher from Cleveland, Ohio (Ballard later ended Washington's twelve-year reign as champion in 1936 in a match in which Washington suffered from sunstroke).

During her twelve years as champion, Washington excelled in both individual and team tennis. She held the ATA singles title from 1929 through 1935, then regained it again in 1937 with a triumph over Catherine Jones. Washington also gave outstanding performances in the women's doubles championships from 1930 through 1936, and was part of the champion ATA women's doubles team for seven years in a row. Washington's primary competitors during these years included Ballard, Jones, Lillian Hines, Emma Leonard, Frances Giddens, Flora Lomax, and Isadore Channels.

At the height of her abilities, Washington was seemingly unbeatable. Arthur Ashe Jr. noted that the *Chicago Defender* of March 14, 1931, stated that, "Ora Washington, now of Chicago, again holds her position as national champion, having gone through the season without a defeat. We don't even recall her losing a set.... Her superiority is so evident that her competitors are frequently beaten before the first ball crosses the net" (Ashe, *A Hard Road to Glory*).

Washington's tennis career and her public acclaim were marked by segregation. Parallel to her twelve-year career of unprecedented championship in the ATA was the career of white tennis star Helen Wills Moody, the dominant player in the United States Lawn Tennis Association. Moody refused Washington's challenges to play to determine America's best in women's singles. As a result, the two finest women players of the era never faced one another on the court.

Analysis of Washington's tennis style is generally qualified by references to her speed and particularities of tennis play for her era. According to Ashe, Washington's approach was unorthodox: "She held the racket halfway up the handle and seldom took a full swing. But no woman had her foot speed, which she honed while playing basketball for the *Philadelphia Tribune* team. She was clearly the first black female to dominate a sport" (Ashe, *A Hard Road to Glory*). In addition to this, Washington's style was characterized by a form of play developed by such African American tennis pioneers as Edgar Brown and James Stocks. Blessed with a terrific overhead game, she was fond of using her forehand, though she also displayed solid backhand drives and slices. A solid server, she depended on strategy and consistency to register her victories.

Washington retired from the ATA on two occasions. After her first retirement, Flora Lomax, who had won the women's singles title, publicly expressed her anger at being unable to challenge Washington because of her decision to hang up her racquet. Washington thus returned to the tennis court, defeating Lomax in the challenge match. She then retired again, feeling it was time to yield the game to younger competitors. *Sepia* magazine described her decision as one that was based on a tennis official's complaint "that her continued presence in the sport 'killed the spirit of young hopefuls who shied away from tennis rather than meet her.'"

Washington was also an outstanding basketball player for many years. She was the star center and captain for the *Philadelphia Tribune* girls squad for eighteen years, and was the team's top scorer for a number of those years. She also played for the Germantown Hornets, leading that team in scoring as well. The Philadelphia girls team was begun in 1931, sponsored by its namesake, a prominent black newspaper. Ashe describes the era's playing style as "the typical six players per team style which had separate threesomes for offense and defense at opposite ends of the court" (Ashe, *A Hard Road to Glory*). Among Washington's teammates were Marie Leach, Sarah Latimore, Gladys Walker, Lavinia Moore, Virginia Woods, Rose Wilson, Myrtle Wilson, and Florence Campbell.

Basketball

Career

Launched

Throughout the 1930s, Washington and her teammates were juggernauts, losing only six games to opposing teams. The Philadelphia team traveled extensively (in February and March of 1938 alone, they made a three-thousand-mile tour of the South covering nearly a dozen states), presenting clinics and demonstrations, and they eventually emerged as "black America's first premier female sports team" (Ashe, *A hard Road to Glory*).

Despite her considerable skills on the basketball court, though, it was as a tennis player that Ora Washington made her biggest impact. "No one who ever saw her play could forget her, nor could anyone who ever met her," remarked Wally Jones and Jim Washington. "She was a quiet person, gracious, yet a fierce competitor on the tennis court" (Jones and Washington, *Black Champions Challenge American Sports*).

In 1961, thirty-seven years after she began her tennis career, Washington was described in *Sepia* as being "as slender and attractive" as she was during her career as a champion. At that time she was not only the owner of an apartment building purchased with earnings from work

Profile by
Laura C. Jarmon

in domestic service, but, more importantly, she was enthusiastically serving her community, conducting free training and coaching for youngsters at the community's tennis courts in Germantown. Her death in 1971 marked the passing of one of America's most enduring sports figures.

MAXINE WATERS

*T*hroughout her political career in the California State Assembly

and the United States House of Representatives, Maxine Waters has been

known as a feisty, articulate, and passionate crusader for her constitu-

ents. Growing up poor, Waters learned as a child to work hard and strive

for success in all of her endeavors. These lessons have served her well in

adulthood, as one observer noted in Essence: "If Maxine Waters maneu-

vers as easily among the makers and shapers of public policy on Capitol

Hill as she does among the welfare mothers, blue-collar workers and

street toughs in Watts [suburb of Los Angeles], it's because she knows,

firsthand, what it's like at both ends of the spectrum" (Harris, Essence).

Maxine Moore Waters was born in St. Louis, Missouri, on August 15,

1938– •

Politician •

1938, to Remus Moore and Velma Lee Carr Moore, who divorced when Maxine was two years old. The fifth of thirteen children (Maxine's mother remarried), Waters grew up determined to make her mark in the world. A conscientious student, she also participated in extracurricular activities such as music, track, and swimming. At thirteen, she secured her first job as a busgirl at a segregated restaurant.

After graduating from high school in 1956, Waters married her childhood sweetheart, Edward Waters. They had two children, Edward and Karen, and secured factory jobs for themselves. In 1961 the couple decided to move to Los Angeles, where Maxine found work in a garment factory and at a telephone company. After suffering a miscarriage in the mid-1960s, though, she had to quit her telephone operator job.

In the aftermath of the 1965 Watts riots, Waters took a job as an assistant teacher in the newly created Head Start program. This nation-wide project was sponsored by the federal government and designed to give children from poor families a more advantageous start in school and life. She soon became the voice for frustrated parents whose children attended the Head Start program. She encouraged parents to make federal budget requests, to contact legislators and agencies for increased funding, and to lobby for Head Start program components tailored for their community.

In 1968, while working at Head Start, Waters decided to attend college. Three and a half years later, in 1972, she graduated from California State University at Los Angeles with a degree in sociology. That year she also divorced Edward Waters. In the meantime, Waters's Head Start work led her to become involved with local elections. She became chief deputy to city council member David Cunningham from 1973 to 1976, and campaigned for several other California politicians.

Sidney Williams, a Mercedes-Benz salesman in Los Angeles and a former Cleveland Browns football player, wooed Maxine Waters for five years before they wed in 1977. He supported her successful candidacy for the California State Assembly in 1976, a legislative body that Waters subsequently served for the next fourteen years. During this time she kept a small apartment in Sacramento, where she stayed during the week, returning home on weekends to attend functions and to meet with constituents.

During her tenure in the state assembly, Maxine Waters became the chairperson of the Ways and Means Subcommittee of State Administration. She was the first woman to serve on the Joint Legislative Budget Committee, the Judiciary Committee, the Elections Reapportionment and Constitutional Amendments Committee, the Natural Resources

Heads to the •

California State

Assembly

Committee, the Joint Committee of Legislative Ethics, and the California Commission on Status of Women.

Waters also served notice that she was unafraid to confront the male-dominated system in the assembly. She made her presence known on often controversial issues with her knowledge and self-confidence, and introduced legislation that reflected her views. Waters sponsored legislation, for example, that prohibited policemen from conducting strip searches and body-cavity searches of persons arrested for misdemeanors. Her membership on the Joint Committee on Public Pension Fund Investments also led to groundbreaking legislation. After eight years of furious lobbying and six different submissions of the bill, she finally secured the passage of a landmark law that required California to divest state pension funds from firms doing business in South Africa, which still operated at the time under laws of apartheid. She also worked tirelessly to get other United States companies to get out of South Africa.

As she became known as the conscience of the California legislature, Waters also evolved into a powerhouse in the state Democratic party. In 1981 she proved influential in garnering the speakership position for Willie Brown Jr. A close friend and ally in the assembly, Brown, in turn, supported her successful bid to become the majority whip. She thus became the first woman in the state to be elected chair of the Democratic Caucus, ranked number four on the leadership team.

One of Maxine Waters's primary concerns was women's rights. To involve more women in Los Angeles in this issue, she, along with Ethel Bradley (wife of Los Angeles's Mayor Bradley) and publisher Ruth Washington, formed the Black Women's Forum. This organization sponsors lectures and strives to motivate women to develop their own lists of important concerns. On a national level, Waters joined with a number of other prominent black women in founding the National Political Congress of Black Women in 1984. The *Washington Informer* noted the primary mission of this nonpartisan, nonprofit organization: "to promote and encourage the participation of Black women in the political process to gain the social, educational and economic empowerment needed to enhance the quality of life for Black women, their families and community."

Waters's commitment to job training for her constituents has been demonstrated through her efforts to build the Maxine Waters Employment Preparation Center, an extension of the Watts Skills Center, founded in 1966. At the center, approximately 2200 students and young adults receive training lasting from three to six months in a range of vocational occupations. Waters also created Project Build, a program to provide much-needed information regarding child care, health, and day care, as well as educational and job-training services, to families in six Los Angeles housing projects. In addition, Waters has sponsored legislation in areas of child abuse prevention, work laws, and environmental protection.

After fourteen years in the California State Assembly, Waters ran for the seat vacated by retiring congressman Augustus Hawkins in the Twenty-ninth Congressional District of California. Although her opponent in the June 1990 primary was endorsed by the Democratic political machine, Waters soundly defeated him, garnering 88 percent of the vote. She also won the general election handily with 80 percent of the votes cast.

Prior to taking on her new responsibilities, Waters commented on the significance of the election of black women to national office: "The women of this country, the Black women,. . . have wanted very much to increase their numbers. So I think our voices are going to be extremely important, not only to articulate the aspirations of Black women, but to add our voices to the voices of Black men" (Collier, *Ebony*).

In 1992, running in the much larger Thirty-fifth Congressional District, Waters accrued 83 percent of the votes cast to win reelection for a second term. Ranked as one of the most liberal members of Congress, she served on the Banking, Finance and Urban Affairs Committee, the Small Business Committee, and the Veterans' Affairs Committee. She also joined several organizations, including the Congressional Black Caucus and the Congressional Caucus for Women's Issues. But while her congressional responsibilities were significant, Waters still actively involved herself in California politics, where her constituency is predominately African American and Latino American. Her congressional district includes South Central Los Angeles, Inglewood, Hawthorne, and Gardena.

Waters's district office burned in the Los Angeles riots that broke out in 1992 after the Rodney King verdict. Waters subsequently invited herself to a meeting at the White House, where President George Bush and top advisors were consulting about how to aid the city. Since the primary people involved were Congressman Waters's constituents, she felt obligated to offer concrete suggestions to improve the quality of life, not just in South Central Los Angeles, but in urban communities across the nation. She was instrumental in ensuring that peace prevailed in the urban Los Angeles area after a second trial of the four policemen in the Rodney King case was held (two of the officers were given thirty-month sentences).

Waters •

Becomes U.S.

Representative

**Profile by
Jacqueline
Brice-Finch**

In recent years Waters has lent her support to diverse corporate and private organizations, including the National Women's Political Caucus, the Elizabeth Jackson Carter Foundation of Spelman College, the National Minority AIDS Project, and the National Council of Negro Women. She was one of the founders of the TransAfrica Foundation, serves on the board of *Essence* magazine, and is a board member of the Overseas Education Fund of the League of Women Voters, which provides Third World women with financial support.

Maxine Waters remains deeply committed to the concerns of the American people. The issues of urban poverty and despair continue to consume her waking moments, and she concedes that her passion to improve the situation has ruffled feathers. "Most people say I'm too pushy, I'm too aggressive, I'm too assertive, I'm too confrontational. That I ask for too much. I've never been considered patient, or even conciliatory in most instances" (*Los Angeles Times,* May 16, 1993). Waters remains unapologetic for her demeanor, however, citing the importance of her work and the needs of the people she represents.

DOROTHY WEST

*D*orothy West is a novelist, short story writer, editor, and journalist

who began her literary career in the 1920s during the Harlem Renais-

sance. Now, in the 1990s, the 1995 release of her novel The Wedding has

sparked a renewal of interest in and appreciation for her writing talent.

As Sybil Steinberg noted in Publishers Weekly in 1995, "Dorothy West,

indeed the last surviving member of the Harlem Renaissance, is having

her own private renaissance" (Steinberg, Publishers Weekly, 34).

1907– •

Writer, editor, •

journalist

West was born June 2, 1907, in Boston, Massachusetts, the only child of Rachel Pease Benson and Isaac Christopher West. Her mother had moved from her native home of Camden, South Carolina, to Massachusetts as a teenager. Years later she met and married the older Isaac West, a former slave from Virginia who owned a wholesale fruit company in Boston, where he was known as the city's "Black Banana King."

West received her formal education in Boston. At the age of two she began lessons under the tutelage of Bessie Trotter, sister of *Boston*

Guardian editor Monroe Nathan Trotter, and then studied under Grace Turner. West entered the Farragut School in Boston at the age of four, but she was able to do second-grade-level work because of the excellent tutoring she had received. The rest of her elementary education was at the Martin School in the Mission Hill District of Boston. Upon graduating from Girl's Latin High School in 1923, West attended Boston University and the Columbia University School of Journalism.

West began writing short stories at age seven. Her first short story, "Promise and Fulfillment," was published in *The Boston Post*. She became a regular contributor to the *Post*, which awarded her several literary prizes for her well-written stories. She developed a passion for Dostoevsky and the theater around this time. Just after high school graduation, still shy of her eighteenth birthday, West and her cousin, poet Helen Johnson, received invitations to attend *Opportunity* magazine's annual awards dinner in New York. The two young ladies attended the dinner and settled in at the Harlem YWCA. West later moved into an apartment that had been vacated by Zora Neale Hurston.

During her stay in New York, West developed her writing skills and established herself among a group of artists and writers who became part of a movement known as the Harlem Renaissance. Other members of the group included such luminaries as Langston Hughes, Zora Neale Hurston, Bruce Nugent, Wallace Thurman, and Aaron Douglas. Of her association with these now well-known figures, West said "I went to the Harlem Renaissance and never said a word. I was young and a girl so they never asked me to say anything. I didn't know I had anything to say. I was just a little girl from Boston, a place of dull people with funny accents" (Washington, 150).

In 1926 West won a second-place short story prize from *Opportunity* magazine for a short story called "The Typewriter." (West shared the award with Zora Neale Hurston.) "The Typewriter" concerned an unfulfilled black man who lives out his dream to be someone important through a series of fantasy letters he dictates to his daughter, who is practicing to increase her typing speed. Each evening he looks forward to this escape from his dull world, but one day he gets home from work and learns that his daughter has returned the rented typewriter; she has gotten a job as a stenographer and no longer needs it. His world is shattered, and he dies.

Other short stories written by West included "Hannah Byde," "An Unimportant Man," "Prologue to a Life," "The Black Dress," and "Mammy." Published in such journals of the day as the *Messenger* and the *Saturday Evening Quill*, as well as *Opportunity*, the stories often contained Dostoevskian elements. Critic Margaret Perry noted that West's stories tend "to emphasize confinement, in moral, psychological, emotional, and physical aspects, [and] the idea of salvation through suffering" (Perry, *Silence to the Drums,* 132). The characters in West's stories are unfulfilled and frustrated people who feel trapped by their environment, by racism, and by sexism.

• **West Founds**

Literary

Magazines

In 1927 West took a bit part in the original stage production of *Porgy* and subsequently went on a three-month tour of the play in London. She traveled to the Soviet Union during the 1930s with a group of twenty-two black Americans to film *Black and White,* a project that was never completed. Despite the failure of this project, West remained in Russia for about a year.

Upon returning to New York, West founded *Challenge* magazine in 1934. Three years later she launched *New Challenge* magazine. These two literary journals sought to provide an avenue for the publication of the high-quality writing being produced by some of the Harlem Renaissance writers, as well as the work of younger writers just beginning their careers. Although West had high hopes for her magazines, their lives were short. Victimized by uneven quality and financial difficulties, the journals were also impacted by West's editorial policies, which shifted to reflect a more proletarian ideology.

After the demise of the two magazines, West worked as a welfare investigator in Harlem for eighteen months. She then joined the Federal Writers Project of the Works Progress Administration, where she remained until the project ended in the 1940s. She continued to write and became a regular contributor of short stories to the *New York Daily News* from 1940 to 1960. In 1945 she left New York permanently and moved to Martha's Vineyard, where she continues to reside.

In 1948 West's novel *The Living is Easy* was published. It is a semi-autobiographical novel in which the main characters, Cleo, Bart, and Judy Judson, are patterned after her mother, her father, and herself, respectively. Like her mother Rachel, the beautiful, light-skinned Cleo Judson is a domineering woman who wishes her dark-skinned daughter, Judy, were more like her in both appearance and personality. Cleo gathers her sisters and their children in the Judson home, a move that ultimately breaks up her marriage with Bart, to whom she is cold and scornful. Bart, however, is the main financial support of the household. The novel satirizes the elite black families of Boston and their often disdainful treatment of "ordinary" black people. Racism, sexism, and class-consciousness are all evident themes in the novel.

The Living is Easy received mixed reviews when it first appeared. Since the reprint of the novel by Feminist Press in 1982, though, critics have examined the book from a more feminist perspective. Modern scholars have focused on the role and importance of the mother in the household, the mother-daughter relationship, and the complexities of the character of Cleo. Robert Bone called the work "a diamond in the rough . . . bitingly ironic," and of "a primarily Renaissance consciousness" (Bone, *Negro Novel in America,* 187, 190). For her part, West noted that "back in 1948 a leading women's magazine refused to publish chapters from . . . *The Living is Easy* because they feared losing subscribers. You see, no one knew what to make of my heroine because the word 'feminist' had hardly been invented yet. *I* didn't know she was a feminist until years later" (Karpen, *New York Times Book Review,* 11).

A long-time resident of Martha's Vineyard, West continued to write, contributing a weekly column to the *Martha's Vineyard Gazette.* And in 1995 she finally unveiled her long-awaited second novel, titled *The Wedding,* which had been begun many years before. According to *Publishers Weekly,* the novel is "a multigenerational story of a family whose marital alliances achieve the acme of 1950s black respectability: light complexions, financial stability and social standing....The impetus to finish *The Wedding* slowly leaked away during the '60s, in part because of the emergence of the Black Panthers, West says. 'I hated them! They scorned the upper middle class. I wanted to write about people like my father, who were ambitious. But people like him were anathema to the Black Panthers, who said that all black people are victims.... It was a discouraging time.'" Editor Jackie Onassis, though, heard of the novel and encouraged West to complete it. Once the book was finally published, commented critic Susan Kenney, "you have only to read the first page to know that you are in the hands of a writer, pure and simple. At the end, it's as though we've been invited not so much to a wedding as to a full-scale opera, only to find that one great artist is belting out all the parts. She brings down the house" (Kenney, *New York Times Book Review,* 12).

**Profile by
Elwanda D. Ingram**

MARION BIRNIE WILKINSON

A skillful leader and producer of numerous statewide clubs and

projects, Marion Birnie Wilkinson improved the quality of life for many.

The seeds she planted throughout the state of South Carolina, and the

nation, continue to flourish and grow today.

1870–1956 •

Humanitarian, •

educator,

clubwoman

Marion Raven Birnie Wilkinson was born June 23, 1870, to Richard and Anna Frost Birnie in Charleston, South Carolina. She and her five sisters and brothers later gained a half-brother after Richard Birnie married Grace Hope. The Birnies were well-to-do blacks, having received their status from earlier family members characterized as free blacks in Charleston.

The Birnie children began their education at Avery Institute in Charleston. While there, Wilkinson became interested in the advancement of her people. When she returned to the historic institution as a teacher, much of her money from her salary was channeled to worthy causes. Her career of education and service mirrored that of several of her ancestors. Her maternal great-grandmother founded a school in Charleston for blacks in 1820 and taught in several schools established for freed blacks after the Civil War. Henry Frost, her maternal grandfather, operated a school on Magazine Street.

Wilkinson married Robert Shaw Wilkinson, also from Charleston, on June 29, 1897. Robert Shaw Wilkinson had been educated at the Robert Shaw Memorial School, Avery Institute, and West Point, and received his B.A. from Oberlin College. His career as an educator began at Kentucky State University, but he moved to South Carolina State University in 1896 and served on its first faculty as a professor of physics and chemistry. After Thomas E. Miller, a former African-American congressman, resigned his presidency of the university in 1911, Wilkinson became president. As his wife, Marion Birnie Wilkinson became "first lady" and emerged as a leader of students, faculty, and the community. The Wilkinsons also started a family, and eventually had four children: Helen Raven, Robert Shaw, Frost Birnie, and Lula Love.

On the campus of South Carolina State, Marion Birnie Wilkinson, affectionately known as "Mother Wilkinson," guided the work of the YWCA for many years. Through this organization, young women developed many characteristics that would serve them well in the workplace and in the community, such as leadership, character, and service. Marion Birnie Wilkinson's leadership led to the construction in 1928 of the only YWCA building on a college campus during that era. Funds were raised by the students for the construction of the building, which was later named the Marion B. Wilkinson Y-Hut. It served the YWCA and YMCA organizations for years and is still being used on the college campus.

Wilkinson also headed the College Boarding Department for many years. Auxiliary services like this department were not provided by the state of South Carolina; faculty and staff thus led the effort to provide students with full college-wide services similar to those enjoyed in other institutions.

The Wilkinsons emerged as leaders of the religious community as well. St. Paul's Episcopal Church, founded in 1912 and eventually located next to the college, had its early beginning in the Wilkinsons' residence. Services were later moved to the Y-Hut, and in 1950 the church moved to its permanent home next to the college campus. Religion played an important role in Marion Wilkinson's family, and evidence indicates significant family activity in the Episcopal church through several generations.

Community and social uplift were Marion Wilkinson's primary concern. She became widely known for her work in these areas in Orangeburg, South Carolina, and nationwide. Cited as a "gift of woman-hood in Ebony," by historian Asa Gordon, she was part of the first group of women at Sidney Park Colored Methodist Episcopal Church (now Christian Methodist Episcopal Church) who in 1909 founded the South

Carolina Federation of Negro Women. Others in the group included Sara B. Henderson, Celia D. Saxon, and Lizella A. Jenkins Moorer. These women spearheaded the growth of several federated clubs in the state, including the Uplift Club (Camden), Louise F. Holmes Literary and Art Club (Charleston), Sunlight Club (Orangeburg), and One More Effort (Sumter). During Wilkinson's leadership as president of the state organization, she received support from all the South Carolina federated clubs for the organization's projects. She gained further support from students, faculty, and staff at the college.

During its infancy, a primary purpose of the South Carolina Federation of Colored Women was to found and support a reformatory school for delinquents. As time passed, the school was used for girls who lacked proper family protection. Known initially as Fairwold, the school later became the Marion B. Wilkinson Home for Girls. Wilkinson and other citizens headed committees that appeared before the state legislature to gain annual financial support for the Fairwold School.

The state withdrew financial support in 1929, placing the burden of all of the fundraising for the home on the local clubs. Fire destroyed the home, but under the leadership of Wilkinson the home was rebuilt in Cayce, South Carolina, on land donated by the Upper Diocese of the Episcopal Church of South Carolina. The Duke Foundation, which would not support the home when it served delinquents, funded the home after it was made an orphanage. The Marion B. Wilkinson Home for Girls became a model for a similar establishment in Virginia.

Wilkinson was known as a sweet and modest woman. The proud history and success of the South Carolina Federated Women's Club during this era, however, was attributed in large part to another Wilkinson trait: her determination. "Why this interest, Why this success: Why this movement to the heroic effort of our women? To this question we exclaim in one, united voice—the great inspiring leadership of the sainted Marion Birnie Wilkinson. Real leadership does not mean standing at the head of an organization—real leadership is that technique so lofty, so skillful, that it induces others to work and perform in like manner" (*Our Book of Gold*).

Wilkinson was also instrumental in the founding of the Sunlight Club, an affiliate of the South Carolina Federation of Negro Women in Orangeburg, South Carolina. In 1909, at the founding of the organization, the Sunlight Club promoted cultural enhancement, education, good character, and better human relations. Charter and early members came from faculty wives, staff of South Carolina State, Claflin College, and the Orangeburg community. The club continues to function, serving various aspects of the community. One of its main fund-raisers is the annual Wilkinson Tea, held every February.

Wilkinson made many notable contributions at the state level as well. She organized recreation centers at Camp Jackson for African American soldiers during World War I. She was responsible for the Better Homes Project, a statewide project to improve homes of the less fortunate, and for the establishment of the Rosenwald Schools in South Carolina, part of a multistate effort in the South funded by the Julius Rosenwald Fund to build schools in rural communities. She worked with the Red Cross, and set up a WPA training school and day nursery during the late 1930s. Her reputation as an effective and knowledgeable activist led President Hoover to seek her advice on child welfare programs.

Wilkinson's responsibilities as a president's wife and community organizer were considerable, yet she remained an attentive and encouraging parent to her four children. The Wilkinson children were well-educated and made important contributions to society in the realms of science, education, medicine, and social welfare.

Profile by Barbara Williams Jenkins

Serving as the wife of the second president of South Carolina State, known then as State Agricultural and Mechanical College, Wilkinson was a gracious, knowledgeable, and intelligent woman. She and her husband were friends of many well-known persons, including Mary McLeod Bethune, Charlotte Hawkins Brown, and Benjamin E. Mays. They were influential on campus, in the city, throughout the state, and nationwide, and their contributions are still remembered. Marian Birnie Wilkinson died on September 19, 1956.

MARION WILLIAMS

arion Williams, the grande dame of gospel music, delighted

1927–1994 •

audiences throughout the world for half a century. As gospel music

historian Bernice Johnson Reagon was widely quoted as stating, "She is

Gospel singer •

simply the best we had during the gospel era of the '40s and '50s." Other

critics and journalists have noted the enduring majesty of her work as

well, and many call her the finest gospel singer of all time.

Born in Miami, Florida, on August 29, 1927, Marion Williams was part of a large family, though the family was victimized by the deaths of a number of infants before their first birthday. Williams's father was a West Indian who worked as a barber and taught music. He died when she was nine years old. Her mother, originally from South Carolina, worked as a laundress and sang in a choir. Williams viewed her mother as a saint and marveled at her upbeat view of life in the face of adversity. The family's poor financial circumstances forced Williams to leave school at age fourteen to work as a maid and child nurse. She subsequently took a job in a laundry, where she worked long and exhausting hours.

Williams was only three years old when she began singing with her mother, a soloist in the church choir of the Church of God and Christ.

Williams remained faithful to this denomination throughout her life. As she grew older she branched out to other area churches, tent revival meetings, and street corner revivals to perform. Her young ears also came in contact with the sounds of blues and jazz during this time.

While visiting her sister in Philadelphia, Pennsylvania, in the mid-1940s, Williams encountered the famous Clara Ward Singers, the pre-eminent gospel group of the 1940s and 1950s, at the Ward African Methodist Episcopal (AME) Church. Upon invitation, Williams sang "What Could I Do (If It Wasn't for the Lord)" at the church. The teenager's stunning performance amazed and captivated the audience. Clara Ward immediately asked Miami's premier gospel soloist to join her group.

Williams eventually accepted the invitation and, between 1947 and 1958, Williams emerged as an important member of the Ward Singers. All Ward Singers were on salary, except family members. When it was later suggested to Williams that the Ward Singers acquired their significant wealth primarily from her singing, she responded, "That's all right. If it wasn't for Gertrude Ward, I'd be taking care of somebody's children, and singing on Sundays" (Heilbut, *The Gospel Sound*).

Williams left the group in 1958, taking group members Frances Steadman, Kitty Parham, and Henrietta Waddy along with her, and organized another gospel group, the Stars of Faith. The Stars of Faith enjoyed tremendous success, but Williams recognized that the group lacked the managerial skills of Gertrude Ward. Nine years later, she joined the Wards for a one-night appearance, the highlight of which was a stunning version of their hit song "Surely God Is Able."

Williams made her theatrical debut in 1961 in the gospel song-play *Black Nativity,* the text of which was written by the noted black author Langston Hughes. Hughes wrote the song-play especially for Williams, and he was pleased with its success. Following an outstanding three-year run in the United States, *Black Nativity* and its star enjoyed fantastic success in Europe. During the Christmas season of 1963, *Black Nativity* was produced for national television.

Gospel diva Williams made her debut as a soloist in 1966 and continued in that capacity until her death. During the late 1960s, she covered the college circuit, appeared at the Antibes Jazz Festival in France and the Dakar Festival of Negro Arts in Africa, performed on several television specials, and received one of Europe's top honors, the International Television Award. Though the popularity of contemporary gospel rose in the 1970s, Williams, a gospel traditionalist, performed less frequently during that time. The 1980s saw a resurgence in her career,

Gospel •

Performer Joins

Ward Singers

Williams Goes •

Solo

though, thanks in part to the efforts of Tony Heilbut and his Spirit Feel label. From the mid-1980s until her death, her concert career thrived, limited only by the physical disabilities she experienced from diabetes.

Over the course of her long career, Williams became entrenched as one of gospel music's legendary voices. A brilliant stage performer, Williams "is simply the most lyrical and imaginative singer gospel has produced," remarked Tony Heilbut in his book *The Gospel of Sound.* "She's a fat sweet-faced woman whose physical graces belie her size. When she sings, she may strut, run, Suzy-Q, sashay, sit or kneel.... Marion's ability to incorporate the best traditional approaches in a uniquely personal way, her vocal range from growl to whoops, from big-mama holler to little girl trill, should impress anybody."

Other critics concurred. "She could shout a church into submission, leaving fans faint, falling into faith," wrote *Washington Post* reviewer Richard Harrington. "Untrained but unlimited, she sang with astonishing rhythmic acumen and perfect timing, displaying a gift for ornamentation to rival makers of illuminated Bibles.... When Williams sang, she was illuminating the Bible in her own inimitable way."

Williams received abundant recognition and praise throughout her professional career, but she never lost her humility or let the adulation go to her head. In her eyes, as she frequently remarked, she was simply doing the Lord's work. She referred to herself as a missionary, one who ministered through her renditions of "We Shall Be Changed," "Standing Here Wondering Which Way to Go," "Packin' Up," "Prayer Changes Things," and "How I Got Over."

Williams's performing venues included nightclubs, jazz festivals, and summer park extravaganzas. She believed that people who refused to go to church also needed to hear the gospel. It was her firm conviction that if she could reach listener's ears, she stood a good chance of reaching their spirits. She did not object to appearing on the same bill as secular singers and was not envious of those who made fortunes in the world of popular music.

There were, of course, those who tried to change Williams's views. The owner of Savoy Records wanted to make Williams another Big Mama Maybelle, a popular 1950s blues shouter, and she was offered $100,000 to cut a blues album. The offer was not at all appealing to Williams. "Secular artists sing about the lovers of their bodies—their baby, their honey, 'my woman' and all that. I sing about Jesus Christ, who is the lover of my soul," Williams told *American Visions* in 1994. The possible financial rewards of a more secular-oriented career did not sway her. As Williams commented in *New York Newsday,* "I've been eatin' all these years. I often tell them, if they don't book me, I'll just sit home and eat my rice and beans.... And enjoy it."

Williams recorded ten albums during her career. She can also be heard on the 1991 film soundtrack for *Fried Green Tomatoes,* which was dedicated to her, and the 1992 movie soundtrack for *Mississippi Masala.* Williams was guest soloist for the 1992 premiere of trumpeter and composer Wynton Marsalis's gospel-influenced jazz suite, "In This House/On This Morning." She was also featured in the PBS presentation *Amazing Grace.*

In 1993, one year prior to her death, long-elusive financial rewards finally came Williams's way. The pioneering gospel singer became the first singer to be honored with a "genius" award by the MacArthur Foundation. The award included a $374,000 payment. When the word reached her, she was preparing an after-service meal in the soup kitchen at her Philadelphia church. "I thought I was in heaven and the angels were talking to me," she told Sharon Fitzgerald for *American Visions.*

Honored with •

Award from the

MacArthur

Foundation

Williams dined at the White House and shared the Presidential Box at the Kennedy Center Opera House with President Bill Clinton, Hillary Rodham Clinton, and other Kennedy Center honorees. She watched from that vantage point as artists such as Aretha Franklin, Little Richard, and Billy Preston paid tribute to her fabulous career. On the day of the Kennedy Center for the Performing Arts event, Williams commented on her career and the future of her art form:

> When I first started out, gospel music was in its infancy. People didn't pay attention to it, really. That didn't bother me; I kept on singing. I loved it and the spirit that I got from it. It just tugged at the very soul of folks. It made me want to live what I sing. I think around 1940, '45 was when people really started to take heed of gospel and know it was an art form.... I think gospel will just bloom. It's opening up more than ever ("Views from the Top," *Washington Post*).

Seven months later, Williams died from vascular disease. She was survived by a son, a brother, and three grandchildren. Mourners noted that Marion Williams brought to gospel a sense of dignity and a capacity for entertaining that exceeded that of most of her peers. Blessed with a vocal range that few could duplicate, she also maintained a humility that was supported by personal and artistic security. These qualities ensure that Marion Williams will always be a treasured part of gospel music's history.

**Profile by
D. Antoinette
Handy**

A CLOSER LOOK

● **DEBBIE ALLEN**

Cohen-Strayner, Barbara Naomi. *Biographical Dictionary of Dance.* New York: Schirmer Books, 1982.

Contemporary Theatre, Film, and Television. Vol. 6. Detroit: Gale Research, 1989.

Current Biography Yearbook. New York: H. W. Wilson, 1987.

"Debbie Allen—Doing It All, Her Way!!" *Ebony* 45 (November 1989): 54-58.

Mapp, Edward. *Directory of Blacks in the Performing Arts.* Metuchen, N.J.: Scarecrow Press, 1978.

"Mothers and Daughters: The Special Connection." *Ebony* 43 (February 1988): 158-62.

New York Theatre Critics' Reviews. 34, No. 26 (1973): 218-21; 51, No. 3 (1980): 366-71.

Ploski, Harry A., and James Williams, eds. *Negro Almanac.* Detroit: Gale Research, 1989.

Who's Who among Black Americans. 5th ed. Lake Forest, Ill.: Educational Communications, 1988.

● **DEL MARIE NEELY ANDERSON**

Anderson, Del Marie. Telephone interview with Dolores Nicholson. July 22, 1992.

The College Handbook, 1993. 30th ed. New York: College Entrance Examination Board, 1993.

"From Fashion Fair Model to Role Model." *Ebony* 47 (April 1992): 112–17.

Peterson's Guide to Two-Year Colleges, 1993. 23rd edition. Princeton: Peterson's Guides, 1992.

"San Jose City College Gets First Woman Prexy, Educator Del Anderson." *Jet* 81 (October 21, 1991): 21.

Williams, Jeannette. Telephone interview with Dolores Nicholson. January 30, 1995.

● **ANITA BAKER**

Current Biography. New York: H. W. Wilson, 1989.

Garland, Phyl. "Anita Baker's Love Songs." *Stereo Review* 55 (December 1990): 118.

Larkin, Colin, ed. *The Guiness Encyclopedia of Popular Music.* Chester, Conn.: New England Publishing Associates, 1992.

Leavy, Walter. "Who's the Greatest." *Ebony* 42 (October 1987): 140–46.

Mapp, Edward. *Directory of Blacks in the Performing Arts.* 2d ed. Metuchen, N.J.: Scarecrow Press, 1990.

Norment, Lynn. "Anita Baker Returns with a Bang." *Ebony* 49 (September 1994): 44–50.

Waldron, Clarence. "Anita Baker Makes Comeback with World Tour, Hit Album." *Jet* 87 (March 13, 1995): 60–63.

Who's Who among Black Americans, 1994–95. 8th ed. Detroit: Gale Research, 1994.

● **KATHLEEN BATTLE**

"The Age of the Black Diva." *Ebony* 46 (August 1991): 74–76.

"Camille Cosby, Kathleen Battle Win Candace Awards." *Jet* 82 (July 20, 1992): 16–17.

Current Biography Yearbook, 1984. New York: H. W. Wilson Company, 1985.

Davis, Peter G. "The Ascent of Mann." *New York* 27 (February 21, 1994): 57–58.

Hine, Darlene Clark, ed. *Black Women in America.* New York: Carlson Publishing, 1993.

For more ●

information

Holland, Bernard. "Classical Music in Review." *New York Times* (November 10, 1992).

———. "Kathleen Battle Pulls out of *Rosenkavalier* at Met." *New York Times* (January 30, 1993).

———. "A Very Special Soprano." *New York Times Magazine* (November 17, 1985).

Jellinek, George. "Kathleen Battle: At Carnegie Hall." *Stereo Review* 67 (December 1992): 123.

Keller, James M. "Kathleen Battle and Jessye Norman: Spirituals." *Musical America* 110 (July 1990): 62–63.

Marsh, Carole S. *The Color Purple and All That Jazz! Black Music, Poetry, Writing and Art.* Bath, N.C.: Gallopade Publishing Group, 1989. "The Met's Battle Royal." *Washington Post* (February 9, 1994).

Musical America: International Directory of the Performing Arts. New York: Musical America Publishing, 1992.

Oestreich, James R. "Classical Music in Review." *New York Times* (October 17, 1992).

Porter, Andrew. "Musical Events." *New Yorker* 60 (April 9, 1984): 114–16.

Rothstein, Edward. "With Emphasis on the Upbeat, the Philharmonic Turns 150." *New York Times* (September 17, 1992).

Stahel, Thomas H. "Lessons in Song and Slaughter." *America* 164 (January 12, 1991): 17.

"Whom Are You Trying to Please?" *Esquire* 106 (December 1986): 208.

• *HALLE BERRY*

"Annual Readers Poll." *Ebony* 50 (September 1993): 92–94, 96.

Collier, Aldore D. "Halle Berry Plays Seductive, Stone Age Secretary in Movie *The Flintstones.*" *Jet* 86 (June 6, 1994): 36–38, 40.

Contemporary Black Biography. Vol. 4. Detroit: Gale Research, 1993.

"Halle Berry and David Justice Purchase New Home in Los Angeles." *Jet* 87 (November 28, 1994): 15.

"Halle Berry: Strictly Business about Show Business." *Ebony* 47 (February 1992): 36, 38, 40–41.

Jones, Lisa. "The Blacker the Berry: Not Just Another High-Toned Ingenue, Halle Berry Is an Activist Actress Who Speaks Her Mind." *Essence* 25 (June 1994): 60–62, 114–16.

Moore, Trudy S. "Halle Berry: Actress Tells Why She Sticks by Male Friend with Aids." *Jet* 81 (June 20, 1992): 34–37.

Randolph, Laura B. "Halle Berry: Hollywood's Hottest Black Actress Has a New Husband, a New Home and a New Attitude." *Ebony* 48 (April 1993): 118–20, 122.

———. "Halle Berry: On Her Roles, Her Regrets and Her Real-Life Nightmare." *Ebony* 50 (December 1994): 114–15, 118–22.

"Running in the Fast Lane." *Ebony* 48 (July 1993): 68, 70, 74.

"Summer Movies Doing Bang-Up Business." *USA Today* (July 10, 1992).

• *WILLA BROWN*

"The Afro-American Airman in World War II." *Aviation Education* (April 1971).

Dixon, Walter T., Jr. *The Negro in Aviation.* Baltimore: Clarke Press, 1950.

Downs, Karl E. "Willa B. Brown: Vivacious Aviatrix." In *Meet the Negro.* Pasadena, Calif.: Login Press, 1943.

Hunt, Rufus A. *The Coffey Intersection.* Chicago: J.R.D.B. Enterprises, 1982.

Johnson, Jesse J., ed. *Black Women in the Armed Forces, 1942–74.* Hampton, Va.: Johnson Publishing, 1974.

Locke, Theresa A. "Willa Brown-Chappell, Mother of Black Aviation." *Negro History Bulletin* 50 (January–June 1987): 5–6.

Naulty, Bernard C., and Morris J. MacGregor, eds. *Blacks in the Military: Essential Documents.* Wilmington, Del.: Scholarly Resources, 1981.

Rose, Robert A. *Lonely Eagles: The Story of America's Black Air Force in World War II.* Los Angeles: Tuskegee Airmen, 1976.

"School for Willa." *Time* (September 25, 1939): 16.

Travis, Dempsey J. *An Autobiography of Black Chicago.* Chicago: Urban Research Institute, 1981.

Waters, Enoc P. "Little Air Show Becomes a National Crusade." In *American Diary: A Personal History of the Black Press.* Chicago: Path Press, 1987.

Who's Who in Aviation, 1942–43. Chicago: Ziff-Davis Publishing, 1942.

"Young Aviatrix To Teach Air-Minded Billikens the Principles of Aviation." *Chicago Defender* (May 16, 1936).

"Young Woman Flyer Gets Pilot's License: Willa Brown, Chicago Aviatrix, Can Carry Passengers, Give Instructions or Make Cross-Country Flights." *Pittsburgh Courier* (July 2, 1938).

• *NANNIE HELEN BURROUGHS*

Afro-American (April 28, 1934).

Barnett, Evelyn Brooks. "Nannie Helen Burroughs." *Dictionary of American Negro Biography*. Eds. Rayford W. Logan and Michael R. Winston. New York: Norton, 1982.

————. "Nannie Helen Burroughs and the Education of Black Women." In *The Afro-American Woman*. Eds. Sharon Harley and Rosalyn Terborg-Penn. Port Washington, N.Y.: Kennikat Press, 1978.

Burroughs, Nannie Helen. "Black Women and Reform." In "Votes for Women." *Crisis* 10 (August 1915): 187.

————. "Eating in Public Places." *Washington Afro-American* (14 April 1934).

————. "Not Color but Character." *The Voice of the Negro* 1 (July 1904): 277-78.

————. "With All Thy Getting." *Southern Workman* 56

Daniels, Sadie I. *Women Builders*. Washington, D.C.: Associated Publishers, 1931.

"Fighting Woman Educator Tells What Race Needs." *Pittsburgh Courier* (December 23, 1932).

Harrison, Earl L. *The Dream and the Dreamer*. Washington, D.C.: Nannie H. Burroughs Literary Foundation, 1956.

Mather, Frank Lincoln. *Who's Who of the Colored Race*. Chicago: Mather, 1915.

"Nannie Helen Burroughs Says Hound Dogs are Kicked but Not Bulldogs." *Afro-American* (February 17, 1934).

Penn, I. Garland, ed. *The United Negro: His Problems and His Progress*. Atlanta: D. E. Luther, 1902.

Pickens, William. *Nannie Burroughs and the School of the 3B's*. n.p., 1921.

Washington Post (May 21, 1961; May 22, 1961).

Who's Who in Colored America. 7th ed. Yonkers-on-Hudson, N.Y.: Christian Burckel, 1950.

Collections

A comprehensive collection of materials related to Burroughs's life and activities can be found in the Nannie H. Burroughs Papers in the Library of Congress.

• *SEPTIMA CLARK*

Blakeney, Barney. "Mourners Recall Extraordinary Life of Septima Clark." *Charlston Post and Courier* (20 December 1987) 1.

————. "Literacy and Liberation," *Freedomways* (First Quarter, 1964): 113-24.

Branch, Taylor. *Parting the Waters: America in the King Years 1954-1963*. New York: Simon and Schuster, 1989.

————. "Writing an American Epic." *Christian Science Monitor* (3 February 1989).

Brown, Cynthia S., ed. *Ready from Within: Septima Clark and the Civil Rights Movement*. Navarro, Calif.: Wild Trees Press, 1986.

Clark, Septima P. *Echo in My Soul*. New York: E. P. Dutton, 1962.

Derkes, Scott. "Dat Not Be My Echo," *South Carolina Wildlife* 26, 4 (July/August 1979): 44-49.

Gallman, Vanessa. "Septima Clark: On Life, Courage, Dedication." *View South* 1, 4 (July/August 1979): 13-16.

Glen, John. *Highlander, No Ordinary School*. Lexington, Ky.: University of Kentucky Press, 1989.

Lanker, Brian. *I Dream a World:* New York: Stewart, Tabori and Chang, 1988.

Tjerandsen, Carl. *Education for Citizenship: A Foundation's Experience*. Santa Cruz, Calif.: Schwarzhaupt Foundation, 1980.

Collections

Clark's papers are held in the College of Charleston in Charleston, South Carolina. Also helpful are the Papers of Highlander Research and Education Center, State Historical Society of Wisconsin, Madison. Documented interviews with Clark are: Eugene Walker, July 30, 1976, and Jacqueline Hall, June 25, l981, housed in Southern Oral History Program Collection, Southern Historical Collection, University of North Carolina, Chapel Hill; and Peter Wood, February 3, 1981, and Eliot Wigginton, June 29, 1981, housed in Highlander Center Archives, Newmarket, Tennessee.

• ALICE COACHMAN

Bernstein, Margaret. "That Championship Season." *Essence* 15 (July 1984): 59, 124, 128.

Herald (Albany), (13 March 1974); (16 August 1984).

Jackson, Tenley-Ann. "Olympic Mind Power." *Essence* 15 (July 1984): 63.

Rhoden, William C. "Good Things Happening for One Who Decided to Wait." *New York Times* (April 27, 1995): B14.

Telegraph (Macon) (2 September 1948).

Times (Albany) (28 March 1979).

Collections
Photographs and news clippings of Alice Coachman (Davis) are available in the Fisk University Library Special Collections.

• CAMILLE O. COSBY

Johnson, Robert E. "Bill and Camille Cosby Discuss the Secrets of Living a Better Life." *Jet* (2 October 1989): 58-62.

———. "Bill and Camille Cosby: First Family of Philanthropy." *Ebony* 44 (May 1989): 25-34.

Norment, Lynn. "Three Great Love Stories." *Ebony* 43 (February 1988): 150-156.

Oliver, Stephanie Stokes. "Camille Cosby: An Intimate Portrait." *Essence* 20 (December 1989): 63-64.

Williams, Lena. "A Private Woman, A Public Cause." *New York Times* (December 15, 1994): C1, C8.

• JULIE DASH

Boyd, Valerie. *"Daughters of the Dust."* *American Visions* 6 (February 1991): 46–48.

Chambers, Veronica. "Finally, a Black Woman behind the Camera." *Glamour* 90 (March 1992): 111.

Dash, Julie. *"Daughters of the Dust": The Making of an African American Women's Film.* Preface by Toni Cade Bambara. New York City: New Press, 1992.

———. Bio. sheet. Geechee Girls Productions.

Flanagan, Sylvia. *"Daughters of the Dust."* *Jet* 81 (March 23, 1992): 62.

Hartman, S. V., and Farah Jasmine Griffin. "Are You as Colored as That Negro?: The Politics of Being Seen in Julie Dash's *Illusions*." *Black American Literature Forum* 25 (Summer 1991): 361–73.

Hine, Darlene Clark, ed. *Black Women in America.* Brooklyn: Carlson Publishing, 1993.

"Julie Dash: Geechee Girl." Promotional material. Atlanta: Moore, Little, Inc.

Kauffman, Stanley. Review of *Daughters of the Dust.* *New Republic* 206 (February 10, 1992): 26–29.

Tate, Gregory. "A Word." In *"Daughters of the Dust": The Making of an African American Women's Film,* by Julie Dash. New York: New Press, 1992.

Thomas, Deborah. "Julie Dash." *Essence* 22 (February 1992): 38.

• THE DELANY SISTERS

"Camille Cosby Acquires the Film, Stage and Television Rights to Delany Sisters' Life Story." *Jet* 85 (January 17, 1994): 26.

"A Century of Being Sisters." *Washington Post* (November 25, 1993).

Current Biography. (November 1995): 14–18

Delany, Sarah, and Elizabeth Delany, in collaboration with Amy Hill Hearth. *Having Our Say: The Delany Sisters' First 100 Years.* New York: Kodansha, 1993.

Good Morning America. Interview with Delany Sisters by Terry Row. November 23, 1993.

Jones, Charisse. "Bessie Delaney Dies at 104; Author of 'Having Our Say'." *The New York Times Biographical Services* (September 26, 1995).

• SUZANNE DE PASSE

Allen, Bonnie. "Suzanne De Passe: Motown's $10-Million Boss Lady." *Essence* 12 (September 1981): 89–92; 141–44.

Black Enterprise 5 (June 1974): 77–80.

Burger, Michael. "Women in Business." *Ebony* 32 (August 1977): 122–23.

"Clothes for the Young Miss." *Ebony* 5 (September 1950): 51.

DeLeon, Robert A. "Suzanne de Passe: Woman behind Motown Stars." *Jet* 48 (June 12, 1975): 24–31.

Igus, Toyomi, ed. *Great Women in the Struggle.* New York: Just Us Books, 1991.

Ingham, John N., and Lynne B. Feldman. *African-American Business Leaders: A Biographi-*

cal Dictionary. Westport, Conn.: Greenwood Press, 1994.

Rothman, Jill. Fax to Jessie Carney Smith. June 21, 1994.

———. Telephone conversation with Jessie Carney Smith. June 23, 1994.

"Suzanne de Passe. Biography." Los Angeles: Rachel McCallister and Associates, 1994.

Who's Who among Black Americans, 1994–95. 8th ed. Detroit: Gale Research, 1994.

Who's Who of American Women. 18th ed. New Providence, N.J.: Marquis Who's Who, 1993.

• DOROTHY DONEGAN

Balliett, Whitney. "Wonder Woman." New Yorker 60 (18 February 1991): 37-38, 40-41.

"Dorothy Donegan Wins In Her Son's Custody Battle." Jet 46 (5 September 1974): 46. "Hazel's Rival?" Time 40 (16 November 1942): 73.

"Is Jazz Going Highbrow?" Ebony 1 (July 1946): 15-19.

Kinkle, Roger D. The Complete Encyclopedia of Popular Music and Jazz: 1900-1950. Vol. 2. New Rochelle, N.Y.: Arlington House, 1974.

"Queen of the Keys." Ebony 13 (March 1958): 84-88.

"People Are Talking About." Jet 34 (27 June 1968): 43.

Reich, Howard. "Dorothy in Dreamland." Chicago Tribune (September 19, 1993): 12.

Reitz, Rosetta. Record notes for Dorothy Romps: A Piano Retrospective 1953-1979. Vol. 9 in Foremothers, Women's Heritage Series. CD 1318. 1991.

Southern, Eileen. Biographical Dictionary of Afro-American and African Musicians. Westport, Conn.: Greenwood Press, 1982.

"Wild But Polished." Time 72 (3 November 1958): 78.

• RITA DOVE

Contemporary Authors. Vol. 109. Detroit: Gale Research, 1983.

Contemporary Literary Criticism. Vol. 50. Detroit: Gale Research, 1987.

Dove, Rita. Fifth Sunday. Baltimore: Callaloo Fiction Series, 1985.

———. Grace Notes. New York: Norton, 1989.

———. Museum. Pittsburgh: Carnegie Mellon University Press, 1983.

———. Thomas and Beulah. Pittsburgh: Carnegie Mellon University Press, 1986.

———. The Yellow House on the Corner. Pittsburgh: Carnegie Mellon University Press, 1980.

Grosholz, Emily. "Marriages and Partings." Hudson Review 40 (Spring 1987): 157-64.

McDowell, Robert. "The Assembling Vision of Rita Dove." Callaloo 9 (Winter 1986): 61-70.

Molotsky, Irvin. "Rita Dove Named Next Poet Laureate; First Black in Post." New York Times (May 19, 1993): C15, C18.

Preston, Rohan B. "Simply Unique." Chicago Tribune (July 5, 1993): 1.

• JOYCELYN ELDERS

"Arkansas Gave Out Defective Condoms." Nashville Tennessean (July 22, 1993).

"Battle Lines Form for Surgeon General Hearings." USA Today (July 7, 1993).

"Battle Looms over Choice for Health Post." Nashville Tennessean (July 14, 1993).

Black, Edwin. "Elders' View on Health Care." Podiatry Today (April 1993).

"Clinton Picks Arkansas Official to Be New U.S. Surgeon General." New York Times (December 15, 1992).

"Colleges as Health Care Models." USA Today (June 3, 1993).

Contemporary Black Biography. Vol. 6. Detroit: Gale Research, 1994.

Current Biography 44 (March 1994): 5. "Doctor Elders: We Need Her." Nashville Tennessean (July 16, 1993).

"Dr. Elders's Prescription for Battle." Washington Post (February 16, 1993).

"Drumbeat Growing against Elders." USA Today (June 29, 1994).

"Elders Is Ideal Choice for Surgeon General." USA Today (July 28, 1993).

Elders, Joycelyn. Interview on "Nightline." ABC-TV, December 9, 1994.

———. Interview in To the Contrary. Public Broadcasting System, n.d.

———. Speech at Group Health Association of America. Washington, D.C., March 1993.

Elders, Joycelyn, and Jennifer Hui. "Making a Difference in Adolescent Health." *Journal of American Medical Association* 269 (March 12, 1993): 1425.

"Joycelyn Elders Joins GW Medical Faculty." *Jet* 85 (April 4, 1994): 6.

"Listening to Elders." *USA Weekend* (June 3–5, 1994).

"Meeting Health Issues Head-on." *USA Today* (July 30, 1993).

Miller, Mark. "A Uncompromising Woman." *Harper's Bazaar* (July 1993): 111.

"Pick for Surgeon General Says She'll Support Medicinal Use of Marijuana." *Nashville Tennessean* (December 20, 1992).

Pone, Tom. "U.S. System More Sick Care than Health Care." *Oncology Times* (May 1993).

Popkin, James. "A Case of Too Much Candor." *U.S. News & World Report* 117 (December 19, 1994): 31.

"President Clinton Fires Elders." *Washington Post* (December 10, 1994).

"Regulate, Not Ban, Smokes Elders Says." *Nashville Tennessean* (March 28, 1994).

"A Unique Individual." *Nashville Tennessean* (July 20, 1993).

"Will Clinton Fall Down on Job of Protecting Elders." *USA Today* (July 9, 1993).

• *JUSTINA L. FORD*

"AIA Awards Fentress for Ford House." *Historic Denver News* (December 1991/January 1992).

Flier. Black American West Museum and Heritage Center. Denver, Colorado, n.d.

Burton, Frances. "A Legacy Continued: Ford Shaped Hopes and Destiny of the Black Community." *Port Charlotte Florida Sun* (February 1989).

"Colorado Medical Pioneer." Resolution. Interim Meeting of the Colorado Medical Society House of Delegates, March 11, 1989.

Denver Post (October 14, 1952).

Denver Weekly News (October 15, 1952).

"Dr. Justina Ford Honored as First Black Female Physician in Colorado." *Colorado Medicine* 15 (February 1989): 60.

"Dr. Justina Ford-Allen; Colorado's First Doctor of Color Passes after 50 Years of Service."

Unidentified newspaper clipping in the files of Jessie Carney Smith.

"Ford House Finds Home." *Denver Weekly News* (February 9, 1984).

"Ford House to be Restored as Black American West Museum." Unidentified newspaper clipping. Black American West Museum.

Gallegos, Magdalena. "Doctor Justina Ford, a Medical Legacy Continues." *Urban Spectrum* 2 (September 1988): 4–5.

Harris, Mark. "The Forty Years of Justina Ford." *Negro Digest* 8 (March 1950): 43–45.

Harris, Ottaw. Letter to Jessie Carney Smith, May 5, 1994.

Hibbard, Bill. "How Blacks Helped Win the West." *Michigan Living*. Undated article.

Johnson, Connie. "Dr. Justina Ford: Preserving the Legacy." *Odyssey West* (March 1988): 4–5.

"Justina L. Ford, M.D. One of Colorado's Medical Pioneers." Biographical sheet. Denver: Black American West Museum, n.d.

"Learning about Dr. Justina Ford." *Denver Post.* Undated article in the files of Jessie Carney Smith.

"She Was Truly 'An Angel of Mercy.'" Guest editorial. *La Voz* (July 27, 1983).

Collections

Biographical information on Justina Ford and a photograph of her home are located in the Denver West Museum and Heritage Center, the Western History Collection of the Denver Public Library, and the Colorado Historical Society.

• *HAZEL B. GARLAND*

Bolden, Frank E. Telephone interview with Phyl Garland, October 20, 1994.

Collins, Jean E. *She Was There: Stories of Pioneering Women Journalists.* New York: Julian Messner, 1980.

"Courier Editor/Journalist Hazel Garland Dead at 75." *New Pittsburgh Courier* (April 6, 1988).

Davis, Marianna W., ed. *Contributions of Black Women to America.* Vol. 1. Columbia, S.C.: Kenday Press, 1982.

"Former Courier Editor Hazel Garland Dies." *Pittsburgh Press* (April 6, 1988).

Garland, Phyl. "Blacks in Journalism." In *Encyclopedia of African-American Culture and History.* New York: Macmillan, 1995.

"Hazel Garland, Pioneer Journalist." *Pittsburgh Post-Gazette* (April 6, 1988).

"Journalist Hazel Garland, Former Courier Editor, Dies." *Jet* 74 (April 25, 1988): 59.

"Nationally Known Journalist, Civic Leader, Hazel Garland Dies at 75." *New York Daily News* (April 6, 1988).

Portis, Connie. Interview with Phyl Garland, July 22, 1993.

• *ZINA LYNNA GARRISON*

Faingold, Noma. "Strike a Pose: Glamour Is Alive in Women's Tennis." *Inside Tennis* 11 (August 1991): 26.

"Garrison Has the Right Stuff." *Inside Women's Tennis* 13 (August 1989): 12–14.

Higdon, David, J. "Zina on Her Own." *Tennis* 24 (March 1989): 33–37.

Hine, Darlene Clark, ed. *Black Women in America*. Brooklyn: Carlson Publishing, 1993.

"Little Steps, Giant Strides." *City Sports* 16 (October 1990): 31–35.

"Living a Dream." *Sports Illustrated* 71 (November 27, 1989): 71–76.

"Tennis Ace Zina Garrison Ties Houston Love Match." *Jet* 77 (October 23, 1989): 52.

Tracy, Steve. "On Center Court." *Spirit* (May 1988): 34–52.

• *FRANCES E. W. HARPER*

Baym, Nina. *Woman's Fiction: A Guide to Novels by and about Women in America 1820-1870*. Ithaca, N.Y.: Cornell University Press, 1978.

Brown, Hallie Q. *Homespun Heroines and Other Women of Distinction*. Xenia, Ohio: Aldine Pub. Co., 1926, 97-103.

Carby, Hazel. Introduction to *Iola Leroy*. Edited by Deborah E. McDowell. Boston: Beacon Press, 1987, 1-20.

Davis, Arthur P., and J. Saunders Redding, eds. *Cavalcade: Negro American Writing from 1760 to the Present*. Boston: Houghton Mifflin, 1971.

Foster, Frances Smith. Introduction to *Iola Leroy*. Edited by Henry Louis Gates, Jr. New York: Oxford University Press, 1988.

Harper, Frances E. W. *Iola Leroy*. Edited by Deborah E. McDowell. Boston: Beacon Press, 1987.

Lerner, Gerda, ed. "Black Women in the Reconstruction South." In *Black Women in White America*. New York: Pantheon, 1973.

McKay, Nellie. Interview by author. 11 April 1991.

Sherman, Joan R. *Invisible Poets: Afro-Americans of the Nineteenth Century*. 2nd ed. Urbana, Ill.: University of Illinois Press, 1989, 62-74.

Shockley, Ann Allen. *Afro-American Women Writers 1746-1933*. Boston: G. K. Hall, 1988, 56-61.

Still, William. Introduction to *Iola Leroy*. Philadelphia: Garigues Brothers, 1892.

• *CHARLOTTE HAWKINS BROWN*

Brown, Charlotte Hawkins. *Mammy: An Appeal to the Heart of the South*. Boston: The Pilgrim Press, 1919.

—. *The Correct Thing To Do, To Say, To Wear*. Boston: Christopher Publishing House, 1941.

Daniel, Sadie Iola. *Woman Builders*. Washington, D.C.: Associated Publishers, 1970.

Dannett, Sylvia G. L. "Charlotte Hawkins Brown." *Profiles of Negro Womanhood*. Vol. 2. Yonkers, N.Y.: Educational Heritage, 1966.

Marteena, Constance Hill. *The Lengthening Shadow of a Woman: A Biography of Charlotte Hawkins Brown*. Hicksville, N.Y.: Exposition Press, 1977.

Stewart, Ruth Ann. "Charlotte Eugenia Hawkins Brown." *Notable American Women: The Modern Period*. Cambridge, Massachusetts: Harvard University Press, 1980.

Tillman, Elvena. "Charlotte Hawkins Brown." *Dictionary of American Negro Biography*. Eds. Rayford W. Logan and Michael R. Winston. New York: Norton, 1982. 65-67.

Wadelington, Charles W. Interview with author, 8 November 8, 1990.

Collections

The Charlotte Hawkins Brown Papers are located in the Schlesinger Library, Radcliffe College, Cambridge, Massachusetts. The collection contains correspondence, speeches memorabilia, materials related to the Palmer Memorial Institute, and biographical material, including a fragmentary autobiography by Brown and an incomplete, unpublished biography, *The Twig Bender,* by Cecie R. Jenkins. The most complete collection of materials on Charlotte Hawkins Brown is located in the Charlotte Hawkins Brown Collection, Division of Archives and History, North Carolina Department of Cultural Resources, Historic Sites Section, Raleigh, North Carolina.

Papers on Charlotte Hawkins Brown's work with the National Council of Negro Women are in the National Council of Negro Women's National Archives for Black Women's History, Washington, D.C.

Collections of materials on Charlotte Hawkins Brown and the Palmer Memorial Institute are located at the Schomburg Center for Research in Black Culture, the New York Public Library, New York City; in the North Carolina Historical Room at the Greensboro Public Library, Greensboro, North Carolina; in the collection of Afro-American Women's materials in the Thomas F. Holgate Library at Bennett College, Greensboro, North Carolina; in the W.C. Jackson Library at the University of North Carolina at Greensboro, Greensboro, North Carolina; and in the Amistad Research Center at Tulane University, New Orleans, Louisiana.

• *ALEXIS M. HERMAN*

"Blacks Held Top Posts at Democratic Confab." *Jet* 82 (August 3, 1992): 10–11.

Dobrzynski, Judith. "Essence Women: Alexis Herman." *Essence* 8 (November 1977): 6.

Herman, Alexis M. Biographical information. White House, 1994.

———. "Black Women in the Labor Force." *Black Collegian* 9 (May/June 1979).

———. "Employment Opportunities for Black Women in the 1980's." *Black Collegian* 10 (April/May 1980): 96–99.

Moreman, Grace E., and Pearl G. Spindler. "Women in the Labor Movement and Organizations." In *The Women's Book of World Records*. Edited by Lois D. O'Neill. Garden City, N.Y.: Anchor Press/Doubleday, 1979.

Who's Who in American Politics. 13th ed. New Providence, N.J.: R. R. Bowker Database Publishing Group, 1992.

"Women in Government: A Slim Past, but a Strong Future." *Ebony* 32 (August 1977): 89–98.

"Women's Job Activist." *Washington Star* (April 1, 1977).

• *ANITA HILL*

"Anita Hill." *People* 36 (December 30, 1991–January 6, 1992): 46–47.

Brock, David. *The Real Anita Hill: The Untold Story*. New York: Free Press, 1993. Garment,

Suzanne. "Why Anita Hill Lost." *Commentary* 93 (January 1992): 26–35.

Guy-Sheftall, Beverly. "Breaking the Silence: A Black Feminist Response to the Thomas/Hill Hearings (for Audre Lorde)." *Black Scholar* 22 (Winter 1991/Spring 1992): 35–37.

Hill, Anita. "Opening Statement before the Senate Judiciary Committee, October 11, 1991." *Black Scholar* 22 (Winter 1991/Spring 1992): 8–11.

"Hill Resigning as Law Professor." *Nashville Tennessean* (March 17, 1995).

"A House Divided." *Essence* 22 (January 1992): 58–59, 92–93.

Hull, Gloria T. "Girls Will Be Girls, and Boys Will . . . Flex Their Muscles." *Black Scholar* 22 (Winter 1991/Spring 1992): 47–48.

Jordan, June. "Can I Get a Witness?" *The Progressive* 55 (December 1991): 12–13.

Leatherman, Courtney. "Once a Little-Known Law Professor, Anita Hill Now Is a 'National Icon.'" *Chronicle of Higher Education* 39 (October 14, 1992): 18A.

Lewis, Earl. "Race as Commodity: Hill and Thomas as Consumer Product." *Black Scholar* 22 (Winter 1991/Spring 1992): 66–68.

Malveaux, Julianne. "No Peace in a Sisterly Space." *Black Scholar* 22 (Winter 1991/Spring 1992): 68–71.

Mayer, Jane, and Jill Abramson. *Strange Justice*. Boston: Houghton Mifflin, 1994.

Morrison, Toni. *Race-ing* Justice, *En-gendering* Power: Essays on Anita Hill, Clarence Thomas, and the Construction of Social Reality. New York: Pantheon, 1992.

Nelson, Jill. "Hill versus Thomas." *Essence* 22 (December 1991): 134.

Patterson, Orlando. "Race, Gender and Liberal Fallacies." *Black Scholar* 22 (Winter 1991/Spring 1992): 77–80.

Sedman, Susan. "Mail Call in Norman, Oklahoma." *Glamour* 90 (March 1992): 30.

"She Could Not Keep Silent." *People* 36 (October 28, 1991): 11–13.

Smolowe, Jill. "Anita Hill's Legacy." *Time* 140 (October 19, 1992): 56–57.

Spencer, Cembalo. "The Chronology of the Clarence Thomas Confirmation." *Black Scholar* 22 (Winter 1991/Spring 1992): 1–3.

Sullivan, Kathleen M. "The Hill-Thomas Mystery." *New York Review of Books* 40 (August 12, 1993): 12–16.

Who's Who among Black Americans, 1994–95. 8th ed. Detroit: Gale Research, 1994.

Winternitz, Helen. "Anita Hill: One Year Later." *Working Woman* 17 (September 1992): 21.

• ANN HOBSON-PILOT

"Capacity Crowd Cheers Chamber Music on St. Maarten." *Symphonium* 2 (Fall 1990): 2.

"Delightful New CD by Harpist Pilot." *Symphonium* 4 (Winter 1992): 1.

Handy, D. Antoinette. *Black Women in American Bands and Orchestras*. Metuchen, N.J.: Scarecrow Press, 1981.

"Harpist Pilot Enjoys Banner Year." *Symphonium* (Fall 1992): 1, 8.

"Harpist Says Her Profession Worth Trouble." *Richmond Times Dispatch,* January 23, 1978.

Hobson-Pilot, Ann. Interview with D. Antoniette Handy. Brookline, Mass., September 16, 1975.

—. Letters to Handy, May 17, 1979; January 20, 1980; January 24, 1994.

—. Telephone conversation with Handy, January 20, 1994.

Row, Steve. "2nd Serenade Is Fiery." *Richmond News Leader,* January 23, 1978.

Southern, Eileen. *Biographical Dictionary of Afro-American and African Musicians*. Westport, Conn.: Greenwood Press, 1982.

• BELL HOOKS

Black Writers. 2d ed. Detroit: Gale Research, 1994.

hooks, bell. *Ain't I a Woman: Black Women and Feminism*. Boston: South End Press, 1981.

———. "Black Is a Woman's Color." In *Bearing Witness: Selections from African American Autobiography in the Twentieth Century*. Edited by Henry Louis Gates. New York: Pantheon, 1991.

———. "Feminism—It's a Black Thang!" *Essence* 23 (July 1992): 124.

———. *Feminist Theory from Margin to Center*. Boston: South End Press, 1984.

Jones, Lisa. "Rebel without a Pause." *Village Voice Literary Supplement* (October 1992): 10.

• WHITNEY HOUSTON

Ansen, David. "*The Bodyguard*." *Newsweek* 120 (November 30, 1992): 80.

Cain, Joy Duckett. "The Soul of Whitney Houston." *Essence* 20 (December 1990): 54–56.

Chappelle, Tony. "The Three Faces of Whitney Houston." *The Black Collegian* 21 (November/December 1991): 128–30.

Current Biography Yearbook, 1986. New York: H. W. Wilson Co., 1986.

"Grammy's High Notes." *Nashville Tennessean* (March 2, 1994).

Jones, James T., IV. "Houston, Boyz II Men Ride 'Soul Train.'" *Nashville Tennessean* (March 10, 1993).

Nashville Tennessean (March 5, 1993; June 6, 1993).

Norment, Lynn. "The Wedding of the Decade." *Ebony* 48 (September 1992): 124–35.

Oermann, Robert K. "Is Whitney Houston Too Perfect?" *Tennessean Showcase* (June 16, 1991): 3.

Sports Illustrated 72 (March 11, 1991): 66.

Time 141 (July 27, 1992): 27; (December 14, 1992): 75.

Turner, Renee D. "How Celebrities Will Celebrate Christmas." *Ebony* 45 (December 1989): 31.

"Whitney Houston: 'Forever Daddy's Girl.'" *Ebony* 45 (June 1990): 13–38.

"Whitney Houston Talks about the Men in Her Life." *Ebony* 46 (May 1991): 110–18.

"Whitney, Toni Top 'Soul Train Awards.'" *Nashville Tennessean* (March 16, 1994).

• ALBERTA HUNTER

Balliett, Whitney. "Let It Be Classy." *New Yorker* 53 (October 31, 1977): 100-112.

Clarke, Gerald. "Good Tune from an Old Violin." *Time* 120 (December 13, 1982): 82.

Gilbert, Lynn, and Gaylen Moore. *Particular Passions: Talks with Women Who Have Shaped Our Times*. New York: Clarkson N. Potter, 1981. 245-53.

Spradling, Mary Mace. *In Black and White*. 3rd ed. Vol. 1. Detroit: Gale Research, 1980. 467-68.

Taylor, Frank C., with Gerald Cook. *Alberta: A Celebration in Blues*. New York: McGraw-Hill.

Videotapes and Films

Alberta Hunter: Jazz at the Smithsonian. Video LP. Sony Corporation, 1982. Catalog no. J0065. Reissued on Keith label 1990.

Alberta Hunter: My Castle's Rocking. Directed by Stuart Goldman. Color. 60 minutes, 16mm film/video. The Cinema Guild.

• *LOUISE E. JEFFERSON*

Badger, T. A. "Louise Jefferson Pursues Many Goals—Illustrator—Photographer." *Torrington and Winsted (Connecticut) Register Citizen* (June 10, 1983).

Banks, T. J. "Artist Honors African Crafts." *Hartford Advocate* (March 7, 1984).

Begnal, Martin. "Portrait of a Unique Lady." *Torrington and Winsted Register Citizen* (September 30, 1993).

Black Women of Connecticut: Achievement against the Odds. Hartford, Conn.: Connecticut Historical Society, 1993.

Granger, Lester B. "The Credit Line Is Lou's." *Opportunity* 25 (Spring 1947): 91–92.

Humphrey, Elizabeth. "Litchfield Artist Knows No Bounds." *Litchfield (Connecticut) Enquirer* (April 2, 1986).

Jefferson, Louise E. Letter to Jessie Carney Smith, July 18, 1994.

Moutoussamy-Ashe, Jeanne. *Viewfinders: Black Women Photographers*. New York: Dodd Mead, 1985.

Murray, Pauli. *Song in a Weary Throat*. New York: Harper and Row, 1987.

• *EVA JESSYE*

Abdul, Raoul. *Blacks in Classical Music*. New York: Dodd, Mead, 1977

Lanker, Brian. *I Dream a World*. New York: Stewart, Tabori and Chang, 1989.

Rush, Theressa G. *Black American Writers*. Vol. 2. Metuchen, N.J.: Scarecrow Press, 1975.

Southern, Eileen. *Music of Black Americans*. New York: Norton, 1971.

Collections

Numerous letters, unpublished materials, and personal mementos of Eva Jessye's, as well as hours of taped conversations with her, are in the possession of the writer. Larger Eva Jessye collections are located at the University of Michigan and Kansas State University at Pittsburg (formerly Pittsburg State).

• *QUEEN LATIFAH*

Collier, Aldore. "Queen Latifah Reigns on and off TV." *Ebony* 49 (December 1933): 118–24.

Gregory, Deborah. "The Queen Rules." *Essence* 24 (October 1993): 56–58, 114–15, 118.

———. "The Queen Mother." *Essence* 24 (October 1993): 58, 121.

Pond, Steve. "Hail to the Queen." *TV Guide* 41 (October 16, 1993): 23–25.

Smith, Dinitia. "The Queen of Rap." *New York* 23 (December 3, 1990): 124–32, 138–46.

• *EDMONIA LEWIS "WILDFIRE"*

Blodgett, Geoffrey. "John Mercer Langston and the Case of Edmonia Lewis: Oberlin, 1862." *Journal of Negro History* 53 (July 1968): 201-218.

Child, Lydia Maria. "Edmonia Lewis." *Broken Fetter* (3 March 1865): 25.

———. "Letter from L. Maria Child." *National Anti-Slavery Standard* 27 February 1864.

Ciovsky, Nicola, Jr., and William H. Gerdts. *The White, Marmorean Flock: Nineteenth-Century American Women Neoclassical Sculptors*. Poughkeepsie, N.Y.: Vassar College Art Gallery, 1972.

Gerdts, William H. *American Neo-Classic Sculpture: The Marble Resurrection*. New York: Viking, 1973.

Goldberg, Marcia. "A Drawing by Edmonia Lewis." *American Art Journal* 9 (November 1977): 104.

Hartigan, Lynda Roscoe. "Edmonia Lewis." In *Sharing Traditions: Five Black Artists in Nineteenth-Century America*. Washington, D.C.: Smithsonian Institution, 1985, 85-98.

James, Henry. *William Wetmore Story and His Friends*. Boston: Houghton, Mifflin, 1903, 357.

Leach, Joseph. *Bright Particular Star: The Life and Times of Charlotte Cushman*. New Haven: Yale University Press, 1970, 335.

Lewis, Edmonia. *The Revolution* (20 April 1871).

Locke, Alain. *The New Negro in Art*. Washington, D.C.: Associates in Negro Folk Education, 1940.

Porter, James A. "Edmonia Lewis." *Notable American Women: 1607-1950*. Vol. 2. Cambridge: Harvard University Press, 1971, 397-99.

Sterling, Dorothy, ed. *We Are Your Sisters: Black Women in the Nineteenth Century*. New York: Norton, 1984. 202, 205-208, 459.

Tuckerman, Henry T. *Book of the Artists: American Artist Life, Comprising the Biographical and Critical Sketches of American Artists*. New York: Putnam, 1867.

Waterston, Anna Quincy. "Edmonia Lewis [the young colored woman who has successfully modeled the bust of Col. Shaw]." *National Anti-Slavery Standard* (24 December 1864).

Wreford, Henry. "Lady Artists in Rome." *Art-Journal* (March 1866): 177.

———. "A Negro Sculptress." *The Atheneum* (3 March 1866): 2001.

Wyman, Lillie Buffam Chase, and Arthur Crawford Wyman. *Elizabeth Buffum 1806-1899*. Boston: W. B. Clarke, 1914, 38.

Collections

Primary sources on Edmonia Lewis are in the James Thomas Fields Collection, Huntington Library, San Marino, California; Oberlin College Archives, Oberlin, Ohio; Robie-Sewall Papers, Massachusetts Historical Society, Boston; and the Anne Whitney Papers, Wellesley College Archives, Margaret Clapp Library, Wellesley, Massachusetts. Extensive primary and secondary research files on Lewis are available in the curatorial department and library of the National Museum of American Art, Washington, D.C. Two photographs of Edmonia Lewis in Chicago, by Henry Rocher, circa 1870, are in the Boston Atheneum, Boston, Massachusetts.

Lydia Maria Child and Annie Adams Fields correspondence is in the James Thomas Fields Collection, F1650, Huntington Library, San Marino, California.

Lydia Maria Child and Harriet Winslow Sewall correspondence is in the Robie-Sewall Papers, Massachusetts Historical Society, Boston, Massachusetts.

• JACKIE "MOMS" MABLEY

Black Writers. Detroit: Gale Research, 1989.

Bogle, Donald. *Brown Sugar*. New York: Harmony Books, 1980, 158-60.

Current Biography Yearbook. New York: H. W. Wilson, 1975, 261-64.

Focus (Summer 1983): 9.

"Moms Mabley Revisited." *Ebony* 46 (February 1988): 124, 126, 128, 130.

"Moms Mabley: She Finally Makes the Movies." *Ebony* 29 (April 1974): 86-88, 90, 92.

New York (14 October 1974).

New York Times (23 May 1975; 25 May 1975).

Newsday (6 April 1967): A-3.

Obituary. *Black Perspective in Music* 3 (Fall 1975): 344-45.

Washington Post (21 August 1972).

Washington Post (4 October 1974): B-1.

Southern, Eileen. *Biographical Dictionary of Afro-American and African Musicians*. Westport, Conn.: Greenwood Press, 1982.

• MARY MAHONEY

Carnegie, M. E. *The Path We Tread*. Philadelphia: Lippincott, 1986.

Davis, Althea T. "Architects for Integration and Equality: Early Black American Leaders in Nursing." Ph. D. dissertation. Teachers College, Columbia University, 1987.

Saunders, Frederick. Interview with Althea T. Davis, 16 January 1987.

• JULIANNE MALVEAUX

Malveaux, Julianne. Biographical statement sent to Jessie Carney Smith. March 1994.

———. Telephone interview with Jessie Carney Smith, August 30, 1994.

• OSEOLA McCARTY

Barbara Walters Presents The Ten Most Fascinating People of 1995. Television program. December 6, 1995.

Bragg, Rick. "All She Has, $150,000, Is Going to a University." *The New York Times*, August 13, 1995: 1, 22.

"The Gift of a Lifetime." *The New York Times*, August 16, 1995: A24.

Hearn, Phil. "Miss McCarty Goes to Washington." *"USM News*, September 28, 1995.

"The Oseola McCarty File." University of Southern Mississippi.

Plummer, William, and Ron Ridenhour. "Saving Grace: A Washerwoman Donates $150,000 to Give Students a Chance She Never Had." *People*, August 28, 1995: 40–41.

Smith, Vern E. "Mississippi Angel." *Newsweek*, November 1995.

"Stephanie Bullock Receives First McCarty Scholarship." *USM News*, August 3, 1995.

"UNESCO to Honor Oseola McCarty in Hattiesburg Nov. 30." *USM News*, November 22, 1995.

Wertz, Sharon. "Oseola McCarty Donates $150,000 to USM." *USM News*, July 26, 1995.

• ROSALIE "ROSE" McCLENDON

Atkinson, Brooks. Review of *Never No More*. *New York Times* (January 8, 1932).

Brown, Sterling A. Review of *Never No More*. *Opportunity* 10 (February 1932): 56-57.

Green, Paul. *The House of Connelly*. Condensed version in Burns Mantle, *The Best Plays of 1931-32*. New York: Dodd, Mead, 1932. 145-78.

————. *In Abraham's Bosom*. Condensed version in Burns Mantle, *The Best Plays of 1926-27*. New York: Dodd, Mead, 1927. 325-52.

Houseman, John. *Run-Through*. New York: Simon and Schuster, 1972. 129, 178-79. Hughes, Langston, and Milton Meltzer. *Black Magic*. Englewood Cliffs, N.J.: Prentice-Hall, 1967.

Kellner, Bruce, ed. *The Harlem Renaissance: A Historical Dictionary for the Era*. New York: Methuen, 1984.

Lewis, Robert. "Rose McClendon." In *Negro: An Anthology*. Edited by Nancy Cunard. New York: Frederick Ungar, 1970. 199-200.

Locke, Alain. *Negro Art: Past and Present*. Washington, D.C.: Associates in Negro Folk Education, 1936. 79.

Rampersad, Arnold. *The Life of Langston Hughes*. Vol. 1, *I, Too, Sing America*. New York: Oxford University Press, 1986. 191, 312-13, 318.

Voorhees, Lillian W. "Rose McClendon." In *Notable American Women 1607-1950*. Edited by Edward T. James and others. Cambridge: Harvard University Press, 1971. 449-50.

Collections

There is a scrapbook of Rose McClendon in the Schomburg Collection on Black Culture. Letters and photographs of McClendon are in the James Weldon Johnson Memorial Collection, Yale University.

• GAY JOHNSON McDOUGALL

Bennett, Lerone, Jr. "15 Days That Shook the World." *Ebony* 49 (August 1994): 60–81.

Brown, Frank Dexter. "Under Specter of Pretoria, Namibia Moves to Freedom." *Black Enterprise* 19 (June 1989): 52.

"Candace Awards Presented to 10 Outstanding Blacks during New York Ceremony." *Jet* 78 (August 6, 1990): 15.

"The Election Onlookers Ogling as History Happens." *Washington Post* (April 26, 1994).

"Farce in Namibia." *The Nation* 249 (August 21–28, 1989): 191–92.

Floyd, Patricia A. Telephone interview with Dolores Nicholson, July 25, 1994.

Johnson, Bill. "Cover Story I—South Africa." *Destiny Magazine* (June 1994): 20–27.

Massaquoi, Hans J. "Namibia: Free at Last." *Ebony* 45 (June 1990): 124–28.

McDougall, Gay J. Professional Resume.

————. Telephone interview with Dolores Nicholson, July 29, 1994.

McKinney, Gwen. "Namibia: On the Road to Freedom." *Essence* 21 (October 1990): 111–14.

Smith, Darren L., ed. *Black Americans Information Directory*. 1st ed. Detroit: Gale Research, 1991.

"South African Odyssey." *Washington Post* (April 26, 1994).

"Speaking of People." *Ebony* 49 (August 1994): 6–7.

"U.S. Expert: Boycott Won't Stop S. Africa Vote." *USA Today* (March 31, 1994).

• PATRICIA CARWELL McKISSACK

Children's Literature Review. Vol. 23. Detroit: Gale Research, 1991.

Contemporary Authors. Vol. 118. Detroit: Gale Research, 1986.

McKissack, Patricia. Letter to Jessie Carney Smith, February 20, 1995.

————. Telephone interviews with Jessie Carney Smith, February 17 and 22, 1995.

McKissack, Patricia, and Fredrick McKissack, Jr. *Black Diamond: The Story of the Negro Baseball Leagues*. Book jacket. New York: Scholastic Press, 1994.

"Patricia C. McKissack." Flyer. New York: Random House, n.d.

"Patricia C. McKissack & Fredrick L. McKissack." Flyer. New York: Scholastic Inc., n.d.

Something about the Author. Vol. 73. Detroit: Gale Research, 1993.

• TERRY L. McMILLAN

Akward, Michael. "Chronicling Everyday Travails and Triumphs." *Callaloo* 1 (Summer 1988): 649–50.

Bates, Karen Grigsby. "Possessing the Secrets of Success." *Emerge* 4 (October 1992): 47–49.

Contemporary Authors. Vol. 140. Detroit: Gale Research, 1993.

Contemporary Literary Criticism. Vol. 50. Detroit: Gale Research, 1988.

Contemporary Literary Criticism. Vol. 61. Detroit: Gale Research, 1990.

Current Biography 54 (February 1993): 36–39.

Edwards, Audrey. "Terry McMillan: Waiting to Exhale." *Essence* 23 (October 1992): 77–78, 82, 118.

Freely, Maureen. "Croaking with Hideous Voices." *The Observer* (May 10, 1987): 20.

McMillan, Terry, ed. *Breaking Ice: An Anthology of African-American Fiction.* New York: Viking Penguin, 1990.

"Profile of a First Novelist: Terry McMillan and *Mama.*" *Writer's Digest* 67 (October 1987): 58.

Sayers, Valerie. "Someone to Walk Over Me." *New York Times Book Review* (August 5, 1989).

Smith, Wendy. "Terry McMillan: The Novelist Explores African American Life from the Point of View of a New Generation." *Publishers Weekly* 239 (May 11, 1992): 50.

Troupe, Quincy. "A Conversation with Terry McMillan." *Emerge* 4 (October 1992): 51–52, 56.

• CAROL E. MOSELEY-BRAUN

"Carol Moseley Braun: First Black Woman Elected to U.S. Senate." *Jet* 83 (September 7, 1992): 8–14.

"Carol Moseley Braun Runs for the Senate." *Chicago Sun-Times,* January 1992. *Indigo* supplement.

Coyne, John R., Jr. "Woman of the Year?" *National Review* 14 (September 1992): 24–25.

Greenburg, Jan Crawford. "Senator Feels Heat of Lobbyists; Moseley-Braun May Decide Legal Reform Bill." *Chicago Tribune* (May 4, 1995).

Hine, Darlene Clark, ed. *Black Women in America.* Brooklyn: Carlson Publishing, 1993.

Levinsohn, Florence Hamlish. "Carol Moseley Braun." *Chicago Reader* (March 6, 1992).

Merida, Kevin. "Senator, Symbol, Self With Three Big Roles to Juggle: Carol Moseley-Braun Always Has Her Hands Full." *Washington Post* (August 15, 1994): C1.

"Moseley-Braun Seeks Women's Health Bill." *Chicago Defender* (February 18, 1993).

Nelson, Jill. "Carol Moseley Braun: Power Beneath Her Wings." *Essence* 23 (October 1992): 57–58, 120, 122, 124.

"Politician 'Can Take Adversity.'" *USA Today,* March 26, 1992.

"Senate Bows to Braun on Symbol of Confederacy." *Washington Post,* July 23, 1993.

"Senator Carol Moseley-Braun of Illinois Appointed to Senate Finance Committee." *Jet* 87 (January 23, 1995): 4.

"Voter Revolt: A Giant-Killer in Illinois." *Newsweek* (March 30, 1992): 38–39.

• JEANNE MOUTOUSSAMY-ASHE

Ashe, Arthur, and Arnold Rampersad. *Days of Grace: A Memoir.* New York: Alfred Knopf, 1993.

Barboza, Steve. "Faces of Africa: Through Jeanne Ashe's Eyes." *Sepia* 30 (December 1981): 38–41.

Contemporary Black Biography. Detroit: Gale Research, 1994.

Dowling, Claudia Glenn. "Daddy and Me." *Life* 16 (November 1993): 61–69. Hine, Darlene Clark, ed. *Black Women in America.* Brooklyn: Carlson Publishing, 1993.

Moutoussamy-Ashe, Jeanne. *Viewfinders: Black Women Photographers.* New York: Dodd Mead, 1986.

———. *Daufuskie Island: A Photographic Essay.* Columbia, S.C.: University of South Carolina Press, 1982.

Randolph, Laura B. "Jeanne Moutoussamy-Ashe: On Love, Loss and Life after Arthur." *Ebony* 48 (October 1993): 27–34.

Willis-Thomas, Deborah. *An Illustrated Bio-Bibliography of Black Photographers, 1940–1988*. New York: Garland Publishing, 1989.

Wilson, Judith. "A Look at Three Contemporary Artists." *Essence* 17 (May 1986): 120–24.

• GLORIA NAYLOR

Andrews, Larry R. "Black Sisterhood in Gloria Naylor's Novels." *CLA Journal* 33 (September 1989): 1–25.

Belenky, Mary Field, Blythe McVicker Clinchy, and Nancy Rule Goldberger. *Women's Ways of Knowing: The Development of Self, Voice, and Mind*. New York: Basic Books, 1986.

Christian, Barbara. "Gloria Naylor's Geography: Community, Class, and Patriarchy in *The Women of Brewster Place* and *Linden Hills*." In *Reading Black, Reading Feminist,* edited by Henry Louis Gates Jr. New York: Meridian, 1990.

Donahue, Deirdre. Review of *The Women of Brewster Place*. *Washington Post* (October 21, 1983).

Holloway, Karla F. C. *Moorings and Metaphors: Figures of Culture and Gender in Black Women's Literature*. New Brunswick: Rutgers University Press, 1992.

Matus, Jill L. "Dream Deferral, and Closure in *The Women of Brewster Place*." *Black American Literature Forum* 24 (Spring 1990): 49–64.

Naylor, Gloria. *Bailey's Cafe*. New York: Harcourt, 1992.

———. *Linden Hills*. New York: Viking Penguin, 1985.

———. *Mama Day*. New York: Vintage, 1988.

———. *The Women of Brewster Place*. New York: Viking Penguin, 1982. Naylor, Gloria, and Toni Morrison. "A Conversation." *Southern Review* 21 (July 1985): 567–93.

Ward, Catherine C. "Gloria Naylor's *Linden Hills:* A Modern Inferno." *Contemporary Literature* 28 (Spring 1987): 67–81.

• HAZEL O'LEARY

"The Clinton Administration's 100 Day Report: Department of Energy Accomplishments." April 30, 1993.

"Clinton Picks Record Number of Blacks for His Cabinet." *Jet* 83 (January 11, 1993): 5.

Contemporary Black Biography. Vol. 6. Detroit: Gale Research, 1994.

Corn, David. "Oprah O'Leary." *The Nation* (June 13, 1994).

Dallas Morning News (December 18, 1992).

"An Energetic Networker to Take Over Energy." *Washington Post* (January 19, 1993).

Haywood, Richette L. "Secretary Hazel O'Leary: Bright, Charming, Tough." *Ebony* 50 (February 1995): 94–100.

"Hazel O'Leary Is Appointed Secretary of Energy." *Ivy Leaf* 17 (Spring 1993): 39.

Healey, Jan. "Hazel R. O'Leary: A Profile." *Congressional Quarterly* 23 (January 1993): 177.

Kaslow, Amy. "Energy Chief Hazel O'Leary On Hot Seat and Enjoying Every Minute." *Christian Science Monitor* (January 5, 1995): 1.

Miller, Alan C. "Energy Secretary's Travel is Costliest Among Cabinet Administration." *Los Angeles Times* (June 25, 1995): 1.

"More Exposure to Radiation Minus Consent Revealed." *Nashville Tennessean* (June 28, 1994).

"New Energy Chief Has Seen 2 Sides of Regulatory Fence." *New York Times* (December 22, 1992).

"Nominee Is a Veteran of Atomic-Waste Battle." *New York Times* (January 9, 1993).

"O'Leary Supports Military-Civilian N-Waste Solution." *USA Today* (August 13, 1993).

Pendleton, Scott. "US Energy Firms Welcome Appointment of O'Leary." *Christian Science Monitor* (January 14, 1993): 8.

"A Plentiful Energy Source Burns Bright." *Washington Times* (February 4, 1993).

Thompson, Garland L. "Four Black Cabinet Secretaries—Will It Make the Difference?" *Crisis* 100 (March 1993): 17–18.

• JENNIE R. PATRICK

Bradby, Marie. "Professional Profile: Dr. Jennie R. Patrick." *U.S. Black Engineer* (Fall 1988): 30–33.

Kazi-Ferrouillet, Kuumba. "Jennie R. Patrick: An Exceptional Black Scientist." *Black Collegian* 14 (January–February, 1984): 102.

Patrick, Jennie R. Letter to Jessie Carney Smith, January 13, 1995.

———. Telephone interview with Jessie Carney Smith, January 13, 1995.

——. "Trials, Tribulations, Triumphs." *Sage* 6 (Fall 1989): 53.

"Speaking of People." *Ebony* 36 (May 1981): 6.

Who's Who among Black Americans, 1994–95. 8th ed. Detroit: Gale Research, 1994.

• *BILLIE GOODSON PIERCE*

The Black Perspective in Music 3 (Fall 1975): 345.

Borenstein, Larry, and Bill Russell. *Preservation Hall Portraits.* Baton Rouge: Louisiana State University Press, 1968.

Carr, Ian, Digby Fairweather, and Brian Priestly, eds. *Jazz: The Essential Companion.* London: Grafton Books, 1987.

Chilton, John. *Who's Who of Jazz.* New York: Macmillan, 1972.

Clark, William. *Preservation Hall: Music from the Heart.* New York: W. W. Norton & Co., 1991.

Dahl, Linda. *Stormy Weather: The Music and Lives of a Century of Jazzwomen.* New York: Pantheon Books, 1984.

Handy, D. Antoinette. *Black Women in American Bands and Orchestras.* Metuchen, N.J.: Scarecrow Press, 1981.

Harris, Sheldon, ed. *Blue's Who's Who.* New Rochelle, N.Y.: Arlington House Publishers, 1979.

Hine, Darlene Clark, ed. *Black Women in America.* Brooklyn: Carlson Publishing, 1993.

New York Times, October 3, 1974.

Plaksin, Sally. *American Women in Jazz: 1900 to the Present.* New York: Seaview Books, 1982.

Southern, Eileen. *Biographical Dictionary of Afro-American and African Musicians.* Westport, Conn.: Greenwood Press, 1982.

The Times Picayune, October 4, 1974, section 1, 8.

Unterbrink, Mary. *Jazz Women at the Keyboard.* Jefferson, N.C.: McFarland, 1983.

Van Vorst, Paige. "Wilhelmina Goodson 'Billie' Pierce." *Downbeat* (November 21, 1974): 10.

• *SARAH FORTEN PURVIS*

Forten, James. Letter to William Lloyd Garrison, 23 February 1831. Anti-Slavery Manuscripts, Boston Public Library.

Purvis, Sarah Forten. Letter to Angelina Grimke('), 15 April 1837. *Letters of Theodore Dwight Weld, Angelina Grimke(') Weld, and Sarah Grimke('), 1822-1844.* Edited by Gilbert H. Barnes and Dwight L. Dumond. New York: D. Appleton-Century, 1934, 379-82.

——. Various poems in *Liberator,* 29 January 1831; 26 March 1831; 21 December 1833; 4 January 1834; 18 January 1834.

Pennsylvania *Freeman* 19 November 1836.

Stevenson, Brenda, ed. *The Journals of Charlotte Forten Grimke(').* New York: Oxford University Press, 1988.

• *CHARLOTTA GORDON PYLES*

Brown, Hallie Q. *Homespun Heroines and Other Women of Distinction.* Xenia, Ohio: Aldine Publishing Co., 1926.

"Called Home." *Burlington Hawkeye,* January 20, 1880. "Died." *Keokuk Daily,* January 21, 1880.

Douglas, Frederick. "Charlotte Piles: A Poem in Her Honor." *Frederick Douglass Paper,* December 12, 1855.

Jones, Mrs. Laurence C. "The Desire for Freedom." *Palimpsest* 8 (May 1927): 153–63.

Register of Deaths. Lee County, Iowa, 1867–1903.

• *MA RAINEY*

Brown, Sterling. "Ma Rainey." In *The Collected Poems of Sterling A. Brown.* Selected by Michael S. Harper. New York: Harper, 1983. 62-63.

Harrison, Daphne Duval. *Black Pearls: Blues Queens of the 1920s.* New Brunswick: Rutgers University Press, 1988. 34-41.

Kellner, Bruce, ed. *The Harlem Renaissance: A Historical Dictionary for the Era.* New York: Methuen, 1987. 293-94.

Lieb, Sandra R. *Mother of the Blues: A Study of Ma Rainey.* Amherst: University of Massachusetts Press, 1981.

Southern, Eileen. *The Music of Black America.* 2nd ed. New York: Norton, 1983. 293-94, 330, 368-69, 452.

Stewart-Baxter, Derrick. *Ma Rainey and the Classic Blues Singers.* New York: Stein and Day, 1970. 35-47.

• *FLORENCE SPEARING RANDOLPH*

Burstyn, Joan N., ed. *Past and Promise: Lives of New Jersey Women*. Metuchen, N.J.: Scarecrow Press, 1990.

"Dr. Florence Randolph." *Star of Zion,* October 10, 1935.

Nichols, James L. *The New Progress of a Race*. Naperville, Ill.: J. L. Nichols and Co., 1929.

"Not to be Ministered Unto, but to Minister." *Chicago Defender,* December 11, 1937.

"Rev. Florence Randolph Given Honorary Degree." *New York Age,* July 8, 1933.

Richardson, Clement. *The National Cyclopedia of the Colored Race*. Vol. 1. Montgomery, Ala.: National Publishing Co., 1919.

"Useful Life of the Reverend Mrs. Florence Randolph." *Baltimore Afro-American,* September 28, 1912.

Who's Who in Colored America. 5th ed. Brooklyn: Who's Who in Colored America, 1940.

"Woman Missionary Honored by Zion." *New York Age,* June 1, 1916.

Collections
The Reverend Florence Spearing Randolph's papers, sermons, and memorabilia are in the possession of Bettye Collier-Thomas.

• *SYLVIA M. RHONE*

Ali, Lorraine. "Exiled in Guyville: A Report on How Women Are Faring in the Music Industry." *Rolling Stone* (October 6, 1994): 57–58.

Baskerville, Dawn, Sheryl Hilliard Tucker, and Donna Whittingham-Barnes. "21 Women of Power and Influence in Corporate America." *Black Enterprise* 22 (August 1991): 76.

Black Book: International Business and Entertainment Reference Guide. Chicago: National Publications Sales Agency, 1994.

Contemporary Black Biography. Vol. 2. Detroit: Gale Research, 1992.

Futrell, Jon, Chris Gill, Roger St. Pierre, and Clive Richardson. *The Illustrated Encyclopedia of Black Music*. New York: Harmony Books, 1982.

Norment, Lynn. "Women at the Top in the Entertainment Industry." *Ebony* 48 (March 1993): 106–14.

Randolph, Laura B. "Women in Dream Jobs." *Ebony* 44 (November 1988): 74–76.

"Sylvia Rhone Named New Head of Elektra/EastWest." *Jet* 86 (August 15, 1994): 55.

Vaughn, Christopher. "Pumping Up the Jam for Profits." *Black Enterprise* 22 (December 1991): 51–56.

Who's Who among Black Americans, 1994–95. 8th ed. Detroit: Gale Research, 1994.

• *LINDA JOHNSON RICE*

"Backstage." *Ebony* 42 (September 1987): 26.

Edelman, Renee. "When Little Sister Means Big Business." *Working Woman* 15 (February 1990): 82–86.

"Linda Johnson Rice." *Black Enterprise* 22 (June 1992): 318.

Norment, Lynn. "Ebony Interview with Linda Johnson Rice." *Ebony* 48 (November 1992): 208–15.

Therrien, Lois. "A Nice Graduation Present: Johnson Publishing." *Business Week* No. 3007 (July 1987): 40.

• *KAY GEORGE ROBERTS*

"Breaking the Sound Barrier." *Nashville Tennessean* (July 7, 1991).

"Conductor Beats Odds with Her Baton." *Detroit Free Press* (February 19, 1992).

"Conductor: Black Woman Musician at U Lowell Succeeds in Field Dominated by Men." *Lowell Sun* (November 9, 1978).

"Good Conduct." *Chicago Tribune* (April 26, 1992).

Grant, Lorrie. "A Maestro with Quiet Confidence." *Emerge* (May 1993): 57, 58.

Handy, D. Antoinette. *Black Women in American Bands and Orchestras*. Metuchen, N.J.: Scarecrow Press, 1981.

———. *Black Conductors*. Metuchen, N.J.: Scarecrow Press, 1994.

Jennings, Patricia Prattis. "1993: A Significant Year for Conductor Kay George Roberts." *Symphonium* 5 (Fall 1993): 4.

"Kay George Roberts, Winida Treepoonpon Score with BSO." *Bangkok Press* (November 1, 1986).

"Kay Roberts Returns for Conducting Debut." *Nashville Tennessean* (May 28, 1976).

"Guest Conductor Inspires Young Dallas Musicians." *Dallas Morning News* (June 21, 1986).

"I Am a Minority within a Minority." *Stuttgarter Nachruchten-Kultur Magazine* (July 20, 1991).

"King Concert Reflects the Binding Power of Music." *Cleveland Plain Dealer* (January 13, 1993).

McDonald, Dianne H. "Conducting Becomes Her." *Newsweek on Campus* (April 1988): 38, 39.

"A Minority within a Minority." *Chattanooga News-Free Press* (February 18, 1993).

Munder, P. "Black Power." *Madame* (September 1989): 56, 107.

Roberts, Kay George. Letters to D. Antoinette Handy. July 28, 1976; March 21, 1986; May 26, 1988; September 7, 1989; December 13, 1989; May 9, 1990; July 10, 1991; July 29, 1991; February 24, 1994.

———. Interviews with D. Antoinette Handy, Washington, D.C., January 13, 1986; January 15, 1986; Philadelphia, Pennsylvania, February 17, 1994.

"A Symphony of Firsts for Woman from Cambridge." *Boston Herald* (August 31, 1986).

Zepernick, Werner. "Nashville Symphony Opens Summer Parks Concerts." *Nashville Banner* (May 31, 1976).

• LEAH J. SEARS-COLLINS

Curriden, Mark. "Rollerblading Justice." *Barrister Magazine* 20 (Summer 1993): 20.

———. "A Jurist of First Impression." *National Law Journal* 16 (September 6, 1993): 27.

"The Female Factor: Influence of Women Growing on High Court." *Savannah Morning News* (July 6, 1993).

Norman, Tyler. "Justifiably Honored: Savannah's Justice Leah Sears-Collins." *Savannah Magazine* (July 4, 1993): 20–23.

Sears-Collins, Leah. Telephone interview with Nagueyalti Warren, March 4, 1992.

Wooten, Jim. "Justice Leah Sears-Collins Is, Indeed, Different." *The Atlanta Journal* (July 8, 1992).

• BETTY SHABAZZ

Cain, Joy Duckett. "Dr. Betty Shabazz: Twenty Years after Malcolm X's Death, His Widow Speaks Out." *Essence* 15 (February 1985): 12.

Conners, Cathy. "Let's Sponsor Our Kids, Dr. Shabazz Tells Confab." *Amsterdam News* (August 4, 1990).

Ebony Success Library. Vol. 1. Nashville: Southwestern Publishing Co., 1973.

"Harlem Honors Dr. Betty Shabazz, Declares Malcolm X Blvd. Drug Free." *Amsterdam News* (March 30, 1991).

Knebel, Fletcher. "A Visit with the Widow of Malcolm X." *Look* 33 (March 4, 1969): 74–80.

Mandulor, Rhea. "Sharing Our Best with Others: An Interview with Dr. Betty Shabazz." *City Sun* (June 9–15, 1993).

Shabazz, Betty. "Legacy of My Husband, Malcolm X." *Ebony* 24 (June 1969): 172–82.

———. "Loving and Losing Malcolm." *Essence* 22 (February 1992): 50–54, 104, 107–9.

• JEANNE C. SINKFORD

Chronicles of Outstanding Leaders in Dentistry: A Conversation with Jeanne Sinkford. Videocassette. Washington, D.C.: International College of Dentists, U.S.A. Section, 1986.

Funnye, Doris Innis, and Juliana Wu, eds. *Profiles in Black: Biographical Sketches of 100 Living Black Unsung Heroes.* New York: CORE Publications, 1976.

"Howard's First Lady of Dentistry." *Ebony* 23 (April 1968): 103–8.

Kidd, Foster, ed. *The Profile of the Negro in American Dentistry.* Washington, D.C.: Howard University Press, 1979.

Sinkford, Jeanne C. "Current Status and Future Trends in Training Dental Practitioners and Dental Auxiliaries to Meet the Needs of the Black Community." *Journal of the National Medical Association* 68 (January 1976): 60–62.

———. "Modern Concepts and Trends in Dentistry." *Journal of the Baltimore College of Dental Surgery* 32 (July 1977): 2–9.

———. "Dental Education: Trends and Assumptions for the 21st Century." *Journal of the National Medical Association* 79 (February 1987): 227–31.

———. "Choose the High Road." In *Legacy, the Dental Profession: The Philosophies and Thoughts of Selected Dental Leaders Worldwide.* Compiled by Clifford F. Loader and Shigeo Ryan Kishi. Bakersfield, Calif.: Loader/Kisher, 1990.

———. "The Future of Dentistry: New Challenges, New Directions." *Journal of the National Medical Association* 82 (May 1990): 353–58.

————. Letter to Jessie Carney Smith, January 26, 1995.

Sinkford, Jeane C., and Joseph L. Henry. "Survival of Black Colleges from a Dental Perspective." *Journal of the National Medical Association* 73 (June 1981): 511–15.

"Two Dental Firsts." *Journal of the National Medical Association* 67 (July 1975): 326–27.

Who's Who of American Women, 1993–1994. Chicago: Marquis Who's Who, 1993.

"Women on the Rise in Dentistry." *Atlanta Daily World,* October 21, 1982.

● *NORMA MERRICK SKLAREK*

Lanker, Brian. *I Dream a World.* New York: Stewart, Tabori and Chang, 1989.

Lewis, S. D. "Professional Woman: Her Fields Have Widened." *Ebony* 32 (August 1977): 115.

● *MARIA W. STEWART*

Davis, Marianna W., ed. *Contributions of Black Women to America.* Vol. 1. Columbia, S.C.: Kenday Press, 1982.

Flexner, Eleanor. "Maria W. Stewart." *Notable American Women.* Vol. 3. Cambridge: Harvard University Press, 1971.

Giddings, Paula. *When and Where I Enter.* New York: William Morrow, 1984.

Loewenberg, Bert, and Ruth Bogin, eds. *Black Women in Nineteenth Century American Life.* University Park: Pennsylvania State University Press, 1977.

O'Connor, Lillian. *Pioneer Women Orators.* New York: Columbia University Press, 1954.

Quarles, Benjamin. *Black Abolitionists.* New York: Oxford University Press, 1969.

Richardson, Marilyn. *Maria Stewart: America's First Black Woman Political Writer.* Bloomington: Indiana University Press, 1987.

Sterling, Dorothy, ed. *We Are Your Sisters.* New York: Norton, 1984.

Stewart, Maria W. *Meditations From the Pen of Mrs. Maria W. Stewart.* The Author, 1879.

● *ELLEN STEWART*

Elsom, John. *Cold War Theater.* London: Routledge, 1992.

Heilpern, John. "La Mama Courage." *Vogue* 182 (August 1992): 138–42.

Henderson, Mary C. *Theater in America.* New York: Abrams, 1986.

Little, Stuart W. *Off-Broadway: The Prophetic Theater.* New York: Coward, McCann and Geoghegan, 1972.

Mapp, Edward. *Directory of Blacks in the Performing Arts.* 2d ed. Metuchen, N.J.: Scarecrow Press, 1990.

Robinson, Alice M., Vera Mowry Roberts, and Milly S. Barranger, eds. *Notable Women in the American Theater.* New York: Greenwood Press, 1989.

Stewart, Ellen. "Finding Ways to Survive." *Backstage* 39 (December 21, 1990): 28.

Wilmeth, Don B., and Tice L. Miller, eds. *Cambridge Guide to American Theater.* New York: Cambridge University Press, 1993.

● *ALETHIA BROWNING TANNER*

Joyner, William A. "Making a School System." *Alexander's Magazine* 1 (March 1906): 35–43, 50–51.

Logan, Rayford W., and Michael R. Winston. *Dictionary of American Negro Biography.* New York: Norton, 1982.

Major, Gerri, with Doris E. Saunders. *Black Society.* Chicago: Johnson Publishing Co., 1976.

Wayman, Alexander W. *Cyclopedia of African Methodism.* Baltimore: Methodist Episcopal Book Depository, 1882.

Williams, George W. *History of the Negro Race in America.* Vol. 2. New York: G. P. Putnam's Sons, 1883.

Collections

Information on the Cook family may be found in the Cook Family Papers, Moorland-Spingarn Research Center, Howard University, Washington, D.C.

● *MARY CHURCH TERRELL*

Current Biography H. W. Wilson, 1942, 1954.

The Delta 10 (January 1941): 4.

Giddings, Paula. *When and Where I Enter: The Impact of Black Women on Race and Sex in America.* Morrow, 1984.

Jones, Beverly Washington. *Quest for Equality: The Life and Writings of Mary Church Terrell.* Carlson Publishers, 1990.

New York Times (29 July 1954).

Shepperd, Gladys B. *Mary Church Terrell—Respectable Person*. Human Relations Press, 1959.

Sterling, Dorothy. *Black Foremothers*. Feminist Press, 1979. Revised 1988.

———. "Mary Church Terrell." *Notable American Women: The Modern Period*. Vol. 4. Harvard University Press, 1980.

Terrell, Mary Church. *A Colored Woman in a White World*. Ransdell, 1940. Reprinted. Arno Press, 1980.

Washington Post (25 July 1954).

Washington Star (25 July 1954).

Wesley, Charles H. *History of the National Association of Colored Women's Clubs, Inc.: A Legacy of Service*. National Association of Colored Women's Clubs, 1984.

● *DEBI THOMAS*

"As Ice Skating Champ Debi Thomas Says the Goal is Gold in '88." *Jet* 69 (March 10, 1986): 48.

Austen, Ian. "Chasing a Crown." *Macleans* 101 (February 1988): 3.

Burazil, Bryan. "With Style and Grace." *Black Enterprise* 16 (June 1986): 86.

Callahan, Tom. "The Word She Uses Is Invincible." *Time* 131 (18 February 1988): 46.

Engeler, Amy. "Blade Runner." *Rolling Stone* (February 25, 1988): 72–84.

"Figure Skating Debi Thomas." *Newsweek* (February 18, 1988): 79.

Kort, Michelle. "Debi Thomas: Skater Extraordinaire." *Ms.* 15 (February 1987): 33.

Norment, Lynn. "The Nation's No. 1 Skating Sensation." *Ebony* 41 (May 1986): 147–51.

Slate, Libby. "Show Stopper." *Essence* 16 (December 1985): 31.

Swift, E. M. "Lashing in on the Lollywobbles." *Sports Illustrated* 64 (February 17, 1986): 29.

———. "Another Miracle on Ice?" *Sports Illustrated* 64 (March 17, 1986): 36.

Who's Who among Black Americans, 1994–95. 8th ed. Detroit: Gale Research, 1994.

● *WILLIE MAE THORNTON*

Aldin, Mary Katherine. "Willie Mae Thornton." *Living Blues*, 60–61 (Summer/Fall 1984): 68.

"Big Mama Thornton Dead at 57; Singer Influenced Early Rockers." In *Variety Obituaries*. Vol. 10. New York: Garland, 1988.

Bolcom, William, Max Harrison, and Paul Oliver. *The New Grove Gospel, Blues and Jazz*. New York: Norton, 1986.

Budds, Michael J. "African-American Women in Blues and Jazz." In *Women and Music: A History*. Edited by Karin Pendle. Bloomington: Indiana University Press, 1991.

Clarke, Donald, ed. *The Penguin Encyclopedia of Popular Music*. New York: Viking Penguin, 1989.

Cohen, Richard. "San Francisco Blues Festival." *Living Blues* 44 (Autumn 1979): 29–30.

Connor, Anthony, and Robert Neff. *Blues*. Boston: David R. Godine, 1975.

Gaar, Gillian G. *She's a Rebel: The History of Women in Rock and Roll*. Seattle: Seal Press, 1992.

George, Nelson. *The Death of Rhythm and Blues*. New York: Pantheon Books, 1988.

Govenar, Alan. *Meeting the Blues*. Dallas: Taylor Publishing, 1988.

Gregory, Hugh. *Soul Music A–Z*. London: Blandford, 1991.

Harris, Sheldon. *Blues Who's Who*. New Rochelle, N.Y.: Arlington House, 1979.

"Heart Attack Claims 'Big Mama' Thornton, 57." *Jet* 66 (August 13, 1984): 63.

Herzhaft, Gérard. *Encyclopedia of the Blues*. Translated by Brigitte Debord. Fayetteville: University of Arkansas Press, 1982.

Hitchcock, H. Wiley, and Stanley Sadie. *The New Grove Dictionary of American Music*. 4 vols. New York: Macmillan, 1986.

Hoke, S. Kay. "American Popular Music." In *Women and Music: A History*. Edited by Karin Pendle. Bloomington: Indiana University Press, 1991.

Larkin, Colin, ed. *The Guiness Encyclopedia of Popular Music*. 4 vols. London: Guiness Publishing, 1992.

Oakley, Giles. *The Devil's Music: A History of the Blues*. London: British Broadcasting Corporation, 1976.

Scott, Frank. *The Down Home Guide to the Blues*. Chicago: Down Home Music, 1991.

Shaw, Arnold. *The World of Soul*. New York: Cowles Book, 1970.

Southern, Eileen. *The Music of Black Americans*. 2d ed. New York: Norton, 1983.

———, ed. *Biographical Dictionary of Afro-American and African Musicians*. Westport, Conn.: Greenwood Press, 1982.

Strachwitz, Chris. *Big Mama Thornton: Ball and Chain*. Arhoolie CD–305, 1989.

Whitcomb, Ian. "Legends of Rhythm and Blues." In *Repercussions: A Celebration of African-American Music*. Edited by Geoffrey Haydon and Dennis Marks. London: Century Publishing, 1985.

• ROSINA TUCKER

Brazeal, Brailsford R. *The Brotherhood of Sleeping Car Porters*. New York: Harper and Brothers, 1946.

Cole, Harriette. "Saluting the Spirit of a Centenarian." *Essence* 16 (May 1985): 168, 170.

"Hall of Fame Recognizes Five Women Who Made a Difference in D.C." *Washington Post* (April 1, 1993).

Holleran, Susan Ellen. "Rosina Corrothers-Tucker: A Bedrock in the Union Movement." *about . . . time* 13 (May 1985): 10–13.

"Labor Group Cites Three Black Women." *Jet* 68 (March 25, 1985): 23.

"Long Life and Civil Rights." *Washington Post* (January 25, 1983).

Pitts, Dave. "A Century of Struggle." *Washington Living* 5 (July 1986): 38–41, 61.

Salem, Dorothy, ed. *African American Women*. New York: Garland Publishing, 1993.

"Still Vocal and Active at Age 103." *Washington Post* (November 8, 1984).

"Tracing Her Roots: Rosina Tucker's Work for the Pullman Porters." *Washington Post* (May 26, 1982).

"A Word from the Wise." *Jet* 67 (October 22, 1984): 22.

• TINA TURNER

Corliss, Richard. "Aye, Tina!" *Time* (June 21, 1993): 64-5.

Current Biography Yearbook. New York: H. W. Wilson, 1984, 410-13.

Hardy, Phil, and Dave Laing. *Encyclopedia of Rock*. New York: Schirmer Books, 1988.

Helander, Brock. *Rock Who's Who*. New York: Schirmer Books, 1982.

Hitchcock, Wiley H., and Stanley Sadie, eds. *New Grove Dictionary of American Music*. Vol. 4. New York: Macmillan, 1986.

Kot, Greg. "Tina! The Film Digs up Pain, but She's Happy Now." *Chicago Tribune* (June 6, 1993): 4.

Norment, Lynn. "Rich, Free and in Controlthe Foreign Affairs of Tina Turner." *Ebony* 45 (November 1989): 166-68, 172.

Pareles, Jon, and Patricia Romanowski, eds. *Rolling Stone Encyclopedia of Rock*. New York: Rolling Stone Press, 1983.

Southern, Eileen. *Biographical Dictionary of Afro-American and African Music*. Westport, Conn.: Greenwood Press, 1982.

Tennessean (30 November 1991).

"Tina Turner Still Sexy and Going Strong." *Jet* 78 (9 July 1990): 56-58, 60.

Turner, Tina, with Kurt Loder. *I, Tina*. New York: William Morrow, 1986.

• CICELY TYSON

Angelou, Maya. "Cicely Tyson: Reflections on a Lone Black Rose." *Ladies Home Journal* 94 (February 1977): 40-41.

"Black Actors Don't Make Any Money: Cicely Tyson." *Jet* 44 (17 May 1973): 62.

Bright, Daniel. "Emmy Award for Cicely." *Sepia* 23 (April 1974): 16-20.

"Cicely, Miles Wed on Thanksgiving Day." *Jet* 61 (17 December 1981): 59.

"Cicely Tyson Scores in TV's Jane Pittman Autobiography." *Jet* 45 (21 February 1974): 62.

Crist, Judith. "Sounder." *New York* 5 (2 October 1972): 70-71.

Current Biography Yearbook. New York: H. W. Wilson, 1975.

Ebert, Albert. "Inside Cicely." *Essence* 3 (February 1973): 40-41.

Grant, Liz. "Beauty Talk with the Stars." *Essence* 4 (January 1974): 38-39.

Kael, Pauline. *New Yorker* (January 28, 1974).

Klemesrud, Judy. "Cicely, the Looker from 'Sounder,'" *New York Times* (1 October 1972).

Norment, Lynn. "Cicely Tyson: Hollywood's Advocate of Positive Black Images Talks about the 'Bo Derek look' Rip-Off, Her New Movie...." *Ebony* 36 (February 1981): 124-126.

Peterson, M. "Black Imagery on the Silver Screen." *Essence* 3 (December 1972): 34.

Ploski, Harry A., ed. *The Negro Almanac*. 5th ed. Detroit: Gale Research, 1989.

Robinson, Louie. "Cicely Tyson: A Very Unlikely Movie Star." *Ebony* 29 (May 1974): 33-43.

Salaam, Kalamu ya [Val Ferdinand]. "Cicely Tyson: A Communicator of Pride." *Black Collegian* 9 (November/December 1978): 52-54, 86-91.

Sanders, Charles L. "Cicely Tyson: She Can Smile Again after a Three-Year Ordeal." *Ebony* 34 (January 1979): 27-36.

Spradling, Mary Mace, ed. *In Black and White*. 3rd ed. Detroit: Gale Research, 1980.

Webster, Ivan. "Woman Called Tyson." *Encore* 7 (November 1978): 24-27.

Who's Who among Black Americans, 6th ed. Detroit: Gale Research, 1990.

Who's Who in America. Wilmette, Ill: Marquis, 1988-1989.

Who's Who in the Theatre. 17th ed. Detroit: Gale Research, 1981.

● SUSAN PAUL VASHON

Brown, Hallie Q. *Homespun Heroines and Other Women of Distinction*. Xenia, Ohio: Aldine Publishing Co., 1926.

Dannett, Sylvia G. *Profiles of Negro Womanhood*. Vol. 1. Chicago: Negro Heritage Library, 1964.

Manning, Erma. *Herstory Silhouettes, Profiles of Black Womanhood*. Saint Louis Public Schools Publication, 1980.

● ORA WASHINGTON

Ashe, Arthur R., Jr. *A Hard Road to Glory: A History of the African-American Athlete 1919–1945*. New York: Warner Books, 1988.

Davis, Marianna W., ed. *Contributions of Black Women to America*. Vol. 1. Columbia, S.C.: Kenday Press, 1982.

"Women in Sports." *Ebony* 32 (August 1977): 62.

Henderson, Edwin Bancroft. *The Negro in Sports*. Washington, D.C.: Associated Publishers, 1949.

Jones, Wally, and Jim Washington. *Black Champions Challenge American Sports*. New York: David McKay, 1972.

"*Sepia* Salutes." *Sepia* 9 (August 1961): 51.

Young, A. S. *Negro Firsts in Sports*. Chicago: Johnson Publishing Company, 1963.

● MAXINE WATERS

Beyette, Beverly. "Maxine Waters." *Ms.* 12 (January 1984): 42–46.

Collier, Aldore. "Maxine Waters Elected to Fill the Seat of Augustus Hawkins." *Ebony* 46 (January 1991): 105, 108.

———. "Maxine Waters: Telling It Like It Is in L.A." *Ebony* 47 (October 1992): 35–36.

Congressional Quarterly 49 (January 12, 1991): 91.

Dowd, Maureen. "Fresh Faces for an Old Struggle." *Time* 122 (August 22, 1983): 31.

Grier, Roosevelt. *Rosey Grier's All-American Heroes: Multicultural Success Stories*. New York: MasterMedia Limited, 1993.

Harris, Ron. "Maxine Waters: The Most Powerful Woman in Politics." *Essence* 14 (March 1984): 79–80.

Hine, Darlene Clark, ed. *Black Women in America*. Brooklyn: Carlson Publishing, 1993.

Los Angeles Sentinel (July 30, 1992); (October 29, 1992).

Los Angeles Times (November 7, 1990); (November 5, 1992); (May 16, 1993).

Malveaux, Julianne. "Maxine Waters: Woman of the House." *Essence* 21 (November 1990): 55–56, 116–17. Marshall, Marilyn. "Maxine Waters: America's Most Influential Black Woman Politician." *Ebony* 39 (August 1984): 56.

"Maxine Waters Rips Vet Committee Chief for Lack of Black Staffers." *Jet* 79 (October 22, 1990): 38.

National Journal 24 (January 18, 1992): 134, 136, 143.

Sweet, Ellen. "Women to Watch in the 80's." *Ms.* 12 (January 1984): 42–46.

Washington Informer (September 30, 1992).

Who's Who in American Politics, 1991–92. 13th ed. Vol. 1. New Providence, N.J.: Bowker, 1991.

Who's Who of American Women, 1993–94. 18th ed. New Providence, N.J.: Reed Reference, 1993.

Women in Public Office. Metuchen, N.J.: Scarecrow Press, 1978.

Zia, Helen. "The King Verdict: Making Sense of It." *Ms.* 3 (July/August 1992): 41–43.

• *DOROTHY WEST*

Bone, Robert. *The Negro Novel in America.* New Haven: Yale University Press, 1965.

Daniel, Walter C. "*Challenge* Magazine: An Experiment That Failed." *CLA Journal* 26 (June 1976): 494-503.

Ferguson, Sally Ann H. "Dorothy West." *Dictionary of Literary Biography: Afro-American Writers, 1940-1955.* Vol. 76. Edited by Trudier Harris. Detroit: Gale Research, 1988.

Johnson, Abby Arthur, and Ronald Maberry Johnson. *Propaganda and Aesthetics: The Literary Politics of Afro-American Magazines in the Twentieth Century.* Amherst: University of Massachusetts Press, 1979.

Karpen, Lynn. "The Last Leaf." *New York Times Book Review* (February 12, 1995): 11.

Kenney, Susan. "Shades of Difference." *New York Times Book Review* (February 12, 1995): 11-12.

Perry, Margaret. *Silence to the Drums: A Survey of the Literature of the Harlem Renaissance.* Westport, Conn.: Greenwood Press, 1976.

Rampersad, Arnold. *The Life of Langston Hughes.* Vol. 1. New York: Oxford University Press, 1986.

Schraufnagel, Noel. *From Apology to Protest: The Black American Novel.* Deland, Fla.: Everett/Edwards, 1973.

Steinberg, Sybil. "Dorothy West: Her Own Renaissance." *Publishers Weekly* (July 3, 1995): 34-5.

Washington, Mary Helen. "I Sign My Mother's Name: Alice Walker, Dorothy West, Paule Marshall." In *Mothering the Mind: Twelve Studies of Writers and Their Silent Partners.* Edited by Ruth Perry and Martine Watson Brownley. New York: Holmes and Meier, 1984.

———. *Invented Lives: Narratives of Black Women 1860-1960.* Garden City, N.Y.: Doubleday, 1987.

West, Dorothy. "Elephant's Dance: A Memoir of Wallace Thurman." *Black World* 20 (November 1970): 77-85.

———. *The Living is Easy.* Boston: Houghton Mifflin, 1948. Reprinted, New York: Arno Press, 1969. Reprinted, Old Westbury, N.Y.: Feminist Press, 1982.

———. "The Richer, the Poorer." In *The Best Short Stories by Negro Writers.* Edited by Langston Hughes. Boston: Little, Brown, 1967.

———. "The Typewriter." In *Opportunity* 4 (July 1926): 220-222.

Collections

The papers of Dorothy West are housed in the Mugar Memorial Library, Boston University, and the James Weldon Johnson Memorial Collection at Yale University.

• *MARION BIRNIE WILKINSON*

Birnie, C. W. "Education of the Negro in Charleston, South Carolina, Prior to the Civil War." *Journal of Negro History* 12 (January 1927): 13–21.

Caldwell, A. B. *History of the Negro.* South Carolina Edition. Atlanta: A. B. Caldwell Publishing Co., 1919.

Drago, Edmund L. *Initiative, Paternalism, and Race Relations—Charleston's Avery Normal Institute.* Athens: University of Georgia Press, 1990.

Fitchett, E. Horace. "The Origin and Growth of the Free Negro Population of Charleston, South Carolina." *Journal of Negro History* 26 (October 1941): 421–37.

Gordon, Asa H. *Sketches of Negro Life and History in South Carolina.* Columbia: University of South Carolina, 1929.

McDonald, Anna Birnie. Interview with Barbara Williams Jenkins, Sumter, South Carolina, January 1994.

National Negro Digest 4, Special Issue (1940): 28–29.

Nix, Nelson C. *A Tentative History of State A & M College.* Unpublished. Orangeburg, S.C.: 1940.

Our Book of Gold. South Carolina Federation of Colored Women's Clubs, 1959.

Who's Who in Colored America, 1930-1932. Edited by Thomas Yenser. Brooklyn: Who's Who in Colored America, 1933.

Wilkinson, Lula Love. Interview with Barbara Williams Jenkins, Orangeburg, S.C.: January 1994.

Zimmerman, Geraldyne Pierce. Interview with Barbara Williams Jenkins, Orangeburg, S.C.: January 1994.

Collections:

Articles, photographs, and memorabilia are available in the Miller F. Whittaker Library, South Carolina State University Historical Collection, Orangeburg, South Carolina.

● *MARION WILLIAMS*

"Amazingly Graced." *Washington Post,* July 10, 1994.

Fitzgerald, Sharon. "The Glorious Walk of Marion Williams." *American Visions* 8 (December/January 1994): 48–51.

Heilbut, Tony. *The Gospel Sound: Good News and Bad Times.* New York: Simon and Schuster, 1971.

Hine, Darlene Clark, ed. *Black Women in America.* Brooklyn: Carlson Publishing, 1993.

"Marion Williams, 40 Years on the Road to Salvation." *New York Newsday* (August 5, 1988).

Nichols, Charles H., ed. *Arna Bontemps-Langston Hughes Letters, 1925–1967.* New York: Dodd, Mead, 1980.

"Singer Marion Williams Influenced Gospel Music." *Chicago Tribune* (July 4, 1994).

Southern, Eileen. *Biographical Dictionary of Afro-American and African Musicians.* Westport, Conn.: Greenwood Press, 1982.

"2 Worlds Meet at Kennedy Center." *New York Times* (December 6, 1993).

"Views from the Top." *Washington Post* (December 5, 1993).

SUBJECT INDEX

A

A. M. Herman and Associates, 123
Abbitt, Cleve, 48
Abbott, Robert, 31
The Abuse of Liberty, 255
"Ada", 254
"Adoration of the Magi", 175
Aeronautical Association of Negro
  Schools, 31
Aeronautical University, 30
African American National Tennis
  Organization, 364
African Meeting House, 135
Agnes Scott College, 202
Aiken, Jim, 178
Aiken, Loretta Mary, 178
Ain't Misbehavin', 4
Alcorn Agricultural and Mechanical
  College, 8
Alice Coachman Foundation, 50
Alice in Wonderland, 4
Alice Tully Hall, 21
Alix, Mae, 151
All-Writing Services, 208
Allen, Andrew, 1
Allen, Andrew "Tex", 1
Allen, Debbie, 1
Allen, Vivian Ayers, 1
Amazing Grace, 180
American Academy of Dramatic Art, 197
American Anti-Slavery Society, 255
American Association of Education of
  Colored Youth, 109
American Film Institute, 59
American Institute of Architects, 309
American Missionary Association, 115
American Nurses Association (ANA), 184
American Tennis Association, 364-365

American Women's Suffrage Association,
  109
Anderson, Del Marie Neely, 7
Apollo Theatre, 168, 179
"An Appeal to Woman", 255
Ariola Records, 14
Armstrong, Lillian Hard, 152
Armstrong, Louis, 179
Armstrong, William H., 354
"Ars Poetica", 81
Ashe, Arthur, 226
Association for the Study of Negro Life
  and History, 37
Association of Southern Women for the
  Prevention of Lynching, 38
Atlanta Offering, 109
Atlantic Records, 276-277
Austin, Chick, 198
Australian Open, 104
The Autobiography of Miss Jane Pittman,
  355
Autumn Leaves, 109
Avery Fischer Hall, 21
Avery Institute, 379
Avicenna Medal, 193

B

"A Bag of Peanuts", 164
Bailey's Cafe, 233
Bailey, Cora, 48
Baker, Anita, 13
"Ball and Chain", 337
Ballet Nacional de Mexico, 3
Baltimore Afro-American, 162
Bangkok Symphony Orchestra, 286
Bannister, Edward Mitchell, 172
Baptist World Alliance, 37
Barbara Watson Modeling School, 353
"Barrel House Blues", 266